THE ANCIENT SEA

The Utopian and Catastrophic
in Classical Narratives and their Reception

The Ancient Sea

The Utopian and Catastrophic
in Classical Narratives and their Reception

edited by

Hamish Williams & Ross Clare

LIVERPOOL UNIVERSITY PRESS

First published 2022 by
Liverpool University Press
4 Cambridge Street
Liverpool
L69 7ZU

British Library Cataloguing-in-Publication data
A British Library CIP record is available

ISBN 978-1-80207-760-5

Typeset by Carnegie Book Production, Lancaster
Printed and bound by CPI Group (UK) Ltd, Croydon CR0 4YY

Contents

Figures

Acknowledgements

First and foremost, I would like to thank Clare Litt from Liverpool University Press (LUP) for supporting this project from the get-go and for guiding us through the proposal preparations and through the review stages. To Anke Eißmann, thank you so much for producing such a beautiful cover illustration for our book. The contributors to this study have acknowledged the assistance of colleagues and funders at the start of their respective essays; personally, my own research and editorial work would not have been possible without the financial support of the Alexander von Humboldt Foundation and the Polish Institute of Advanced Studies, realized during research stays in Jena, hosted by Professor Thomas Honegger, and in Warsaw, hosted by Professor Przemysław Urbańczyk, from 2019 to 2022.

Hamish Williams
Wednesday 30 March 2022

Editor's Notes

Hamish Williams

This book was edited according to the stylistic conventions of the so-called "Notes and Bibliography" variant of the Chicago Style from *The Chicago Manual of Style* (seventeenth edition, 2017). For a guide to the abbreviations used for ancient authors, ancient texts, and standard modern collections of ancient inscriptions, fragments, and iconography (etc.) (e.g. *CIL*, *FGrH*, *LIMC*), see Simon Hornblower and Anthony Spawforth, eds., *The Oxford Companion to Classical Civilization*, second edition (Oxford: Oxford University Press, 2014), xix–xxvii. Abbreviations not in this guide are introduced in the individual papers. For the dating of calendar years, the modern system of BCE and CE has generally been used throughout the volume; however, in two chapters, AD is preferred to CE on account of prevailing scholarly conventions when referring to certain historical events. Abbreviations for periodicals and journals from classical studies can be found in *l'Année Philologique*. Spelling conventions are set according to UK English.

Introduction

Hamish Williams and Ross Clare

The sea has become an important *topos* (place) in recent classical studies scholarship: Beaulieu's *The Sea in the Greek Imagination* (2015); De Souza, Arnaud, and Buchet's (eds.) *The Sea in History: The Ancient World* (2017); and Beaulieu's (ed.) *A Cultural History of the Sea in Antiquity* (2021).[1] Connecting the ancient world with other spheres, scholarship has also adopted a cultural-historical perspective of the sea, tracking changing representations from antiquity, towards medieval times and early modernity, and into the contemporary period; some representative examples include Harris' (ed.) *Rethinking the Mediterranean* (2005) and Mack's *The Sea: A Cultural History* (2013).[2] These works must also be read

We would like to thank the anonymous peer reviewer of the volume and the LUP editorial board for the helpful comments on this introduction and other chapters.

   1 Marie-Claire Beaulieu, ed., *A Cultural History of the Sea in Antiquity*, Volume 1. A Cultural History of the Sea (London, Oxford, and New York: Bloomsbury, 2021); Marie-Claire Beaulieu, *The Sea in the Greek Imagination* (Philadelphia: University of Pennsylvania Press, 2015); Philip de Souza, Pascal Arnaud, and Christine Buchet, eds., *The Sea in History: The Ancient World* (Woodbridge, Suffolk: Boydell Press, 2017). Beyond classical scholarship on the sea rests a body of wider studies on water in ancient worlds; see Georgia Irby, *Conceptions of the Watery World in Greco-Roman Antiquity* (London: Bloomsbury, 2021). This focus is unsurprising considering water's centrality to human life, but also considering that a history of the ancient Mediterranean region is almost always, in part, a history of the Mediterranean Sea. So, Part Two of Greg Woolf's *The Life and Death of Ancient Cities: A Natural History* (Oxford: Oxford University Press, 2020) is all about the development of societies around the Mediterranean in relation to the sea, its attendant inland watercourses, and the islands upon which humans lived. This feeds right into the more "down-to-earth" studies about water in "real life"; see, for example, Dora P. Crouch, *Water Management in Ancient Greek Cities* (New York: Oxford University Press, 1993); Anne O. Koloski-Ostrow, *The Archaeology of Sanitation in Roman Italy: Toilets, Sewers, and Water Systems* (Chapel Hill, NC: University of North Carolina Press, 2015).

   2 William V. Harris, ed., *Rethinking the Mediterranean* (Oxford: Oxford University Press, 2005); John Mack, *The Sea: A Cultural History* (London: Reaktion Books, 2013).

alongside the vast scientific literature on the sea, from environmental, oceanographic, and climate-change perspectives.[3]

Encouraged by the spatial turn in studies of classical narratives,[4] by growing interdisciplinarity between classics and the sciences, and by our modern environmental consciousness of the sea as an essential theatre of human activity (not to mention human-induced change),[5] classical

3 Scholarship on marine science is enormous. For an all-round introduction, see Peter S. Meadows and Janette I. Campbell, *An Introduction to Marine Science* (New York: Springer, 1988); for a broader look at the sea from the perspective of social sciences, see Hubert Zapf, ed., *Handbook of Ecocriticism and Cultural Ecology* (Berlin: De Gruyter, 2016).

4 Space has been a late bloomer in studies of cultural (literary, historical, social) narratives. Narratives have traditionally been examined through the analysis of the features of narrator and time; see, for example, Gérard Genette, *Narrative Discourse: An Essay in Method* (Ithaca, NY: Cornell University Press, 1980), 228–244. In contrast, there has been, until quite recently, a comparative neglect of theory and critical analysis focusing on the aspect of space; see, for example, Mieke Bal and Christine van Boheemen, *Narratology: Introduction to the Theory of Narrative*, third edition (Toronto: University of Toronto Press, 2009), 134; Irene J. F. de Jong, "Introduction," in *Space in Ancient Greek Literature: Studies in Ancient Greek Narrative, Volume 3*, ed. Irene J. F. de Jong (Leiden: Brill, 2012), 1; Gabriele Zoran, "Towards a Theory of Space in Narrative," *Poetics Today* 5, no. 2 (1984): 310. For the bias of literature as a "temporal art" rather than a "spatial art," see Jenny S. Clay, *Homer's Trojan Theater: Space, Vision, and Memory in the Iliad* (Cambridge: Cambridge University Press, 2011), 29–30; de Jong, "Introduction," 1; Christos Tsagalis, *From Listeners to Viewers: Space in the Iliad* (Cambridge, MA: Harvard University Press, 2012), 1; Zoran, "Space in Narrative," 30. This simplified belief has become ingrained in popular approaches to narrative texts such that space can often be regarded as an inert background setting to a narrative, like the painted backdrop to a theatrical stage, in front of which the "real narrative" unfolds; in this way of thinking, space has no meaningful effect other than to create the immediate physical context in which the story may unfold and is not greatly significant in the production of meaning; see Bal and van Boheemen, *Narratology*, 139; de Jong, "Introduction," 1–2, 13. Scholars across the human and social sciences have, however, slowly begun to appreciate the relevance of space to our understanding of a story, and how it is indeed an integral part of narrative art itself; see de Jong, "Introduction," 1ff. As late as discussions on space entered into discourses of literary and cultural studies, they have only begun to be acknowledged in classics in the last ten to fifteen years of critical study; see Tsagalis, *From Listeners to Viewers*, 2. Since the 2000s, there has been a growing interest in the narratives roles, cultural values, and different types of space in classical texts; see, for example, Katherine Clarke, *Between Geography and History: Hellenistic Constructions of the Roman World* (Oxford: Oxford University Press, 1999); Irene J. F. de Jong, ed., *Space in Ancient Greek Literature: Studies in Ancient Greek Narrative, Volume 3* (Leiden: Brill, 2012); Jeremy McInerney and Ineke Sluiter, eds., *Valuing Landscape in Classical Antiquity: Natural Environment and Cultural Imagination* (Leiden: Brill, 2016); Tsagalis, *From Listeners to Viewers*.

5 Classical studies has been characteristically slow in eliding with environmental studies and ecocriticism, but there are, to date, some essential works to refer to. Foremost are Lukas Thommen's *An Environmental History of Ancient Greece*

scholars have shown us how the sea in the ancient Mediterranean world of Greece and Rome (and beyond) was an essential domain for trade, cultural exchange, identity making, communication, exploration, colonization, and of course the consolidation of power. In tandem with the reality of the sea and of seafaring experiences in antiquity, a parallel experience of the sea also emerged in narrative representations from ancient Greece and Rome, of the sea as a *cultural imaginary*. The sea is not a mere backdrop in front of which the daily events of social and political life play out; it is, rather, a site over which complex webs of meaning are spun. Often, in truth, it is hard to extricate the "imagined" from the "real": where Beaulieu's *The Sea in the Greek Imagination* (2015) focuses on the myths of heroes and divine intervention, she concludes that the sea is *both* "real and imaginary."[6] Schliephake's edited volume *Ecocriticism, Ecology and the Cultures of Antiquity* (2017)[7] collects some extraordinary papers that find within antiquity the same kinds of environmental problems that the present age of modernity faces: therefore, it might seem like a more realistic, pragmatic, even social-scientific study of ancient environments – but for the fact that many of the contributions skilfully draw out both practical *and* ethical issues from philosophical, historical, and mythical literature. Likewise, while this volume sits within the wider tradition of the sea as a constituent of the ancient (and modern) cultural imagination, we also appreciate that we cannot do so without actively co-operating with more concrete realities such as the pragmatic potential of colonization for a better life (Beek), the effect of piracy on seafarers (Mataix Ferrándiz), or the lived experiences of average Greeks and Romans who risked the waves (Irby).

One noticeable thread within this web of thalassic meanings concerns the specific tension which the ancient sea exhibits in narratives between representations of the *utopic* and the *catastrophic* – and, indeed, of ambiguous imaginaries which drift between these two poles. This collection of essays puts into sharper focus this archetypal topographic antithesis of the sea in ancient narratives: it constitutes a way of life, an open road of potential exploration and adventure, and even the discovery

---

and Rome, translated by Philip Hill (Cambridge: Cambridge University Press, 2012), and Christopher Schliephake's (ed.) *Ecocriticism, Ecology and the Cultures of Antiquity* (Lanham, MD: Rowman & Littlefield, 2017). Richard Buxton's *Myths and Tragedies in their Ancient Greek Contexts* (Oxford: Oxford University Press, 2013) also ruminates deeply on landscapes as major components of ancient stories.

6 Beaulieu, *Greek Imagination*, 197.
7 Schliephake, *Ecocriticism, Ecology.*

of paradise, a utopic sphere in different respects; yet it also represents an untameable, unknowable, and intimidating site of natural disaster, societal collapse, and death, a catastrophic sphere.

The tension between the sea as utopic and catastrophic is evident across a number of ancient Greek narratives. In mythic narratives, Odysseus' seafaring voyages across a preternatural Mediterranean introduce him to a number of seaside, seafaring, or sea-related societies which approach, in different respects, visions of perfection: for example, the isolated Phaeacians, who maintain a golden-age, blissful existence on Scheria, are sailors who possess a magical relationship with the sea itself, agents of an expedited, safe trip home over the sea, in spite of its Poseidonic, catastrophic tendencies, which Odysseus knows all too well;[8] Aeolus, the god of the winds, representing an ideal of Greek hospitality, provides not only bountiful fare to the Ithacan sailors but also a guest-gift which can transport them home in accelerated time over a placated sea;[9] and even the island of the Cyclopes, along with the nearby Island of the Goats, appears initially to the landbound sailors to be a place of pastoral plenty, a fantasy for a colonial seafaring Greek, rather like Crusoe's goat-filled island near the Orinoco was for the Englishman (see Easterbrook).[10] Yet in the case of the Cyclopes, the vision of paradise is soon disfigured by the monstrous acts of the man-eating Polyphemus, who forces the Ithacans back out onto the sea, mourning the loss of their companions and "grieving as they sailed onwards."[11] The cruel sea introduces further catastrophes for the sailors: the dysmorphic beast Scylla, against whom martial heroism is no match, slaughters yet more of Odysseus' crew, plucking them out of the ship as they pass by her cliff (see Irby); the Sirens present a tempting vision of a past Iliadic glory, a nostalgic heroic paradise, but such a temptation leads only to ruin as the rotten corpses on their island bear testament to;[12] worst of all, Charybdis literally embodies the immeasurable capacity of the sea to swallow up everything and to turn humans and their histories to oblivion.

In historical narratives, Thucydides starts his story of the conflict between Athens and Sparta with a trip to the mythical past, back to the Cretans who ruled the Aegean Sea under King Minos. These Cretans are

8 Hom. *Od.* 6–8.
9 10.
10 9.
11 9.565–566. All translations and paraphrasing are our own unless otherwise stated.
12 Charles Segal, "Kleos and its Ironies in the *Odyssey*," AC 52 (1983): 39–40.

said by Thucydides to construct the first navy, which imposes order across the seas through the eradication of piracy.[13] The Greek historian shows, on the one hand, the importance of this foundational "civilizing" act by subsequently commenting on the prevalence of piracy in this early period of the Aegean, on the raids on smaller communities, and on the dominant attitude of acceptance towards piracy in these pre-thalassocratic times.[14] At the same time, Thucydides' comment is a back-handed compliment, in contrasting the eradication of piracy by King Minos with the imposition of imperial taxes and a colonial empire that functions through nepotism. Some have, accordingly, viewed Thucydides' comment as a contemporary criticism of the imperial–moral decline of Athens as a seafaring power.[15] From a historical perspective, does the Minoan–Athenian attempt to create order out of the catastrophic sea, as embodied by "free piracy," lead to an ideal of interconnected civilized societies (at least in the initial imperial periods), a federal utopia of united Greek city-states? Or, rather, to the destructive disaster of tyranny (in liberal terms) – oppression and violence? Papers by Bartninkas, Crosson, Mataix Ferrándiz, and Easterbrook all home in, in different respects, on these imperial, thalassic dimensions. Certainly, the question as to whether the "Minoans" were peace-loving, free-trading utopians or tyrannical thalassocrats who brought violence upon the Greek mainland (and ultimately catastrophe upon themselves) has been tackled (and reimagined) by several fictional writers during the twentieth century, including Robert Graves and Mary Renault (see Williams).

In philosophical narratives, Plato's story of Atlantis in his *Timaeus* and *Critias* is an invitation for his readers to undertake not only a temporal journey into mythic prehistory (via, characteristically ancient, Egyptian records) but also a spatial journey over the sea, westwards to an isolated island beyond the known Mediterranean, much like other classical paradises such as the Homeric Elysium and the Blessed Isles (from Hesiod to Plutarch and beyond) which are separated from the known Greco-Roman world by the sea. The sea-girt Atlantis conforms, in some respects, to the Hesiodic, golden-age environment which is a pervasive *topos* in ancient literature: entailing close divine connections, material abundance, and a self-sustaining natural domain. While Atlantis presents the utopian

---

13 Thuc. 1.4. See Diod. Sic. 4.60.2; Hdt. 3.122.
14 Thuc. 1.5.
15 Sterling Dow, "The Minoan Thalassocracy," *Proceedings of the Massachusetts Historical Society* 79 (1967): 8.

possibility of a blessed existence for its islanders, the tale in the *Timaeus* is ultimately one of catastrophe and collapse as the island, along with the rest of the prehistorical world, sinks below the sea into near oblivion. The *Critias*, unfortunately, breaks off in the narrative which starts to describe the divine punishment, but it is clear, at any rate, that there is some kind of degeneration from Atlantis' early blessedness which is realized through a decline in the inhabitants' divine essence[16] and, perhaps, by their hubristic drive towards materialism. Atlantis maintains, thus, an uneasy tension between its reflection of earlier golden-age paradises and its status as a corrupted kingdom, perhaps an Athenian reflection of the collapse of their powerful enemy; Atlantis might well be "Persia transformed, and transported from the east to the west, and way back from the fifth century to an earlier, dreamlike time."[17]

The concepts of utopia and catastrophe are far from absent in the Roman historical and literary record. Sea-girt island utopias were often borrowed from the Greek mythographic tradition.[18] The first "paradise" that comes to mind is that of Elysium: admittedly, first attested to in the earliest Greek literature as a "land where living is made easy for mankind";[19] this was, nonetheless, carried through into Latin poetry as "the land of joy, the lovely glades of the fortunate woods and the home of the blest," a place where "spirits have their own sun and their own stars" and where everyone has a wonderful time "on the golden sand."[20] Similarly, Panchaea, the near-utopic island described by the Hellenistic writer Euhemerus, gained far more traction in later Roman eras, where, for example, the island would be re-implemented by Lactantius to

16 Pl. *Critias* 120e.

17 Christopher Rowe, "Plato and the Persian Wars," in *Cultural Responses to the Persian Wars: Antiquity to the Third Millennium*, ed. Emma Bridges, Edith Hall, and P. J. Rhodes (Oxford: Oxford University Press, 2007), 102.

18 On the Roman inheritance from Greek mythography, see Alan Cameron, *Greek Mythography in the Roman World* (Oxford: Oxford University Press, 2004). For studies on the Greek mythographic tradition, see Robert L. Fowler, *Early Greek Mythography, Volume 2: Commentary* (Oxford: Oxford University Press, 2013); Allen J. Romano and John Marincola, eds., *Host or Parasite: Mythographers and their Contemporaries in the Classical and Hellenistic Periods* (Berlin and Boston: de Gruyter GmbH, 2019); Stephen M. Trzaskoma and R. Scott Smith, eds., *Writing Myth: Mythography in the Ancient World* (Leuven, Paris, Walpole: Peeters, 2013).

19 And "where no snow falls, no strong winds blow and there is never any rain" (Hom. *Od.* 4.563–569); as in E. V. Rieu and D. C. H. Rieu, trans., *Homer: The Odyssey* (London: Penguin, 2003).

20 Verg. *Aen.* 6.637ff.; as in David West, trans., *Virgil. The Aeneid* (London: Penguin, 2003).

outright dispel the myth of the old gods and to bolster the veracity of his favoured religion, Christianity.[21] The word "catastrophe" is often invoked in the modern world to conjure images of the very real, if oft disputed, "fall of Rome."[22] Long before this, earlier Roman history painted images of water-based, in some cases specifically sea-based, catastrophes. In Propertius' work, the aftermath of the Battle at Actium reveals a "seascape marked not by the spoils of a victor, but by the bones of Roman soldiers killed in the engagement" – a space of unquantifiable violence and death, and one which cannot easily be commemorated as a triumph perhaps because the sea is "perpetually shifting."[23] For a more "popular" watery example, one need only consider Caesar's crossing of the Rubicon: a dramatic moment that, depending on political perspective, represents either the death of the Republic or the beginning of a long-lasting Empire (see Crosson). The notion that Caesar "crosses the Rubicon" has become proverbial, applied to the point within an event after which the actant can no longer turn back – in tragic terms, the *peripeteia* engendering the dramatic *katastrophē*.

The utopia–catastrophe dichotomy of sea imaginings in Greek and Roman literature, moreover, seems to have a significant afterlife in modern cultural-historical narratives, as is discussed in the third section of this volume. Of course, it is quite likely that modern, popular narratives receive a far greater part of their "thalassic data" from our inherited cultural imaginings of the early modern period and, often, of the imperial–colonial period involving nineteenth-century European nation-states.[24] The image of Jack Aubrey on his frigate might be more familiar to

---

21 See Lactantius *Divine Institutes* 1.11.55ff. For more on Panchaea, with an emphasis on Roman (and to a smaller extent Greek) literature, see Rhiannon Evans, "Searching for Paradise: Landscape, Utopia, and Rome," *Arethusa* 36, no. 3 (2003): 285–307.

22 For a critique of the application of "catastrophe" to the "event" that was Rome's fall, see Bryan Ward-Perkins, *The Fall of Rome and the End of Civilization* (Oxford and New York: Oxford University Press, 2005), 3–5. For a similar deconstruction of coastal catastrophes in this volume, see Middleton's chapter.

23 Marian W. Makins, "Dissenting Voices in Propertius' Post-War Landscapes," in *Landscapes of War in Greek and Roman Literature*, ed. Bettina Reitz-Joosse, Marian W. Makins, and Christopher J. Mackie (London: Bloomsbury, 2021), 131–154. For another paper on Actium and Propertius, see also Bettina Reitz-Joosse's "Land at Peace and Sea at War: Landscape and the Memory of Actium in Greek Epigram and Propertius' Elegies," in *Valuing Landscape in Classical Antiquity: Natural Environment and Cultural Imagination*, ed. Jeremy McInerney and Ineke Sluiter (Leiden: Brill, 2016), 276–296.

24 For an introduction to the sea in this period, see Claire Jowitt, Craig Lambert, and Steve Mentz, eds., *The Routledge Companion to Marine and Maritime Worlds, 1400–1800* (London: Routledge, 2020).

a modern, popular readership than that of Alcibiades on a trireme (unless they have read their Renault). Some contributions to this volume certainly reflect on the influences of the Enlightenment and colonial periods (for example, Easterbrook, Williams), although, importantly, they do so in interesting ways such that utopia and catastrophe can be seen as both ancient and modern ideas simultaneously. Looking closely at examples of classical reception can further help us to conceptualize history itself as a moving, reactive continuum that is full of ideas. This is because "each reception [can be] located synchronically in a wider context of lateral relationships that may extend across space rather than time"[25] – that is, not only as an interesting connector between ancient and modern, but as a complex mode of thinking about places and spaces, in which notions such as utopia and catastrophe live, change shape, act upon, and are acted upon by diverse constituents.

*

To sum up, the notion that the "ancient sea" as imagined provided both the potential for a better future, approaching a utopian state, and the potential for imminent catastrophe is not new to scholars of Greek and Roman studies; in this volume, however, we do try to explore the *sheer diversity in narrative representations* of the ancient sea as utopic and catastrophic. Such a study naturally encompasses an array of different ancient narrative genres, including mythic, literary, philosophical, historiographic, legal, religious, and social narratives – not to forget their post-classical afterlives in, for example, socio-religious, theatrical, and popular-novelistic narratives as well as their intersection with "non-nar-rative" material culture such as visual art, sculpture, and archaeological remains.

Thus, we ask, how exactly do these narratives present the ancient sea as *utopic*? From a physical or topographic perspective, utopia can be found, or founded, by prospective colonists in some imaginary island paradise far away and across the distant sea (see Beek, Williams); the sea can hold an unknown, mysterious utopia below its surface, where humanity transgresses its normal limits and approaches the divine

---

25 Lorna Hardwick and Christopher Stray, "Introduction: Making Connections," in *A Companion to Classical Receptions*, ed. Lorna Hardwick and Christopher Stray (London: Bloomsbury, 2008), 5.

(Denson, Easterbrook); and the sea itself as a watery body, just like rivers and lakes, can hold utopian potential, in providing a check to human ambition and violence (Crosson). This utopic quality of the sea can transcend literal explorations on the spatial plane and even move into the analogical: as an avenue for ships and seafaring, the sea can become a powerful metaphor for articulating political notions of utopia, the ideal state (Cornelli); or as an avenue for the emotions, the sea can connote an individual's sense of hope and subjectivity (Martorana). Many of these utopian imaginings are not without their ideological problems, from modern, postcolonial perspectives; in imperial-minded narratives, the sea can represent the utopian potential for immeasurable wealth and power – through commercial gains and, ultimately, through political expansion across its apparently neutral territories (Bartninkas, Mataix Ferrándiz).

On the other hand, contributors in this study also help us to contrast the utopic quality of the sea with its role as a *catastrophic* sphere. This dimension of the sea can often be realized through alarming physical representations: along the coasts of human habitation, the sea threatens natural disaster, involving floods, tsunamis, and earthquakes (Middleton); further out, the danger of the sea is realized through storms and the accompanying monsters (Irby); and the sea can even pose extinction (physical or cultural) to entire (lost) civilizations (Williams). From the literal to the metaphorical, the catastrophic sea can symbolize the distress of the helpless (Martorana), or it can stand as a metonym for nature itself, as a necessary check on excessive order and thus tyranny (Crosson). As with the utopic sea, the sea as catastrophic brings with it an array of different connotations: as representing violence or instability, from raiding pirates to shipwrecks, which needs to be restrained by political and legal structures (Bartninkas, Mataix Ferrándiz); as the archetypal symbol of chaos, eternally tussling with order (Álvarez-Martí-Aguilar); or even as a realm for expressing a savage alterity which can be colonized by imperial imaginings (Easterbrook).

Beyond studies of the sea, an investigation into the topics of utopia and catastrophe in classical studies also provides much food for thought for the study of these imagined phenomena in other cultural and sociological fields. Utopian studies is, after all, a fast-growing interdisciplinary field, invoking political studies, cultural studies, and philosophy, and is a response to what many twentieth-century historians have viewed as a century of (failed) utopias; similarly, studies on crises, collapse, and extinction have experienced a rapid growth, again a response to "the decade of crisis"

(2010–2020).[26] From the perspective of ethics (in philosophical or religious studies), for example, the recurrent discursive orientation between utopia and catastrophe (or crises) has been regarded as the dominant myth of our modern culture,[27] a polarity which informs our orientation in decision-making processes. From the viewpoint of political philosophy, many critics in the school of political realism have viewed the twentieth century as entailing a ruinous series of catastrophic utopian experiments (so realizing dystopias in practice);[28] such utopianism is to be countered by the "ideologically free" mechanism of liberalism[29] or the apparent "true" utopia of libertarianism,[30] which can help limit the disaster. From the perspective of cultural and literary studies, the late nineteenth and twentieth century has witnessed an explosion of new genres which place utopian and catastrophic thinking at the fore: the golden-age Lothlóriens and Hellish Mordors of fantasy writer J. R. R. Tolkien,[31] the progressive science fiction of *Star Trek*,[32] and the satirical tracts of George Orwell.[33]

In line with this general interest for the topics of utopia and catastrophe (including crisis, disaster, collapse) in cultural and sociological studies, classical studies has slowly started to appreciate the importance of these topics in the ancient world: significant treatments for the former have been covered by John Ferguson (1975), Rhiannon Evans (2008), and Pierre Destrée, Jan Opsomer, and Geert Roskam (eds.) (2021);[34] and for the latter,

---

26 Andy Beckett, "The Age of Perpetual Crisis: How the 2010s Disrupted Everything but Resolved Nothing," *The Guardian* (17 December 2019): https://www.theguardian.com/society/2019/dec/17/decade-of-perpetual-crisis-2010s-disrupted-everything-but-resolved-nothing. Accessed 19 September 2021.

27 Darrell J. Fasching, *The Ethical Challenge of Auschwitz and Hiroshima: Apocalypse or Utopia* (New York: State University of New York Press, 1993), 2–3.

28 Thus, see Martin E. Marty, "'But Even So: Look at That': An Ironic Perspective on Utopias," in *Visions of Utopia*, ed. Edward Rothstein, Herbert Muschamp, and Martin E. Marty (Oxford: Oxford University Press, 2003), 82.

29 See Edward Rothstein, "Utopia and its Discontents," in *Visions of Utopia*, ed. Edward Rothstein, Herbert Muschamp, and Martin E. Marty (Oxford: Oxford University Press, 2003), 5, 12.

30 Robert Nozick, *Anarchy, State, and Utopia* (Oxford: Blackwell, 1999), 297–313.

31 Rothstein, "Utopia and its Discontents," 3.

32 Matthew W. Kapell, *Exploring the Next Frontier: Vietnam, NASA, Star Trek and Utopia in 1960s and 1970s American Myth and History* (New York and London: Routledge, 2016), 3ff.; George Kovacs, "Moral and Mortal in *Star Trek: The Original Series*," in *Classical Traditions in Science Fiction*, ed. Brett Rogers and Ben Stevens (Oxford: Oxford University Press, 2015), 199–216.

33 Rothstein, "Utopia and its Discontents," 3–4.

34 Pierre Destrée, Jan Opsomer, and Geert Roskam, eds., *Utopias in Ancient Thought* (Berlin, 2021); Rhiannon Evans, *Utopia Antiqua: Readings of the Golden Age and Decline at*

in the case of collapse and disaster, by Guy Middleton (2010, 2017) and Edward Watts (2021).[35] We believe, however, that the field of classical studies can contribute far more to broader treatments of these themes in cultural studies, and this volume seeks to bring into closer conversation the inherent tension between utopia and catastrophe (and imaginings which lie between or mix these two together) by focusing on the *ancient sea as an archetypal narrative space* which opens up this conflict.

*

The chapters in this volume are divided into three sections: Section 1, "Ancient Society: History, Historiography, Philosophy, and Politics" (Chapters 1 to 5), covers archaeological, historiographic, legal, and philosophical texts; Section 2, "Ancient Literature and Myth" (Chapters 6 to 9), covers literary, mythological texts in both Greek and Latin writings, with evidence from the visual arts also playing a role; and Section 3, "Classical Receptions" (Chapters 10 to 12), covers religious, theatrical, and novelistic "texts." The various chapters intersect with each other beyond these boundaries, and we encourage the reader to make their own thematic and conceptual connections between both papers and sections.

Chapter 1. Starting the section on ancient history and society, Middleton's chapter examines three infamous coastal disasters in the ancient world, all of which are believed to have entailed "catastrophic" tsunamis: the Thera eruption and its effect on Minoan Crete in the late Bronze Age, the inundation and destruction of Classical Helike in the fourth century BCE, and the "AD 365 Tsunami" and its effect on Alexandria. In all these cases, Middleton juxtaposes the facts of scientific evidence from archaeological, geological, and seismological studies at and around the purported sites of disaster with the narrative representations of these events, whether in ancient texts or in modern scholarship (the latter in the case of Minoan Crete). What emerges is that these coastal catastrophes only become "catastrophes," as such, through the conjuncture of a natural event

Rome (London and New York: Routledge, 2008); John Ferguson, *Utopias of the Classical World* (London: Thames and Hudson, 1975).

35 Guy D. Middleton, *The Collapse of Palatial Society in Late Bronze Age Greece and the Postpalatial Period* (Oxford: Archaeopress, 2010); *Understanding Collapse: Ancient History and Modern Myths* (Cambridge: Cambridge University Press, 2017); Edward J. Watts, *The Eternal Decline and Fall of Rome: The History of a Dangerous Idea* (Oxford: Oxford University Press, 2021).

causing physical destruction, a human population, and, consequently, the imaginative transformation of the event through cultural narratives. On the one hand, Middleton warns us against assuming a literal, scientific truth in the narratives of catastrophic tsunamis and coastal disasters which we have inherited (or even constructed) from the ancient world; scientific investigation creates a far more ambiguous, complex picture, questioning, for example, ideas of significant, total destruction during a single natural event and pointing, instead, to social continuity at disaster sites. On the other hand, Middleton suggests important religious motivations behind the construction of narratives of total catastrophe, as a characteristic anthropological means of dealing with death and destruction; the link between catastrophe and religion, interestingly, is not confined to "primitive superstition," with many moderns even in the "developed world" turning to religion in the wake of natural disasters.

Chapter 2. Bartninkas' chapter draws our focus further towards the conceptualization of sea power by the ancient Greeks, particularly the Athenians, who in their formalization of societal organization (the *polis*) were all but forced to take account of and to evaluate the sea. Bartninkas breaks down classical Athens' preoccupation with the sea by offering a comparative, chronological reading of three essential Greek writers: the Old Oligarch (Pseudo-Xenophon), Thucydides, and Plato. Bartninkas finds at the heart of the Old Oligarch's text a positive justification for oligarchic-minded readers of democratic government; more precisely, he identifies a reciprocal relationship between sea power (the navy) and the urban class making up a great percentage of the *dēmos*. The sea provides the utopian boons of increased commerce and territorial expansion, while at the same time allowing for the cosmopolitan life and institutions which defined Athens. That the sea remained an essential component of the way Athens thought about itself is then prompted by a reading of Thucydides directed at the interaction between city, money, and the maritime empire. Of particular interest here is the discussion of Thucydides' *Archaeology*, of different Greek thalassocracies from the Minoans to the Corinthians which culminated in Athens as a kind of utopic, hyper-technological sea power. Finally, Bartninkas deploys the thought of Plato: where many of his dialogists defend the apparent morality of Athens' sea-based empire, there remains within his writings certain elements of potential opposition, even condemnation of maritime imperial power and the effects of the chaotic sea upon morality. Ultimately, Bartninkas uses these classical texts to reignite debates on Athens' self-conception in such a way that the 'reality' of Athens and the "imagined" Athens as recorded in the written record are shown to be in constant conversation. The result of this conversation is an ever-fluctuating tradition of thought incorporating the physical walled *polis*, the naval empire that funded it, the people in receipt of it, and more abstract questions of stability – whether Athens would crash head-first into catastrophe or sail into a utopian future.

Chapter 3. From the historiographic narratives examined in the first two chapters, Cornelli's chapter suitably takes up the concluding Platonic discussion in Bartninkas' paper with a close reading of an important passage in Plato's *Republic*. Here no literal sea is encountered in the philosopher's dialogue; rather the sea and, more particularly, seafaring and a ship are envisioned for their allegorical potential. Cornelli places the image of Plato's ship in line with other important symbolic figures in the philosopher's work (including the image of the Sun, the cave, and the line), and he argues that the discussion of how this imagined ship should operate – versus how it actually operates – has important implications for the urban utopia which Plato imagines, *Kallipolis*. In short, the Athenian philosopher's distaste for democracy (and demagogues) and his "oligarchic" preference for a philosopher state (a kind of "sophocracy") are articulated by his dissection of the picture of the ship, which faces catastrophe through the mob rule which tries to take command of the vessel, in opposition to the skilled, knowledgeable *gubernator*–philosopher who should steer the ship on its correct path. Such a broken ship of state is contextualized in the light of the Athenian civil war – the allegory becomes, then, a persuasive, joint project on the part of Plato for his readers to not only imagine but also realize a different, utopian Athens, which is just, beautiful, and good.

Chapter 4. From discussions of ancient Greek contexts, Beek's chapter moves the discussion into the Roman world. His analysis is built on a fascinating episode in the period of late-Republican civil war and strife – the account of General Sertorius, who, as both Sallust and Plutarch reflect, desired to sail westwards to the Blessed Isles in order to escape the turmoil in Rome and find, or found, a new "utopian" state. Rather than focusing exclusively on the nature of this event in light of late-Republican history, Beek contextualizes this intriguing event within a Greek tradition of seafaring, colonial narratives, whether in mythological (Hesiod), historio-graphical (Herodotus), or philosophical texts (Plato), which were concerned with the possibility of new, isolated, perfective lands to be acquired across the seas. The nature of this perfection, Beek shows us, seems to have fluctuated between two conceptual models of constructing utopia in the Greek imagination – "finding" or "founding" utopia abroad: of discovering idyllic paradises in the far reaches over the sea, lands which could, for example, breed forms of environmental determinism (in geographic and historiographic narratives) and of starting a new city-state from scratch (in philosophical traditions). Interestingly, the surviving narratives on Sertorius seem to preserve both discourses. Apart from the contribution of the finding/founding dichotomy to classical studies on utopias, Beek's paper also draws our attention to the tension between theory and practice: such utopias were not simply a pure thought exercise in the Greco-Roman imagination but likely had implications on how statesmen and colonists approached the thalassic unknown.

Chapter 5. Given that the sea loomed large in Greek and Roman thought and that this marine-centric historical and philosophical tradition directly impacted proposed or actually undertaken action, the ancient world needed a formalized legal framework by which its inhabitants could live and through which the government could institute "rules" for the sea and prosecute (or attempt to prosecute) those who disobeyed those laws. Mataix Ferrándiz' paper shows how legal attitudes conceived of the sea as a space of violence. It was, after all, an unpredictable, ever-changing landscape, a savage place that was at once catastrophic in nature, a host to piracy and plunder. Mataix Ferrándiz, however, utilizes Roman law to demonstrate how the Romans saw such an unruly frontier not as an insurmountable barrier, but as a challenge to be accepted. In the end, we see the sea is a catastrophic opportunity for utopia with imperial undertones: a place that, once tentatively overcome, could act as an instrument for the accumulation of imperial power and the spreading of propaganda to consolidate that power.

Chapter 6. In the next section of the volume, on ancient literature and myth, Irby makes clear how ancient narrative constructions of the sea often regarded it as a dangerous space of the unknown and the unhuman, the province, in other words, of various sea creatures, great monsters, sea nymphs, and gods. Through a wealth of primary-source evidence across various genres of Greco-Roman writing, including literary, historiographic, and social narratives (inscriptions), in comparison often with the material evidence of surviving artwork on vases and mosaics, Irby shows how the sea can be thought of as both utopic and catastrophic at the same time. The utopic dimension is certainly not anthropocentric; rather, the sea becomes an isolated, pleasurable, even timeless site of enjoyment for Nereids and for those few mortals who manage to encroach upon this milieu. But for most mortals, as Irby shows, the sea is a site of catastrophic ruin, of shipwrecks, drownings, and whirlpools – fears which are most memorably captured through narrative encounters with sea animals and monsters, of which Irby provides us a full catalogue. Most interesting is the link made in these narratives between the natural disaster of sea storms and sea monsters in the Greco-Roman imagination – that the creatures of the deeps that populate classical mythology quite possibly instigated, were involved in, or were even created by the cataclysmic storms that tear up the real and imaginary Mediterranean seascape. This is an unambiguous demonstration of the ancients' fear of the sea and of the meteorological events happening upon it, manifested through terrifying entities.

Chapter 7. In the next chapter, Denson inverts our accustomed examination of ancient sea narratives in horizontal terms, along the surface; instead, we plunge into the depths, into the hidden realm of Poseidon's underwater kingdom. Unlike modern science fiction and historical fiction narratives, from Jules Verne's *Twenty Thousand Leagues Under the Sea* (1869–1870) to Madeline Miller's *Circe* (2018), there is scant data in ancient narratives which allow us to dive below the surface, as it were; nevertheless, Denson rounds up some early literary allusions to the underwater home of Poseidon along with related references in, among others, Homer, Hesiod, Euripides, and Apollonius of Rhodes, before moving to his two key texts: the myth of Theseus' dive into the underwater halls of his father, in Bacchylides' seventeenth ode; and the submergence of Enalus, a mythic story preserved by Athenaeus. Denson draws our attention to details in classical texts that upend our understanding of their approaches to the very depths of the sea: it is not always unknown, unknowable, dark and dangerous. It might also be a site of utopia: promising divine interaction and the transcending of mortal limits; a regal, luxurious realm which offers untold riches to a few lucky mortals; a beautifully ordered, stable, even domestic vision of the sea in the form of Poseidon's palace, and in contrast to chaotic, tumultuous visions of the ocean; and, lastly, perhaps even a site for (heroic) rebirth, the return from the katapontic voyage being perhaps analogous to the successful katabasis into and anabasis out of the underworld.

Chapter 8. In the next chapter, Martorana provides a shift in thematic focus with a re-reading of Latin literature to isolate the literary female; in particular, she examines several of the epistolary poems of Ovid's *Heroides*, exploring the relationship between the sea and the various female mythic-historical characters who speak in these poems, including Penelope, Phyllis, Dido, Ariadne, and Sappho. Re-orientation is, in fact, key to our understanding here. Martorana demonstrates that the proposed (that is, male-written) heroines of Ovid attempt to fundamentally redefine the sea so that the text itself speaks of the seascape as a subjective space: one which can act upon the heroine, be acted upon by them, and can reflect their thoughts and feelings. The papers in this volume so often emphasize the active nature of the sea: here, however, it is in a sense interactive, a vehicle for the formulation of feelings and a medium for the expression of emotions. Martorana, therefore, at once proffers new insights into the *Heroides* text even as she submits an almost entirely new mode of seeing the sea not as an object but as a fluid participant in the construction of gender and personal identity. This analysis challenges us to view the sea not necessarily as both catastrophic and utopic, but as neither – as an ambivalent, ambiguous, subjective arena.

Chapter 9. Rather like Martorana's chapter, Crosson's takes us on a close textual reading of specific episodes in a Latin text; more particularly, his paper homes in on an interesting watery narrative in the fifth book of Lucan's *Pharsalia*, wherein Julius Caesar, engaged in a civil war against Pompey, tries to master a stormy Adriatic Sea by himself. According to Crosson, Lucan paints a hubristic picture of Caesar, a man who is becoming godlike in his ambitions, who commits acts of outrage (*nefas*) against, for example, sacred groves (drawing on an Ovidian motif), and who disrespects traditional religious rites such as hospitality. While there does not seem to be a manifest divinity directing his "nemetic" wrath against Caesar, Crosson argues that the Adriatic Sea performs such a function, providing a prelude to Caesar's ultimate tyrannicide. Water, indeed, appears to mark a clear obstacle against Caesar, with both the Rubicon and the River Nile providing challenges to the rampant leader before he tries unsuccessfully to cross the Adriatic. Lucan treats of the Adriatic Sea in his *Pharsalia* as a space of untameable power greater than that of any human, one so powerful that it disarms Caesar's over-ambitious, hubristic attempts to control Nature; but it is also a space imbued with utopian potential for those who oppose Caesar's tyrannical enterprise. Crosson goes further, reflecting on our own modern preoccupation with Nature as a force that fights back and argues that Lucan will not allow arrogance to impinge upon cosmic laws and to go unpunished. Thus, the sea itself becomes an almost characterful entity, if an inherently sublime and inhuman one, that takes its revenge against the hubristic Caesar. Crosson regards the constructed Adriatic Sea as in Lucan as a *utopian dystopia* – illustrating how the sea is utopic in its fight against tyranny, even if that very sea is shown to be intrinsically dangerous and chaotic to humanity.

Chapter 10. The third section, on classical receptions, opens with a broader cultural-historical approach to the theme by Álvarez-Martí-Aguilar, whose study ranges across instances of sea catastrophes (floods and tsunamis) in Mesopotamian, biblical, Roman, and early-modern narratives (and their present-day memories). This chapter views the ocean as essentially a spatial symbol of original chaos, embedded in cosmogonic accounts in both the Hebrew and Greco-Latin traditions wherein a divinity imposes order on the heaving seas, restraining them from invading the land. On the basis of earlier cosmogonic and flood narratives in the Western tradition, Álvarez-Martí-Aguilar interprets the cultural narratives of two historical tsunamis – the "AD 365 Alexandria tsunami" and the "AD 1755 tsunami" off the Iberian Peninsula – as attempts by the chaotic sea to break the divinely installed boundaries which protect the land. Despite the catastrophe which results from the tsunamis, at certain sites such as Epidauros (Croatia), Alexandria, and Cadiz, the sea is narrated to have been detained on its violent journey by divinely inspired mortals, priests who arrest the advance of original chaos. Álvarez-Martí-Aguilar focuses on the similarities between these acts of tsunamis being stopped by priests with the original divine arresting of the chaotic ocean; so too, the similarities between the religious-historiographic narratives on the Alexandria tsunami and the local traditions and legends of the Miracle of 'Our Lady of the Palm' are broached.

Chapter II. Easterbrook's chapter examines the crossover between Greco-Roman myth, the early-modern novel *Robinson Crusoe* (1719), and especially the Victorian theatre performances (pantomime) based on Defoe's story to demonstrate just how much classical material can achieve in modern contexts. Victorian pantomime (a form of musical comedy) was often fascinated with seafaring narratives, with the tales of Sinbad the Sailor and Robinson Crusoe proving popular source materials. The Robinsonade pantomimes which developed from *Robinson Crusoe* greatly changed the original subject matter of Defoe's work and contextualized it in manners which made it relevant for audiences in late-Victorian Britain. While for Defoe the sea was a *topos* by which the main character could, like Jonah, go through a Protestant moral progression, from exhibiting sin to pleading for forgiveness to seeking redemption, the Crusoe story in Victorian pantomime characterized the sea in quite different fashions. Important, to this end, is the role of classical characters, wherein Robinson Crusoe might be rescued by an amorous Aphrodite, encounter a vengeful Neptune (an encounter with which many British voyagers who crossed the Equator were familiar), or hear tell of amoral Amazons. Easterbrook aligns these classical encounters with the theme of the volume by showing, on the one hand, how Aphrodite or Venus could appear in their paradisiacal underwater caves which we might regard as "somatopias," spaces which are aimed at colonizing the female body (in line with contemporary gender politics); on the other hand, the catastrophic element of the sea could be identified with the violence and vengeance of Neptune. Importantly, though, this classical god is no match for British maritime might, which defeats the ancient god and his business partners. Thus, Greek and Roman mythology, refracted through a novel-turned-pantomime(s), contributed to the British imaginary and encouraged reflection upon both British society and the wider empire.

Chapter 12. Williams' paper retains the British-centred reception focus of Easterbrook's analysis but jumps forward about half a century to the post-Second World War period, when the balance of global power (cultural, military, political, but also thalassic) had definitively shifted to the US and USSR, and when Britain was certainly in a post-imperial period, with its mighty, trading sea empire and *Pax Britannica* now things of the past. Classics, again, provides a means for cultural reflection. While the peaceful, seafaring Minoans and their island utopia were, essentially, invented (and subsequently owned) by British archaeologist and, in today's terms, "influencer" Sir Arthur Evans and so coloured according to Victorian–Edwardian nostalgia for *Great* Britain, for British writers in the aftermath of the Second World War such idealism was no longer possible; concurrently, the mythologization of a Minoan utopia had to transform to reflect changing political sensibilities. These appropriations and reimaginations of British Minoans are interpreted by Williams through a close reading of two post-Second World War novels which draw on utopian ideas of Minoan Crete and/or Minoans: Lawrence Durrell's *The Dark Labyrinth* (1947) and Robert Graves' *Seven Days in New Crete* (1949). For Durrell's modern English characters, finding their way through the dangerous "labyrinth" of Minoan Crete presents the chance of arriving at an isolated, landlocked, alpine paradise, a Minoan Shangri-La, an inward utopia which is far removed from the dangerous tossings and turnings of the deathly sea and, by extension, the worldly distractions (false, "social utopias") which prevent characters from discovering themselves and, importantly, a sense of ontological, almost Buddhist bliss. For Graves' futuristic, but also retrospective New Cretans, the sea is a place of contamination through interaction with a corrupted outside world; New Crete is a terrestrial utopia which draws on many common Minoan ideals in twentieth-century writings, not least as a place of feminine superiority and poetic potential.

Ancient Society: History, Historiography, Philosophy, and Politics

From the Edge of the Deep Green Sea: Tsunamis and Coastal Catastrophes in the Ancient Aegean and Eastern Mediterranean

Guy D. Middleton

Introduction

The sea has been recognized throughout history as a dangerous, threatening, and untameable element, to be treated with caution and reverence, and placated through divine favour with prayers and offerings. Those on land are not immune to dangers from the sea, the most dramatic of which must be the world-reversing and terrifying tsunami. Since 1992, tsunamis including the Indian Ocean (2004) and Japan (2011) waves have killed 300,000 people and left scars in communities, landscapes, and psyches.[1] These two tsunamis were generated by earthquakes and the uplifting of the sea bed, which generated waves 40 metres in height that devastated coastal regions. The Mediterranean is not immune from tsunamis, being an area of seismic, tectonic, and volcanic activity.[2] Tsunamis in the ancient eastern Mediterranean, and whether or not they were the cause of coastal catastrophes, will be the main focus of this chapter.

Tsunamis, earthquakes, and volcanoes are not automatic causes of "catastrophes" or "disasters"; rather these come about because of the

I would like to thank Rachel Kulick for discussing her work on Palaikastro and the Minoan tsunami question, Stathis Stiros for sending me several recent papers on AD 365, and Olafur Arnalds for sending me his paper on the effects of volcanic tephra on ecosystems.

1 Jose C. Borrero, "Tsunami," in *Encyclopedia of Marine Geosciences*, ed. Jan Harff et al. (Dordrecht: Springer, 2014). DOI 10.1007/978-94-007-6644-0_146-3.

2 Mohammad Heidarzadeh and Aditya R. Gusman, "Source Modeling and Spectral Analysis of the Crete Tsunami of 2nd May 2020 along the Hellenic Subduction Zone, Offshore Greece," *Earth Planets Space* 73, article no. 74 (18 March 2021): https://doi.org/10.1186/s40623-021-01394-4.

conjunction of a natural hazard with a vulnerable human population.[3] Considering tsunamis, and the examples mentioned above, a catastrophe can occur due to direct (and indirect) loss of life as well as loss of facilities, infrastructure, and services (such as homes, roads, and drinking water). The catastrophe is not momentary but part of a process that continues after the given hazard has struck. This is the sense in which "catastrophe" is understood in this chapter.

Tsunamis have been identified by both textual and material evidence as real natural hazards that affected the ancient world and caused catastrophes, although there is no specific word to describe them. The earliest Greek literary source, the *Iliad*, tells of a wave that Poseidon caused to wash away the victorious Greeks' defensive wall after the end of the Trojan War.[4] The area was wiped clean and left covered with sand. In the fifth century BCE, Herodotus mentions "an exceptionally low tide which lasted a long time" at Potidaea, followed by a "flood" which "according to the people thereabouts [was] higher than it had been before."[5] This was during the Persian invasion of 479 BCE. Many Persian troops, taking the opportunity to try to cross the exposed sea bed, were drowned. This was a catastrophe for the Persians, if not for the locals. Recently a team has reported evidence from core samples that support the reality of this tsunami event.[6] Thucydides, writing of events he was contemporary with, also tells us of earthquakes and tsunamis in 426 BCE. He recorded that "the sea at Orobiae, in Euboea, retiring from the then line of coast, returned in a huge wave and invaded a great part of the town, and retreated leaving some of it still under water; so that what was once land is now sea; such of the inhabitants perishing as could not run up to the higher ground in time."[7]

Over time, recorded observations of natural phenomena increased, and some authors even produced earthquake catalogues, such as the one by

3 See, for example, Anthony Oliver-Smith and Susanna M. Hoffman, "Introduction: Why Anthropologists Should Study Disasters," in *Catastrophe and Culture: The Anthropology of Disaster*, ed. Anthony Oliver-Smith and Susanna M. Hoffman (Santa Fe, NM: School of American Research Press, 2002), 3–22.

4 Hom. *Il.* 12.1–30.

5 Hdt. 8.129; Alfred D. Godley, trans., *Herodotus, The Histories* (Cambridge, MA: Harvard University Press, 1920).

6 Margret Mathes-Schmidt et al., "Event Deposits in the Eastern Thermaikos Gulf and Kassandra Peninsula (Northern Greece): Evidence of the 479 BC 'Herodotus Tsunami'," *Zeitschrift für Geomorphologie*, Supplementary Issues 62, Supplementary Issue 2 (2019): 101–125.

7 Thuc. 3.89; Richard Crawley, trans., *Thucydides, The Peloponnesian War* (London: J. M. Dent, 1910).

Demetrius of Callatis, mentioned by Strabo;[8] these may well have recorded unusual waves too. Although there were no "instrumental" observations, as we have now, knowledge of earlier earthquakes and tsunamis nevertheless became part of the inherited tradition such that even in Roman times authors as varied as the poet Ovid, the philosopher Seneca, and the historian Diodorus Siculus could draw on examples of these phenomena from hundreds of years before and attempt to discern their cause.

In this chapter, I examine three cases in which coastal catastrophes have been proposed. In the first example, we go back to Late Bronze Age Crete, where the eruption of the Thera volcano has been associated with the decline and collapse of Minoan civilization. This is a modern catastrophe narrative, which can be evaluated through archaeological and geological research on Crete and in the Aegean. The second case is the destruction in 373 BCE of the Classical city of Helike,[9] in the northern Peloponnese (on the south coast of the Gulf of Corinth), which was characterized as a coastal catastrophe in then-contemporary and subsequent textual sources. The third case, the devastating tsunami of AD 365, was vividly described by the contemporary Ammianus Marcellinus.[10] In the second and third cases, we can attempt to test the literary record against the archaeological data and other research. In the process of approaching these supposed coastal catastrophes through a combination of evidence, it is hoped that we can come to understand both the nature of the events they are associated with, the tsunamis, and the archaeological and literary evidence itself more closely.

The Thera Eruption and Minoan Crete

The Late Bronze Age eruption of Thera (Santorini) "was the greatest event of natural destruction in human history," generating a ten-metre-high wave that, "after an unbroken run to Crete, cast itself on Knossos" and, at least in part, "precipitated the downfall of the Minoan civilization," as one book on volcanoes explains.[11] Luce has mentioned casualties

---

8 Strabo 1.3.20; Horace L. Jones, trans., *The Geography of Strabo* (Cambridge, MA: Harvard University Press, 1924).

9 For consistency I use the spelling "Helike" throughout the main text of this chapter, including in quotations that employ other conventions.

10 For further discussion of this tsunami, see Álvarez-Martí-Aguilar's chapter in this volume.

11 James Hamilton, *Volcano: Nature and Culture* (London: Reaktion Books, 2012), 11.

possibly in the tens of thousands, damage to settlements and buildings, the destruction of ships, years of failed crops and famine in the east, and the relocation of people.[12] There is no evidence that Knossos, at over five kilometres inland and 95 metres above the current sea level, was ever drowned in a tsunami, but the basic narrative above is widely known, and all of the effects Luce listed are known from other historical examples of earthquakes, volcanoes, and tsunamis. The Thera tsunami and its impact on Minoan Crete require re-examination in the light of developments in the field.

Archaeologists place the final Minoan "collapse" long after the Neopalatial Thera eruption of Late Minoan IA (LM IA; 1600–1500 BCE),[13] with more or less than a century between the eruption and the LM IB (1500–1425 BCE) destructions and loss of cultural features that indicate the collapse of the established Neopalatial order.[14] Although many sites were destroyed in LM IA, it is not always possible to tell whether destructions were prior to or contemporaneous with the Thera eruption; many sites continued or were rebuilt and occupied in LM IB.[15] Sometimes these had modifications for restricting access, subdividing spaces, and making room for production and storage, and were on a reduced scale. A change in Minoan religious practices can be seen after the eruption – peak sanctuaries are largely abandoned. Theran pumice seems to be used in ritual contexts. There were destructions away from the north coast for which a tsunami cannot be blamed, many of which are attributed to earthquakes.[16] Destructions seem to happen throughout LM IA and B, probably with a range of immediate causes.[17]

---

12 John V. Luce, *The End of Atlantis* (London: Paladin, 1969), 79–80; John V. Luce and Kathleen Bolton, "Thera and the Devastation of Minoan Crete: A New Interpretation of the Evidence," *American Journal of Archaeology* 80, no. 1 (Winter 1976): 9–18.

13 The dates supplied here follow those of L. Vance Watrous, *Minoan Crete: An Introduction* (Cambridge: Cambridge University Press, 2021), xv.

14 Jan Driessen, "The Santorini Eruption: An Archaeological Investigation of its Distal Impacts on Minoan Crete," *Quaternary International* 499 (2019): 195–204; Jan Driessen and Colin F. MacDonald, "The Eruption of the Santorini Volcano and its Effects on Minoan Crete," in *The Archaeology of Geological Catastrophes*, ed. W. J. McGuire et al. (London: Geological Society, 2000), 81–93.

15 Jan Driessen and Colin F. MacDonald, *The Troubled Island: Minoan Crete before and after the Santorini Eruption* (Liège: Université de Liège, 1997), 36.

16 Paul Rehak and John G. Younger, "Review of Aegean Prehistory VII: Neopalatial, Final Palatial, and Postpalatial Crete," *American Journal of Archaeology* 102, no. 1 (January 1998): 91–173.

17 Driessen, "Santorini Eruption," 199; Driessen and MacDonald, *Troubled Island*, 35; Rehak and Younger, "Review," 149.

The Minoan collapse must be seen in a longer context. Neopalatial Crete was organized into larger and smaller states, which appear to have competed with each other, sometimes violently – there are defensive structures and weapons.[18] What seems to have happened is that a potentially unstable socio-political arrangement on the island unravelled.[19] In LM II (1425–1390 BCE) only the Knossos palace remained in use and in LM IIIA (1390–1330 BCE) its Mycenaean (?) administrators were using Greek written in Linear B rather than "Minoan" written in Linear A. Long seen as taking advantage of the destruction of the Minoan navy, the chronology suggests that Mycenaeans did not simply step straight into a power vacuum and take over wholesale. The picture is undoubtedly much more complicated, with a combination of natural and human factors.[20] As Driessen comments, "Santorini's destruction and what happened on Crete in LM IB are two chronologically different events. Whether the second has some relationship to the first remains a hypothesis."[21]

A natural disaster such as an earthquake, volcanic eruption, or tsunami can have other effects with far-reaching consequences. Certainly, the psychological effects of Thera should not be understated – the sound and sight of the eruption, the darkening sky and ash fall, the huge volumes of pumice ejected and transported by the sea. Driessen and MacDonald have discussed the range of impacts of a disaster, such as the panic, shock, or disbelief that might have resulted, the allocation of blame to gods, leaders, or the system, possible religious responses, including human sacrifice, and the impact of local responses and the formation of new groups that would compete with the previous order.[22] Materially, the new "Marine style" pottery, associated with the elite and perhaps with some ritual function, might also have appeared in response to coastal catastrophe. But given the above "history," was there actually a coastal catastrophe in LM IA?

---

18   Watrous, *Minoan Crete*, 87–88.
19   Rehak and Younger, "Review," 149.
20   Jan Driessen and Charlotte Langohr, "Rallying 'round a 'Minoan' Past: The Legitimation of Power at Knossos During the Late Bronze Age," in *Rethinking Mycenaean Palaces II*, ed. Michael L. Galaty and William A. Parkinson (Los Angeles: Cotsen Institute of Archaeology, 2007), 178–189.
21   Jan Driessen, "*The Troubled Island...* 15 years later," paper presented at the January 2013 Heidelberg meeting on the relations between Crete and Santorini (2013): https://www.academia.edu/2971816/The_Troubled_Island._15_years_later. Accessed 25 July 2021.
22   Driessen and MacDonald, *Troubled Island*, 94–102.

The earthquake–volcano–tsunami theory was originally proposed by Marinatos in 1939 to explain the LM IA destructions. He argued that "there is little reason to doubt that the devastation of the coast-sites of Minoan Crete was caused by the waves from the eruption of Thera."[23] Foremost in his mind was Krakatoa, with its massive Plinian eruption, pyroclastic flows, caldera collapse, and tsunami. Marinatos thought that sites such as Amnisos, north of Knossos, showed evidence of destruction by wave action. In a much more recent study, Driessen and MacGillivray have also suggested that a number of site destructions and the patterns left in the archaeological record for LM IA, from Chania along the north and east coasts to Zakros, could fit with the action of a tsunami sweeping in and then retreating.[24] Sedimentary analysis of the Aegean sea floor has been generally accepted as showing the effects of tsunamis shifting sediments around.[25]

The site reckoned to provide the most compelling evidence of a megatsunami is Palaikastro, on the east coast of Crete.[26] There, Bruins and colleagues identified seven sedimentary features consistent with a tsunami.[27] These included a sharp boundary of sediment with underlying rock, redeposited grains of Theran ash (intraclasts), tumbled building stones, marine shells, marine microfauna (including coral algae and foraminifera), overlapping (imbricated) pottery sherds, masonry, bones and rounded pebbles, and a mixed-up stratigraphic layer comprising a variety of materials (for example, ceramics, bone, and rounded pebbles). The best explanation for such a "chaotic" layer of sediment seemed to

23 Spyridon Marinatos, "The Volcanic Destruction of Minoan Crete," *Antiquity* 13, no. 52 (December 1939): 425–439.

24 Jan Driessen and J. Alexander MacGillivray, "Swept Away in LM IA? Explaining Debris Deposition in Coastal Neopalatial Crete," in *Proceedings of the 10th Cretological Congress of Chania 2006*, ed. Maria Vlasaki-Andreadaki (Iraklion: Society for the Study of Cretan Historical Studies, 2011), 233–244.

25 Beverly Goodman-Tchernov et al., "Tsunami Waves Generated by the Santorini Eruption Reached Eastern Mediterranean Shores," *Geology* 37, no. 10 (1 October 2009): 943–946; Kim A. Kastens and Maria B. Cita, "Tsunami-Induced Sediment Transport in the Abyssal Mediterranean Sea," *GSA Bulletin* 92, no. 11 (1 November 1981): 845–857; K. Minoura et al., "Discovery of Minoan Tsunami Deposits," *Geology* 28, no. 1 (1 January 2000): 59–62.

26 Driessen, "Santorini Eruption," 196.

27 Hendrik J. Bruins et al., "Geoarchaeological Tsunami Deposits at Palaikastro (Crete) and the Late Minoan IA Eruption of Santorini," *Journal of Archaeological Science* 35, no. 1 (January 2008): 191–212; Hendrik J. Bruins, Johannes van der Plicht, and J. Alexander MacGillivray, "The Minoan Santorini Eruption and Tsunami Deposits in Palaikastro (Crete): Dating by Geology, Archaeology, ¹⁴C, and Egyptian Chronology," *Radiocarbon* 51, no. 2 (2009): 397–411.

be tsunami action. They proposed that a nine-metre-high wave that travelled 300 metres inland "inundated the town completely."[28]

Other work carried out at Palaikastro may contradict the tsunami hypothesis, and at least some of the evidence taken as indicative of a tsunami can be explained in other ways. Kulick undertook a micromorphological analysis of 35 soil samples from three newly excavated structures. She suggests that "it does not appear that the mechanisms that deposited the tephra, sediments, and LM IA archaeological debris in this location were rapid or violent," which challenges "the hypothesis [of] [...] a catastrophic LM IA event," such as a tsunami.[29] Evidence from other coastal sites such as Priniatikos Pyrgos and Papadiokampos may support Kulick's point.[30] It is possible that flooding from the landward side, caused by rain, damming, and dam breaking, could explain the formation of at least some of the evidence adduced to a tsunami. Such flooding on Crete can be incredibly destructive. Whether or not a tsunami inundated Palaikastro, or it was flooded from the landward side, it was not abandoned, but rebuilt and inhabited through LM IB.

On the ground in northern Crete, geological evidence of a megatsunami is limited. Dominey-Howes undertook a study of 41 coastal sites on Crete and Kos, where core samples were taken and examined for macro and micro marine fossils, such as foraminifera and molluscs, that would have been deposited by a tsunami.[31] He found no evidence indicative of a tsunami and concluded that any tsunami generated by the Thera eruption may have been limited to the immediate vicinity of the island or may have spread only in a westerly direction.

Our understanding of the generation of the proposed tsunami has also changed. Initially it was thought that the collapse of the massive Theran caldera would have caused a huge tsunami, as at Krakatoa, but other research has cast doubt on this.[32] Nomikou and colleagues' bathymetric

---

28 Bruins et al., "Geoarchaeological Tsunami Deposits," 209.

29 Rachel Kulick, "Urban Micromorphology: A Microecological Narrative of a Neopalatial Neighborhood at Bronze Age Palaikastro, Crete," *Geoarchaeology* 34, no. 4 (2019): 430–447.

30 Barry P. Molloy et al., "Of Tephra and Tsunamis: A Secondary Deposit of Tephra Sealing LM IA Activity at Priniatikos Pyrgos," in *A Cretan Landscape Through Time: Priniatikos Pyrgos and Environs*, ed. Barry P. Molloy and Chloë N. Duckworth (Oxford: Archaeopress, 2014), 43–53.

31 Dale Dominey-Howes, "A Re-analysis of the Late Bronze Age Eruption and Tsunami of Santorini, Greece, and the Implications for the Volcano-Tsunami Hazard," *Journal of Volcanology and Geothermal Research* 130, nos. 1–2 (15 February 2004): 107–132.

32 Marinatos, *Volcanic Destruction*, 430–432; Floyd W. McCoy and Grant Heiken,

and seismic study of the Theran sea floor suggests that the caldera was neither flooded nor open to the sea before the eruption; this means that caldera collapse could not have generated any large tsunami.[33] Even if it was flooded, they note, any tsunami waves would have been directed through the northwest and southwest channels rather than towards Crete. A tsunami hitting Crete, then, might have been generated only from pyroclastic flows and the slumping of ash, rock, and pumice and might have been much less powerful than previously thought.

Unambiguous archaeological and geological evidence of a megatsunami and coastal catastrophe on Minoan Crete has been generally difficult to find. One reason for a lack of archaeological visibility could be that communities were quite effective at cleaning up afterwards. Sea-level and coastline change and the alteration of local land forms also affect the coastal archaeology; geologically clear tsunami deposits may no longer be accessible. In archaeology, it must always be remembered that "absence of evidence is not evidence of absence." Recently published research from coastal Turkey, however, might provide evidence of a Theran tsunami in that region.[34]

Another point worth considering is that a tsunami could have been smaller than imagined. The psychological and social impact of a tsunami may have been much greater than any physical destructions caused by it. Even a relatively low and non-destructive wave, if affecting a long stretch of coastline, would have been a remarkable event. The sea creeping over the land is something to see. This would have been a phenomenon that everyone on the island would have heard about and that many in the north and east would have experienced directly. Possibly preceded by earthquakes, with darkness and ash fall, then pumice arriving by sea later, it may well have seemed that the world was ending. Rain-driven floods may have added into a tradition of "catastrophe." The Cretans may have thought that the sky, the earth, and the sea were coming against them, but whether there were coastal catastrophes is still uncertain.

"Tsunami Generated by the Late Bronze Age Eruption of Thera (Santorini), Greece," *Pure and Applied Geophysics* 157, no. 6 (2000): 1227–1256.

33 P. Nomikou et al., "Post-Eruptive Flooding of Santorini Caldera and Implications for Tsunami Generation," *Nature Communications* 7, article no. 13332 (8 November 2016), 1–10.

34 Vasıf Şahoğlu et al., "Volcanic Ash, Victims, and Tsunami Debris from the Late Bronze Age Thera Eruption Discovered at Çeşme-Bağlararası (Turkey)," *Proceedings of the National Academy of Sciences* 119, no. 1 (December 2021): e2114213118. https://doi.org/10.1073/pnas.2114213118.

The Destruction of Classical Helike in 373 BCE

Classical Helike was an important city in Achaea in the Peloponnese, famous for its sanctuary of Poseidon. The destruction of the city and its neighbour Bura in 373 BCE was widely known in antiquity; its story was retold by authors well into Roman times, some of whom provide the clearest descriptions. It may have been the inspiration for the fate of Atlantis and the Athenians in Plato's Atlantis myth (a political allegory not a history).[35] In the story, there were earthquakes and floods and Atlantis "was swallowed up by the sea and vanished"; the Athenian soldiers, who had defeated the Atlanteans, were "swallowed up by the earth."[36]

Strabo explained that "the sea was raised by an earthquake and it submerged Helike, and also the temple of the Heliconian Poseidon."[37] He quoted two earlier sources thus:

> Eratosthenes says that he himself saw the place, and that the ferrymen say that there was a bronze Poseidon in the strait, standing erect, holding a hippocampus in his hand, which was perilous for those who fished with nets. And Heracleides says that the submersion took place by night in his time, and, although the city was twelve stadia distant from the sea, this whole district together with the city was hidden from sight.[38]

Heracleides, contemporary with the event, also stated that a rescue party of 2,000 Achaeans "were unable to recover the bodies."[39] Diodorus also tells us of the earthquake and that falling buildings killed most people in their panic and confusion; then there was a "greater and still more incredible danger. For the sea rose to a vast height, and a wave towering even higher washed away and drowned all the inhabitants and their native lands as well."[40] Pausanias added that "the tide was so deep in the grove of Poseidon that only the tops of the trees remained visible. What with the sudden earthquake, and the invasion of the sea that accompanied

---

35 Richard Ellis, *Imagining Atlantis* (New York: Vintage, 1998), 237–244; A. E. Taylor, *A Commentary on Plato's Timaeus* (Oxford: Oxford University Press, 1928), 56.

36 Pl. *Ti.* 25; Walter R. M. Lamb, trans., *Plato in Twelve Volumes*, Volume 9 (Cambridge, MA: Harvard University Press, 1925).

37 Strabo 8.7.2.

38 8.7.2.

39 8.7.2.

40 Diod. Sic. 15.48; Charles L. Sherman, trans., *Diodorus Siculus, Library of History, Volume VII: Books 15.20–16.65* (Cambridge, MA: Harvard University Press, 1952).

it, the tidal wave swallowed up Helike and every man in it."[41] Apparently in his time "the ruins of Helike" were "visible, but not so plainly now as they were once, because they are corroded by the salt water."[42] With no people and no city left, the territory of Helike was divided up amongst its neighbours and the city-state ceased to exist.[43]

The Gulf of Corinth region is known as being at high risk of tsunamis, so the historical accounts have usually been taken seriously.[44] But although Helike's location was described in the ancient sources, some way inland between the Selinous and Kerynites rivers, no city or remains are visible in modern times, though a coin minted at Helike was found in the area in 1861. The modern search for Helike began again with Marinatos.[45] He noted that aerial photographs of the area revealed nothing and that the sea bottom nearby was covered in mud, hiding whatever lay beneath. Marinatos and Harold Edgerton, who had developed a sonar "mud-pinger," mapped the topography of the sea bed but, despite finding one "unusual configuration" almost 400 metres offshore, did not discover the lost city.[46] In 1988 the new Helike Project also used sonar technology to survey eight square kilometres of sea floor, but again no trace was found of the city.[47]

At the end of his article, Marinatos had suggested that, whatever happened beforehand, the Classical city had eventually been buried by fluvial deposits from the rivers – it may have been buried by sediment under the sea or on land.[48] The new Helike team, having had no luck searching the sea bed, turned their attention to the coastal plain between

41 Paus. 7.24.12; William H. S. Jones, trans., *Pausanias: Description of Greece*, Volume III (Cambridge, MA: Harvard University Press, 1918).

42 Paus. 7.24.13.

43 Emily Mackil, "Wandering Cities: Alternatives to Catastrophe in the Greek polis," *American Journal of Archaeology* 108, no. 4 (October 2004): 493–516.

44 M. Papathoma and D. Dominey-Howes, "Tsunami Vulnerability Assessment and its Implications for Coastal Hazard Analysis and Disaster Management Planning, Gulf of Corinth, Greece," *Natural Hazards and Earth System Sciences* 3, no. 6 (31 December 2003): 733–747.

45 Spyridon Marinatos, "Helice: A Submerged Town of Classical Greece," *Archaeology* 13, no. 3 (1960): 186–193.

46 *New York Times*, "Discovery Off Greece Stirring Hope in Quest for Ancient City," (1 December 1966): https://www.nytimes.com/1966/12/01/archives/discovery-off-greece-stirring-hope-in-quest-for-ancient-city-sonic.html. Accessed 25 July 2021; Harold Edgerton, "Underwater Archaeological Search with Sonar," *Historical Archaeology* 10, no. 1 (1976): 46–53.

47 Steven Soter and Dora Katsonopoulou, "Submergence and Uplift of Settlements in the Area of Helike, Greece, from the Early Bronze Age to Late Antiquity," *Geoarchaeology: An International Journal* 26, no. 4 (July/August 2011): 584–610.

48 Marinatos, "Helice," 193.

the two rivers and between 1991 and 2002 drilled 99 boreholes. In numerous cores, they found evidence of occupation and fragments of pottery deposited in coarse and gravelly soil, possibly deposited by water action. They examined nine sites in more detail through excavations.

Their search was successful: Classical material was found in several locations. At the Balalas site, the corner of a Classical-period building was found, along with some worn fragments of pottery. A part of the walls had fallen to seaward; the team thought it could have been pushed/pulled by the flow and backwash of a tsunami. At the Papafilippou area, Classical remains were also uncovered, with walls, roof tiles, pottery, and coins found. In some layers in the Classical trenches freshwater and marine microfauna were identified. It seemed that not only had Helike been found, but also there was evidence of it having been destroyed by a tsunami. However, on balance, Soter and Katsonopoulou concluded that "while the historical evidence for the earthquake and tsunami in 373 BC is strong, evidence based on stratigraphy and archaeological excavation is merely suggestive."[49]

The excavations of the Helike Project and exploration by other researchers have revealed that the area of Helike had a very long history of habitation, probably owing to the good agricultural land between the rivers. There was an Early Bronze Age settlement and Mycenaean material. Near some late Mycenaean graves a Geometric-period temple was found in the village of Nikoleia.[50] There were examples of Archaic, late Classical, and Hellenistic material, including walls, tiles, and coins, with some destruction layers dated to slightly after the supposed tsunami destruction (330–300 BCE). A Hellenistic temple was found and excavated by Petropoulos.[51] The Helike team found Roman, Late Roman, and Byzantine remains too, including a major Roman road, likely to have been the one travelled by Pausanias.[52] A study of coins found in the Helike area concluded that some were minted shortly after 373 BCE, and its author suggested that post-373 BCE Helike still existed as a political unit in some form.[53] Bura, which according to Strabo was swallowed up by the earth, was refounded by survivors who had been away from the city when it was destroyed.[54]

---

49 Soter and Katsonopoulou, "Submergence and Uplift," 604.

50 Erophile Kolia, "A Sanctuary of the Geometric Period in Ancient Helike, Achaea," *The Annual of the British School at Athens* 106, no. 1 (November 2011): 201–246.

51 Kolia, "Sanctuary," 203.

52 Soter and Katsonopoulou, "Submergence and Uplift," 591.

53 Robert Weir, "Exaggerated Rumours of Death and the Downdating of Helike's Coinage," in *Helike V: Ancient Helike and Aigialeia. Poseidon, God of Earthquakes and Waters*, ed. Dora Katsonopoulou (Athens: The Helike Society, 2017), 33–61.

54 Paus. 7.25.5; Strabo 1.3.18.

The sources seem clear on blaming a tsunami from the sea for the destruction of Helike and the death of its inhabitants. So, given the presence of Hellenistic and Roman material, including the remains of a Hellenistic temple, how can the very clearly described and well-known story of the coastal catastrophe be made sense of? Those who have studied the landscape around Helike in trying to find the Classical city have found that the area is and has been subject to numerous types of change, including the shifting course of rivers, siltation, and tectonic uplift and slippage.[55] Marinatos knew this already, having talked with locals who told him about the shifting shoreline – one example they gave was of a vineyard that had only a few years before been next to the sea but was now 300 feet inland.[56]

The most recent study by Koukouvelas and colleagues sets aside previous "coastal disaster models" and instead proposes an "inland-driven disaster model."[57] They dismiss the tsunami idea as generally unsupported and propose that tectonic processes were to blame for the destruction. In their study, they suggest that "the wave that 'washed away and drowned all the inhabitants' was not a tsunami, but rather the frontal wave of a catastrophic mud flow formed by bursting of a natural dam formed during the 373 BC Helike earthquake."[58] An example of precisely this kind of occurrence, they note, happened in the nearby Krathis River area. Heavy rainfall and an earthquake caused landslides which obstructed the river and created two new lakes. Lake Krathis was some three kilometres long with a dam of 80 metres in height. In January 1914, the dam failed and caused a 13 kilometre and metre-deep flood. Another recent study by Engel and colleagues suggests that a minor tsunami may have hit Helike, but also that the city was probably submerged in the formation of a lake or lagoon.[59] It lay on a gradually submerging area of land, and an earthquake could have led to a more rapid subsidence, as well as soil liquefaction, changes to the courses of

55 A. Koutsios et al., "Sedimentological and Geophysical Observations in the Delta Plain of Selinous River, Ancient Helike, Northern Peloponnesus Greece," *Bulletin of the Geological Society of Greece* 43, no. 2 (2010): 654–662.

56 Marinatos, *Helice*, 192.

57 Ioannis K. Koukouvelas et al., "Earthquake-Triggered Landslides and Mudflows: Was this the Wave that Engulfed Ancient Helike?" *The Holocene* 30, no. 12 (August 2020): 1653–1668.

58 Koukouvelas et al., "Landslides," 1665.

59 Max Engel et al., "New Sediment Cores Reveal Environmental Changes Driven by Tectonic Processes at Ancient Helike, Greece," *Geoarchaeology: An International Journal* 31, no. 2 (2016): 140–155.

rivers, and landslides. Thus a sea wave may not have been the major factor in the destruction of the city.

Perhaps the dynamic nature of the local environment and traditions about changes in it stretching far back in time were what made the cult of Poseidon so prominent at Helike – it was a highly appropriate place for the worship of the god of the sea and of earthquakes. What exactly happened to the cities of Helike (and Bura) is still not clear. There is no need to doubt significant destruction, but perhaps it was not total; and whatever the risks – and these were surely known by communities in the area – people continued to live there after 373 BCE.

Alexandria and the AD 365 Tsunami

Alexandria has become both more famous and more infamous over the past few decades. On the one hand, underwater archaeologists have explored and mapped the sunken parts of the city, revealing many exciting details about the ancient city.[60] On the other, Alexandria has become increasingly endangered by rising sea levels and by subsidence, which threaten not only its antiquities but its modern infrastructure, its population, and its very existence.[61] The city has been very resilient up to now, despite having been imperilled by natural and human action. One event the city survived is the great tsunami of AD 365, which is recorded by a number of historical sources, but which continues to puzzle.

The AD 365 earthquake has been associated with a massive tectonic uplift event, which raised western Crete by six to nine metres.[62] This may have been caused by a slip of 20 metres along a fault line 100 kilometres long, west of the island.[63] Archaeology has demonstrated that some sites on Crete have destructions contemporary with the earthquake, for example Gortyn and Kisamos, and the harbour at Phalasarna was raised up by over six metres.[64] Other areas from Sicily and into the Adriatic to Cyprus and

---

60 Franck Goddio and Andre Bernand, *Sunken Egypt: Alexandria* (London: Periplus, 2004).

61 Samy Magdy, "Rising Seas Threaten Egypt's Fabled Port City of Alexandria," *Associated Press* (30 August 2019): https://apnews.com/article/e4fec321109941798cd-befae310695aa. Accessed 25 July 2021.

62 P. A. Pirazzoli et al., "Historical Environmental Changes at Phalasarna Harbor, West Crete," *Geoarchaeology* 7, no. 4 (July 1992): 371–392.

63 B. Shaw et al., "Eastern Mediterranean Tectonics and Tsunami Hazard Inferred from the AD 365 Earthquake," *Nature Geoscience* 1, no. 4 (9 March 2008): 268–276.

64 Stathis C. Stiros, "The AD 365 Crete Earthquake and Possible Seismic Clustering

North Africa may have suffered earthquakes too.[65] A region-wide tsunami is inferred from sediment deposits taken from southwest Crete and the Ionian Sea, and from core samples and trenching at El Alamein and Kefr Saber, west of Alexandria.[66] One estimate proposes that the tsunami ran up as high as 9.5 metres.[67]

The late-fourth-century historian Ammianus Marcellinus is the key ancient source on this global tsunami. He reported that the massive earthquake and tsunami "spread through the entire extent of the world."[68] His description of the event is a *tour de force* and worth quoting at length:

> For a little after daybreak, preceded by heavy and repeated thunder and lightning, the whole of the firm and solid earth was shaken and trembled, the sea with its rolling waves was driven back and withdrew from the land, so that in the abyss of the deep thus revealed men saw many kinds of sea-creatures stuck fast in the slime; and vast mountains and deep valleys, which Nature, the creator, had hidden in the unplumbed depths, then, as one might well believe, first saw the beams of the sun. Hence, many ships were stranded as if on dry land, and since many men roamed about without fear in the little that remained of the waters, to gather fish and similar things with their hands, the roaring sea, resenting, as it were, this forced retreat, rose in its turn; and over the boiling shoals it dashed mightily upon islands and broad stretches of the

During the Fourth to Sixth Centuries AD in the Eastern Mediterranean: A Review of Historical and Archaeological Data," *Journal of Structural Geology* 23, nos. 2–3 (February 2001): 545–562; Stathis C. Stiros and Sofia Papageorgiou, "Seismicity of Western Crete and the Destruction of the Town of Kisamos at AD 365: Archaeological Evidence," *Journal of Seismology* 5, no. 3 (July 2001): 381–397.

65 Stathis C. Stiros, "The 8.5+ Magnitude, AD 365 Earthquake in Crete: Coastal Uplift, Topography Changes, Archaeological and Historical Signature," *Quaternary International* 216, nos. 1–2 (April 2010): 54–63.

66 Alina Polonia et al., "Mediterranean Megaturbidite Triggered by the AD 365 Crete Earthquake and Tsunami," *Scientific Reports* 3, article no. 1285 (15 February 2013): https://doi.org/10.1038/srep01285; Asema Salama et al., "Paleotsunami Deposits Along the Coast of Egypt Correlate with Historical Earthquake Records of Eastern Mediterranean," *Natural Hazards and Earth System Sciences* 18, no. 8 (17 August 2018): 2203–2219; Vera Werner et al., "The Sedimentary and Geomorphological Imprint of the AD 365 Tsunami on the Coasts of Southwestern Crete (Greece) – Examples from Sougia and Palaiochora," *Quaternary International* 473, Part A (15 April 2018): 66–90.

67 Amr Z. Hamouda, "A Reanalysis of the AD 365 Tsunami Impact Along the Egyptian Mediterranean Coast," *Acta Geophysica* 58, no. 4 (2009): 687–704.

68 Amm. Marc. 26.10; John C. Rolfe, trans., *Ammianus Marcellinus. Rerum Gestarum* (Cambridge, MA: Harvard University Press, 1935–1940).

mainland, and levelled innumerable buildings in the cities and wherever else they were found; so that amid the mad discord of the elements the altered face of the earth revealed marvellous sights. For the great mass of waters, returning when it was least expected, killed many thousands of men by drowning; and by the swift recoil of the eddying tides a number of ships, after the swelling of the wet element subsided, were seen to have foundered, and the lifeless bodies of shipwrecked persons lay floating on their backs or on their faces. Other great ships, driven by the mad blasts, landed on the tops of buildings (as happened at Alexandria), and some were driven almost two miles inland, like a Laconian ship which I myself in passing that way saw near the town of Mothone, yawning apart through long decay.[69]

Ammianus' account rings true, but he does not claim to have been an eyewitness to the disaster, and he is probably reliant on common knowledge, discussions with witnesses, and other people's writings. Indeed, as Kelly points out, Ammianus is mute on who saw the things he described; those people picking up fish would not have survived the return of the sea.[70] After referring to "the whole circle of the world," he mentions only two places specifically, Alexandria and Methone, but by ending the passage with his own observation, he gives authority to the preceding description, as if he has seen what he describes. Ammianus' text can be taken in a number of ways, as a relevant and factual aside in his broader narrative, as a literary device or flourish, as metaphor, or as a combination of these.

Yet, as Stiros observes, "the impacts of the 365 tsunami in Alexandria remain a matter of debate, ranging from total destruction (50,000 victims) to marginal effects [...] and to [a] rather fabricated story."[71] One of the key issues is the dating of the earthquake and tsunami, and another is reconciling the various sources which disagree in the details. Stiros has tabulated data from 21 ancient sources dating from the fourth (contemporary) to the eleventh centuries, which give a range of dates and details.[72] Ammianus is the clearest, giving the date of 21 July AD 365 for a

69 Amm. Marc. 26.10.16–19.

70 Gavin Kelly, "Ammianus and the Great Tsunami," *Journal of Roman Studies* 94 (2004): 141–167.

71 Stathis C. Stiros, "The AD 365 Ammianus Tsunami in Alexandria, Egypt, and the Crete ca. 365 Fault and Tsunami," *Arabian Journal of Geosciences* 13, article no. 716 (23 July 2020): 716.

72 Stathis C. Stiros, "Was Alexandria (Egypt) Destroyed in A.D. 365? A Famous

universal earthquake and tsunami. Another contemporary, Athanasius, an Alexandrian bishop, gives the same date for the earthquake and tsunami from the east in his *Festal Letter* 37. Two other fourth-century sources, Hieronymus and Libanius, mention earthquakes and tsunamis, but the former places these in AD 363 and Libanius from AD 363 to 368. The much later sources must derive from earlier ones, but dates from AD 355 to AD 383 are given. Some of the sources mention an earthquake but no tsunami, and the seventh-century John of Nikiu describes how Alexandria was saved from the tsunami by a miracle.

The second issue is the impact on Alexandria. Ammianus' ship on a roof suggests a major tsunami wave, and the three-kilometre run-up (though this may not be at Alexandria) agrees with this. The city lies only five metres above sea level on a spit of land at the western end of the Nile Delta, with Lake Mareotis behind it, and around three kilometres from sea to lake. A wave this big would certainly have been catastrophic, as Stiros notes. Running up over the walls, seawater would have been concentrated and then trapped in the streets, which would have serious longer-term effects on habitability and use, human health, and the fresh water supply, which was provided by a complex system of cisterns, tunnels, wells, and aqueducts.[73] However, there is no indication of tumbled columns or statues or of building collapse, no evidence of commemorative inscriptions that would have followed rebuilding, and no mention of imperial funding or tax relief, which could be expected as a recovery measure. Athanasius' annual *Festal Letters* continue without any further mention of the catastrophe.[74]

John of Nikiu's story dates the earthquake and tsunami to AD 363 and is different to the others; it goes against the catastrophe narrative:

> When the sea rose against the city of Alexandria and, threatening an inundation, had already advanced to a place called Heptastadion, the venerable father [St Athanasius, the patriarch of Alexandria] accompanied by all the priests went forth to the borders of the sea, and holding in his hand the book of the holy Law he raised his hand to heaven and said: "O Lord, Thou God who liest not, it is Thou that didst promise to Noah after the flood and say: 'I will not again bring

a flood of waters upon the earth'." And after these words of the saint the sea returned to its place and the wrath of God was appeased.[75]

Like John, Sozomen, writing in the fifth century, also placed the earthquake and tsunami during the rise to power or reign of Julian, who died in AD 363. This may be because Sozomen was giving his own pro-Christian perspective. He wrote that God was displeased with the polytheistic Julian, and immediately prior to his description of the earthquake and tsunami, he stated that "it is, however, very obvious that, throughout the reign of this emperor, God gave manifest tokens of His displeasure, and permitted many calamities to befall several of the provinces of the Roman Empire."[76] He also points out excessive drought, bad air, agricultural failure, hunger, and disease in Julian's empire; clear signs of divine displeasure.

If Christian authors could move historical events around to fit their own purposes, pagan authors such as Ammianus could also use events to reflect on the wider situation. Kelly has argued that the tsunami episode in Ammianus is a deliberate and calculated metaphor for "the grand narrative of the Roman Empire," and for the world after the death of the emperor Julian; it is not a disinterested and disconnected aside.[77] Ammianus, and other authors, may even have confused several events for a single one, or deliberately conflated them. Ammianus' account is interesting also for what it does not tell us – the detail he omits whilst remaining plausible: "Ammianus offers a dramatized, rhetorical, and elusive account of the tsunami, which nevertheless maintains for modern readers the semblance of comprehension and balance [...]."[78]

There appears to be little or no archaeological evidence for a "catastrophic" tsunami at Alexandria in or around AD 365, and the historical sources do not indicate a crisis of the kind we would expect from Ammianus' description. The city's physical, political, and social infrastructures did not fail, and the city remained important. It continued to exist through Late Antique and Byzantine times and still later after its

75 John of Nikiu, *Chronicle* 82.9–21; Robert H. Charles, trans., *The Chronicle of John, Bishop of Nikiu: Translated from Zotenberg's Ethiopic Text* (Merchantville: Arx Publishing, 2007), 84.

76 Sozomen, *Ecclesiastical History* 6.2; Philip Schaff and Rev. Henry Wallace, eds., *Nicene and Post-Nicene Fathers: Second Series Volume II Socrates, Sozomenus: Church Histories* (New York: Cosimo, Inc., 2007), 347.

77 Kelly, "Ammianus," 165.

78 Kelly, "Ammianus," 155.

conquest by the Arabs in AD 646.[79] There is no break in the ecclesiastical history of the city at AD 365, it remained the seat of a bishop, there is no reported cessation in the functioning of the library, and apparently no damage to the Pharos lighthouse, which survived for a millennium, its integrity eroded by repeated earthquakes over its long life, and described as there but ruined in AD 1349.[80]

The harbour and some palaces and other buildings of the coastal and harbour areas of ancient Alexandria are now underwater, adding to the "mysterious" history of the city.[81] Like other deltas, the Nile Delta area is prone to subsidence, and during earthquakes this can be exacerbated by soil liquefaction and slumping. Subsidence is also caused because of building on unstable or water-saturated soils.[82] It can happen gradually over the years as well as suddenly in subsidence events. It is this that appears to have caused the harbour zones of Alexandria to sink.

While the city experienced earthquakes and probably tsunamis too, a severe coastal catastrophe in AD 365 seems hard to find. Ammianus may not have been a disinterested recorder of events, but, like other authors, made use of events with metaphorical intent; he may have conflated events, hearsay, and testimony, referring to multiple locations to weave together his dramatic description of a global catastrophe.

Catastrophe and the Divine

Attempts to accommodate catastrophes and disasters are often made through the medium of religion – even today. Although there is a progressivist narrative in which human understanding developed from the primitive, superstitious, and religious to the rational and modern in

---

79 Petra M. Sijpesteijn, "The Arab Conquest of Egypt and the Beginning of Muslim Rule," in *Byzantine Egypt*, ed. Roger S. Bagnall (Cambridge: Cambridge University Press, 2007), 437–459.

80 Goddio and Bernand, *Sunken Egypt*, 166–173.

81 Franck Goddio and David Fabre, "Port of Alexandria: Underwater archaeology," in *Encyclopedia of Global Archaeology*, ed. Claire Smith (New York: Springer, 2014), 6020–6027.

82 Jean-Daniel Stanley, Thomas F. Jorstad, and Franck Goddio, "Human Impact on Sediment Mass Movement and Submergence of Ancient Sites in the Two Harbours of Alexandria, Egypt," *Norwegian Journal of Geology* 86 (2006): 337–350; Jean-Daniel Stanley and Marguerite A. Toscano, "Ancient Archaeological Sites Buried and Submerged along Egypt's Nile Delta Coast: Gauges of Holocene Delta Margin Subsidence," *Journal of Coastal Research* 25, no. 1 (1 January 2009): 158–170.

the eighteenth-century European and American "Enlightenment," this is misleading – part of a wider web of discourses about backwardness, superiority, and even imperialism.[83] A closer look at the evidence makes it clear that, whilst scientific explanations have become much more dominant and accepted, religious interpretations and responses have never gone away, not even in "developed" countries.[84] Some people do still see disasters as divine retribution for some human fault, whilst some religious people are able to explain why good or innocent people can be struck by catastrophes. Recent studies of the population in Christchurch, New Zealand, struck by an earthquake in 2011, suggested that some of the affected people turned to religion.[85] Also, it is widely accepted that religion can play a role in post-disaster recovery, both on a personal and community level.[86] Religious responses may vary within populations, and this can be one way of negotiating social change, as one study of post-tsunami Samoa demonstrates.[87]

Whatever the responses of ancient people to natural hazards or catastrophe, we should not dismiss them as "primitive." It is possible that some people's confidence in the dominant religious system on Crete was undermined, whilst others' beliefs may have become stronger, and perhaps taken new forms; there may have been religious and social conflict in response to a Theran tsunami – and the definite and dramatic eruption of Thera. For the Minoans, as well as the Greeks and later the Romans, "the whole ancient conception of the world was influenced by religious ideas."[88] One or more goddesses of the sea seems to have been worshipped on Crete,

83 David K. Chester and Angus M. Duncan, "Responding to Disasters within the Christian Tradition, with Reference to Volcanic Eruptions and Earthquakes," *Religion* 40, no. 2 (2010): 85–95.

84 David K. Chester and Angus M. Duncan, "Geomythology, Theodicy, and the Continuing Relevance of Religious Worldviews on Responses to Volcanic Eruptions," in *Living under the Shadow: The Cultural Impacts of Volcanic Eruptions*, ed. John Grattan and Robin Torrence (Walnut Creek: Left Coast Press, 2007), 203–224.

85 Chris G. Sibley and Joseph Bulbulia, "Faith after an Earthquake: A Longitudinal Study of Religion and Perceived Health before and after the 2011 Christchurch New Zealand Earthquake," *PLoS ONE* 7, no. 12 (5 December 2012): e49648. https://doi.org/10.1371/journal.pone.0049648.

86 Lei Sun et al., "Religious Belief and Tibetans' Response to Earthquake Disaster: A Case Study of the 2010 Ms 7.1 Yushu Earthquake, Qinghai Province, China," *Natural Hazards* 99, no. 1 (10 August 2019): 141–159.

87 Sanne B. Holmgaard, "The Role of Religion in Local Perceptions of Disasters: The Case of Post-Tsunami Religious and Social Change in Samoa," *Environmental Hazards* 18, no. 4 (15 November 2018): 311–325.

88 Mark Humphries, "Religion," in *A Companion to Ancient History*, ed. Andrew Erskine (Chichester: Wiley-Blackwell, 2009), 301–311.

offered votives such as shells, clay boats, and fish both to obtain good favour and to offer thanks for success.[89] Images show goddesses holding dolphins, holding fish, on ships, or amongst the waves. Later, the interconnection of the motions of the earth and sea was embodied in the god Poseidon; Poseidon was god of the sea and of earthquakes.[90] The god had various epithets, such as "earth-shaker" and "he who keeps things steady," and was held responsible for causing earthquakes, storms, and tsunamis. Poseidon was worshipped in the Late Bronze Age, as shown by the Mycenaean Linear B texts from Knossos and Pylos.[91] Poseidon-worship in Crete may have been an import from mainland Greece, as the god is not known from Minoan Linear A – perhaps a post-tsunami borrowing makes sense.

In his story about the tsunami at Potidaea, Herodotus suggests that there were different ways a catastrophe could be explained.[92] He tells us that the Potidaeans' explanation was that the Persians who were killed had desecrated a shrine of Poseidon and also that he himself agrees with this – and not any other – explanation. There certainly were other ways of explaining what happened. Thucydides thought no tsunami possible without an earthquake – perhaps contrasting his way of thinking with that of Herodotus. And there was Pythagoras' idea of constant change and transformation, related beautifully by Ovid in the *Metamorphoses* (15). Earlier and contemporary thinkers had also engaged with explanation: Anaximenes blamed earthquakes on the drying or wetting of the earth, Anaximander on trapped subterranean rising air, and Democritus on a saturated, water-filled earth. Later, Aristotle and others would add their own theories. Some of these we might call "rational" or "scientific" because they privilege an understanding of the earth as a system which experiences natural processes.

Diodorus also explained the diversity of accepted ways of explaining catastrophes. He wrote the following of Helike and Bura:

These disasters have been the subject of much discussion. Natural scientists make it their endeavour to attribute responsibility in such

---

89 Watrous, *Minoan Crete*, 159–160.

90 Paus. 7.21.3.

91 Michael H. Jameson, "Poseidon," in *The Oxford Classical Dictionary*, fourth edition, ed. Simon Hornblower, Antony Spawforth, and Esther Eidinow (Oxford: Oxford University Press, 2012): https://www-oxfordreference-com.libproxy.ncl.ac.uk/view/10.1093/acref/9780199545568.001.0001/acref-9780199545568-e-5270.   Accessed 25 July 2021.

92 Hdt. 8.129.

cases not to divine providence, but to certain natural circumstances determined by necessary causes, whereas those who are disposed to venerate the divine power assign certain plausible reasons for the occurrence, alleging that the disaster was occasioned by the anger of the gods at those who had committed sacrilege.[93]

Interestingly, he also adds a little detail that "the Peloponnese has beneath its surface huge caverns and [great] underground accumulations of flowing water" and mentions how some rivers had disappeared, whilst others flowed underground, appearing elsewhere.[94] This is the kind of detail that the "philosophers" would have noted. As for the religious view, there were also "proofs": that Poseidon was god of earthquakes and waves and that the Peloponnese was special to Poseidon and he was greatly honoured there. Diodorus at least superficially appears to support the religious view but leaves us to make our own conclusions.

In ancient Christian times too, catastrophes have been viewed from a religious perspective, often as punishment for human misbehaviour. Sozomen records religion in both cause of and response to disasters: "they [the inhabitants of Nicomedia] went about the streets of their own city and Constantinople as if some earthquake, or pestilence, or other visitation of Divine wrath had occurred, and sang psalms, and offered supplications."[95] About the Alexandria catastrophe, Sozomen explained that the people celebrated the day of the "inundation [...] by a yearly festival; a general illumination is made throughout the city; they offer thankful prayers to God, and celebrate the day very brilliantly and piously."[96] John of Nikiu's story shows the recognition of the power of a saint to intervene with God when catastrophe loomed. This way of thinking has never disappeared, despite modern science.

Final Thoughts

Coastal catastrophes were a part of the experience of life around the shores of the Mediterranean Sea in ancient times, understood through the twin lenses of religion and rational thought. These liminal areas

93 Diod. Sic. 15.48.4.
94 15.49.5.
95 Sozomen, *Ecclesiastical History* 8.6.
96 6.2.

experienced changes both sudden and gradual, from the sea and the land. Earthquakes, volcanoes, and tsunamis were constant threats, as were floods, tectonic shifts, subsidence and uplift, changes in the course of rivers, siltation, and changing sea levels – they still are. Yet despite our scientific knowledge of these phenomena, the three cases of coastal catastrophes discussed here, Thera and Minoan Crete, Classical Helike, and Alexandria in AD 365, all turn out to be surprisingly elusive. For each, we still have difficulties in understanding and reconstructing exactly what happened, when, and what the causes and effects were. The discussion about each will continue.

A lack of clarity about these three "events" should not be seen as disappointing, or as a failure of archaeology, history, geology, or science, but rather quite the opposite. Attempting to piece together "what actually happened," being critical about the stories that become popular, and then going back to the evidence and finding new data, are interesting and revealing. In the process, we become more aware of how archaeological and historical evidence might tell us different things – and where the gaps in our knowledge are. More questions appear that drive research on and new methods of research are devised. The challenge of exploring ancient coastal catastrophes weaves together techniques from a range of disciplines to cast light on the real and lived experiences of ancient people and communities.

CHAPTER TWO

The Greek Notions of Sea Power

Vilius Bartninkas

Introduction

The division between land-based and sea-based powers is one of the most enduring conceptual legacies of Greek geopolitical thinking that is still widely used both in contemporary academic discussions and in the media. Commenting on a recent conflict between China and America in the South China Sea, the *Economist* writes:

> The manoeuvres are a clear assertion of America's sea power, which remains supreme – but no longer unchallenged [...]. Sea power of both the hard, naval kind and the softer kind that involves trade and exploitation of the ocean's resources is as vital as ever. Bits and bytes move digitally, and people by air. Physical goods, though, still overwhelmingly go by sea [...]. A strategy that used to put local sea control first now emphasises China's expanding economic and diplomatic influence. The primacy China once gave its land forces has ended. The traditional mentality that land outweighs the sea must be abandoned, and great importance has to be attached to managing the seas and oceans and protecting maritime rights and interests. It is necessary for China to develop a modern maritime force structure commensurate with its national security.[1]

Here we see two familiar attributes of sea power (or thalassocracy): a commercial activity and a naval fleet. Add to them a political aspect,

I would like to thank Ross Clare and Hamish Williams for their particularly helpful comments and suggestions on this chapter. My overall argument owes much to past discussions with Petras Dirgėla on maritime states and history. I dedicate these reflections to my dear friend Rytis Martikonis, who encouraged me to investigate this topic all those years ago.

1 "Who rules the waves?" *The Economist* (17 October 2015): https://www.economist.com/international/2015/10/17/who-rules-the-waves. Accessed 6 August 2021.

that is an inclusive republican or oligarchic government, and one may discover what Andrew Lambert considers to be the core principles constitutive of every great historical sea power working backwards from the British Empire to the Dutch Republic, Venice, Carthage, and eventually Athens.[2] It is no surprise that this list originates with and perhaps is even modelled on classical Athens; our cultural imagination intuitively associates the city (*polis*) with its remarkable sea battles and the maritime empire that controlled the Aegean Sea. But it is worthwhile to investigate more closely whether the Greeks themselves regarded these three principles (that is, commerce, fleet, and an inclusive constitution) as the key to the Athenian domination.

Greek intellectuals began to ponder over this question precisely after the unprecedented military success of the Athenian navy against Persia in the fifth century BCE. Our first extant text exploring this problem is Herodotus' *Histories*. Although its final books give a detailed account of the Athenian enterprises at sea by discussing their preparations for the Persian invasion, examining the sea battle of Salamis (480 BCE) and showing how it cracked the Persian fleet, Herodotus limits his reflections on sea power to a short passage in Book 7.[3] He tells a story there about the Athenian consultations with the Delphic oracle, who gave them the baffling advice to build wooden walls against the Persians, and how the Athenian statesman Themistocles persuaded the citizens to interpret the message as a suggestion to create a fleet of 200 triremes, which was fortunately attainable thanks to the newly discovered silver mines at Laureion.[4] Thus, we find two rudimentary elements for the establishing of sea power: a considerable fleet of warships and the revenues to support them.[5] It is interesting to note that these two aspects are also highlighted in the case of Polycrates, the tyrant of Samos, whom Herodotus considers to be the first of the Greeks "to control the sea" (θαλασσοκρατέειν;

2 See Andrew D. Lambert, *Seapower States: Maritime Culture, Continental Empires and the Conflict that Made the Modern World* (New Haven, CT: Yale University Press, 2018), 32–47.

3 Hdt. 7.141–144.

4 For a discussion of the actual number of ships in Themistocles' naval bill, see Herman T. Wallinga, *Ships and Sea-Power before the Great Persian War: The Ancestry of the Ancient Trireme* (Leiden: Brill, 1993), 148–157; for the Athenian navy before Themistocles, see Christopher J. Haas, "Athenian Naval Power before Themistocles," *Historia: Zeitschrift für Alte Geschichte* 34, no. 1 (1985): 29–46.

5 In spite of the later more refined theories of sea power, such a simplistic explanation continued to have its attraction – see, for example, how the roots of the potential Thessalian sea power is discussed in Xenophon's *Hellenica* (6.1.8–12).

thalassokrateein).[6] Undoubtably, Polycrates is a convenient figure since his large-scale piracy in the region and political meddling in the conflict between Egypt and Persia in the second half of the sixth century BCE give a certain prehistory to the thalassocracy of Athens.[7] His accession to power and downfall is a complicated subject, but it seems that Samos under Polycrates' leadership acquired around 100 penteconters and 40 triremes,[8] which allowed him to dominate the western Mediterranean, and large funds, which enabled him to maintain the fleet and to initiate significant infrastructural projects in the island of Samos.[9]

We can detect a consistent picture of sea power in Herodotus; nonetheless, it differs considerably from the abovementioned factors that Andrew Lambert deems to be essential for sea power, that is, commerce and a republican constitution.[10] The disagreement between the ancients and the moderns on what constitutes sea power poses a series of questions that are crucial for understanding the essence of this phenomenon. What kind of elements and how many of them are necessary for creating sea power? Can sea power change over time and acquire new distinguishing facets? And how does sea power affect society and its culture? However one may wish to answer them, these questions lead us back to Athens as the city provides the paradigm for Western thought about sea powers. And any discussion of this matter is not a discussion of sea power *per se*, as if we could have an unmediated and direct access to this phenomenon in ancient society, but first and foremost it entails an analysis of the literary sources that identified sea power as a geopolitical issue and provided a theory for it.

6 Hdt. 3.122.2; Andrea L. Purvis, trans., and Robert B. Strassler, ed., *The Landmark Herodotus* (New York: Anchor Books, 2009).

7 Thucydides relocates the origins of thalassocracy to the mythical past by introducing Minos as the first ruler of the seas. Although such a claim may strike as less critical than Herodotus' suggestion, Elizabeth Irwin ("The Politics of Precedence: First Historians on First Thalassocrats," in *Debating the Athenian Cultural Revolution: Art, Literature, Philosophy, and Politics 430–380 BC*, ed. Robin Osborne (Cambridge: Cambridge University Press, 2007), 204) is right to observe that Minos serves a rhetorical role to naturalize the Athenian sea power by showing that "how things are now is how they must always have been, and in turn how they will always be κατά τὸ ἀνθρώπινον."

8 Hdt. 3.39, 3.44.

9 3.60. For Polycrates' fleet and political changes in Samos, see Graham Shipley, *A History of Samos, 800–188 BC* (Oxford: Clarendon, 1987), 69–99; and then Anthony Papalas, "Polycrates of Samos and the First Greek Trireme Fleet," *The Mariner's Mirror* 85, no. 1 (1999): 3–19.

10 It seems that commercial activity with Egypt and the pharaoh's interest in counterweighting the growing Persian naval power may have been the real building blocks of Polycrates' political rise, see Wallinga, *Ships and Sea-Power*, 84–101.

This chapter explores three classical authors, the Old Oligarch, Thucydides, and Plato, whose texts lay the conceptual foundation for the Greek notions of sea power. What unites them is the presumption that the sea is a medium to obtain and project the *polis'* power. And from this standpoint a vigorous debate unfolds on whether thalassocracy is an inherently subversive phenomenon responsible for exerting damaging, even catastrophic effects on the Greek geopolitical scene or a dynamic force of change that through its special measures can transform the Mediterranean into a fundamentally better place. So the key question of this chapter is to determine the overall political assessment of sea power in classical Greek authors, especially concerning the impact of sea power on civic life and geopolitical relations. We begin our analysis with the Old Oligarch, who aims to show that the destructive vision of sea power is rooted in an oligarchic value system that needs to be suspended in order to see the true nature of sea power. On this deeper level of analysis, the Athenian sea power is envisaged as a combined result of the constitutional framework of the *polis*, its imperial and economic policy, and the social realities behind the manpower of the navy, all of which accounts for the flourishing life of the ordinary citizens. The second section takes us to Thucydides, who adds a historical dimension to sea power by examining its gradual development towards structural, techno-logical, organizational, and cultural complexity. On this approach, the Athenian sea power emerges as the latest product of a long thalassocratic tradition that challenged the political order by perfecting a multi-layered symbiosis between the ships and the people. We will see that both the Old Oligarch and Thucydides uncover an ostensibly utopian aspect of Athenian imperialism, which vastly improved the welfare and status of the ordinary citizens at the expense of the oppressed *poleis*. And this will bring us to the final section on Plato, who investigates the implications of these principles for the moral fabric of society and who questions the potential of sea power to unlock utopian politics.[11]

---

11 There are further salient contrasts between these authors. The Old Oligarch and Thucydides discuss real constitutions, while Plato invents an imaginary consti-tution. What is more, the first two accounts are markedly historical: the Old Oligarch writes a pamphlet concerning the current state of affairs in Athens; Thucydides constructs a chronological arrangement of sea powers. Plato has some remarks on historical Athens too, but the framework of a philosophical dialogue makes him more interested in the normative and, therefore, atemporal aspects of sea power. Despite these differences in subject matter and genres, the three authors share the aim of giving an accurate, if not "objective," assessment of sea power.

The Old Oligarch on the City and Sea Power

If there is one classical Greek text which is exclusively devised to determine the relation between sea power and Athens, then it is a curious short pamphlet written in the early years of the Peloponnesian War by an anonymous author, whom the tradition passed down as Pseudo-Xenophon or the Old Oligarch.[12] The treatise is addressed to the oligarchs, their sympathizers, and more generally anyone hostile to the Athenian democracy in order to explain the logic of this constitution. The heart of the matter is that the oligarchs see democracy as a bad constitution run by even worse people, who (to the utter surprise of the social elite) managed to create an empire and established a military superpower instead of driving themselves into political chaos. For this reason, the author intends to explicate the rationality of those aspects of democracy that the oligarchs see as inherently mistaken and to reveal why the Athenian constitution is a rational, efficient political mechanism that works against all the odds.[13] The text discusses a number of such problematic aspects, but one overarching topic is the complex interconnection of the Athenian constitution, the people, and the naval forces.

The author adopts the social bias of an oligarch. It leads him to define the Athenian democracy as a constitution governed by the people (ὁ δῆμος; *ho dēmos*), who are interchangeably referred to as the poor (οἱ πένητες; *hoi penētes*),[14] the common people (οἱ δημοτικοί; *hoi dēmotikoi*),[15] the worthless (οἱ πονηροί; *hoi ponēroi*),[16] the inferior (οἱ χείρους; *hoi cheirous*),[17] the mob (ὁ ὄχλος; *ho ochlos*),[18] the masses (τὸ πλῆθος; *to plēthos*),[19] and the morally worst (τὸ κάκιστον; *to kakiston*).[20] Such heavily loaded language shows that the author attaches pejorative and evaluative senses to the term *dēmos*, which accentuate its bad ethical and social qualities. It is

12 For dating in the years 431–413 BC, see Robin Osborne, *The Old Oligarch: Pseudo-Xenophon's Constitution of the Athenians*, third edition (London: London Association of Classical Teachers, 2017), 4–6, 10–16; for a useful overview of the alternative dates, see John L. Marr and Peter J. Rhodes, eds., *The "Old Oligarch": The Constitution of the Athenians Attributed to Xenophon* (Oxford: Aris & Phillips, 2008), 31–32.

13 An alternative way to approach this text is as an ironic parody of democratic ideology, which is discussed and dismissed in Osborne, *Old Oligarch*, 3–11.

14 Old Oligarch 1.2.

15 1.4.

16 1.4.

17 1.4.

18 2.10.

19 2.18.

20 3.10.

clearly based on a deeper conviction that the rule of the ordinary people
had a harmful effect on public morality and the high culture of the city.[21]
But more importantly, "the people" here does not refer to the whole
political body of Athens, which would include every citizen from the
wealthiest landowners and the knights to the average farmers, who can
serve as the hoplites, the artisans, and the landless labourers. Levystone
accurately observes that the Old Oligarch narrows down the term to a
specific class, whose members are distinguished by their low birth, lack
of education, economic poverty,[22] and a military function to serve in the
navy.[23] It is an extremely restricted sense of the term *dēmos*, limited to
"the urban proletariat."[24] The Old Oligarch, therefore, draws a partisan
and yet an intriguing picture of the Athenian democracy: its institutions
and political life are dominated not by, as one would suspect, several
conflicting classes and interest groups but, rather, by a single class of the
urban poor.

What is so special about the urban poor that the author regards them
as the cornerstone of democracy? From the outset, the Old Oligarch
claims that the people ensure the protection, stability, and power of the
constitution in a variety of maritime roles:

> The poor and the *dēmos* are justified there in having more than
> the well-born and the rich, because of the fact that it is the *dēmos*
> who operate the ships and who confer its strength on the city; the
> steersmen, the boatswains, the lieutenants, the look-outs and the
> naval engineers – these are the people who confer its strength on
> the city, much more so than the hoplites and the well-born and the
> valuable.[25]

Thus, the existing political order and the exclusive position of the *dēmos*
are supported by the mass participation in the fleet. The Athenian navy,
the author continues, managed not only to preserve democracy but also
to grow the status of Athens in the global scene to such an extent that
they became the rulers of the sea (θαλασσοκράτορες; *thalassokratores*).[26]

---

21 Cf. 1.7–13.

22 1.5.

23 1.2. See David Levystone, "La constitution des Athéniens du Pseudo-Xénophon:
D'un despotisme à l'autre," *Revue Française d'Histoire des Idées Politiques* 1, no. 1 (2005):
15–20.

24 This point is developed in Marr and Rhodes, eds., *The "Old Oligarch"*, 20–22.

25 Old Oligarch 1.2; Marr and Rhodes, *The "Old Oligarch"*.

26 Old Oligarch 2.2.

However, the Old Oligarch examines neither the reasons for the Athenian sea power nor the process that established its status. For him, sea power and the necessary skills to maintain it emerged almost spontaneously.[27] The author is more interested in the already-existing strategic advantages conferred by sea power, among which he finds the following: the subjugation of larger *poleis* and islands and the control of their trade;[28] the capacity for mobile and long-distance raids of the stronger enemies;[29] the economic independence from land production and the capacity to import both necessary and luxury goods from foreign countries;[30] a rich and cosmopolitan cultural life;[31] and an easy acquisition of the materials necessary for maintaining the fleet through sea trade.[32] These are not sporadic observations concerning the economic and military benefits of sea power. They show a systematic way in which Athens can gather and control the goods and, by using them, simultaneously support democratic institutions, maintain the fleet, and build an empire in the region. The combined force of these advantages depicts Athens as a new type of global economy that can provide a firm foundation to the utopian life of the demos by financing entertainment and cultural institutions, and providing an access to the material goods that would be otherwise limited to the elite few.

We can see here some new layers of sea power in comparison to Herodotus. Once again, the starting point of sea power is the fleet, but the Old Oligarch promptly suggests looking into the social factors determining the nature of the naval forces – as opposed to the land forces, which are based on the farmers and the wealthier landowners.[33] According to him, the navy draws its manpower from the urban class, the very group that also dominates the political scene of Athens. In this way, the navy gives military support to the democratic constitution, while the democratic

---

27 1.19.
28 2.2–3. For the historical importance of the Athenian control of islands, see Christy Constantakopoulou, *The Dance of the Islands: Insularity, Networks, the Athenian Empire, and the Aegean World* (Oxford: Oxford University Press, 2007), 84–88; for the significance of naval bases for ancient sea powers, see Vincent Gabrielsen, "Naval Warfare: Its Economic and Social Impact on Greek Cities," in *War as a Cultural and Social Force: Essays on Warfare in Antiquity*, ed. Tønnes Bekker-Nielsen and Lise Hannestad (Copenhagen: Det kongelige Danske Videnskabernes Selskab, 2001), 73.
29 Old Oligarch 2.4–5.
30 2.6–7.
31 2.8–10.
32 2.11–12.
33 1.2, 2.14.

politics gives military priority to the navy, and the link between the two is the urban class. Scholars usually note the special position of the Old Oligarch among the other theorists of sea power who emerge, because of his insistence on the special relationship between democracy and thalassocracy.[34] But they tend to miss the additional two elements in the proposed model of the Old Oligarch, which are economic hegemony and empire. Although Herodotus also notices the potential of sea power for conquest and economic exploitation,[35] the Old Oligarch uncovers the systematic way in which sea power can subdue the coastal cities, control their sea trade, and thus accumulate the required goods. As a result, the complete model of sea power contains five different elements: a democratic constitution, a naval fleet, the urban class, a global economy, and a geopolitical hegemony.

The Old Oligarch has been severely criticized for the sociological inaccuracy of this model. In particular, his assertion that the *dēmos* should be understood as the urban class has been dismissed as an exaggeration unsupported by the demographics of Athens. Marr and Rhodes estimate that "at most only 25% of the citizen body were landless men" (a significant figure, nonetheless, as any politician seeking to win an election would tell us), while the majority were farmers living in the countryside.[36] Moreover, even if one could imagine a majority entailing the poor and the landless citizens in Athens, there still remains the near impossibility of a total coherence in terms of their social and economic interests.[37] However, Robin Osborne is right to contend that a sociological misjudgement does not deny the relevance of the author's analytical findings on the more basic dynamics of the *polis*. Take an unstructured view of the Athenian society, and it becomes puzzling as to why maritime interests prevailed in a civic body the majority of whose members were in one way or another dependent on the land and agriculture. In this respect, the Old Oligarch reveals which social group had the greatest profit from both

---

34 A notable exception is Lys. 13.14–16, cf. 28.11; see also Arist. *Ath. Pol.* 27. The most comprehensive treatment of this subject is found in Paola Ceccarelli, "Sans thalassocratie, pas de démocratie? Le rapport entre thalassocratie et démocratie à Athènes dans la discussion du Ve et IVe siècle av. J.-C.," *Historia: Zeitschrift für Alte Geschichte* 42, no. 4 (1993): 444–470; see also a classical study of Arnaldo Momigliano, "Sea Power in Greek Thought," *The Classical Review* 58, no. 1 (1944): 1–7.

35 Hdt. 3.39, cf. 3.58–59.

36 See Marr and Rhodes, *The "Old Oligarch"*, 22.

37 An important differentiating criterion is the communities, their needs and priorities, to which the poor and landless citizens belonged, see Osborne, *Old Oligarch*, 9.

the constitutional order and the military organization of the city. In the end, he aims to show how the interaction between the *dēmos* and Athens and, more generally, sea power increased the welfare of the *polis* and thus laid the grounds for a new arrangement that must have been utopian for the urban poor. This insight, however, leaves the oligarchic readers at a certain impasse: what seemed to be a constitutional havoc is a powerful, resource-rich utopia, and unless the oligarchs want Athens to lose its hegemonic status, there is hardly any way to maintain it without endorsing the *dēmos* and sea power.

Thucydides on the Development of Sea Power

Thucydides' reflections on sea power are ingrained in the so-called *Archaeology*,[38] a theoretical prelude to *The History of the Peloponnesian War* as a whole. Its objective is to accustom the reader to the idea that this war was "the greatest movement" in history,[39] which also implies the demonstration that its participants had immense resources for the war in terms of power (δύναμις; *dynamis*), far greater than any other actor in any previous war. Among the most prominent themes of the *Archaeology* are power and the causes by which it can be obtained or lost. From the very beginning,[40] it is clear that Thucydides is particularly interested in the financial factors, the unity of the people, and their capacity for common action.[41] And he is also at pains to show that it is not land power as such but sea power, in particular, that has shaped Greek history. Thus, the *Archaeology* produces a list of thalassocracies, which represents a succession and development of maritime states and which culminates with imperial Athens.[42]

---

38 Thuc. 1.2–1.19.

39 1.1.2; Richard Crawley, trans., and Robert B. Strassler, ed., *The Landmark Thucydides* (New York: Free Press, 1996).

40 Thuc. 1.2–3.

41 For this point, see Virginia J. Hunter, *Past and Process in Herodotus and Thucydides* (Princeton, NJ: Princeton University Press, 1982), 44–48. For the rhetorical construction and the audience of the *Archaeology*, see Nino Luraghi, "Author and Audience in Thucydides' *Archaeology*. Some Reflections," *Harvard Studies in Classical Philology* 100 (2000): 227–239.

42 I shall not consider another famous list of thalassocracies, which is found in Eusebius' *Chronicle* and is based on the lost Book 7 of Diodorus Siculus' *Library*. Its dating is controversial; see John K. Fotheringham, "On the List of Thalassocracies in Eusebius," *The Journal of Hellenic Studies* 27 (1907): 75–89; Molly Miller, *The Thalassocracies* (New York: State University of New York Press, 1971); John L. Myres,

Thucydides locates the origins of all power in the Creto-Mycenaean period. He regards Minos as the first to have created a naval fleet,[43] a tool for power that allowed the mythical king of Crete to conquer and colonize the islands of Cyclades, to suppress piracy, and to ensure a steady flow of revenues.[44] It is worthwhile to note that despite the aggression and expansionism of Minos' Crete, this sea power is not treated as a univocally calamitous political force, since it offered at least some inhabitants of the Mediterranean a prospect of a better life. It brought security to the occupied region, which enabled the coastal cities to use the cleared sea for navigation, communication, and commerce, thus increasing their own capital (χρήματα; *chrēmata*) and obtaining the money to build defensive walls.[45] The second notable sea power was in the hands of another mythical king, Agamemnon, though the matters here are more complicated. Thucydides credits Agamemnon's Mycenae with assembling the largest and strongest fleet in his times,[46] but the problem was twofold: Agamemnon used his ships in a primitive way as transportation vessels rather than as weapons in their own right;[47] and he did not have sufficient funds to maintain them.[48] Thucydides claims that otherwise Agamemnon would not have embroiled himself in such a prolonged siege of Troy, which forced him to build a fortified camp there, subsist on agriculture, and undertake piratical raids in order to obtain more supplies. Agamemnon's failures provide a telling contrast to Minos' sea power. Agamemnon's fatal weakness was the lack of financial resources, whereas Minos' possession of capital was precisely the key to the efficient subjection of various islands and *poleis*.[49] And if this specific flaw eventually undermined Agamemnon's power and reduced it to piratical exploitation, the absence of financial

"On the List of Thalassocracies of Eusebius," *The Journal of Hellenic Studies* 26 (1906): 84–130. There were attempts to use the list as a resource to reconstruct the forgotten sea powers, but Constantakopoulou (*Dance of the Islands*, 91–92) is right to conclude that "the list should not be seen as a form of early history of sea power, let alone be used as evidence for its existence for specific states in the seventh and early sixth centuries. The list is useful only in that it articulates the idea of succession in a clear form: that of a list [...]. Indeed, the list reflects Thucydides' analysis of thalassocracies and it sits well within the context of Athenian attempts to appear as the natural successors of a long series of historical thalassocrats in the Aegean area."
43 Thuc. I.4.
44 I.4.1–I.5.1; cf. I.8.2–I.8.4.
45 I.7.
46 I.9.3–I.9.4.
47 I.10.4.
48 I.11.
49 I.8.3.

deficit enabled Minos to eliminate pirates from the region and instead to build an empire, which produced further revenues for the Cretan hegemony. So in the earliest form, the sea can be subdued by a delicate triangulation between ships, money, and empire. And sea power can be further increased by raising the walls around the *polis* and thus ensuring its security.[50]

Thucydides' critical take on Agamemnon's primitive ships prepares the reader for the next phase of sea powers, which is brought forth by the city of Corinth in the age of tyrants. Thucydides claims that the source of the Corinthian rise was their expedient location, suitable for both land and sea trade. It allowed them to accumulate an abundance of financial reserves,[51] which funded the creation of the fleet characterized by two innovations. In terms of technology, Corinth is regarded as the inventor of the modern type of warship,[52] the trireme, designed as a "floating missile"[53] to target and ram other ships. In terms of organization, Corinth's sea power marked a transition from private to public ownership of ships: the naval fleet became the property of the *polis*.[54] The new generation of sea powers brought a novel quality to Greek warfare, which changed the understanding of the use and purpose of ships. The new technology decidedly moved the theatre of war to the sea by initiating the first large-scale battles there,[55] while the organizational development implied that the material and political benefits of operating the ships as well as the responsibilities of maintaining them passed to the whole city and its citizens. The full potential of the latter aspect, however, will be fully materialized only later in Athens, which will use its sea power to increase the welfare of the *dēmos*.

This period also marks a sudden proliferation of sea powers. Immediately after Corinth, we find a quick succession of various maritime states: the Ionians "attained to great naval strength" (πολὺ γίγνεται ναυτικὸν; *polu gignetai nautikon*) and controlled the eastern Aegean, after whom Polycrates

50   For the causal relationship between these elements, see Lisa Kallet-Marx, *Money, Expense, and Naval Power in Thucydides' History 1–5.24* (Berkeley, CA: University of California Press, 1993), 24–30; Josiah Ober, "Thucydides Theoretikos/Thucydides Histor: Realist Theory and the Challenge of History," in *Thucydides*, ed. R. J. Rusten (Oxford: Oxford University Press, 2009), 440–443.

51   Thuc. 1.13.5.

52   1.13.2–3.

53   I borrow this image from Gabrielsen, "Naval Warfare," 73.

54   For this dual progress, see Wallinga, *Ships and Sea-Power*, 20–32, though he is sceptical about the possibility of Corinth having an exclusively trireme fleet.

55   Thuc. 1.13.4.

of Samos obtained "a powerful navy" (ναυτικῷ ἰσχύων; *nautikō ischuōn*) and used it to subdue the adjacent islands, and finally the Phocaeans used their fleet to defeat the Carthaginians and to establish the colony of Marseilles.[56] But the importance of these three sea powers, Thucydides adds, was diminished by the fact that, from a technological perspective, they were still dependent on the old type of ships, the penteconters and longboats,[57] which is a critique that Thucydides also applies to the sea power of Aegina and Archaic Athens.[58] Thucydides ascribes the trireme fleets only to the Sicilian tyrants and the island of Corcyra, a former colony of Corinth.[59] So what are we to make of this crowded list?[60] It seems that sea power of this period no longer marked a sole domination in the sea but, rather, a limited capacity to project one's strength through the navy and thus to compete with the other *poleis* for resources. But Thucydides still contends that significant geopolitical power was obtained through one's capacity to manoeuvre between the ships, the money (χρήματα), and the empire (ἀρχή)[61] rather than through land warfare.

The highpoint of the *Archaeology* is the naval supremacy of imperial Athens in the Classical period. Thucydides briefly notes two exclusive traits of Athenian sea power and leaves the specific details for the rest of *The History of the Peloponnesian War*. First, the Persian wars shaped the Athenians as a political community and changed the identity of the *polis*. The wartime experiences made them a naval people (ναυτικοὶ ἐγένοντο; *nautikoi egenonto*),[62] which is to say that a significant portion of the population became highly skilled in seafaring.[63] This claim opens another important theme in Thucydides, the maritime culture and its society. In later books, we repeatedly find the stress on those Athenian values and character traits that are a direct reflection of trireme technology. The triremes empowered the city to advance boldly into foreign territories with unprecedented speed and freedom of action,[64] and as a consequence

---

56   1.13.6.

57   1.14.1.

58   1.14.3.

59   1.14.2.

60   For the (problematic) historical accuracy of this list, see Wallinga, *Ships and Sea-Power*, 13–32, 63–83; Philip de Souza, "Towards Thalassocracy? Greek Naval Developments," in *Archaic Greece: New Approaches and New Evidence*, ed. Nick Fisher and Hans van Wees (London: Duckworth, 1998), 277–287.

61   Thuc. 1.15.1.

62   1.18.2.

63   1.142.5–1.143.1.

64   2.39, 2.41.4, 2.62.

the Athenians became known for their quickness, confidence, appetite for danger, and long-distance travel.[65]

Second, Athens used the success in the Persian Wars to impose a tribute (φόρος; *phoros*) on her allies and deprive them of their ships.[66] This points to a new financial mechanism. The tribute was collected by the Athenians as deposits to the common treasury (ταμιεῖον; *tamieion*), which built up currency reserves and thus increased the financial stability of the fleet maintenance.[67] Eventually, it became an instrument to expand the Athenian hegemony by slowly transforming the league dependent on the Athenian navy into an empire subjugated by it.[68] In addition, the reserves promoted the public wellbeing of the city and substantially improved its material conditions.[69] Among the latter, Thucydides attaches a special importance to the defensive infrastructure projects, namely the rebuilding of the city walls, the fortification of Peiraeus,[70] and the connection of the city and its harbour with the Long Walls:[71] this was foreseen as the basis for future naval supremacy because it allowed an increase in the manpower of the navy as Athens no longer needed a large contingent of defensive land forces.[72]

Let us gather the results of our discussion. From Minos' Crete to Classical Athens, Thucydides maintains a coherent model of sea power, which stems from the basic interaction between the walled *polis*, the revenues, the naval fleet (what Josiah Ober calls "the material triad"), and finally the empire.[73] This received a particularly positive assessment from modern historians of classical antiquity, who agree that one common denominator of historical Greek sea powers is the size of the fleet and their wealth.[74]

---

65 1.70.2–4, 8.96.5. For the Athenian maritime identity and trireme technology, see also Xen. *Hell.* 7.1.2–11.

66 Thuc. 1.19.

67 1.96. On Athenian financial resources, see Kallet-Marx, *Money, Expense, and Naval Power*, 184–206.

68 Thuc. 1.97–1.99.

69 2.38, 2.60.2–4.

70 1.90–1.93.

71 1.107.1.

72 Cf. Andocides (3.5–9, 3.37–39), an Attic orator, who argues the walls and the fleet were the actual basis of the Athenian power.

73 Ober, "Thucydides Theoretikos," 443.

74 See, for example, Gabrielsen, "Naval Warfare," 75; Eric W. Robinson, *Democracy beyond Athens: Popular Government in the Greek Classical Age* (Cambridge: Cambridge University Press, 2011), 237; Jacqueline de Romilly, *The Mind of Thucydides* (Ithaca, NY: Cornell University Press, 2012), 157; Chester G. Starr, *The Influence of Sea Power on Ancient History* (Oxford: Oxford University Press, 1989), 24–27.

Another layer of this model, which emerges in Thucydides' developmental account, entails certain historical changes in technology, organization, economic resources, and cultural identity that increased the complexity of sea power. The original and the latest sea powers do share the same core structure, but there are significant differences in their overall architecture and practical implementation: some improved the technology of warships, others worked on the financial mechanisms to maintain the fleet; some fleets belonged to a single ruler, others became the property of the *polis*; some used them to fight pirates, others employed them to extend geopolitical importance. In addition, Thucydides shows that the Greek world was never a stable place and its motions reflected the rising and falling sea powers. The dynamism initiated by thalassocracies had an ambiguous character: on the one hand, it introduced a destructive dimension to Greek political life by turning it into a heated competition for resources and hegemony; on the other hand, it also allowed some *poleis* to use the obtained resources for the public good. Finally, we saw a number of political communities with varying constitutions that had a significant naval strength at certain periods of time.[75] The reader is invited to approach sea power as a recurring historical phenomenon, whose roots lie in a successful command of the abovementioned factors rather than Athenian exceptionality.[76] So although the Athenians perfected the connection between sea power and the *dēmos*, we are encouraged not to think of a democratic constitution as the sole foundation of sea power.[77]

75 Thucydides is supported through a meticulous analysis by Robinson (*Democracy beyond Athens*, 236), who compellingly shows that "democratic thalassocracies were not the norm."

76 For this point, see Ober, "Thucydides Theoretikos," 444.

77 Some may even say that Thucydides' work hints at the inherent tensions between democracy and sea power: "[Thucydides] Theoretikos' optimism regarding potential human understanding of state behavior is complicated by [Thucydides] Histor's narrative, which shows that a democracy-as-hegemon may be unstable under extreme pressure and might even collapse under the weight of its attempt to square the ideal of democratic rule by public discourse at home with self-interested, 'tyrannical' rule abroad" (Ober, "Thucydides Theoretikos," 475). It also raises questions about the conceptual and historical relationship between this text and the Old Oligarch, for which see Simon Hornblower, "The Old Oligarch (Pseudo-Xenophon's Athenaion Politeia) and Thucydides. A Fourth-Century Date for the Old Oligarch?" in *Polis and Politics: Studies in Ancient Greek History Presented to Mogens Herman Hansen on His Sixtieth Birthday*, ed. Pernille Flensted-Jensen, Thomas H. Nielsen, and Lene Rubinstein (Copenhagen: Museum Tusculanum Press, 2000), 363–384; Osborne, *Old Oligarch*, 5–6; Jacqueline de Romilly, "Le Pseudo-Xénophon et Thucydide. Étude sur quelques divergences de vues," *Revue de Philologie* 36 (1962): 225–241; Chester G. Starr, "Thucydides on Sea Power," *Mnemosyne* 31, no. 4 (1978): 343–350.

Plato on the Morality of Sea Power

Unlike Thucydides and the Old Oligarch, Plato's take on foreign affairs and geopolitical issues is minimalistic. His ideal *poleis*, Kallipolis of the *Republic* and Magnesia of the *Laws*, are arranged to sustain an autarkic socioeconomic life, where military means are employed only for defensive purposes. Specifically, Magnesia is envisaged as a land power of the Spartan manner, which specializes in a conventional hoplite warfare[78] and abstains from protecting itself with defensive walls.[79] It is clear that Magnesia will lack some of the basic recurring facets of sea power, such as an intensive sea trade, shipbuilding materials, skilled seafarers, and a navy.[80] Plato's analysis, however, is no longer a reconstruction of thalassocratic models but, rather, an evaluation of their impact on society. In all these passages, we find the repeated contention that every military organization has strong implications for morality and that traditional land warfare in particular contributes towards virtuous life by nurturing courage (ἀνδρεία; *andreia*) and excellence (ἀριστεία; *aristeia*).

A naval state, on the other hand, is something to be avoided due to its negative influence on morals and social habits.[81] The underlying problem of sea power is already to be found in Plato's earlier works: ships, ports, and imperial tributes may satisfy various material desires, but they cannot cultivate the virtues of moderation and justice (σωφροσύνης καὶ δικαιοσύνης; *sōphrosunēs kai dikaiosunēs*).[82] This thesis is expanded in the *Laws*, which gives a few examples of how maritime interests may produce ethical damage. First, an economic reliance on sea trade stimulates the people to do the profit-seeking business, which increases distrust among them and thus breaks the unity of the *polis*.[83] Second, a competition between sea powers for supremacy provokes them to imitate each other, especially in military matters, which means an influx of new habits as

78 Pl. *Leg.* 8.830c–e, 8.832e–834c, 12.943a–b.

79 6.778d–779a. Along with Sparta, Crete is also presented as a constitution exemplifying political conservatism, which can teach a lesson or two to the future founders of Magnesia (for example, 1.634d–e). Plato seems to downplay the long-term influence of Minos' thalassocracy (4.705a–b) on the Cretans and their character, who are primarily discerned by their military capacities in the highlands and the mountainous environment (1.625c–626b; cf. 8.834a–d).

80 4.704d–707c.

81 Cf. Aristotle (*Pol.* 7.6, 1327a11–1327b18), whose ideal state will have both a harbour and a navy for defensive reasons as well as an effective geopolitical role.

82 Pl. *Grg.* 519a2. See also *Alc.* 134b–c; *Grg* 517b–c; *Resp.* 371a–b.

83 Pl. *Leg.* 4.705a.

well as instability.[84] Third, naval tactics are in tension with the traditional notions of courage since they prioritize mobile attacks, strategic retreats, and deceitful positioning over the conventional hoplite ideal of standing one's ground and defending one's land.[85] And lastly, considering the social profile of the rowers of the ships, sea powers are bound to give more military honours to the lower sectors of society, which is a polite way to refer to the mob of not particularly worthy people (οὐ πάνυ σπουδαίων ἀνθρώπων; *ou panu spoudaiōn anthrōpōn*), rather than the social elite or the agrarian middle class.[86]

This evidence is generally used to pair Plato with the Old Oligarch and present him as a leading critic of the morality of sea power. It is true that the abovementioned arguments indicate how unnecessary social practices and moral dispositions may arise out of maritime activities and that sea power is fundamentally in tension with the utopian life. However, they do not make a compelling case for the absolute immorality of sea power. They point to an inbuilt tendency of sea power to rely on the wrong sort of people and to facilitate social change and diversity, which eventually translates into political instability. But naval states as such are not treated as inherently bad polities. This careful assessment of sea power is also confirmed by Plato's account of the Persian wars, which shows that despite the Athenian possession of a fleet, the Persian threat increased civic friendship and the general observation of the laws in Athens.[87] And even if naval warfare has no educational value, it still does not have a bad influence:

CLEINIAS: All the same, my friend, it was the sea battle at Salamis – Greeks against barbarians – which according to us Cretans was the salvation of Greece.

ATHENIAN: Yes, that is what the majority of Greeks and barbarians do say. But what we say, I and Megillus here, is that it was the land battle at Marathon, and the one at Plataea – Marathon marking the beginning of the Greek's salvation, Plataea its completion. These battles, we say, made the Greeks into better people, whereas the sea battles made them no better [καὶ τὰς μὲν βελτίους τοὺς Ἕλληνας

---

84   4.705c–706b.
85   4.706b–707a.
86   4.707a–b.
87   3.698a–699d.

ποιῆσαι, τὰς δὲ οὐ βελτίους] – if we can say that about battles which
did help to secure our safety at that time.[88]

The sea battles did not make the Athenians better, but this is not to say
that they made them worse. Instead, Plato locates the roots of moral flaws
in the Athenian *dēmos* and specifically in their excessive use of freedom
that first affected their cultural tastes and fashions and gradually spread
to other areas of society until it subverted respect for the laws.[89]

A similar lesson appears to be drawn in Plato's diptych the *Timaeus–
Critias*, which tells a captivating fictional story about primeval Athens,
Atlantis, and their war. The first time the two cities are presented
together is also the very moment when the contrast between their power
is revealed: Atlantis is an island empire that used its navy to subject other
cities, while Athens is an autarkic land community that used its forces
to defend Greek liberty and defeat Atlantis.[90] The maritime identity
of Atlantis, moreover, is reaffirmed by emphasizing its intricate naval
infrastructure,[91] massive fleet of triremes as well as colossal marine
forces,[92] and religious worship of the sea god Poseidon.[93] But Atlantis is
also depicted as a flourishing place that at least for some generations had
good government, material wellbeing, and a decent civic life. So given the
later imperial ambitions, is sea power considered as the effective reason
for the moral deterioration of this imaginary utopia? The answer is
negative, for the downfall of Atlantis started with the failure to reproduce
good rulers, who then misused their vast material possessions.[94] Of
course, sea power is not a neutral factor in terms of moral influence
since the exponential growth of the city brought these possessions in the
first place. That being said, a vicious disposition towards external goods
was aroused not because of sea power but because of the lack of proper
education and cultural institutions. So, despite the usual presentation
of Plato as an outright critic of sea power, it is safer to conclude that sea

---

88 4.707b4–c6; M. Schofield, ed., and T. Griffith, trans., *Plato: Laws* (Cambridge:
Cambridge University Press, 2016).

89 Pl. *Leg.* 3.700d–701c.

90 Pl. *Ti.* 24d–25c. For the historical and political allusions to the main actors of the
Persian Wars and the Peloponnesian War in the Atlantis story, see Christopher Gill,
Plato's Atlantis Story: Text, Translation and Commentary (Liverpool: Liverpool University
Press, 2017), 27–30.

91 Pl. *Critias* 115d–116c.

92 117d, 119b.

93 116c–d, 119c–120c.

94 120d–121b.

power has potential for corruption, but unless there are other contributing factors, it does not in itself make the city evil.[95]

A wholesale moral condemnation of sea power is not so frequent among the Greek intellectuals, and there is even some textual evidence pointing to the opposite view. For instance, Lysias claims that the Athenian navy was a force of both political and moral good:[96] it provided the Greeks with security and ensured their freedom from barbarian rule thanks to Athenian moderation and moral excellence (τοσαύτην σωφροσύνην καὶ δέος ἡ τούτων ἀρετὴ πᾶσιν ἀνθρώποις παρεῖχεν).[97] Similarly, Isocrates' *Panegyricus* responds to various political charges against Athenian sea power by arguing that it instilled discipline in its subjects rather than bad rule, served their interests, and spread harmony,[98] all of which was due to Athenian virtue (ἀρετή).[99] Xenophon reports the courage of ordinary sailors.[100] But then again, Isocrates' position was fluctuating over this matter.[101] His later speech *On the Peace* denounces the latent imperialism intrinsic to sea power, arguing that it corrupts its owners to such an extent that they unconsciously bring upon themselves self-destruction,[102] a pattern that was repeated by both the Athenians and the Spartans (when the latter acquired thalassocracy).[103] So the morality of sea power remained a controversial subject among the Greek thinkers. Its deceitful nature was duly exposed by showing the way in which sea power intensifies the life of the *polis* and opens up an ambiguous space for political action. It is true that the destructive side of sea power that emerged from its impact on moral habits and social stability was counterweighed to some extent by other authors and their positive assessment of its role in providing security and material welfare. But ultimately sea power appeared to be too volatile,

95 Cf. Momigliano, "Sea Power in Greek Thought," 4–5; Glenn R. Morrow, *Plato's Cretan City* (Princeton, NJ: Princeton University Press, 1960), 96–100.

96 Lys. 2.55–60.

97 2.57.4–5.

98 Isoc. *Paneg.* 4.100–105.

99 4.119.2.

100 Xen. *Hell.* 1.1.28. See also David M. Pritchard ("The Fractured Imaginary: Popular Thinking on Military Matters in Fifth Century Athens," *Ancient History* 28, no. 1 (1998): 53–55), who argues that sailors received a positive moral characterization in Athenian comedy and tragedy.

101 For the change of Isocrates' views on sea power, see Josiah Ober, "Views of Sea Power in the Fourth-Century Attic Orators," *Ancient World* 1 (1978): 126–128. More generally, Ober's paper shows that the Attic orators were mostly interested in the military benefits of sea power.

102 Isoc. *On the Peace* 8.64.

103 8.100–103.

agonistic, indeed too exploitative to build a lasting moral foundation for a political utopia.

Conclusions

The first theories of thalassocracy began with the idea that material factors, such as building ports and warships, ensure the capacity to dominate at sea. But later authors found that sea power required creating something else: a way of life that enables a psychological, political, cultural, and economic reorientation of society towards the sea. The Greeks had a plurality of notions of sea power and no single way of thinking about this phenomenon. We found a variety of ideas pertaining to thalassocracy, such as a military and economic model to increase the welfare of the *polis*, a democratic empire based on the needs of the urban class, and a social process that revolutionizes the values of society. On an even more abstract level, the phenomenon of sea power appears to embody broader principles of expansionism and mobility, which are bound to threaten the stability of the existing political order and lead to either a catastrophic subversion of it or the creation of a new utopian arrangement. Thus, at their core, the Greek notions of sea power mediate between a profound transformation of the political sphere and a conspicuous challenge to the good life of citizens.

CHAPTER THREE

Plato Sailing against the Current: The Image of the Ship in the *Republic*

Gabriele Cornelli

The Frame of the Image: The Ship and the Third Wave

The image of the ship opens up a series of images which are essential to Platonic philosophy in general and to the sixth and seventh books of the *Republic* in particular. Here the images of the Sun, the line, and the cave are found, and this is the reason why these two books of the *Republic* are among the most studied of Plato's works.[1] However, as Keyt has noticed, this ship image has received much less attention from the commentators, especially when compared to the other three.[2] In fact, even if almost every work of political science has a footnote on the ship image, the critical attention still does not adequately reflect the important role this image plays in the *Republic*.

In general, Long rightly argues against a uniform interpretation of the use of images in Plato's work.[3] One of the problems in analyzes is that Plato reveals a deep contradiction and a clear ambivalence regarding the use of images in his work: on the one hand, he is infamous for his condemnation of images and poetry as a whole; on the other hand, the dialogues are full

---

1 For an exhaustive commentary on these three passages (with references), see Mario Vegetti, *Platone. La Repubblica. Vol. V, Libri VI–VII* (Napoli: Bibliopolis, 2003), 13ff.; see also Veronica Santini, *Il filosofo e il mare: Immagini marine e nautiche nella Repubblica di Platone* (Milan: Mimesis, 2011), 112. For Proclus' reading of the *Republic*, see Michele Abbate, "Gli aspetti etico-politici della Repubblica nel commento di Proclo (dissertazioni VII/VIII e XI)," in *La Repubblica di Platone nella tradizione antica*, ed. Mario Vegetti and Michele Abbate (Napoli: Bibliopolis, 1999), 207–218.

2 David Keyt, "Plato and the Ship of State," in *The Blackwell Guide to Plato's Republic*, ed. Gerasimos Santas (Malden: Blackwell, 2006), 189. For the images of the Sun, the line, and the cave, see Pl. *Resp.* 507b (ff.), 509d (ff.), and 514a (ff.).

3 A. G. Long, "The Ship of State and the Subordination of Socrates," in *Plato and the Power of Images*, ed. Pierre Destrée and Radcliffe G. Edmonds III (Leiden: Brill, 2017), 158.

of images such as allegories, analogies, similes, characters, metaphors, and models. So, images are both, in some respect, a hindrance and a powerful tool for philosophical communication. We will find some of this ambiguity in the following pages. There is no pretension here of solving the problem of metaphoric or analogical language – a problem that not even Plato himself seems to have solved.[4]

Before the meaning of the image of the ship itself is investigated, we first need to analyze its frame or, that is, its context. The first pages of Book VI are the starting point of a long *addendum* that plays an important role within the dialogue. This *addendum* has a clear narrative and argumentative function. In these pages, what is at stake is the viability of the proposal made by Socrates, according to which the philosophers should rule the city.[5] As we all know, this proposal has been widely received in Platonic tradition, but Adeimantus, Socrates' main interlocutor in this sequence of the dialogue, has a strong negative reaction to Socrates' proposal and actually threatens Socrates with an armed attack.[6] It seems that Socrates is aware that his proposal would cause a feeling of strangeness, and, in some way, he was already expecting this excessive reaction as he himself mentions: "Well, I've now come to what we likened to the greatest wave. But I shall say what I have to say, even if the wave is a wave of laughter that will simply drown me in ridicule and contempt."[7]

Yet Socrates takes the risk of looking ridiculous because he wants his proposal for a just, "utopian" city, *Kallipolis*, to overcome unscathed the turbulence expected from the image of the third wave. Thus, the image of waves meaningfully anticipates the nautical imagery that will resume a few pages later with the allegory of the ship.[8] The third wave is expected to have a huge impact not only on the conversation but also on the city itself, and, for this reason, Socrates is afraid of looking ridiculous or of getting a violent reaction from the city. This is the reason why Socrates begins a long debate that brings up the image of the ship in Book VI.

In the passage between 474b and 487a, the discussion focused on epistemological questions which aim to determine what the nature of

4 For a wider discussion of images in Plato, see Pierre Destrée and Radcliffe G. Edmonds III, eds., *Plato and the Power of Images* (Leiden: Brill, 2017).

5 Pl. *Resp.* V 473d. The text used here is based on the following edition: S. R. Slings, ed., *Plato. Platonis Rempublicam* (Oxford: Clarendon Press, 2003).

6 VI 473e–474a.

7 V 473c. All translations of ancient sources are my own, unless otherwise stated.

8 The first wave concerns the role of women in the city (V 457b); the second the abolition of the nuclear family (V 457c).

the philosopher appointed as guardian of the city would be. In Socrates' words, the philosopher is able to reach the truth and avoid being deceived by opinion because his soul aims to achieve *what is*, instead of paying attention to *what would be*. Obviously, we are immersing ourselves here in Platonic vocabulary. This contemplation of the unchanging will provide the philosopher with the two necessary conditions that qualify the philosopher for city government: a well-ordered soul from an ethical point of view and the guidelines for representing the beautiful, the just, and the good which are required for government.[9] However, despite all the effort made to define the true nature of the philosopher and even if Socrates is praised for the rhetorical strength of his discourse, Adeimantus and the other interlocutors remain unpersuaded. The idea of philosophers becoming guardians seems to be very far from a consensual one as these are usually seen as eccentric and useless people, or often as simply bad (παμπόνηροι; *pamponēroi*).[10] The abyss of aporia is now getting close.

Plato is, then, sailing against the current, against the flow: his utopian proposal is not only an object of ridicule but also profoundly scandalous. The scandal of the proposal clearly derives from a particular feature of Platonic utopia, one that directly concerns the pages of the *Republic* we are studying here: Plato's *Republic* must be seen more as a "projectual utopia"[11] than as the kind of utopia of evasion typically found in modern times. What is at stake here, according to Vegetti,[12] is not a utopian design intended to be a "book of dreams," mostly because its realization is desirable and possible or, at least, not impossible, although difficult and necessarily imperfect. Plato claims that that project was constructed in the manner of a narrative fiction, a mythical tale.[13] The utopian design is then presented as a gesture of powerful philosophical imagination, a discursive act already endowed in itself with efficacy. Hence the scandal.

The place of philosophers within the public arena was a wider debate in which not only comedy but also many other cultural and

---

9 V 484b.

10 See VI 487d.

11 Mario Vegetti, *Um Paradigma no Céu: Platão político de Aristóteles ao século XX* (São Paulo: Annablume, 2010), 162.

12 Mario Vegetti, "Beltista eiper dynata. The Status of Utopia in the Republic," in *The Painter of Constitutions*, ed. Mario Vegetti (Sankt Augustin: Academia Verlag, 2013), 120.

13 Pl. *Resp.* 376d, 501e; Pl. *Ti.* 26c.

educational Athenian institutions of the fifth and fourth centuries BCE were engaged. The philosophy of the geometers of the Academy that is depicted in Isocrates' *Antídosis*, a text that constitutes a sort of intellectual self-apology by the great orator, reveals the vitality of the then-current debate.[14] Isocrates states that he partially agrees with the criticism of the majority regarding the usefulness of the philosophy of geometers. For him, it is useful only as an introductory tool (propaedeutic) to the most important disciplines, which are all linked to the practice of oratory and are, therefore, political. On the other hand, Isocrates states that philosophy is of no use when it turns to idle speculation about useless issues such as those of the ancient sophists who are worried about abstract topics such as the infinity of being.[15] The target of this criticism is obviously Socratic and Platonic philosophy. Isocrates and his school seem to be competing with Plato and his Academy not only for a prominent role in the education of the new Athenian generations (and Greeks, in general) but also for influencing the definition of philosophy itself as well as its role in the utopian city.[16] The same charge of futility against astronomical and geometric research can be seen in the same central pages of the *Republic* that we are analyzing. It is exactly in this context that the relevance of the image of the ship becomes clear: not only as part of the Platonic argument in favour of the utopia proposal in the *Republic* but also as Plato's important contribution to the *ongoing* speculation in Athens.

If this is the actual pragmatic dimension of the *Republic*, the statement that Socrates addresses to Adeimantus is nothing but surprising: "When

14 Isoc. *Antid.* 262. See Andrea W. Nightingale, *Genres in Dialogue: Plato and the Construct of Philosophy* (Cambridge: Cambridge University Press, 1995), 28–29, who shows that the text *Antídosis* explicitly relies on the Platonic *Apology* model (cf. especially *Antid.* 15) since both share motifs and themes. This is another consequence of the intense ongoing debate between the two schools and also an obvious reference to Isocrates' criticism against Plato. On the geometers in relation to Socrates, see Long, "The Ship of State," 190ff. Geometry clearly acts as a propaedeutic to philosophical dialectics in Plato's Academy, as a result of a great capacity for abstraction that arithmetic and geometry revealed to fifth-century BCE thinkers. Plato, in *Republic* Book VI, within the metaphor of the line, considers mathematics as still halfway (*metaxú*) between the sensible world (*pístis*, "belief"; *eikasía*, "conjecture") and the intelligible world.

15 Cf. Isoc. *Antid.* 268–269.

16 Bibliography about Isocrates' anti-Platonism is certainly very extensive; see Ingemar Düring, *Herodicus the Cratetean: A Study in Anti-Platonic Tradition* (Stockholm: Wahlström & Widstrand, 1941), 143–146; R. L. Howland, "The Attack on Isocrates in the Phaedrus," *The Classical Quarterly* 31, nos. 3–4 (1937): 151–159; Nightingale, *Genres in Dialogue*, 13–59.

I'd heard him [Adeimantus] out, I said: Do you think that what these people say is false [i.e. that philosophers are bad]? [...] You'd hear that they seem to me to speak the truth."[17] Adeimantus, just like any other reader of the dialogue, is obviously surprised by this unexpected change of direction in Socrates' argument. But, says Adeimantus, disappointed, "[h]ow, then, can it be true to say that there will be no end to evils in our cities until philosophers – people we agree to be useless – rule in them?"[18] The lexicon here is clearly utopian: "the end to evils in the city" is probably the central goal and a manifesto for any utopian agenda.

Once again, Socrates uses an aporetic strategy which forces the interlocutor to back off. Here is Socrates' answer to Adeimantus: "The question you ask needs to be answered by means of an image or simile."[19] Adeimantus finds himself twice misguided. First, Socrates seems to agree with the common view according to which philosophers are useless to the city, and when he tries to explain this apparent contradiction in his argument, he adds that the only way to answer it is by means of images. At this point, the course and the style of the argument change completely. Adeimantus' protest is thus of no use: "And you, of course, aren't used to speaking in similes!"[20] Socrates, however, proceeds undeterred, and he spares no irony regarding Adeimantus' surprise at his own proposal: "So! Are you making fun of me now that you've landed me with a claim that's so hard to establish? In any case, listen to my simile, and you'll appreciate all the more how greedy for images I am."[21]

The image that Socrates announces and proposes to draw is exactly the image of a ship. The description of the frame (context) of the picture allows us to make a preliminary remark. The dramatic and argumentative strength of this image seems to rely precisely on this long and controversial route during which Socrates has to cope with the waves that prevent the construction of his utopian *Kallipolis*. It is thus the third and last of these waves, the biggest of all, which entails showing the predominant place of philosophers in the government of the city and in explaining the relevance of using the ship's image and its place in these central pages of the dialogue.

17 Pl. *Resp.* VI 487d–e.
18 VI 487d–e.
19 VI 487e.
20 VI 487e.
21 VI 478e–488a.

The Legend of the Image

Even before going through the image in question, Socrates seems to be adding a sort of "legend to the picture," a note, as if he wanted to provide the interlocutors and the reader with a key for understanding the meaning of the image of the ship as well as the technique used for its construction:

> What the most decent people experience in relation to their city is so hard to bear that there is no other single experience like it. Hence to find an image of it and a defence for them [the most decent people], I must construct it [the image] from many sources, just as painters paint chimeras by combining the features of different things.[22]

First of all, it is worth explaining the reason why I am translating τραγέλαφος (*tragelaphos*), a crucial term in our passage, as "chimera." This Greek term can also be translated in a literal way as "goat–stag," a hybrid imaginary creature, half goat and half deer. This fantastic animal is already present in ancient literature, having been mentioned in Aristophanes' *Frogs*.[23] As the meaning of this word seems, in this case, to refer more to a hybrid and fantastic image in general, I choose to use a similar image which is more generic and also more present in the modern imagination: the idea of "chimera."[24]

What matters most, however, is to see how the image becomes a sort of legend to the image of the ship: Socrates seems to be emphasizing the reverse of the image, that is, as something hybrid or abnormal. This abnormality, this hybrid monstrosity of *tragelaphos*, is mainly supposed to highlight the abnormality and monstrosity of the painful situation of the civil war – one notices the repetition of the verb πάσχω (to suffer) in the passage – that the best citizens are enduring. This image below the image is, therefore, proposed as a key for reading and a warning: something strange is being shown, and other elements in the image of the ship will contribute to emphasize this monstrosity. The reason why this image had to take this hybrid form is mentioned beforehand: the current reality of the city is so monstrous and strange that the use of this type of fantastic image is rendered necessary. After this initial legend, the reader is then made to believe that there is something in the image that is not right, as

22 VI 488a.
23 Ar. *Ran.* 935–939.
24 For a comprehensive study of the origins and use of *tragelaphos*, see Giovanna Sillitti, *Tragelaphos: Storia di una metafora e di un problema* (Napoli: Bibliopolis, 1980).

if it were upside down. The ship image is thus introduced as "an inverted image,"[25] which represents the reversal of political roles as well as the reversal of the values of the city itself.

The Image of the Ship

Socrates then begins to depict the ship. "Imagine" (νοέω), no longer "listen" (ἀκούω), as he said immediately before.[26] By using this particular verb, Socrates is, in some respect, inviting Adeimantus to participate actively in the construction of the image of the ship. The image to be drawn becomes thus a shared project which aims to make something present, a common effort of "representation." I believe that the emphasis on the idea of sharing this project bears, in itself, a political dimension:

> Imagine, then, that something like the following happens on a ship or on many ships. The shipowner is bigger and stronger than everyone else on board, but he is hard of hearing, a bit short-sighted, and his knowledge of seafaring is equally deficient. The sailors are quarrelling with one another about steering the ship, each of them thinking that he should be the captain, even though he's never learned the art of navigation, cannot point to anyone who taught it to him, or to a time when he learned it.[27]

The strangeness of the image is striking due to the chaotic situation of characters that should be predisposed to navigation. However, there is nothing surprising about the use of a ship allegory to represent a city. This comparison of a city with a ship has a long and well-established literary tradition.[28] The closest image to the one mentioned in Plato can be found in the elegies of Theognis, written in the sixth century BCE:

> If I had, oh Simonides, the riches I once had, I would not be sad to be in the company of the nobles. Yet now fortune passes far away: I see it passing but am speechless for necessity; for I should have understood better than my fellow-citizens that we gather up the

---

25   Santini, *Il filosofo*, 126.
26   Pl. *Resp.* VI 487d.
27   VI 488a–b.
28   Silvia Gastaldi, "L'allegoria della nave," in *La Repubblica. Vol. 5, Libri 6 e 7*, ed. Mario Vegetti (Napoli: Bibliopolis, 2003), 193.

white sails and in the dark night are drifting on the waters of Melos. They refuse to empty the hold, though the water is reaching the edges. It's hard for anyone to be saved if they do what they do. They have dismissed a valiant captain, who kept watch knowing what he was doing [κυβερνήτην μὲν ἔπαυσαν ἐσθλόν, ὅτις φυλακὴν εἶχεν ἐπισταμένως]. They give bottom to riches with violence, order has disappeared, and there is no longer an equitable sharing of goods. The porters are in charge, the commoners rule over the nobles. I fear that the ship will be swallowed by the waves. I say this in riddles [ἠινίχθω] for the nobles, but even a plebeian [κακός] of obtuse mind would understand them.[29]

Revealing a clear oligarchic perspective, Theognis' allegory has traces in common with the image of Plato, anticipating key elements of the image of the ship. There can be little doubt that this previous allegory inspired the image of the ship drawn by Socrates in the *Republic*. The description of the figure of the captain of the ship in Theognis' allegory is thus very meaningful. The phrase φυλακὴν εἶχεν ἐπισταμένως anticipates at the same time, as Santini noticed,[30] both the Platonic image of the philosopher as a guardian (*phylax*) and the connection between the *technē* of government (whether of the city or the ship) and knowledge (*epistamenōs*).

The first character that Socrates introduces in the image of the ship is the ναύκληρος, that is, the shipowner. The ship of the Platonic image in question can be compared to a commercial sailing ship, such as those crossing the Mediterranean by then, probably since the time of the Phoenicians. The maritime trade in the ancient Mediterranean would certainly have relied on a fixed structure composed of specific roles, from that of the importer or exporter of goods to the person responsible for the wholesale. Normally, the exporter, who wished to sell goods overseas, would rent a ship (or part of it) from the shipowner.[31] In turn,

29 Thgn. 667–682; text based on the following edition: Douglas Young, ed., *Theognis: Elegiae* (*post* Ernestum Diehl) (Leipzig: Teubner, 1971). In my translation, I follow closely that of Franco Ferrari, *Teognide, Elegie. Introduzione, traduzione e note* (Milan: Biblioteca Universale Rizzoli, 1989), with Bruck's emendation, which reads κακός in the last line instead of κακόν. In the second case, the sense of the passage would still be understandable, of course: "but anyone, if he is wise, can recognize the actual calamity." Douglas E. Gerber, *Greek Elegiac Poetry* (Cambridge, MA: Harvard University Press, 1999), 273.
30 Santini, *Il filosofo*, 70.
31 Lionel Casson, *The Ancient Mariners: Seafarers and Sea Fighters of the Mediterranean in Ancient Times* (New York: Macmillan, 1959), 114.

the shipowner of course owns the ship but not the load that it is carrying. He hires naval officers, from the captain to the last of the sailors who will make up the crew.

In the Platonic passage, all the terms that express the idea of captaining or leading the ship are related to the *kubernētēs* figure, which brings together positions and roles that are usually in practice distributed among a larger number of crew members or officers of merchant shipping: the *kubernētēs* refers at the same time to the captain of the ship, to the pilot, to the navigator, and to the helmsman. It is clear that the position of *kubernētēs* has multiple roles, especially if we consider the number of occurrences throughout Plato's own work. In the first book of the *Republic*,[32] for example, the *kubernētēs* is also named ἄρχων ναυτῶν (*archōn nautōn*), "commander of the crew," while in the *Statesman* the *kubernētēs* is the helmsman of the universe, who leaves the helm and retires to his observation post.[33]

The precarious nautical knowledge of the Greeks, along with the inherent dangers of a sea voyage, makes sailing something dangerous and prone to dramatic outcomes either because the shipowner might lose the ship's position or because the voyage puts the lives of the crew at risk.[34] In the Socratic image, the shipowner is described as "bigger and stronger than everyone else on board, but he is hard of hearing, a bit short-sighted, and his knowledge of seafaring is equally deficient."[35] These features of the shipowner immediately remind us of another parallel – very often mentioned in scholarship – with the character Demos, the protagonist of Aristophanes' *Knights*. The comedy in question takes place in a house and not on a ship, but the similarities are obvious.

Demos, the owner of the house, is obviously an allegory for the people (*dēmos*), as his servants introduce him: "It's Demos of the Pnyx, an intolerable old man and half deaf."[36] In the comedy, Demos is continually

---

32 Pl. *Resp.* I 341C–341d.

33 Pl. *Plt.* 272e. For other Platonic passages that reinforce these multiple *kubernētēs* roles, see Keyt, "Plato and the Ship of State," 192.

34 See also Casson, *Ancient Mariners*, 38: "Whether under sail or oars, working these ships was strenuous, uncomfortable, and dangerous. They were much less sturdy than the robust craft of the Vikings, and the Greeks were correspondingly far less bold than those reckless sea raiders."

35 Pl. *Resp.* VI 488a.

36 Ar. *Eq.* 42–43. All subsequent translations from Aristophanes follow: Gilbert Murray, *Aristophanes. The Knights* (London: George Allen & Unwin, 1956). The following edition of the Greek text is used: Nigel G. Wilson, ed., *Aristophanis Fabulae* (Oxonii: E typographeo Clarendoniano, 1935–2007).

flattered by a servant called Paphlagonian, who symbolizes the demagogue: "an arrant rogue, the incarnation of calumny. This leatherworker knows his old master thoroughly,"[37] meaning he knows how to deceive him. The outraged servants of the household steal a set of oracles that Paphlagonian keeps in secret, and they discover that these are prophecies about who will rule the city: firstly, it will be a dealer in oakum, then a sheep-dealer, and finally one sausage seller (Ἀλλαντοπώλης).[38] Having been invited to take on this responsibility, the sausage seller claims that he is not prepared to take it over, but the servant replies: "Some secret virtue? No? Don't say you came of honest parents?"[39] The sausage seller replies immediately: "Honest? Lord, not them! Both pretty queer."[40] Soon after, he confesses: "But I don't see yet how ever I shall learn to rule a state." The reply of the servants is sarcastic:

> Easy as lying! [Φαυλότατον ἔργον] Do as now you do.
> Turn every question to a public stew.
> Hash things, and cook things. Win the common herd
> By strong sweet sauces in your every word [ἀεὶ προσποιοῦ].
> For other gifts, you have half the catalogue
> Already, for the perfect demagogue [ὑπογλυκαίνων ῥηματίοις
>   μαγειρικοῖς];
> A blood-shot voice, low breeding, huckster's tricks [φωνὴ μιαρά,
>   γέγονας κακῶς]
> What more can man require for politics? [ἄπαντα πρὸς πολιτείαν
>   ἃ δει][41]

Thus, although Socrates does not explicitly say that the shipowner is an allegory of the people, the parallel with the passage from Aristophanes seems to be a clear reference to it. Two more pieces of evidence make this connection clearer. A few pages after, Socrates mentions that some people (in other words, the Sophists) raise a big, strong animal; they then learn its emotions and the best way to manipulate it.[42] The allegory of the animal is quickly revealed: these are the πολλοί (*polloi*),[43] the many gathered in assemblies and theatres, that is, the people. A second clue is granted from

37 Ar. *Eq.* 46.
38 143.
39 184: ἐκ καλῶν εἶ ἀγαθῶν.
40 186: εἰ μὴ 'κ πονηρῶν γ'.
41 213–218.
42 Pl. *Resp.* VI 493a–b.
43 VI 493d.

reading Aristotle: when he is explaining the difference between metaphor and allegory in the *Rhetoric*, he states that Plato's *Republic* draws the image of the people as a shipowner.[44] I believe, therefore, that there cannot be any doubt that the shipowner symbolizes the people.[45]

Even if the shipowner is bigger and stronger than the others (because it is the people, the owner of the city–ship), he has, however, no skills to lead the ship. This limitation is the dramatic and theoretical note that inspires the whole picture: sailors (as servants of Demos) are ready to do anything in order to take over the government.[46] In the image of the ship, the lack of sailing *technē* in those who aspire to become captains is the scandal: it is unthinkable that those who intend to take over the government have no education. The absolute lack of education for politics and the sarcastic statement denying the need for any training or education for those who aim to take over the government also constitute a fundamental convergence between the two images. As the parallel with Aristophanes' sarcastic allegory made clear, the insistence on the importance of education is also found in Plato's image; it is not mentioned *where* exactly these captains were educated and *when* this actually took place. This emphasis is hardly surprising: the theme of the education of the rulers is exactly one of the key issues of the *Republic* and, more generally, of Plato's political thought. Accordingly, the insistence of the sailors on stating that the art of sailing was not teachable is not unprecedented. Their line of thought certainly reminds us of Protagoras' words regarding the original myth of the city; at the beginning of that homonymous Platonic dialogue, it is mentioned that all citizens are capable of being politicians as politics does not require any previous education.

The image of the ship is precisely the cornerstone of Plato's criticism against rhetoric, sophistic, and also the democratic party: the lack of any necessity to hold special political training is, in fact, the "fundamental postulate of democracy."[47] Plato, however, cannot accept the democratic

---

44 Arist. *Rh.* II 4 1406b 34–36.

45 For the suggestion that the image of the owner is to be associated with that of Athenian politicians of the time, see Bruno Centrone, *Platone. Repúbblica*, trans. Franco Sartori, foreword by Mario Vegetti, notes by Bruno Centrone (Bari: Laterza, 2011), VI, n12.

46 In Plato's image, the shipowner seems to suffer from not only deafness but also visual problems. This is certainly a reference to the importance of sight for navigation, but it is also a Platonic note on the relevance of this ability for the guardians, which is precisely associated with the necessary exercise of *theoria*. The sailor of the ship is also a close observer of the sky, as in the allegory of the cave, just a few pages after; cf. Keyt, "Plato and the Ship of State," 197; Santini, *Il filosofo*, 129.

47 Gastaldi, "L'allegoria della nave," 197.

thesis that anyone, without education, is able to be in politics – not so much, or not only, because of his clearly oligarchic political preference. Plato is convinced that without a reform of the political class (a reform which consists mainly in the education of those expected to be guardians), the only possible scenario of justice is the one expressed by Thrasymachus at the beginning of the *Republic*, for whom "justice is nothing other than the convenience [συμφέρον; *sympheron*] of the stronger."[48] It is in seeking to respond to this theoretical position that Plato apparently writes the rest of the dialogue. The convenience of the stronger and the idea of politics driven by the pursuit of self-interest are exactly what the Platonic image describes:

> Indeed, the sailors claim that it is not teachable and are ready to cut to pieces anyone who says that it is. They are always crowding around the shipowner, begging him and doing everything possible to get him to turn the rudder over to them.[49] And sometimes, if they do not succeed in persuading him, they execute the ones who do succeed or throw them overboard [...].[50]

Violence is, therefore, the hallmark of this ship, and also of the city that is under the conditions described in the picture. It is impossible not to see a tragic reference to the figure of Socrates himself in the shattered figure who defends the idea that the art of navigation (thus, politics) is teachable.[51] The reference to the violence against each other, which takes the shape of a civil war, is also clear. It is not a coincidence that Plato uses the expression στασιάζοντας (*stasiazontas*) applied to the same sailors in their continuous struggle to get command of the ship. The reference to the idea of στάσις (*stasis*), to the city's internal struggle, as well as to the civil war that took place in Athens in the last years of the fifth century BCE cannot go unnoticed. I believe, however, that the term *stasis* summarizes, more generally, in the literary context of the time the broad lexicon of civil war, which clearly refers to the Athenian background by then.

---

48 Pl. *Resp.* I 338c: τὸ δίκαιον οὐκ ἄλλο τι ἢ τὸ τοῦ κρείττονος συμφέρον.

49 Ancient sailboats did not have a "helm" yet: the πηδάλιον (*pēdalion*) was composed of two steering oars, one on each side of the ship. The helm, being located at and attached to the stern of the ship, and the compass for navigation were invented only in the Middle Ages, around 1200 CE (Casson, *Ancient Mariners*, 246). For a more technical description of the Athenian trireme and how it works, see John S. Morrison and John F. Coates, *The Athenian Trireme* (Cambridge: Cambridge University Press, 1986); and especially, John F. Coats, "The Trireme Sails Again," *Scientific American* 260, no. 4 (1989): 96–103.

50 Pl. *Resp.* VI 488b–c.

51 See also Gastaldi, "L'allegoria della nave," 198.

The *sympheron* idea, of justice as the interest of the stronger, is expressed not only by physical violence but also by other sailors' behaviour:

> [A]nd then, having stupefied their noble shipowner with drugs, wine, or in some other way, they rule the ship, using up what is in it and sailing while drinking and feasting, in the way that people like that are prone to do. Moreover, they call the person who is clever at persuading or forcing the shipowner to let them rule a "navigator," a "captain," and "one who knows ships," and dismiss anyone else as useless.[52]

Persuasion and violence are here meaningfully at the same level. The argument against rhetoric and sophistic cannot be more explicit. Mandrake and wine are used in order to make the shipowner docile. The same type of narcotic effect is expected from persuasion.[53]

The shipowner is said to be γενναῖον (*gennaion*), "noble," "well-born." Although this term might possibly be ironic, as Keyt noticed,[54] the term can, however, simply be referring to the noble origin or to the economic power of the one who owns the ship. I believe that it is possible to agree with the classic comment of Adam,[55] according to which the shipowner, due to his position, would fundamentally be a victim of the violence (and persuasion) of the sailors.[56] The one who does not act like this – the one who does not seek power through deceit and violence – is called *achrēston*, "useless." The uselessness of philosophy is here recovered again. Lastly, a double pernicious outcome results from the sailors' command: the goods of the ship are wasted in feasting and drunkenness, and the sailing is consequently compromised. The route of a ship with such a command cannot be anything but tragic, both in image and in what it means. The danger of shipwreck for the city is, thus, the expected result when justice is replaced by a reckless private management of public affairs.

---

52 Pl. *Resp.* VI 488c–d.

53 See, among others, what Gorgias says about the narcotic effects of bad persuasion in *The Encomium of Helen* (14).

54 Keyt, "Plato and the Ship of State," 195.

55 James Adam, *The Republic of Plato*, 2 volumes (Cambridge: Cambridge University Press, 1902), 9.

56 On this, see Adam, *Republic of Plato*, 9: "though unwieldy, sluggish, and dull-witted (cf. Ap. 30), he is placid, and not deliberately vicious." I distance myself from Santini's reading (*Il filosofo*, 135) which suggests a fault or, at least, a lack of responsibility on the part of the owner, who should be ready and able to pilot the ship.

The True Captain

Immediately after such a vivid description of the city, Plato finally puts on the scene, as an *ex-machina*, the utopia. This is represented by the figure of the *true captain*:

> They do not understand that a true captain must pay attention to the seasons of the year, the sky, the stars, the winds, and all that pertains to his craft, if he is really to be the ruler of a ship. And they do not believe there is any craft that would enable him to determine how he should steer the ship, whether the others want him to or not, or any possibility of mastering this alleged craft or of practising it at the same time as the craft of navigation. Do you not think that the true captain will be called a real stargazer, a babbler, and a good-for-nothing by those who sail in ships governed in that way, in which such things happen?[57]

The *alēthinos* captain, the *true* captain, is a guarantee that the route of the ship cannot lead to sinking. The image is consistent with the general idea in these pages of the *Republic* in which the guardian philosophers are the only possibility of salvation of a city otherwise doomed to shipwreck. The *true* captain, trained in the art of sailing, fundamentally puts the *epimeleia* into practice, which I have translated as "to pay attention to (to mind)," but of course the meaning is far more complex, combining both the idea of study or training with one of careful and concrete surveillance. Both tasks can easily be seen as responsibilities assigned to a captain. The practice of *epimeleia* is carefully described in the list of the things that a captain should pay attention to: the weather conditions, the seasons, the sky, the stars, and the wind.

Thus, the captain's position seems to require multiple cares, which ultimately consist of knowledge of astronomy and geometry. The theoretical training of the captain, as it is described, is mainly covered by astronomy, which has seasons and stars as its object, according to a similar description in Plato's *Symposium*.[58] In astronomy, as in sailing, the observation of celestial phenomena is especially relevant (οὐρανοῦ καὶ ἄστρων). This emphasis on the heavens makes us think of the two central allegories that will be explored in the following pages of the *Republic*: the

---

57 Pl. *Resp.* VI 488d–489a.
58 Pl. *Symp.* 188b.

Sun and the cave. For instance, in the allegory of the cave, the released prisoner also looks at the stars at night and towards the Sun during the day: here is another sign of how the ship image is deeply intertwined with the other onto-epistemological images used by Plato in these central pages of the *Republic*. The science of geometry is implicit not only in the astronomy but also in the reference to the winds because, as a sailor knows very well, sailing is a constant search for the best angles between the sails and the wind. Geometry and astronomy, as we have seen, represent the trademarks of Platonic philosophy as attacked by Isocrates.

As is to be expected, the true captain would not meet the favour of the crew: on the contrary, he would be considered by the crew to be a "star-gazer" (*meteōroskopos*), "babbler" (*adoleschēs*), or "useless." The *meteōroskopos* and *adoleschēs* epithets are often associated, in the literature of his time, with Socrates himself; already in Aristophanes' *Clouds*, in fact, the Athenian master is called *meteōrosophistēs*[59] and also *adoleschēs*.[60] However, it is the double allegory of sailing and medicine linked by Plato in the pages of the *Statesman*[61] to which these two epithets are more closely related. In this dialogue, the captain of the ship is also called: *meteōrologos*, *adoleschēs*, and *sophistēs*,[62] or "a star-gazer, some babbling sophist."[63] This expression with the addition of the term *sophistēs* is quite revealing because it signifies the intention of Plato to refer, once again, to Socrates and his tragic historical fate. Immediately after, the same character, the very one who takes care of navigation or medicine (ἐπιτίθεσθαι κυβερνητικῇ καὶ ἰατρικῇ), is accused of corrupting the youth (νεωτέρους διαφθείροντα).[64] As is widely known, the corruption of the youth is the main charge against Socrates,[65] and these pages of the *Statesman* must have been constructed in order to make a reference to that.[66]

59 Ar. *Nub.* 360.
60 1480; for other references, see Keyt "Plato and the Ship of State," 198.
61 Pl. *Plt.* 296e (ff.).
62 299b.
63 Translated by Rowe in John M. Cooper, *Plato: Complete Works* (Indianapolis and Cambridge: Hackett, 1997). This is not the context to dedicate a more comprehensive study of the rich parallels between the *Republic* and the double image of the *Statesman* in order to understand Plato's political proposal, especially with regard to the democratic possibilities involved. I hope to be able to write on it very soon.
64 Pl. *Plt.* 299b–c.
65 See Pl. *Ap.* 24b–c.
66 Therefore, the reference to the master's fate is, once again, one of the main reasons for the construction of the image of the true captain. In the same reference, one of the main meanings of the allegory is also implicit: the captain that sails with knowledge of the art required for navigation does not really need the consensus of the crew. This same

The third epithet with which the crew associates the true captain is *achrēstos*, "useless." Linked to the other two epithets, however, the term has a more precise meaning which is decisive for understanding the allegory. The uselessness of Socrates and his followers is, in fact, also strictly linked to the babbler mentioned in Aristophanes' *Clouds*. The *adoleschia* of Socrates and his disciples is mentioned in the comedy when Strepsiades sets fire to the "Thinkery." It is a fairly common sarcastic criticism of this type of theoretical knowledge of philosophy and – more precisely – to the Socratic education itself. This philosophical education is perceived as misleading due to a lack of practical use, in the same way as the education of the captain in the Platonic image is considered by the crew also to be useless for the seizure of power. There is a reference to Isocrates' criticism of Platonic philosophy mentioned in the *Antídosis*, according to which the philosophy of astronomers and geometricians (as seen above) is called ἀδολεσχίαν and μικρολογίαν, "empty talk" and "hair-splitting."[67]

That it is Socrates' political tragedy – and the Socratics with him, among them certainly Plato – that lies beneath the captain image is also clear in the final passage, which seems to be recovering the initial note[68] about the hard and difficult position of those who hold leading positions:

> I do not think that you need to examine the simile in detail to see that the ships resemble cities and their attitude to the true philosophers, but you already understand what I mean.
> [...]
> Then first tell this simile to anyone who wonders why philosophers are not honored in the cities, and try to persuade him that there would be far more cause for wonder if they were honored.[69]

The hermeneutic circle of the image is thus completed here: we are referring to cities, especially a city that does not take into account the philosophers, as was the case for Socrates and his followers. We are

---

idea is explored again in the image of the *Republic*, as well as in the very long excursus of the *Statesman* quoted above. On Socrates' condemnation on religious grounds and, in particular, the corruption of the young, see also A. Chevitarese and Gabriele Cornelli, "(Almost) Forgotten Complicity: Socrates (and Plato) between the Oligarchic Coup of 404 BC and the Democratic Restoration of 403," in *New Perspectives on the Ancient World*, ed. Pedro Paulo A. Funari, Renata Senna Garraffoni, and Bethany Letalien (Oxford: Archaeopress/FAPESP, 2008), 161–167.

67 Isoc. *Antid.* 269; cf. also Gastaldi, "L'allegoria della nave," 202.
68 Pl. *Resp.* VI 488a.
69 VI 489a.

referring to Athens. Therefore, the following expression is not surprising: Οὐ δή οἶμαι δεῖσθαί σε ἐξεταζομένην τὴν εἰκόνα; "I do not think that you need to examine the simile in detail." The allegory of the ship is the crude representation of the Athenian political reality at that time, the same that hits the eyes of Adeimantus every day. Hence the observation of Socrates on the fact that the image does not require close examination: the image represents the reverse of the philosopher's utopia which is obviously the contemporaneous reality of Athens, as Plato constantly suggests, making indirect references to Socrates and to his followers. What the simile tells us is that with political actors such as those, it is impossible to find a place for philosophers. There is no need to figure it in detail – as Plato seems to suggest: just look at the recent historical events and at Athens nowadays!

There is, however, another invitation to Adeimantus, and this time it is a positive one: an invitation to move towards the action which is expressed by two verbs that were mentioned throughout the development of the image – *didaskō* (teach) and *peithō* (persuade). Adeimantus should be able to explain or to teach the image in order to persuade those that do not understand why philosophers are not taken into consideration, that is, the reason why they are not captaining the ship of the city. In this final legend, the image of the ship reveals itself to be an invitation to political activity that aims at education and persuasion. What is being said here is that the reverse of the utopia of the city, in which philosophers are not rulers, should not be surprising. This is, of course, an invitation to go through the history of the last decades of Athens in order to persuade the audience of the dramatic need to overcome the three waves. The strongest appeal can be found in the third wave: the need to put the government into the hands of philosophers because this would definitely put the city–ship on a safer route. A political project and an educational project that are, therefore, once again standing against the flow. This last invitation, made to Adeimantus to retrace (and to help to retrace) the recent history of Athens closes the image as such. The meaning of the image and its role within the argument of the central books of the *Republic* are thus provided to the readers: the government of the ship–city requires qualities that can only be found in philosophers.

Conclusion

In the central books of Plato's *Republic*, the image of the ship represents, therefore, a last attempt to convince the interlocutor of the need to put the government into the hands of philosophers: it is the representation of utopia in reverse that is the sinking of Athens. The image reveals in dramatic tones the need for the education of the true captain of the ship, as someone who stands out from the other applicants just for having been educated in the art of sailing. It shows in first-hand what will be discussed by Socrates in the following pages, namely the argument according to which the training of the guardians requires a theoretical supplement. This supplement will represent a guarantee that they would be equipped with the ethical and theoretic skills needed to be rulers. In Books VI and VII of the Republic, the assumption of this guarantee will lead to the construction of an onto-epistemological horizon at which the captain–guardian can look or can bear in mind while he is piloting the ship of the city.

The reverse of the utopia here represented by the image of the ship also seems to play a controversial role within the political debate of fourth-century Athens that took place immediately after the city's defeat in the civil wars between the end of the fifth century and the beginning of the fourth. This debate was probably very common and widespread on the comedy stage, as well as on the benches of the squares and gardens such as those of Isocrates and of the Academy itself. In this debate, Plato sails against the current, against the flow. While his proposal to put the government into the hands of philosophers comes into direct collision with the democratic ideology, the philosophy curriculum intended to train these guardians is strongly criticized by Isocrates and other institutions of Athenian political education.

Plato, on the one hand, re-uses a well-known traditional image that links ship and city and which defends his oligarchic proposal for a just city if its government is given to true captains, or in other words the philosophers. On the other hand, once again, Plato introduced, in this controversy, a clear reference to the tragic fate of Socrates, the real prototype of a captain. It is Socrates who is, in fact, the one sailing against the flow both in political and in educational areas. For this reason, he was eventually killed and thrown overboard by the crew. The image of the ship therefore constitutes a renewed apology for his master's actions and also those of the Socratic fellows (among them Plato himself) during the Athenian civil war.

CHAPTER FOUR

Sailing to Find Utopia or Sailing to Found Utopia? The Pragmatic and Idealistic Pursuit of Ideal Cities in Greek and Roman Political Philosophy

Aaron L. Beek

Introduction

What did classical writers think of as an ideal world before More invented Utopia? Ideas of "utopia" prompt some combination of two philosophical threads. First appears the idea that there is a rich land, one where the land produces food of its own accord, the climate is pleasant, and people are free from strife and toil. This bounty of the land means that there is no need to contest over it. For examples, we see hints of such in Pindar's pleasant afterlife in *Olympian 2*, Hesiod's *Works and Days*, and Homer's Phaeacia.[1] The second thread, however, is rather different – rather than resting in the bounty of the land, men come together and design the perfect state. This new state is generally stable, allows for generational change, and is free from corruption and petty politics. The citizens of such a state must work, but the work is not burdensome. The people of such utopias often are depicted with unusual customs to ensure this, such as Iambulus' Children of the Sun eschewing marriage, living in groups no larger than 400, and being ruled by the oldest.[2]

These two images are not exclusive, of course, and in our classical utopia-like states, these images are often combined, such as in the paradox-ographers' descriptions of the Indian islands. There remains an implicit

Many thanks are due to both Hamish Williams and Ross Clare for their organization of this volume and the accompanying conference.

1 Pind. *Ol.* 65–73; Hes. *Op.* 117–120, 170–173; Hom. *Od.* 7.114–132.
2 Diod. Sic. 2.55–60.

underlying question: is an ideal land rooted in an idyllic landscape or is it rooted in the excellent features of its governance? Is a utopia something that can be created or only something that can be discovered? This is not simply an academic question about the nature of paradise, because it has long-reaching impact in terms of affecting the actions of prominent political figures in the Greek and Roman world. Moreover, the sense of sailing away from the existing world in order to place a sea between the utopian state and the former state is a theme with roots in the familiar myths of the founding of prominent cities such as Thebes, Rome, and Carthage, but it is also a commonplace in the isolation of the utopian settlements depicted in the geographical writers.

There are many ways to categorize ideas of utopia. Doyne Dawson presented a distinction between "high" utopias and "low" utopias, in which the first type was theoretical, but the second was meant to actually be put into place.[3] As framed by Ian Storey, one can divide ideas of paradise in Old Comedy into past, present, and future. In this model, past utopias are lost paradises, present paradises are to be discovered, and future paradises could be regained.[4] For John Ferguson, utopian thought presented a unique intersection of the idealizing of the natural world (ideal places) and of the man-made (ideal states).[5] Historians have long recognized utopian fiction as presenting insight on the ills of contemporary society; while many such utopias are satirical rather than philosophical (see Lucian's *True History* or the *Birds* of Aristophanes), that does not necessitate that the satire is devoid of philosophy. Others have differentiated between a "hard" paradise and a "soft" paradise. This is rooted in the idea that a soft land would eventually generate soft people, in a form of environmental determinism.[6] There is no shortage of discussion of *loci amoeni*, that is, pleasant places, in classical literature. At

---

3 Doyne Dawson, *Cities of the Gods: Communist Utopias in Greek Thought* (Oxford: Oxford University Press, 1992), 7. Dawson's work is more clearly invested in the "high" type, while this chapter is more invested in the "low" type or, at the least, in actual changes intended to come about through the philosophical musing.

4 Ian Storey, *Fragments of Old Comedy. Vol. 1* (Cambridge, MA: Harvard University Press (LCL), 2011), xxi–xxii.

5 John Ferguson, *Utopias of the Classical World* (London: Thames and Hudson, 1975), for example, 9, 15, 16, 25.

6 For Herodotus, this partly explained the Persian defeat at the hands of the Greeks and justified Greek (and particularly Spartan) austerity compared to Persian excess. While he makes the point throughout, he closes his work (9.122) with a particularly forceful version. Even the Greeks were not immune – the Greeks of Colophon were said to have been originally tough and hardy but then softened by dealings with the Lydians (Ath. 526a = Xenophanes frag. 3).

the risk of overgeneralizing, the classical ideal tends to aim for something rustic and idyllic, not bustling and urban (despite its close association with city-founding), tends to reinforce life as simple and almost austere, and, curiously, tends to be fairly anti-marriage. The intersection of utopian philosophy and city-founding may be particularly affected by the writings of Hippodamus of Miletus, famous in antiquity both for political philosophy and for urban planning.[7] And last but not least, Rhiannon Evans extensively explored narratives of decline and averting decline as a crucial aspect of utopia/dystopia.[8]

This paper sets aside questions of past, present, and future paradises as well as distinctions of hard and soft paradises to focus on a different distinction. Is a paradise something to be discovered or something to be created? Are the protagonists of utopian literature presented as sailing forth intending to find utopia in a promised land, or do they instead set forth to found utopia, having escaped from the dysfunctional states left behind them? Once again, there are arguments in favour of each. Those pieces more devoted to philosophical inquiry, such as we find in Plutarch's *De facie* and Plato, do tend to present an ideal city as something that can be theoretically created.[9] Others, however, are rooted in the geographical and paradoxographical tradition: travellers' tales of faraway wondrous lands that are paradises that can be found, even if they have admirable institutions. Likewise, many tales of past golden ages present paradise as something that was once found and then lost or ruined. These differences matter to those setting out to colonize new lands and affect how they approach these lands. Sertorius is said to have debated sailing off to the Isles of the Blessed to set up his own "true" Roman state rather than continue to contend with Sulla and Pompey for the Roman Empire. This episode is presented as an opportunity for both senses of utopia, though we may fairly question how much this image is reflecting the actual goals of Sertorius versus reflecting the presentations of Sallust and Plutarch and their own philosophical ideas of the ideal state.

---

7 For Hippodamus, see Roger Paden, "The Two Professions of Hippodamus of Miletus," *Philosophy and Geography* 4, no. 1 (2001), 25–48. For the influence of utopian philosophy on modern city planning, see Gábor Betegh, "Plato's Magnesia and Costa's Brasilia," in *Political Theory and Architecture*, ed. Duncan Bell and Bernardo Zacka (London: Bloomsbury, 2019), 59–77.

8 Rhiannon Evans, *Utopia Antiqua: Readings of the Golden Age and Decline at Rome* (London and New York: Routledge, 2008), esp. 3–5.

9 Plut. *De facie* 26 (*Mor.* 940F–942C).

Sertorius and the Blessed Isles

While in many authors utopia is either a curiosity or perhaps a philosophical thought experiment, we cannot discount the fact that such philosophy motivated political leaders on occasion to undertake real actions to try to achieve such a utopia, whether through finding it or making it. Because of their importance to Sertorius, the Blessed Isles are an interesting place to start. Appearing first in Book 4 of the *Odyssey*, the Blessed Isles are a clement paradise. Homer describes them as devoid of snow or storms, while Pindar asserts there is no need to toil in these islands, and here the night and day are of equal length.[10] These islands were initially considered to be referencing a post-mortem paradise of Elysium, but these islands were soon to be associated by historians, geographers, and paradoxographers with either the Canary Islands or the Madeira archipelago.[11] While not always utopian, they do tend to be idyllic in some way.[12] For the most part, in Roman thought, these islands spend several centuries merely as distant curiosities, with a minor surge of interest following the (unfortunately non-extant) geographical writings of Juba II, who apparently discussed these islands in some detail.[13] But in approximately 81 BCE, they take on a special importance to the Roman commander Sertorius.

Rome, in the early first century BCE, was beset by a series of civil wars and conflicts that brought characters such as Marius, Sulla, and Pompey to positions of power and caused the Romans to question the status of their state. Quintus Sertorius was sent to Iberia during the civil wars of the 80s BCE, in which he was more a supporter of Cinna than of Marius.

---

10 Hom. *Od.* 4.563–568; cf. Hes. *Op.* 170–173.

11 Strabo 3.12. The precise location of the Blessed Isles was a debated question in antiquity, and writers such as Agatharcides (fr. 7) and Pliny (*HN* 6.37) were relatively open about the debate. For further discussion of the location, see Joseph McAlhany, "Sertorius between Myth and History: The Isles of the Blessed Episode in Sallust, Plutarch and Horace," *Classical Journal* 112, no. 1 (2016): 57–76; Philip Spann, "Sallust, Plutarch, and the Isles of the Blest," *Terrae Incognitae* 9, no. 1 (1977): 75–80. For the fragments of Agartharcides, see Stanley Burstein, *Agatharchides of Cnidus, On the Erythraean Sea* (London: Ashgate, 1989).

12 For islands as utopias, see the later section of this chapter "The Island Utopia."

13 Juba's writings were very well-regarded and referenced extensively by Pliny (for example, *HN* 5.1, 5.10, 6.30–37, 8.4–5, 8.13–19) and somewhat more sparingly by Plutarch (for example, *Sertorius* 9, *Caes.* 55, *Rom.* 15). From his time as governor of Africa, Sallust was personally acquainted with Juba's grandfather and father and with their library (see *Iug.* 17–18), though his *Bellum Iugurthinum* preceded Juba's writings (Juba being roughly eight years of age at that time).

Indeed, several passages mentioning Sertorius hint at him fleeing to Spain as the supporters of Sulla took control in Rome.[14] Nevertheless, the Sullan faction sent him away with a double purpose: to rein in Iberia and to remove him from interfering in matters in Rome.[15] Sertorius is an unusual figure, and the pro-Pompey histories of his day painted him as an utter villain, while the later pro-Caesarian accounts (like Sallust) rebranded Sertorius as a great man.[16] Past examinations of Sertorius in this sense have thought to connect him more with the revolutionary aims of the Gracchi, of Catiline, or of Caesar, but I think we have a good argument to connect him with Greek history and philosophy instead.[17] In a sense, Sertorius is partaking in both sides of this finding/founding dialectic.

Regarding the sources on Sertorius and his flirtation with settling the Blessed Isles, we are mostly reliant upon Plutarch and Sallust. Regrettably, the short (and very late) account by Julius Exsuperantius nowhere records

14 These passages, for example, Orosius, *Historiae Adversus Paganos* 5.23, Ampelius 18.17, are really quite short, and the fuller accounts of Appian and Plutarch concur that Sertorius was formally appointed praetor in Spain.

15 The account of Exsuperantius (50) clearly suggests these two motives, though he may be working with disagreeing sources: *Tum consules principesque alii factionis, tanto verborum pondere castigati, sive ut aemulum ac vehementem negligentiae correctorem ab oculis removerent, sive ut feroci provinciae, cuius infidelitatem timerent, idoneum praeponerent ducem, misere in Citeriorem Hispaniam, eique mandatum est, ut transiens res in Gallia Transalpina componeret.* "Then the consuls and the leaders of the other factions, chastened by the great import of these words [the accusations of Sertorius], in order either to remove a rival and a fierce corrector of their negligence from their sight, or to appoint a capable commander for a savage province which they feared might become disloyal, sent him to Nearer Spain, and ordered him to settle matters in Transalpine Gaul on the way." All translations of ancient sources, unless otherwise stated, are my own.

16 For a fuller description of these sources, see Joseph McAlhany, "Sertorius," 57–58; and for the hostile tradition in particular, surviving in Livy and Appian, see Philip Spann, *Quintus Sertorius and the Legacy of Sulla* (Fayetteville, AR: University of Arkansas Press, 1987), 155–157. The key account, Plutarch's *Life of Sertorius*, appears to follow Sallust most closely; cf. Spann, "Isles of the Blest," 75–80. For Plutarch's version of Sertorius, see Christoph F. Konrad, *Plutarch's Sertorius: A Historical Commentary* (Chapel Hill, NC: University of North Carolina Press, 1994); Luis Garcia Moreno, "Paradoxography and Political Ideals in Plutarch's Life of Sertorius," in *Plutarch and the Historical Tradition*, ed. Philip A. Stadter (London and New York: Routledge, 1992), 132–158; see, especially, 140–142 for Sallustian language in Plutarch. See also Christopher Pelling, *Plutarch and History: Eighteen Studies* (Swansea: Classical Press of Wales, 2002), whose magisterial treatment of Plutarch leaves the *Life of Sertorius* relatively untouched, though his study remains influential in his treatment of Plutarch's assessments of Roman leaders' goals.

17 For example, Ferguson (*Utopias*, 156–158) presents Sertorius as such a revolutionary.

either the episode of the North African campaign or the flirtation with sailing into the Atlantic.[18] Similarly, the even briefer account of Florus spares a bare mention of the *Fortunatas Insulas*.[19] Livy, Appian, and the other sources for Sertorius do not mention this diversion at all.[20]

The Blessed Isles in Sallust's account can be seen both as a place for Sertorius to find utopia and to found a utopia. Consider fragments 1.88–90 and 92 of Sallust,[21] which indicate both aspects:

1.F88 McG = 86R = 99M
Quom Sertorius neque erumpere, tam levi copia, navibus
"When Sertorius could neither rush out from the ships with such a light-armed force, [nor...]."

1.F89 McG = 87R = 103M
more humanae cupidinis ignara visendi
"with the customary human desire of seeing unknown lands"

1.F90 McG = 88R = 100M
Quas duas insulas propinquas inter se yet decem <milia> stadia procul a Gadibus sitas, constabat suopte ingenio alimenta mortalibus gignere
"These two islands, situated close to each other and ten thousand stades from Gades, produced food for men of their own accord."

1.F92 McG = 90R = 102M
Traditur fugam in Oceani longinqua agitavisse
"He is said to have considered escape in the far reaches of Ocean."

18   For discussions of the relative value of Exsuperantius for understanding Sallust's *Histories*, see Andreas Beschorner, "Das 'Opusculum' des Iulius Exuperantius," *Hermes* 127, no. 2 (1999): 237–253.
19   Florus 2.10.
20   Nevertheless, the appearance of it in Florus, who normally follows Livy quite closely, suggests that Livy did discuss it in the lost books of *Ab Urbe Condita*, even if it does not appear in the *Periochae*. See also Spann, "Isles of the Blest." Diodorus likewise mentions Sertorius in the fragments (38.F22a), but we cannot readily tell how much detail he originally gave the topic.
21   This work uses the fragment numbers from the commentary of Patrick McGushin, ed. and trans., *The Histories*, Volume 1 and 2 (Oxford: Oxford University Press, 1992–1994); however, my translations are closer to the 2015 Ramsey Loeb edition; see John T. Ramsey, ed. and trans., *Sallust: Fragments of the Histories, Letters to Caesar* (Cambridge, MA: Harvard University Press (LCL), 2015). To aid the reader who may have other editions, reference is also included to the fragment numbers in both Ramsey (R) and to the earlier edition of Maurenbrecher (M).

Short though they are, these four fragments illustrate a series of rationales for the journey: that Sertorius had a force that disproportionately consisted of light-armed infantry (and thus was poorly suited to further engagement with Rome), that he desired to see (or discover) new lands, that such a land was relatively near at hand (Sertorius was already on the Atlantic coast), and the land could support him and his men, and that this was a potential flight from Spain.[22] In F92, it is indicated that a fair amount of this musing rested upon the desire to escape. His abortive attempts to find a new home elsewhere in Africa and the Balearics similarly suggest a desire to escape rather than to explore. As we see in F90, there is no need for Sertorius and his men to cultivate the islands to have sustenance. This idea of the land producing enough without cultivation is a standard motif of either paradisiacal places or legendary golden ages.[23] If one seeks to *find* a utopia, this is a necessary aspect. If one seeks to *found* a utopia, however, this aspect would be largely unnecessary, although certainly nice to have.[24] In short, this all seems like a standard paradise description from mythic narrative, except that we have a historical figure contemplating setting out to settle them.

Sallust is not alone in this presentation: before Sertorius embarked on his North African adventure, Plutarch claims in *Life of Sertorius* 9.1 that Sertorius desired to sail to the Blessed Isles and implies he was only thwarted in this aim by the mutinous departure of his best sailors, the piratic Cilicians. Sertorius then decided to intervene in a civil war in Mauretania, where he was successful. And Plutarch may perhaps also hint at such a desire again at 10.1 after Sertorius' successful campaign in North Africa. Here in 10.1, this overt pause has little place in such a short narrative except to subtly underline again how the decisions Sertorius was making were pressed upon him. Plutarch partially justifies

---

22   As Ramsey points out (*Sallust*, 84), Pseud-Acro adds the clarification that Sertorius is defeated (*victum*) at this point. He does not resume contesting with Rome until offered the leadership of the Lusitani.

23   For example (in chronological order), Hom. *Od.* 7.120–121; Hes. *Op.* 117–118; Aratus, *Phaenomena* 110–114; Ov. *Met.* 1.101–102. It should also be noted that while this is a common motif to find in the discussion of golden ages, it is not ubiquitous. For many writers, a key aspect of a golden age was that a hard, rustic life led to a primitive form of Stoic virtue.

24   However, for the island utopia creating an ideal "blank slate" upon which to build, see the below section "The Island Utopia." Sallust (*Hist.* 2 frag. 10–11 McG = 10–11R = 8, 83M) may use similar language for Sardinia. Like Maurenbrecher, I agree that fragment 11's depiction of a rich and fertile land does not go with Sardinia, but unlike Maurenbrecher, I suspect it connected rather to the Balearic Islands, drawn by the similarity in name of the Sardinian Balari tribe; see Strabo on the Balearics, for example, 3.5.1–2.

his decisions by implying Sertorius only had bad options from which to choose. Without a proper fleet, however, Sertorius could not venture into the Atlantic but was forced to opt for a night crossing even to cross to Spain from Mauretania.[25] After returning to Spain, he then instead chose to found a Rome-in-exile, complete with its own senate, trained his local Spanish recruits in Roman discipline, and treated with foreign powers as consul of Rome.[26]

The further question prompted here is that of what political philosophy might have prompted these thoughts. Perhaps nowhere in the comparison of Stoics and Epicureans is such a great contrast noted as in their implications for what a utopian city would be like. An Epicurean paradise would be reflected in the lack of needless toil, while a Stoic paradise would be one in which a simple, rigorous life would lead to highly virtuous lives. This dichotomy might be more familiar to many as the hard–soft distinction found in Lovejoy and Boas' *Primitivism* (1935) or in Hartog's *Mirror of Herodotus* (1980).[27] Xenophon likewise utilizes this hard–soft distinction, arguing that a good land makes a weak people.[28] It can be argued that the intact utopian traditions from Hellenistic philosophy tend to represent an idealization of the "hard" type of paradise of disciplined honest citizens.[29] The fragmentary traditions, however, as well as those

25 For the crossing, see Sall. *Hist* 1 frag. 94 McG = 93R = 105M. This lack of a navy was temporary: Sertorius soon seized several harbours and came to a new deal with the Cilicians (perhaps through Mithridates) so that by 75 BCE Sertorius had the upper hand at sea again.

26 For treating with Mithridates, see Appian, *Mithridatic Wars* 68; cf. Sall. *Hist.* 2 frag. 76 McG = 80R = 93M. For more in-depth discussion of how this Blessed-Isles episode fits into the history of Sertorius, see Garcia Moreno, "Plutarch's Sertorius," 143–146; McAlhany, "Sertorius," esp. 61–62; Spann, "Isles of the Blest."

27 For the hard–soft distinction in Lovejoy and Boas, see Arthur O. Lovejoy and George Boas, *Primitivism and Related Ideas in Antiquity* (New York: Octagon Books, 1973), 10–11. For their discussion of Stoic ideals of paradise, see 260–286; see also Dawson, *Cities of the Gods*, 164–166.

28 Xen. *An.* 3.2.25; cf. Rosie Harman, "Colonisation, Nostos, and the Foreign Environment in Xenophon's Anabasis," in *The Routledge Handbook of Identity and the Environment in the Classical and Medieval Worlds*, ed. Rebecca Futo Kennedy and Molly Jones-Lewis (New York: Routledge, 2016), 134–135; Harman also connects the soft land and soft people more explicitly at page 138. This association explains (at least for Xenophon) why the Greeks are better soldiers. Xenophon considers founding a city himself near Sinope at 5.6.15ff., but his thoughts are on the strength of his force relative to the surroundings, not the wealth of the land, unlike his earlier observations in Cilicia.

29 And has been argued: see Dawson, *Cities of the Gods*, 160–222, esp. 165–166 on Stoic utopias; Page DuBois, "The History of the Impossible: Ancient Utopias," *Classical Philology* 101, no. 1 (2006): 10; Ferguson, *Utopias*, 140.

from the geographical writers, represent more hints of the "soft" paradise, focused upon the beneficence of the land.

Whether the real, historical Sertorius sought to *find* a utopian paradise by sailing away to the Blessed Isles, where life would be easy, or sought to *found* a utopian state untroubled by constant warfare, Plutarch presents a Sertorius more interested in the latter. While insufficient material from Sallust remains to be certain about the aims of Sertorius, Sallust was likewise of the opinion that the nature of first-century BCE politics created bad men from good.[30] Plutarch's Sertorius is more invested in state-creation, as we see from Plutarch's portrayal of Sertorius as a civilizing influence upon his allies. While Plutarch was fairly anti-Stoic in specific tenets, he seems to be in agreement with them at a more general level.[31] Certainly, Plutarch's overall depiction of Sertorius is not that of a luxury-seeker but of a man both disciplined and able to instil discipline.[32] Plutarch's presentation of the Spartans is also worth noting here, for he presents the Spartans' drastic reconfiguring of their society as an attempt to create a utopia-like state.[33]

It is fairly unusual to find this merger of trying to find a utopia with trying to found a utopia within the same figure. Plutarch and Sallust sought to represent Sertorius in engaging with thinking about the ideal state. Moreover, this account suggests either that Sallust and Plutarch are embellishing the account of Sertorius with latter-day concerns about ideal states or that Sertorius may have read fairly widely in philosophy (or both).[34] To understand another aspect of the thoughts of Sertorius, his actions are potentially rooted less in contemporary and Hellenistic thoughts of rectifying the state, from which we get the sense of his desire to *found* utopia, but more akin to the earlier narratives of colonial

30 This opinion can be found throughout Sallust, but especially in the opening passages of the *Bellum Catalinae*, for example, Sall. *Cat.* 3, 5, 10–11.

31 On the relation of Plutarch and Stoicism, see Dawson, *Cities of the Gods*, 165–166; Jan Opsomer, "Plutarch and the Stoics," in *A Companion to Plutarch*, ed. Mark Beck (Malden, MA: Blackwell, 2014), 88–103. For Plutarch's direct statements on Stoicism and Epicureanism, see Plut. *Mor.* 1033–1106, passim.

32 Plut. *Sertorius* 10.2–3, 13.1–2. Indeed, the depiction of Sertorius is not unlike the "noble bandit" motif we see with figures such as Viriathus and Spartacus. McAlhany ("Sertorius," 69–70) notes (correctly, in this author's view) that Plutarch's depiction of the Blessed Isles is atypical diction for Plutarch and likely stems from Sallust.

33 Plut. *Lyc.* passim, but 8–11 in particular. For how idealization of the Spartans played out in other philosophical utopias, see also Dawson, *Cities of the Gods*, 198–204.

34 Garcia Moreno ("Plutarch's Sertorius," 148) observes a conflict between Plutarch and Sallust over this episode – that the seeking of utopia is against the nature of a good leader (according to Plutarch).

settlement found in Herodotus, Diodorus, or Archaic Greek poetry, from which we glean his desires to *find* utopia. Sallust and Plutarch may have even downplayed these ideas of seeking new lands in keeping with their philosophical ideas.[35] Alternatively, these are separate desires, with Sertorius changing goals along with the changing situation – for Sertorius apparently does not contemplate finding utopia in the Blessed Isles before what had appeared to be a penultimate defeat and apparently does not contemplate founding a new Rome in Spain until after the option to sail into the Atlantic is taken away.

Later, in the Roman world, we do see renewed interest in founding utopia. A long tradition of geographic writers relayed ideas of what territories were most ideal and why.[36] While Greek writers in the Roman world, most notably Diodorus Siculus and Strabo, express interest in finding utopias in distant realms, Latin authors appear to double down on Plato and the Stoics and consider founding utopia here and now. There is no linguistic monolith, however. Beyond recording some of the accounts of Euhemerus, Diodorus also appears to follow some of his Sicilian forebear's Euhemerist philosophy.[37] Strabo, in turn, though invested in an accurate geographical description of the Mediterranean, was also prone to a degree of environmental determinism in which the equation of poor agricultural resources with banditry led to circular reasoning – Strabo reinforced this correspondence by making fertile lands peaceful and rugged lands prone to banditry, and he even intensified the landscape in areas of known banditry.[38] Both Strabo and Diodorus were inclined to take earlier geographical utopias as genuine accounts describing real geography, while Plutarch appears more inclined to see these accounts as literary thought experiments in the vein of Plato.[39] Perhaps of particular

35 For the observation that the Sertorian view of utopia conflicts with the Greek philosophical tradition, see also McAlhany, "Sertorius," 70.

36 For some discussion, including modern discussions of the value of geography, see William Koelsch, *Geography and the Classical World: Unearthing Historical Geography's Forgotten Past* (London: I. B. Tauris, 2014).

37 See Iris Sulimani, "Imaginary Islands in the Hellenistic Era," in *Myths on the Map: The Storied Landscapes of Ancient Greece*, ed. Greta Hawes (Oxford: Oxford University Press, 2017), 223–224. Diodorus and Euhemerus seem to have shared a penchant for rationalizing myth or extracting "real" knowledge from the world of myth; see also Sulimani, "Imaginary Islands," 237n38.

38 See Strabo's description of Liguria (4.6), the Balearics (3.5), and Cilicia (14.5), respectively.

39 The credulity of Diodorus, in particular, accounts for the survival of the fragments of Iambulus, Euhemerus, and Dionysius Scytobrachion, *inter alia*. Diodorus presents mythic history on the level of real geography; even when the events are incredible, the

interest here is the example of Plotinus, who, amidst the chaos of the third century, sought permission from the emperor of the day to sail forth and found a utopian philosophers' city in accordance with the precepts of Plato. While it remains unclear which precepts of Plato he intended to follow, he did have a location in mind – a largely abandoned city in southern Italy, perhaps reminiscent of the Pythagorean settlements in Magna Graecia in the sixth century BCE, such as at Croton, or the Panhellenic philosopher's colony at Thurii in the mid-fifth century.[40]

The narrative shows that the proliferation of such works at least occasionally led to real-world decisions by leaders. Despite the influence of Sallust, Plutarch, and Stoic thought, all likely favouring the sense of founding a new idealized state, complete with newer and better customs, the Sertorian narrative may have more in common with the exotic descriptions in the geographical tradition seen in Diodorus and Strabo or the historical tradition found in Herodotus and Thucydides, all presenting descriptions and opportunities to find an ideal land in which to place an ideal city.

Herodotus, Thucydides, and the Western Greeks

Our historians of Classical Greece present us with an unusual set of accounts of the so-called "colonization" of the western Mediterranean, which of course occurred centuries earlier.[41] The term "colonization" is a faulty one by modern definitions as these colonies rarely retained

locations are credible, as has been noted by Iris Sulimani, *Diodorus' Mythistory and the Pagan Mission: Historiography and Culture-Heroes in the First Pentad of the* Bibliotheke (Leiden and Boston: Brill, 2011), 165. While Plutarch's own utopia-tale in *De facie* 26 clearly appears to be such a literary usage, one highly speculative article posits that the directions given could indeed get sailors to the coast of Canada: Ioannis Liritzis et al., "Does Astronomical and Geographical Information of Plutarch's *De facie* Describe a Trip beyond the North Atlantic Ocean?" *Journal of Coastal Research* 34, no. 3 (May 2018), 651–674.

40 For Pythagorean and Neoplatonic ideas of the ideal city, see Dawson, *Cities of the Gods*, 15–16. Hippodamus was said to have designed the city of Thurii and Herodotus to have settled there, but neither man is mentioned in our longest account of the founding and constitution of Thurii (Diod. Sic. 12.9–19).

41 My presentation of Archaic colonization here is heavily indebted to two volumes: Carol Dougherty, *The Poetics of Colonization: From City to Text in Ancient Greece* (Oxford: Oxford University Press, 1993) and Irad Malkin, *The Returns of Odysseus: Colonization and Ethnicity* (Berkeley, CA: University of California Press, 1998). Malkin's later article, "Networks and the Emergence of Greek Identity," *Mediterranean Historical Review* 18, no. 2 (2003), 56–74, has also influenced my thoughts here.

close ties to the mother city.[42] Nevertheless, the rhetoric of colonization in the early modern period is, to some degree, rooted in the philosophy of ancient colonization.[43] Thucydides presented most Greeks, excepting the Arcadians and Athenians, as displeased with the poverty of their land and entirely willing to depart for more fertile lands.[44] Notably, both the Arcadians and Athenians took pride in their claims of autochthony.[45] Thucydides also strove to rationalize his observations that the cities away from the coast were substantially older than those on the coast. Accordingly, Thucydides tells us that in the Archaic period, settlements near the coast were vulnerable to piracy.[46] This development, if true, meant that the first waves of Greek and Phoenician colonization in the Archaic period were able to settle harbour sites in the western Mediterranean with little opposition.[47] Whereas the earliest Greek settlements in mainland Greece were far from the sea for safety (according to Thucydides), these new settlements posed the sea as a barrier and a defence, particularly with fortified islets. For Herodotus, the age of Greek colonialism was already ending. The waves of Greek (and Phoenician) colonists settling along the

---

42 For more on why "colonization" is a poor term for ancient settlement in the western Mediterranean, see Franco de Angelis, "Ancient Greek Colonization in the 21st Century: Some Suggested Directions," *Bollettino di Archeologia Online* 1 (2010), 18–30.

43 This issue is beyond the scope of the present project, though a recent presentation on this topic may be worth mentioning: Aaron L. Beek, "Founding an Isolated Utopia: Utopian and Colonial Ideas in Classical and Postclassical Thought" (online presentation, 27th International Conference of Europeanists, 21–25 June 2021).

44 For this aspect of colonization as flight, see also Philip Kaplan, "Location and Dislocation in Early Greek Geography and Ethnography," in *The Routledge Handbook of Identity and the Environment in the Classical and Medieval Worlds*, ed. Rebecca Futo Kennedy and Molly Jones-Lewis (New York: Routledge, 2016), 299–314.

45 For some discussion of these myths of autochthony, see Kaplan, "Location and Dislocation," 303–304.

46 Thuc. 1.2; cf. Diod. Sic. 5.80, Sall. *Hist.* 1 frag. 4 McG = 9R = 9M.

47 The narrative of "empty land" was often used even when native peoples were present; however, as Malkin (*Returns of Odysseus*, 69–70) and Christy Constantakopoulou (*The Dance of the Islands* (Oxford: Oxford University Press, 2007), 8) have pointed out, colonial settlement on offshore islands often represented settlement on genuinely unsettled territory. For examinations of Greek settlements in the west, I chiefly consulted Gocha R. Tsetskhladze, *Greek Colonisation: An Account of Greek Colonies and Other Settlements Overseas*, 2 volumes (Leiden: Brill, 2006–2008); but see also Kathryn Lomas, *Rome and the Western Greeks 350 BC–AD 200* (London: Routledge, 1993); Jean-Paul Morel, "L'expansion phocéenne en Occident: dix années de recherches (1966–1975)," *Bulletin de correspondance hellénique* 99, no. 2 (1975): 853–896; Christel Müller and Claire Hasenohr, *Les Italiens dans le Monde Grec (BCH 41)* (Paris: Ecole française d'athènes, 2002). For future directions, see also Franco de Angelis, "Ancient Greek Colonization," 18–30.

sparsely settled coastlines and islands in the eighth century had taken the choicest harbours and claimed their territory. The later expeditions of the late sixth and early fifth centuries did not simply find natural harbours unoccupied by the locals but rather bargained with those who had come before, negotiated alliances, and invaded. In Herodotus, the old stories of Dorian invasion made the Greeks naturally a mobile people inclined to sail away to settle new lands.

For both Herodotus and Thucydides, there was a clear desire among the Archaic Greeks to settle unpopulated lands... but if such could not be found, they would settle for depopulated lands. Two of the more famous Herodotean episodes should illustrate this issue: Battus (4.150–160) and Dorieus (5.42–48). Battus of Thera, prompted by the oracle of Delphi, went forth to set up a colony and sought unsettled land, first an island off the coast of Libya (which the oracle at Delphi said did not count), then on the Libyan coast, and then, on the advice of the native Libyans, at Cyrene in the mid-seventh century. According to Herodotus, this colony at Cyrene became prosperous and remained peaceful for two generations before falling into war with the Libyans and the Egyptians. Overall, this may fall under the category of a utopia one could find. Noteworthy here is the language describing Cyrene as idyllic.

Dorieus the Spartan, on the other hand, has a tale not so pleasant. A century and a half or so after the foundation of Cyrene, this Dorieus attempted to found a colony at Cinyps in Tripolitania "in the fairest land of Libya" but was driven out by the locals. Regrouping in the Peloponnese, he then set forth again, aiming to seize Phoenician territory in Sicily. After failing in that endeavour as well, Dorieus then seized power first in Heraclea Minoa and then in Selinus. The rhetoric of the find/found distinction is absent, but the colonial endeavours of Dorieus include five invasions of inhabited territory.[48] Malkin described Dorieus as justifying his actions through charter myth – the settlement was in some sense an inheritance from Hercules.[49] Herodotus clearly presents the struggles of

---

48 Herodotus also tells a similar story of the Samians, who set forth to found a colony in northern Sicily but were persuaded to attack and seize Zancle instead (Hdt. 6.22–23).

49 See Malkin, *Returns of Odysseus*, 20–21. Kaplan ("Location and Dislocation," 310) argues that we cannot normally see any sense of a "promised land" in Greek colonization, but he notes that the Return of the Heraclidae may serve as an exception. Dorieus, as a descendant of those Heraclidae, might even have used this mythological basis instead of seeking the blessing of Delphi. Dionysius of Halicarnassus preserves a story that it was the influence of Heracles that caused mingling of the men of the coasts and the barbarians inland (Dion. Hal. *Ant. Rom.* 1.41.1).

Dorieus as rooted in the folly of not consulting the oracles, which had a long association with colonial endeavours.[50] These attempts may serve as an example of trying to found a utopia. Dorieus was not drawn by the idea of perfect lands, nor even by taking better lands from others, but convinced that he deserved to be the ruler of a city and that the quality of its location was not the most important consideration, only the quality of his followers.

While it would be fairly pointless to arbitrarily categorize the Greeks' settlements in the western Mediterranean as each falling into these two types, the desire to find utopia versus the desire to found utopia are still useful concepts for understanding some of the motivations of the *oikists* and their followers. Given the Thucydidean presentation of the Greeks as mobile and seeking better lands, and the depiction of soldiers as willing to settle for land allotments in both Roman and Hellenistic history, the desire for new lands seems likely to have been a significant motivator for many of the colonists, even if the *oikist* had other ideas for the new state. Moreover, this Archaic pair of concepts of the perfect settlement reappears first in the literature of Classical Athens (seriously in Plato and mockingly in comedy) and then again in Hellenistic philosophy. In particular, we see the idealization of islands and otherwise-isolated lands in siting the perfect settlement, and while the sea features prominently in these settlements, the important factor is not the sea's role in facilitating trade and prosperity, as one might expect, but rather the sea's ability to afford security, to enforce separation from others, and to serve as a barrier.

The Island Utopia

Two factors in ancient utopian thinking which seem to be commonplaces (even if not strictly necessary) are settlement on an island and establishing self-sufficiency. The ideal community is therefore construed as one with no connection to the outside world. Time and time again, the sea appears as a crucial divider in determining utopia. The Blessed Isles in Plutarch's *Life of Sertorius* and in other classical writers, Plato's Atlantis, Euhemerus' Panchaia, Iambulus' Islands of the Sun, More's Utopia, and Bacon's New Atlantis – all depict their utopias far away off on islands.[51] Indeed Diodorus

---

50 Hdt. 5.42.2; on this passage, cf. Dougherty, *Poetics of Colonization*, 19.
51 Marek Winiarczyk (*The Sacred History of Euhemerus of Messene* (Berlin: De Gruyter, 2013), 16) adds several others to the list. On the work of Euhemerus, see Winiarczyk,

Siculus preserves his utopian accounts perhaps not because they are utopias but because they were on islands.[52] The third-century BCE writer Dionysius Scytobrachion even depicts not one but two island utopias, one far to the west in the Atlantic, the other far to the south on a riverine isle in inland Libya, presumably far up the Nile, and thereby far to the east as well.[53] In Plutarch's *De facie* and an excerpt of Theopompus preserved in Aelian, the utopian land, though not an island, is nevertheless across a sea, but larger than the known *oikoumene*.[54]

We might also consider early modern European legends of earthly paradises unspoiled by connection to the world (for example, Cibola, Shangri-La) or attributions of perfection applied to remote lands such as Timbuktu or Tibet.[55] Apparently, utopia required isolation, if not necessarily literal islands. Nor is the idea of an island utopia limited to European utopias: Taoist philosophy also had legends of supernaturally

---

Sacred History, esp. 16–19; Franco de Angelis and Benjamin Garstad, "Euhemerus in Context," *Classical Antiquity* 25, no. 2 (2006), 211–242; for further bibliography on island utopias, cf. Marek Winiarczyk, *Die hellenistischen Utopien* (Berlin: De Gruyter, 2011), esp. 261–263. For Lucian, see Wolfgang Fauth, "Utopische Inseln," *Gymnasium Helveticum* 86 (1979), and esp. 39–40 for further bibliography on the island utopia motif; see also Evans, *Utopia Antiqua*, 14–15. For a discussion of the island utopia as it pertains to insularity and the Aegean, see Constantakopoulou, *Dance of the Islands*, 5–7, 163–173. Notably, Constantakopoulou points out that Athenian utopia was closely related with the perception of Attica as an island of sorts.

52 Emilio Gabba, "True History and False History in Classical Antiquity," *Journal of Roman Studies* 71 (1981): 56; cf. Sulimani, "Imaginary Islands," 221.

53 For Dionysius Scytobrachion, see *FGrH* 32 (frags. 7–8 for these two utopias) = Diod. Sic. 3.53, 368–369; cf. Gabba, "True and False History," 58; Jeffrey S. Rusten, *Dionysius Scytobrachion* (Wiesbaden: Springer, 1982); Winarcyck, *Sacred History*, 20, 37–38, 125–128. For the dating of Dionysius to the third century rather than the second century (*contra* Gabba and Jacoby) on the strength of Papyri Hibeh 2.186, see Rusten, *Dionysius Scytobrachion*, 27–29, in particular. Dionysius here puts the western utopia on an island in Lake Tritonis, famous for its association with the Argo, but he relocates the lake beyond the Strait of Gibraltar. Herodotus (for example, 4.179) and other classical writers put this lake in southern Tunisia (where it exists today in much reduced form as the Chott-al-Djerid and is used by filmmakers as a site of desolation instead, most notably as Tatooine in the *Star Wars* films). The Nysa associated with Dionysus is normally located in Arabia or India, not Libya, and Diodorus (3.3.62–69) indeed preserves a multitude of accounts of Nysa. Either Scytobrachion or Diodorus may be duplicating the account of a far-off Dionysiac utopia. For Dionysus being associated with a utopia across the sea, see also the farcical *True Story* of Lucian which places his rivers of wine across the Atlantic (1.7–9).

54 *FGrH* 115,75 = Ael. *VH* 3.18; Plut. *De facie* 26.

55 This ideal of the remote, idealized, unsettled land was used extensively in propaganda of the colonial era; cf. Thomas W. Africa, "Thomas More and the Spartan Mirage," *Historical Reflections* 6, no 2 (1979): 343–344.

happy islands of the blessed far off in the ocean.[56] Thomas More was familiar with the tales of Plato, Lucian, Plutarch, and (via Diodorus) those of Euhemerus and Iambulus, as well as the farcical ideal states of Aristophanes.[57] Thus it is hardly surprising to see many classical ideas emerge in his *Utopia*. And the simple idea of the island society having greater stability likely had some appeal to an Englishman as well. While undoubtedly useful in utopian fiction to explain lack of contemporary access, the utopian island sees its place in the real world as islands become sought-after sites for colonial endeavours.

Utopian ideas often come with a backdrop of chaos and warfare. Plato wrote his *Republic* after the defeat of Athens and wrote of Atlantis among the striving for hegemony and subsequent defeat of Sparta and Thebes. Euhemerus wrote during the wars of the Diadochi, Cicero's *De Re Publica* came out in the late days of the Roman Republic, and Augustine's *City of God* was penned in the latter days of the Western Roman Empire. Even More's *Utopia* (1516) was responding to the same chaotic world as Machiavelli's *Prince* (1513).[58] The interest in ideal states would appear to reflect a dissatisfaction in the contemporary government(s) for the authors. The implications of this for the present volume (begun in 2020) are not lost on this author. Many early tales of Archaic Greek settlement also bear a literary motif of crisis at home that prompts the *oikist* to depart.[59] In such cases, the departure is not a choice, only the destination.

This dissatisfaction with the politics of the day led ancient writers to posit that an ideal society would perhaps only suffer from dealing with the

---

56 For more on the Taoist text of Lieh-tzu, see Angus C. Graham, trans., *The Book of Lieh-tzu: A Classic of the Tao* (New York: Columbia University Press, 1990). My thanks to my colleagues at NWU for pointing me in this direction. For comparisons of utopian imagery, including Eastern and Western ideas of utopia, see Diskin Clay and Andrea Purvis, *Four Island Utopias: Being Plato's Atlantis; Euhermos of Messene's Panchaia; Iamboulos' Island of the Sun; Sir Francis Bacon's New Atlantis, With a Supplement on Utopian Prototypes, Developments, and Variations* (Newburyport, MA: Focus, 1999).

57 See Africa, "Spartan Mirage," esp. 345–346 for the specific classical influences on More.

58 That these thinkers were responding to the same contemporary moments is clear; whether More may have read Machiavelli is more controversial; for further discussion (concluding there is no evidence that More had read Machiavelli), see John F. Tinkler, "Praise and Advice: Rhetorical Approaches in More's *Utopia* and Machiavelli's *The Prince*," *The Sixteenth Century Journal* 19, no. 2 (1988): 187–207.

59 For a description of the poetic motif, see Dougherty, *Poetics of Colonization*, 15–18. The presence of these crises in the literary representation of Greek settlements should not be taken as proof of historic crises. Nevertheless, the association of crisis with both utopian thought and with narratives of settlements should be seen as closely related.

outside world, and so these island communities tend to interact little with outsiders. The sea here thus serves as a barrier rather than a connector; a defence against dangers both physical and moral. The sea remains vilified even in utopian premises. We are presented with a χαλεπὴ...θάλασσα, a "dangerous sea," in Aratus, while Hyginus informs us that the golden age involved little seafaring: *neque navigio quemquam usum esse*.[60] Trade is likewise vilified. The Spartans famously eschewed trade and coinage, while the Romans cast port cities as corrupt.[61] Even the historians' story that Pompey settled pirates "far from the sea" may have its root in the vilification of the sea as a corrupting force.[62]

While it is difficult in the extreme to draw out what Sertorius was thinking about the Isles of the Blessed in the tiny references which survive, it is clear that the pattern fits. Sallust presents trade and seafaring as fairly directly corrupting, while Livy attributes the corruption rather to the seeking of *luxuria*.[63] Sallust was firmly blaming the lust for power and luxury as the root of Rome's ills (and even includes himself among the guilty), critiques the Carthaginians' reliance on trade, and extols the virtues of these islands that produce enough food to live on without need for cultivation. Plutarch notes also the Spartan disdain of trade.[64] Cynic philosophy painted existing institutions as a drag on society and proposed a less formally organized society.[65] In this sense, the utopia is framed in negative terms: it is the absence of all these ills which make utopia.

Similarly, many politicians and philosophers have praised rivers as boundaries, conceiving of a body of water as a barrier, serving as a wall rather than a road. This does not always reflect actual practice in the ancient world well. Indeed, the Roman defences of the German border on the Rhine were famous, yet archaeologically speaking, we find dozens of

---

60   Aratus, *Phaenomena* 110; Hyg. *Poeticon Astronomicon* 2.25.

61   Dion. Hal. *Ant. Rom.* 2.28.1–2; Plut. *Lyc.* 9. The most famous, however, is the speech of Censorinus (Appian, *Pun.* 86–90). Famously, the 146 BCE destruction of Corinth and Carthage were partially attributed to the weakness gained from seaborne trade.

62   Pompey's pirate settlements at Soli in Cilicia and Dyme in the Peloponnese, *inter alia*, were in fact on the sea or not far away on navigable rivers; see Plut. *Pomp.* 28.3–4.

63   For Livy's thoughts, see 39.6–7, esp. 39.6.6: *luxuriae enim peregrinae origo ab exercitu Asiatico invecta in urbem est*; "For the origin of foreign luxury was brought into the city by the army stationed in Asia." For Sallust's thoughts, see Sall. *Cat.* 10; *Iug.* 2; *Hist.* 1 frag. 11–14 McG = 11–14R = 15,12,16,13M; cf. Florus 1.47; Vell. Pat. 2.1.1.

64   Plut. *Lyc.* 9.

65   For Cynic philosophy and utopia, see Dawson, *Cities of the Gods*, 111–159, and particularly 143–145 for returning to a more "primitive" form of society.

Roman forts upon the east bank of the Rhine, with the Rhine serving as a vital supply line as much as the first line of defence.

Since the islands were self-contained, untainted by the outside, they also had to be self-sufficient. Our authors, however, feel obliged to explain how such self-sufficiency was possible. Geographers also repeatedly asserted the fertility of known Mediterranean islands such as Corsica, Sardinia, Sicily, Zacynthos, and Mallorca.[66] In Diodorus, the self-sufficiency of the Children of the Sun is partially climatic, with different crops ripening at different times.[67] Diogenes Laertius asserts that self-sufficiency so as to avoid needless toil and profit-seeking was a core tenet of Epicureanism.[68] Without the need to procure necessities through struggle, one could live contentedly. Likewise, the anarchic Cynics also praised *autarkeia* (self-sufficiency), though through a rather lower standard of living.[69]

This allows us to return to the dialectic of *finding* a utopia versus *founding* a utopia. If self-sufficiency is desirable or even necessary, then one cannot readily impose a utopian society reliant upon the export of a valuable commodity such as olive oil or woollen cloth.[70] These sorts of export economies are not framed as importing for the sake of necessities but rather for luxuries. The seeking of luxury is thus a vice that prevents the existence of a more desirable society. Florus even goes so far as to claim the general origin of civil war is too much prosperity (*nimiae felicitates*).[71]

This establishment of self-sufficiency, besides being an intrusion of the Phaeacian-style utopia into the Stoic political utopia, may well represent the introduction of some of the ideas of Epicureanism as well as the long-standing Roman suspicion of trade.

66 For Corsica, see Diod. Sic. 5.14; for Sardinia, see Diod. Sic. 14.29.6; Luc. 3.74–76; Strabo 5.2.7; for Sicily, see Bacchyl. *Epinician* 3.1; Diod. Sic. 5.2.1; cf. *Pind. Ol.* 2.9–10; for Zacynthos, see Plin. *HN* 4.54; for Mallorca, see Strabo 3.5.1. See also Constantakopoulou, *Dance of the Islands*, 5–6. It should be noted that Plato's Atlantis was similarly fertile (Pl. *Critias* 117a).
67 This aspect also appears outside his recounting of Iambulus, as he asserts that the multiple crops planted by the Indians never fail at the same time.
68 Diog. Laert. 10.130–131; cf. Porph. *Abst.* 1.48.
69 It may be strange to juxtapose a philosophy of asceticism and a philosophy of comfort in this way, but both philosophies taught that one should be content with one's circumstances.
70 These being the mainstays of Plato's Athens and More's England, respectively. More (*Utopia*, para. 23) explicitly critiques the way the value of wool as an export product had consequences that were to the detriment of English peasants.
71 Florus 1.47.

Conclusions

In a sense, the single biggest obstacle to establishing the idyllic community was the existence of the current dysfunctional community, and the "find/found" dichotomy illustrates how different ancient participants might differ in their goals. The idea of the "blank slate" as ideal continued into the Roman period, particularly in mythological discussions of the past, including new renditions of the "golden age."[72] The desire to start fresh and to have a self-sufficient idyllic colony also appears repeatedly in the settlement of Roman soldiers from the first to the third century. This desire, however, is an ideal held by the founders and by the grantees; by the consuls or the emperors – it does not appear to be a desire held by the veterans themselves. A simple pastoral life is not what many of these retired soldiers wanted. Rather than escaping the rat race and the profit-seeking world, these veterans instead sought higher station within it.

And just like Sertorius' Cilicians seeking plunder and booty, or Pompey's resettled pirates taking to piracy again after his death, we see soldiers selling their allotments, re-enlisting, resorting to brigandage, and complaining about the site of settlements. Accordingly, the late Republic and the Empire switch to settling veterans in pre-existing towns rather than totally new foundations, while the poets praise idyllic meadows and wax on about, and bemoan the lack of, a blank slate to start new cities. Veterans flock to settle near provincial capitals, and complain about being settled in borderlands.[73] Nevertheless, there appears to be something of a disconnect between the colonial thought of the founders and of the colonists (who preferred to find utopia). In this sense, the sailing away becomes a necessary component of founding a utopian state (at least in literature). This is perhaps surprising given the widespread fear of the sea with its dangers of storms, shipwrecks, and pirates. Perhaps it was philosophically (or poetically) more compelling for settlers to bravely face the unknown than for them to bravely face the *known*.

In the end, the tension between finding utopia and founding utopia is intrinsically tied up with the sea as well as with disparate thoughts on philosophical and geographical matters. To different ancient thinkers, the sea posed opportunity or threat. The danger of the sea served to

---

72 For an extensive discussion of how the rendition of the Myth of the Ages in Ovid, Vergil, and Statius reflects Roman thought, see Evans, *Utopia Antiqua*, 36–71.

73 This, admittedly, may have less to do with any form of utopian thought and more to do with the obvious implicit dangers in living in a settlement on the border.

deter some from looking for utopia but encouraged others to see it as a guard against threats to utopia. While the larger body of real settlers and colonists of history appear to have frequently sought to find a utopian place, they rarely if ever bought into the ideas of founding a utopian state promoted by philosophers. The same cannot be said for their leaders, however, who utilized both concepts as needed.

CHAPTER FIVE

Ruling the Catastrophic Sea: Roman Law and the Gains of a Utopic Mediterranean

Emilia Mataix Ferrándiz

Introduction

The dichotomy between the secure land and the savage or catastrophic sea seems to be one of the oldest metaphors for life, as exemplified in Blumenberg's famous essay on shipwrecks.[1] Blumenberg based his study on the fact that, at some level, we have all witnessed the wrecks of others, while standing in safety and knowing that there is nothing we can do to help, remaining fixed – whether comfortably or uncomfortably – in our ambiguous role as spectators. However, the necessities of exchange and trade as well as the need to harvest the sea have forced humans to live and experience coastal dwellings and the sea itself; these interactions have, therefore, associated the sea, the foreshore, and the coastal margin with particular significances.

In the Roman case, one could argue that their terrestrial society was established first and that, subsequently, the sea–land relationship followed. This is really a question concerning the identity and cultural memory of people in relationship to their physical context and their life activities. On the one hand, in the Roman life cycle, time was organized in relation to labour and production, and space in relation to the rural

I would like to thank Dr Hamish Williams and Dr Ross Clare for inviting me to contribute to this volume. I would like especially to thank Dr Williams and the two anonymous reviewers, whose comments and suggestions have improved this piece immeasurably. Any ideas expressed here are the author's own. This publication was made possible through a fellowship awarded by the Käte Hamburger Kolleg "Legal Unity and Pluralism" at the University of Münster, funded by the Federal Ministry of Education and Research (BMBF).

1 Hans Blumenberg, *Shipwreck with Spectator: Paradigm of a Metaphor for Existence* (Boston: MIT Press, 1979).

and urban landscape.[2] After all, Rome was founded in a world of farmers that turned into a global empire.[3] On the other hand, despite the general view of the Roman aversion or lack of interest in the sea,[4] the truth is that Rome evolved from its agricultural beginnings to become a global power, and that would not have been possible without their overcoming the initial reluctance towards seafaring and the sea. For example, a passage of Cicero's, depicting the sea as "the most violent of nature's offspring," refers to the art of seafaring as being able to tame its wilderness and obtain supplies.[5] The latter source highlights three key points: (1) that the sea was considered a catastrophic realm; (2) but that in order to overcome its catastrophic nature, it was also a source of utopian endeavours in creating profit, wealth, political power, and so on; and (3) that people, therefore, discovered different ways to cope with this wilderness and to obtain gains.

Accordingly, there was a clear tension between the untamed nature of the sea and the needs that compelled the Romans to brave its waves. Because of these two aspects, the Romans elaborated legal and political conceptualizations of the maritime spaces so as to cope on an institutional level with the issues associated with sea ventures. Thus the catastrophic sea, as a violent realm in which the civil laws of the Romans were ineffective, could be ultimately managed by other legal tools and the categorizations employed by them. In addition, these legal categorizations could transform the violent sea into a space of utopian potential through commercial gains and ultimately political expansion. Therefore, in this chapter, the Roman perceptions of the sea as both catastrophic

2   Andrea Carandini, "Urban Landscapes and Ethnic Identity of Early Rome," in *Urban Landscapes and Ethnic Identity of Early Rome*, ed. Gabriele Cifani and Simon Stoddart (Oxford: Oxford University Press, 2012), 5. That perception of the land can be appreciated in the careful work of the *agrimensores*; see Brian Campbell, ed. and trans., *The Writings of the Roman Land Surveyors: Introduction, Text, Translation and Commentary* (London: Society for the Promotion of Roman Studies, 2000).

3   This is one of the main points of Astrid Van Oyen's *The Socio-Economics of Roman Storage: Agriculture, Trade, and Family* (Cambridge: Cambridge University Press, 2020), esp. 14–16. However, even if the Romans' economy was primarily devoted to farming, that does not mean that they did not have maritime activity in the Archaic period; see Gabriele Cifani, "Aspects of the Origins of Roman Maritime Trade," in *Roman Law and Maritime Commerce*, ed. Emilia Mataix Ferrándiz and Peter Candy (Edinburgh: Edinburgh University Press, 2021), 11–22.

4   This image is partly based on Polybius' narration of the Roman–Carthaginian treaties (Polyb. 1.20, 1.21.1–2).

5   Cic. *Nat. D.* 152. All translations of ancient sources are my own, unless otherwise specified.

and utopian will be understood through the ways that terrestrial and maritime affairs are identified and sorted through legal conceptualizations, whether these were imposed by the central authority or by the peoples living in an area.

The Sea in the Roman Legal Imagination

The opportunities and dangers of seafaring were a prominent theme in ancient Roman life. The sea loomed large in the ancient society's imagination, in as much as it shaped the seasonal rhythms and habits of areas ostensibly tucked away from its textured coasts.[6] The sea and its personifications were present in everyday metaphors and writings of different kinds, and even if many authors may have not lived by the sea, or even the coast, they possessed a set of ideas about the sea and its nature. For many literary authors, plying over the sea was often seen as violating a sacred domain banned to mortals, and drowning meant that one's spirit remained in a place from which there was no return.[7]

The sea appears as a problematic element in legal articulations of property since no one could either possess it or exclude others from it. Indeed, if one looks at the writings of Roman land surveyors (*agrimensores*), their accounts definitely refer to the sea as a boundary in their area calculations, and they therefore excluded it from their maps.[8] Polybius gives a list of the categories that in Republican Rome were considered property of the Roman people; he includes rivers, lakes (or harbours), lagoons, public lands, and mines but does not mention the seashore or the sea.[9] Some texts from jurists ascribed to the imperial period do describe the legal characterizations of the land facing the sea.

6 For the Greek case, see Marie-Claire Beaulieu, *The Sea in the Greek Imagination* (Philadelphia: University of Pennsylvania Press, 2015).

7 Boris Dunsch, "Describe nunc Tempestatem. Sea Storm and Shipwreck Type Scenes in Ancient Literature," in *Shipwreck in Art and Literature: Images and Interpretations from Antiquity to the Present Day*, ed. Carl Thomson (London: Routledge, 2013), 42–59; Boris Dunsch, "Why Do We Violate Strange Seas and Sacred Waters?" in *The Sea as Bridge and Boundary in Greek and Roman Poetry*, ed. Marta Grzechnik and Heta Hurskainen (Cologne: Böhlau Verlag, 2015), 17–42; Henry Huxley, "Storm and Shipwreck in Roman Literature," *Greece & Rome* 21, no. 63 (1952): 117–124.

8 Campbell, *The Writings*, 177, 197, 390; Oswald A. Dilke, *The Roman Land Surveyors: An Introduction to the Agrimensores* (New York: Barnes and Noble, 1971), 115; Jean-Yves Guillaumin, *Sur quelques notices des arpenteurs romains* (Besançon: Institut des Sciences et Techniques de l'Antiquité, 2007), 109–110, 138, 143, 151.

9 Polyb. 4.17.2.

Marcianus, a jurist of the third century AD, summarizes the general Roman juristic views on the sea: it was a *res communis* or *nullius*, a thing that by nature was common to all (citizens and non-citizens), while the Roman land was bounded by the civil law which was only applicable to Roman citizens.[10] A similar approach can be read in an earlier fragment from Pomponius (first century AD), in which the author indicates that a building constructed in the sea can be private, but that the power of the sea running over that building can take property away from the owner and make it part of the public realm.[11] Another jurist from the imperial period, Celsus (second century AD), shared a similar definition of the sea and indicated that shores were the property of the Roman people.[12] The latter are quite strong arguments for the agency of the sea in affecting human lives and private property rights.

That these legal sources date to the Empire and not the Republic does not change the fact that the Roman legal mind in earlier periods would have generally conceived of the sea as an unruly space, as we will appreciate in the Republican legal sources from the following sections. The developments in legal culture and the less likely survival of texts belonging to Republican jurists both play a part in ensuring that the sources we possess describing the interactions between sea and land belong to later periods.[13] In sum, these legal texts describing sea–land interactions are not so much a map of the physical archaeology of their landscapes but, rather, social conceptions from which their image of the sea has been constructed.[14]

---

10 Justinian, *Digest* (*D.*) 1.8.2.1. (Marcian, Book Three, *Institutiones*); *D.* 1.8.4. pr.1. (Marc. 3 *Inst*). And indeed, non-Roman citizens needed to benefit from different legal tools to claim ownership of Roman lands; see Georgy Kantor, "Property in Land in the Roman Provinces," in *Legalism: Property and Ownership*, ed. Georgy Kantor, Thomas B. Lambert, and Hannah Skoda (Oxford: Oxford University Press, 2017), 55–74.

11 *D.* 1.8.10 (Pomponius 6 *ex Plaut.*): *Aristo ait, sicut id, quod in mare aedificatum sit, fieret privatum, ita quod mari occupatum sit, fieri publicum*; "Aristo says that only as a building erected in the sea becomes private property, so too one which has been overrun by the sea becomes public"; as in Charles H. Monro, trans., *The Digest of Justinian* (Cambridge: Cambridge University Press, 1904). All subsequent translations from the *Digest* are taken from Monro.

12 *D.* 43.8.3 (Celsus, 39 *Dig.*); also, in Cic. *Top.* 32.

13 Ulrike Babusiaux, "Legal Writing and Legal Reasoning," in *The Oxford Handbook of Roman Society and Law*, ed. Clifford Ando, Paul Du Plessis, and Kaius Tuori (Oxford: Oxford University Press, 2016), 176–185.

14 David Berg Tuddenham, "Maritime Cultural Landscapes, Maritimity and Quasi Objects," *Journal of Maritime Archaeology* 5, no. 1 (2010): 10.

There are two points to note from the texts of Marcianus, Pomponius, and Celsus. First, the sea is not subject to an individual or to any concrete population's dominion and, consequently, not subject to Roman governance. Second, the land was governed by *ius civile*, the law of the Romans,[15] while the sea was the realm of *ius gentium*, the law of the peoples (Romans and non-Romans).[16] As in most ancient empires, the basic legal tenet was that law applied to people based on a personality principle (in other words, the community to which one belongs) not to an area principle, as is common in modern states (for example, laws applied to those living in Judea or in Egypt).[17] In sum, even if a Roman citizen resided in Egypt, his applicable law would be the law of the Romans, not that of Egypt. This last point, in connection to the sea as a limit for civil law, essentially means that at least in theory, the Romans could not claim their exclusive rule over the sea since this was a space governed by general laws which applied equally to citizens and non-citizens.

In that sense, on the basis of what has already been discussed in this chapter, the Roman legal imagination, at least from the focus of Roman western law, was characterized by a divide between a secure, firm land, which could be governed by the law of the Romans, and the sea, which was a savage entity that could be at best domesticated by the law of the peoples (for example, through treaties between two different countries). In these circumstances, the law defined the limit of some space and imposed rules on them. For the range of spaces included in such a fashion, norms did apply within their limits, leaving the external world largely or entirely beyond their reach.[18]

In that (legally) imagined scenario, shipwrecks appear as events which took place between sea (when the wreck happened; governed by the law of the peoples) and land (if the salvaged goods arrived on shore; governed by civil law), and they, accordingly, create some issues in terms of the spatial, land–sea divide as conceptualized in the Roman legal mind. In Roman legal writings, the sea had an agency over the subjects suffering a shipwreck, since this event could give and take ownership of goods lost

15 *D.* 1.1.6pr. (Ulpian, *Institutionum* 1).

16 Kaius Tuori, "The Savage Sea and the Civilizing Law: The Roman Law Tradition and the Rule of the Sea," in *Thalassokratographie: Rezeption und Transformation antiker Seeherrschaft*, ed. Hans Kopp and Christian Wendt (Berlin: De Gruyter, 2018), 210–211.

17 Clifford Ando, *Law, Language, and Empire in the Roman Tradition* (Philadelphia: University of Pennsylvania Press, 2011), 2–4.

18 Daniel J. Gargola, *The Shape of the Roman Order: The Republic and its Spaces* (Chapel Hill, NC: University of North Carolina Press, 2017), 189.

at sea[19] or could free a shipper from liability in the case of wreckage.[20] In their texts, Roman jurists reflect on different kinds of sea-storm scenes, to which they apply legal tools in order to organize and provide solutions to the catastrophes suffered by people in what was considered a space free from the rule of Roman civil law.[21] In that respect, shipwrecks appear as events that bridge the gap between land and sea because of the different legal remedies provided to deal with these catastrophes, which in turn enlarged the scope of land-based legal rulings. Therefore, the legal regimes targeting violence in connection with these events demarcated territorial and extraterritorial limits for the application of Roman law to a catastrophic environment, as was the sea.

Plundering, Utopian Visions, and Legal Borders

The Archaic conception of plundering is represented by the *ius naufragii*, which constituted a practice by which a shipwreck or its remains, upon reaching a foreign coast outside a recognized trading hub, belonged to those who took the remains as their own.[22] This practice was initially conceived of as an individual right but was later developed as a right of the diverse communities around the Mediterranean,[23] whose governments supported it since they found in this activity a means of subsistence, enrichment, and affirmation of their power.[24] The latter connects with the

---

19 *D.* 41.2.21.1 (Iavolenus 7 *Ex Cass.*); *D.* 41.1.58 (Iav. 11 *Ex Cass.*); *D.* 41.7.7 (Jul. 2 *Ex Min.*); *D.* 14.2.8 (Jul 2 *Ex Min.*); *D.* 41.1.9.8 (Gaius 2 *Rer. Cott.*); *D.* 14.2.2.7 (Paul 34 *ad Ed.*); *D.* 47.2.43.11 (Ulp. 41 *ad Sab.*).

20 That constitutes the so-called *exceptio Labeoniana*, located in *D.* 4.9.3.1 (Ulp. 14 *ad Ed.*): "Hence, Labeo writes that if anything is lost through shipwreck or an attack by pirates, it is not unfair that a defence be given to the 'seaman'."

21 See, for example, *D.* 9.2.27.24 (Ulp. 18 *ad Ed.*); *D.* 47.9.3.7 (Ulp. 56 *ad Ed.*).

22 See Amm. Marc. 2.2–3; Apollod. *Epit.* 6, 7; Dionysius, *Periegeta* 47–49; Hdt. 3.137–138; Plin. *HN.* 2.73 (71) and 7.57.11; Polyb. 2, 8; Strabo 5.4.2, 89.5.2, 17.3.20. The existence of coastal areas with a large number of wrecks sunk near the sandy shores probably indicates that the act of shipwrecking vessels by attracting them to the coast with signs was usual; see. *D.* 47.9.10 (Ulp. 1 *Opin.*); Gianfranco Purpura, "Rinvenimenti sottomarini nella Sicilia Occidentale," *Archeologia subacquea* 3, no. 37–38 (1986), 156.

23 Gian-Luigi Andrich, "Naufragio," *Digesto Italiano* 15, no. 2 (1904–1911); Pietro Janni, *Il Mare degli Antichi* (Bari: Dedalo, 1996), 453–470; Cesare Maria Moschetti, "Naufragio," *Enciclopedia del Diritto* 27 (1977); Jean Rougé, *Recherches sur l'organisation du commerce maritime en Méditerranée sous l'Empire romain* (Paris: S.E.V.P.E.N, 1966), 109; Julie Velissaropoulos-Karakostas, *Les nauclères grecs: recherches sur les institutions maritimes en Grèce et dans l'Orient hellénisé* (Paris: Droz, 1980), 162.

24 Genaro Chic García, "Violencia legal y no legal en el marco del estrecho de

idea of the sea as an environment where utopian visions of power could be projected – especially in the sense of being a place which, when subdued, could provide a substantial degree of power to the conqueror.

In sum, *ius naufragii* was part of the economic activities sustaining coastal populations. Indeed, it is possible to find cases in which the rights of different communities to a wreck collided and where they needed to find an arrangement.[25] These assaults were part of a "raid mentality," and that way of thinking and acting, in consequence, were mostly linked to a cultural and traditional way of acquiring goods rather than a socio-political act of war (also common at the time).[26] This conception of plundering was unavoidably linked with the ancient understanding of the sea and its shores, which were used to divide humanity into different spheres: us (the community) and the others. However, the Roman victory over Carthage in the Punic wars (second century BCE) marked the starting point of the Roman hegemony in the Mediterranean and, accordingly, the rise of the Roman conceptualization of plundering as a noxious practice that should be prosecuted.[27] In that way, the Romans were trying to promote unity and peace in the Mediterranean, while preparing for their large-scale expansion on land and sea. Indeed, during the First Punic War, the Romans acquired a navy and some familiarity with maritime warfare;[28] similarly, during the Illyrian Wars, ruling the sea to safeguard merchants (which was also an effort to advance the Roman elite's needs) became a part of Roman strategic thinking.[29]

Gibraltar," in *Piratería y seguridad Marítima en el Mediterráneo Antiguo*, ed. Alfonso Álvarez-Ossorio Rivas, Eduardo Ferrer Albelda, and Enrique García Vargas (Seville: Universidad de Sevilla, 2013), 17.

25 For example, the inhabitants of Salmidessos delimited the coast in order to share what came to their banks from the wrecks; see Xen. *An.* 7.5.2; Henri van Effenterre, "Querelles cretoises," *REA* 44, no. 1 (1942): 32–40 (see *Inscriptiones Cretenses* I, XVI, n° 4 B = *Inscriptiones Delos*, 1513 B); Velissaropoulos-Karakostas, *Nauclères*, 161. In another case illustrating this practice, a ship was wrecked in Knossos and two communities contested the cargo; this led to an agreement being reached between Knossos and Tylissos, prohibiting looting from each other before settling the share of the common booty; see Hermann Bengston, *Die Staatsverträge des Altertums*, second volume (Munich: Beck, 1975), 148.

26 Vincent Gabrielsen, "Economic Activity, Maritime Trade and Piracy in the Hellenistic Aegean," *REA* 103, no. 1 (2001): 226.

27 Jean Rougé, "Le Droit de Naufrage et ses limitations en Mediterranée avant l'établissement de la domination de Rome," in *Mélanges Piganiol 3*, ed. Raymond Chevalier (Paris: S.E.V.P.E.N, 1966), 1467–1469.

28 For this narrative, see, for example, Zeev Rubin, "The Mediterranean and the Dilemma of the Roman Empire in Late Antiquity," *MHR* 1, no. 1 (1986): 12–26.

29 John Wilkes, *The Illyrians* (Chichester: Blackwell, 1992), 170–180.

Notwithstanding that, even if it is true that political changes also cause developments in society, one should bear in mind that all cultural and historical processes take time to settle, and changes in the realm of ancient maritime customs would not have been an exception. In that sense, after the Romans had imposed their hegemonic rule over the Mediterranean, plundering practices were not going to disappear immediately as a maritime practice. In that sense, for those people who had always relied on looting as part of their economic income, it would have been difficult to be told that this practice was not acceptable anymore.[30] Indeed, the first ruling openly attesting the unlawfulness of *ius naufragii* and its associated practices appears during the second half of the first century BCE,[31] and even in the high and late Empire, it is possible to appreciate that many populations still plundered for profit.[32] The latter highlights the fact, on the one hand, that the maritime custom of sinking ships was still considered by many coastal populations as a means of subsistence and, on the other hand, that the Roman state lacked enough power to coerce the complete elimination of this practice.[33] In these historical and cultural contexts, the process of establishing the limits to these violent aggressions within space caused a dynamic negotiation of legal conceptions, politics, power, and identity.

One of the first examples of border delimitation are the treaties agreed to by Rome and Carthage (509–279 BCE). The first treaty is succinctly described by Polybius and indicates that Romans should not sail beyond the Fair Promontory (Cap Bon), and from this note the treaties designated areas for safe navigation.[34] The Carthaginian

---

30 Raids were a source of economic income in the Archaic Mediterranean for several populations, such as those of Dalmatia, Cilicia, and Liguria; see Diod. Sic. 5.39.8; Strabo 4.203.

31 *D.* 47.9.1pr. (Ulp. 56 *ad Ed.*); see Emilia Mataix Ferrándiz, "De incendio ruina naufragio rate nave expugnata. Origins, Context and Legal Treatment of Shipwrecking in Roman Law," *RIDA* 66 (2019): 153–195.

32 See, for example, *D.* 47.9.4.1 (Paul 54 *ad Ed.*), *D.* 47.9.10 (Ulp. 1 *Opin.*); see also Emilia Mataix Ferrándiz, "'Washed by the Waves'. Fighting against Shipwrecking in the Later Roman Empire," in *Seafaring and Mobility in the Late Antique Mediterranean*, ed. Antti Lampinen and Emilia Mataix Ferrándiz (London: Bloomsbury Academic, 2022), 133–148.

33 Christopher Fuhrmann, *Policing the Roman Empire: Soldiers, Administration, and Public Order* (Oxford: Oxford University Press, 2012), 49–52; Benjamin Kelly, "Riot Control and Imperial Ideology in the Roman Empire," *Phoenix* 61, no. 1–2 (2007): 158.

34 Polyb. 3.22: "There shall be friendship between the Romans and their allies, and the Carthaginians and their allies, on these conditions: Neither the Romans nor their allies are to sail beyond the Fair Promontory, unless driven by stress of weather or the

treaty is deeply embedded on a territorial limitation: Romans could navigate only around some Carthaginian areas and would only have access to land for five days in the case of repairs. This legal instrument constituted a bilateral agreement created in the context of an envisioned or ongoing war, and in which it is possible to see the Carthaginian superiority over the Romans at the time.[35] In addition, it is possible to appreciate a different conceptualization of the sea on the part of the Carthaginians. Until now, we have seen how, according to Roman sources, the sea was a space free from the dominion of the law of the Romans; with this treaty, however, the Carthaginians were establishing navigational limits in the sea surrounding their shores, as imposing order (their rule) over an area traditionally demarcated as chaotic or catastrophic for humans (the sea).

Other treaties established friendship or alliances among the parties, such as in the case of the Roman treaty with Maroneia (167 BCE), which indicates the following:

[ποιεῖν τὸν δῆμον τὸν] Ῥωμαίων καὶ τὸν δῆμον τὸν [Μαρωνιτῶν καὶ] Αἰνίων τοὺς κεκριμένους ὑπὸ Λευκίο[υ Παύλου] ἐλευθέρους καὶ πολιτευομένους με[τ᾽ αὐ]τῶν· Φιλία καὶ συμμαχία καλὴ ἔστω καὶ κατὰ γῆν καὶ κατὰ θάλασσαν εἰς τὸν ἅπαντα χρόνον [...].

The [Alliance of the demos] of the Romans and the demos of [the Maronitai and] those of the Ainioi judged by Lucius [Paulus] to be free and sharing in their state: There shall be friendship and good alliance by land and by sea for all time [...].[36]

The wording is like several other treaties between the Romans and Greek states in the second century BCE – in particular, the treaty with Astypalaia (105 BCE):

---

fear of enemies. If any one of them be driven ashore he shall not buy or take aught for himself save what is needful for the repair of his ship and the service of the gods, and he shall depart within five days." Evelyn S. Shuckburgh, trans., *The Histories of Polybius* (London and New York: Macmillan, 1889; Bloomington, IN: Indiana University Press, 1962).

35 Jean-Louis Ferrary, "Traités et domination romaine dans le monde hellénique," in *I trattati nel mondo antico*, ed. Luciano Canfora, Mario Liverani, and Carlo Zaccagnini (Rome: L'Erma di Bretschneider, 1990), 235.

36 *SEG* XXXV.823. ll.6–11; Roger Bagnall and Peter Derow, eds. and trans., *The Hellenistic Period: Historical Sources in Translation* (Malden, MA, and Oxford: John Wiley and Sons, 2007), 90–92.

[...] τω δήμω τω] ['Ρωμαίων καὶ] τω δήμω τω Αστυπαλαιεων ειρήνη καὶ
[φιλία] [καϊ συμμαχία] ἔστω καὶ κατὰ γήν καὶ κατὰ θάλασσαν [εις τον α-]
[πάντα χρόνον] πόλεμος δε μη ἔστω.

This friendship and alliance shall be good for all time, both by land
and by sea. [...] between the People of the Romans and the People of
the Astypalaians let there be peace, friendship, and alliance both on
land and on sea for all time; let there be no war.[37]

These documents demonstrate the role of law in negotiating the gap
between sea and land with the aim of avoiding violence and war.
Nevertheless, are we only dealing with acts of public violence, such as
war raids? These treaties may have prevented the exercise of *ius naufragii*
between both communities, perhaps not considering the act of plundering
as unlawful *per se* but rather on account of the community against which
it was committed. These sources attest to a fragmented Mediterranean
and how, to establish limits to sea violence, different populations needed
to enable agreements which would establish what was lawful or unlawful
based on territorial or personal principles. Both treaties from Astypalaia
and Maroneia establish a bridge between land and sea, and in that
way they allowed Rome to extend its spatial governance, because these
supposed treaties of friendship were in reality tools for political expansion
for Rome, which was increasing its power at the time.[38]

Sea Governance and Power

This section reflects chronologically on some legal sources that mirror how
the violence threatening the Roman expansionist project at times impelled
the Romans to open the spatial limits of the legal sources. This exercise
contributed to a change in how the sea was perceived in the areas where
these regulations were applied as well as to the configuration of the sea in
the Roman expansionist project that was in turn being gradually defined.

---

37 IG. XII 3.173. ll.26–29 (= *IGRR* IV 1028); Robert K. Sherk, trans., *Roman Documents
from the Greek East* (Baltimore, MD: Johns Hopkins Press, 1969), 56–58. Iota subscripts
(or adscripts) and some accents are missing in the Greek of the Astypalaia inscription,
but these are absent in the original inscription.

38 David J. Bederman, *International Law in Antiquity* (Cambridge: Cambridge
University Press, 2001), 189–192; Arthur Nussbaum, *A Concise History of the Law of
Nations* (New York: The Macmillan Company, 1947), 11.

The first example brought here is the *lex de provinciis praetoris* (100 BCE),[39] also known as the *lex de piratis persequendis*.[40] Between the end of the nineteenth and the beginning of the twentieth century, three inscriptions were discovered at Delphi and Cnidos, being identified, despite their fragmentary state and poor preservation, as the Greek version of a Roman *lex* that represented the Roman struggle against piracy in the Mediterranean.[41] Although most of the Cnidos inscription has nothing to do with the Delphic inscription, there is a section, between columns II and IV, corresponding to the beginning and end of the law, which coincides with the Delphic inscription, although this is not a literal but rather a content-based match:

Delphi copy, block B, lines 8–12:

ὁμοίως τ]ε καὶ πρὸς τὸν βασιλέα τὸν ἐν τ[ῆ ν]ήσῳ Κύπρωι βασιλεύοντα
καὶ πρὸς τὸν βασιλ[έα τὸν ἐν Ἀλε]-|ξανδρείαι καὶ Αἰγύπ[τωι βασιλεύοντα
καὶ ρὸς τὸν βασιλέα τὸν ἐπὶ Κυ]ρήνη βασιλεύοντα καὶ πρὸς τοὺς βασιλεῖς
τοὺς ἐν Συρίαι βασιλεύον[τας, πρὸς οὓς] | φιλία καὶ συμμαχία ἐ[στὶ τῶι
δήμωι τῶι Ῥωμαίων, γράμματα ἀποστελλέ]τω καὶ ὅτι δίκαιόν ἐστ[ιν
αὐ]τοὺς φροντίσαι, μὴ ἐκ τῆς βασιλείας αὐτ[ῶν μήτε] τῆ[ς] | χώρας ἢ
ὁρίων πειρατὴ[ς μηδεὶς ὁρμήσῃ, μηδὲ οἱ ἄρχοντες ἢ φρούραρχοι οὓς
κ]αταστήσουσιν τοὺ[ς] πειρατὰς ὑποδέξωνται, καὶ φροντίσαι, ὅσον [ἐν

---

39 The Roman aim to control piracy might well be dated to an earlier period: for example, one might consider the case of the Aetolians, whose public economy seems to have been regularly based on state-sponsored piracy, which the Romans certainly sought to control in the third century BCE; see, for example, Frank William Walbank, ed., *The Cambridge Ancient History, Volume VII, Part 1: The Hellenistic World* (Cambridge: Cambridge University Press, 1984), 232, 255.

40 Knidos, column II, 1–31 and Delphi, block B, 8–14; see also Michael Crawford et al., "Lex de provinciis praetoriis," in *The Roman Statutes, Vol. 1*, ed. Michael Crawford (London: Bulletin of the Institute of Classical Studies Supplement 34, 1996), 231–270.

41 The text of the law can be found in *SEG* III, 378; *FIRA* I, 121–123 (text from Francesco Riccobono). A few years after its discovery, some authors erroneously identified this law with the *Lex Gabinia de bello piratico* (67 BCE); see Edouard Cuq, "La Loi Gabinia contre la Piraterie de l'an 67 av. J.C. d'àprés une Inscription de Delphes," *CRAI* (1923); Stuart H. Jones, "A Roman Law Concerning Piracy," *JRS* 16, no. 2 (1926): 158. An extensive study of the epigraphic problems of both inscriptions can be found in Jean-Louis Ferrary, "Retour sur la loi des inscriptions de Delphes en de Cnide (Roman Statutes n.12)," in *Epigrafis 2006. Atti della XIVe Rencontre sur l'epigraphie in onore di Silvio Panciera*, ed. Maria Luisa Caldelli, Gian Luca Gregori, and Silvia Orlandi (Rome: Quasar, 2008), 102; Lucia Monaco, *Persecutio piratarum. Battaglie ambigue e svolte costituzionali nella Roma Reppublicana* (Naples: Jovene, 1996), 116–118. The Greek version was not an official translation made in Rome and sent to the provinces, but was made by the governor of the Asian province.

αὐ]τοῖς ἐσ[τι] | τοῦτο, ὁ δῆμος ὁ Ῥωμαίω[ν ἵν᾽ εἰς τὴν ἁπάντων σωτηρίαν συνεργοὺς ἔχῃ.

[And likewise] to the king who reigns in the island of Cyprus and the king [who reigns in] Alexandria and Egypt [and the king] who reigns in Cyrene and the kings who reign in Syria [who] have a relationship of friendship and alliance [with the Roman people [he] sends letters] [in which it is said] that it is right that they take care that from their kingdom [or] from their territory or from their borders [does] not [escape] [any] pirate [and that the magistrates or the commanders of garrisons that [they] designate give asylum to the pirates, and that [they] take care, as far as this [it will be possible], that the Roman people [them] have [as] coadjutors for security of all.[42]

Cnidos copy, column II, lines 6–11:

[---] τῶι δήμωι Ῥωμαί-|ων κατὰ τοῦτον τὸν νόμον, ὅπως τῶν | ἐ[θν]ῶν μή τ[ι]σιν ἄδικα πράγματα [μήτε] | [--- c.10 ---] πρά[γ]ματα γένηται, εἴπερ | κατεδίδοτο πράγματα, κατὰ δύνα-|μιν ποιεῖν ἄνευ δόλου πονηροῦ οἵ τε πο-|λῖται Ῥωμαίων οἵ τε σύμμαχοι ὀνόμα-|τος Λατίνου ὁμοίως τε τῶν ἐθνῶν, οἵτι-|νες ἐν φιλίαι τοῦ δήμου Ῥωμαίων εἰσίν, | ὅπως μετ᾽ ἀ[σ]φ[α]λείας πλοΐζεσθαι δύνων-|ται καὶ τῶ[ν] δ[ι]καίων τυνχάνωσιν [...].

[it has seemed good (?)] to the Roman people according to this statute, so that to none of the nations may there befall injury or [insult], for [who]ever (?) shall have received a charge (?), insofar as it shall be possible, to act without wrongful deceit, so that the citizens of Rome and the allies and the Latins, likewise those of the nations who are friends of the Roman people may sail in safety and obtain their rights.[43]

The provisions contained in the law ensure navigation safety for Romans, Latins, and Roman allies by classifying these areas as Roman praetorian provinces.[44] In this way, this regulation forced eastern countries to undertake

42 Riccardo Braga, trans. (Italian), *La lex de prouinciis praetoriis* (Milan: EDUCatt Università Cattolica, 2014), 33; translated from Italian to English by the author of this chapter.
43 Michael Crawford, trans., *The Roman Statutes, Vol. I* (London: Institute of Classical Studies, School of Advanced Study, University of London, 1996), 253.
44 Cnidos copy, col. II, lines 6–11; col. III, lines 28–37; Delphi copy, block B, lines 8–12.

activities to prevent pirates from maintaining bases in their lands and to forbid them from seeking shelter in their ports.[45] The legal problem of suppression of piracy was compounded by the question of jurisdiction.[46] To the need of establishing clear frontiers between territorial units, the Romans responded by classifying provinces and establishing their rule of law. In that way, jurisdiction was not in question.[47] By contrast, the sea offered no such defined frontiers other than coastlines and, therefore, these laws created a bridge between law and sea by allowing Roman jurisdiction to penetrate into foreign lands and waters.

By classifying these spaces as praetorian provinces, these areas came to have a legal significance, because in that way the existing Roman law was susceptible to be created and applied to govern these areas and their inhabitants.[48] In the case of the *lex de provinciis praetoris*, it is possible to observe how many of the limits that would normally apply to Roman regulation were trespassed in order to fight violence (even if the commercial and expansionist interests of Rome played a role as well).[49] We can see how a statute applies to Romans and non-Romans, and how it is valid on land but also at sea, since it was aiming to allow for safe navigation. The urgency of the measures taken to target piracy would have justified the exceptionality of these enactments.[50] An inscription from Astypalaia indicates that the inhabitants of that area had fleets capable of capturing cities and were able to defeat pirates on their own; this does not mean that Rome's support was not necessary to challenge piracy successfully in these areas.[51] In addition, these laws bear witness to the increasing power of Rome, which was managing violence via legal statutes and not by bilateral treaties, as before.

45 Jean-Louis Ferrary, "Recherches sur la législation de Saturninus et Glaucia," *MEFRA* 89, no. 2 (1977), 619–660; Anna Tarwacka, *Romans and Pirates: Legal Perspective* (Warsaw: Wydawnictwo Uniwersytetu, 2009), 39–41.

46 John L. Anderson, "Piracy and World History: An Economic Perspective on Maritime Predation," *Journal of World History* 6, no. 2 (1995): 178.

47 Strabo 10.5.4, 14.5.2.

48 The latter effect has also been observed by Christer Westerdahl, "Holy, Profane and Political. Territoriality-Extraterritoriality: A Problem with Borders," in *Papers in Cartography, Numismatics, Oriental Studies and Librarianship Presented to Ulla Ehrensvärd* (Stockholm: Kungl. biblioteket, 2003), 468–470; the concept of land in Scandinavia has, among other things, a direct legal significance; a "land" (province) is thus the area of validity of a formulated law.

49 This is also the argument of Tarwacka, *Romans and Pirates*, 63–66; see also Anna Tarwacka, "Some Remarks on Piracy in Roman Law," *Annuaires de droit maritime et oceanique* 36 (2018): 299.

50 Strabo 14.5.2.

51 *IG* XII³. 171; see Clemens Geelhar, "Some Remarks on the *lex de provinciis praetoriis*," *RIDA* 49 (2002): 115–117.

In terms of jurisdiction, these laws represent the first hints of empire since their expansion was based on the creation of provinces.[52] Indeed, that supposed anti-pirate alliance allowed Rome to establish a tighter control of the oriental provinces and to become, in a way, more formidable than the pirates themselves.[53] Thus the catastrophic image of the sea, mirrored through the piratic danger as depicted by the Romans, allowed them to enforce legislation which helped the expansion of their empire.

A different way of delineating the land and sea limits can be perceived in the *Lex Gabinia de bello piratico*, approved in 67 BCE by the tribune Aulus Gabinius.[54] At that time, the violent threat of the pirates in the Mediterranean (partly due to their strong position in the slave market) had even affected the grain routes, which in turn had provoked an increase in grain prices, and which, consequently, heightened the risks of suffering famines in Rome.[55] This climate of crisis led to one tribune proposing that the Senate should grant *imperium infinitum* to the general Pompey during a three-year campaign to fight piracy.[56] On the territorial plane, Pompey was entrusted with the area from the Black Sea to the Pillars of Hercules, along with the coasts extending 80 kilometres inland in order to strike against the caves where pirates were hiding.[57] The reason for defining such an extended territory was to ensure that the leader had the ability to persecute the pirates wherever they appeared or fled.[58] Pompey's campaign to suppress piracy throughout the Mediterranean was a significant step towards the consolidation of the idea of Mediterranean as *mare nostrum*, with only Roman interests given full legitimation within its circuit.[59]

From a constitutional point of view, the *Lex Gabinia* has an important role in the construction of the maritime legal landscape of the Roman Republic. The *imperium* granted to Pompey the Great was not extended to all the provinces but still gave him the right to use his power over a very

---

52 Clifford Ando, "Public Law and Republican Empire in Rome, 200–27 BCE," in *Empire and Legal Thought: Ideas and Institutions from Antiquity to Modernity*, ed. Edward Cavanagh (Leiden: Brill, 2020), 119.

53 Monaco, *Persecutio*, 177–179.

54 Asc. *Pro Cornelio* 72a–c; Cass. Dio. 36.

55 Peter A. Brunt, *The Fall of the Roman Republic and Related Essays* (Oxford: Oxford University Press, 1987), 179.

56 Tac. *Ann.* 15.25.

57 Vell. Pat. 2.31.2.

58 Philip de Souza, *Piracy in the Graeco-Roman World* (Cambridge: Cambridge University Press, 1999), 114.

59 Cic. *Leg. Man.* 314; cf. Balb. 6.16; Plut. *Pomp.* 24–30. The term *mare nostrum* is also referred to in Cic. *Leg. Man.* 314; cf. Balb. 6.16; Plut. *Pomp.* 24–30.

large territorial area. The latter constituted a breach of the Republican constitution[60] since such a wide range of power resulted in a collision with the authority of the governors of individual provinces.[61] Politically, to grant such extensive power to a single person was an entirely new situation, as also was the fact that his power could be used on both land and sea.[62] The latter demonstrates how flexible the limits of the law could be regarding its application in defined spaces when there was a public emergency, as was the Roman claim of the necessity of eradicating piracy in relation to the Republic's maintenance of order.

In addition, Cicero's discourse in defence of the *Lex Manilia* (66 BCE) – a legal enactment that Pompey the Great be given sole command in the Third Mithridatic War – provides details on the spatial extent of his powers such as that which can be seen in the *Lex Gabinia*. Another important impact of this disposition for the spatial discourse, which is the focus of our study, can be clearly read in Cicero's words:

> *Itaque una lex, unus vir, unus annus non modo nos illa miseria ac turpitudine liberavit, sed etiam effecit, ut aliquando vere videremur omnibus gentibus ac nationibus terra marique imperare.*[63]

> And the result was that one law, one man, and one year not only set you free from that distress and that reproach, but also brought it to pass that you seemed at last in very truth to be holding empire over all nations and peoples by land and sea.[64]

These phrases constitute the first literary reference to a victory "on land and sea" in the broad sense of all lands and all seas.[65] The latter not only demonstrates an entanglement between land and sea but also appeals to the extension of Roman power and jurisdiction over both areas. However, the concept of *imperium*, generally associated with Roman power, did not translate into *dominium* in the Roman case, and, therefore, it did not

---

60 Monaco, *Persecutio*, 224–226.

61 Vell. Pat. 2.31.2. According to Velleius Paterculus, Pompey had the same *imperium* in relation to the governors as the rank of proconsul.

62 As was the case for other governors, such as Agron, the king of Illyria; see Polyb. 2.2.

63 Cic. *Leg. Man.* 56.

64 Humfrey Grose Hodge, trans., *Cicero IX: Pro Lege Manilia. Pro Caecina. Pro Cluentio. Pro Rabirio. Perduellionis Reo* (Harvard, MA: Harvard University Press, 1927).

65 Claude Nicolet, *Space, Geography, and Politics in the Early Roman Empire* (Ann Arbor, MI: University of Michigan Press, 1991), 36.

translate into a territorial extension of the state jurisdiction seaward.[66] Therefore, we are again facing the same challenge as with the imperial jurists' texts indicated in the first section, since these legal enactments do not represent a map of the archaeology of Roman dominion; instead, while the sea was still recognized as a space free from being governed by the law of the Romans, they established their governance by other means, through supposed acts of pacification and piratical suppression. This is obviously a political act, but within that act, there was a conceptual spatial change that bridged the gap between the civilized land and the catastrophic sea. It may even be that some "political" borders were indeed symbolic in some sense, rather than fixed geographically.[67]

Finally, around 44 BCE, Cicero labelled piracy as a "global danger that should be eradicated" in his book on duties, *De officiis*.[68] That qualification legally justified that combating pirates was an obligation of all countries, who could take the measures that they considered appropriate to do so, even justifying crossing borders and jurisdictions.[69] In that sense, one may wonder if the orator was being partial when defining and qualifying piracy with his rhetorical abilities in order to justify the Roman expansion. Also in the first book on the commonwealth, *De republica*, Cicero had drawn a sharp distinction between, on the one hand, political communities that were united by the consensual commitment of their members towards a shared conception of law and right and that were bound by common utility and, on the other hand, mere gatherings of persons, who came together for whatever reason.[70] Therefore, piracy could not simply be defined as "armed

---

66   Percy T. Fenn, "Justinian and the Freedom of the Sea," *The American Journal of International Law* 19, no. 4 (1925): 716–727; John Richardson, "Imperium Romanum: Empire and the Language of Power," *JRS* 81 (1991): 1–9; John Richardson, "The Meaning of imperium in the Last Century BC and the First AD," in *The Roman Foundations of the Law of Nations: Alberico Gentili and the Justice of Empire*, ed. Benedict Kingsbury and Benjamin Straumann (Oxford: Oxford University Press, 2010), 21–29; Bo J. Theutenberg, "Mare Clausum et Mare Liberum," *Arctic* 37, no. 4 (1984): 482; Tuori, "Savage Sea," 203, 214.

67   See also a similar approach in Westerdahl, "Holy, Profane," 493.

68   Cic. *Off.* 3.108.

69   Anna Tarwacka, "Piracy in Roman Law and the Beginnings of International Criminal Law," *Polish Review of International and European Law* 1, no. 1–2 (2012): 70, 73; Tarwacka, "Some Remarks on Piracy in Roman Law," 302, 309.

70   Cic. *Rep.* 1.39 (50 BCE); see also August. *De civitate Dei* 4.4: "And so if justice is left out, what are kingdoms except great robber bands? For what are robber bands except little kingdoms? The band also is a group of men governed by the orders of a leader, bound by a social compact, and its booty is divided according to a law agreed upon. If by repeatedly adding desperate men this plague grows to the point where it holds territory and establishes a fixed seat, seizes cities and subdues peoples, then it more

violence exercised through the use of ships" since the characterization of these actions does not depend solely on the force exerted over something or someone but also on how these are perceived in different places and by diverse cultures.[71] In that sense, the criminalization and prosecution of piracy would not be based on principles of natural law[72] but, rather, on unilateral solutions to act against specific situations and was closely related to the notion of, if not empire, at least a politically organized community.[73] The Republican episode, however, was of great significance from the perspective of the theory of law, and it should not be omitted in research on Roman maritime landscapes. The Roman Republican fight against piracy constitutes another episode in which it is possible to observe how the boundaries of the dichotomies between sea and land, the catastrophic sea (as reflected by piracy and attitudes to plundering) and the utopian sea (tamed, ordered – albeit with imperial overtones) were crossed.

Conclusions

The sea may appear in the ancient mind as a catastrophic environment, but, at the same time, that chaos promoted the utopian dream of taming such a savage space. In that sense, that dichotomy of wildness and

conspicuously assumes the name of kingdom, and this name is now openly granted to it, not for any subtraction of cupidity, but by addition of impunity. For it was an elegant and true reply that was made to Alexander the Great by a certain pirate whom he had captured. When the king asked him what he was thinking of, that he should molest the sea, he said with defiant independence: "The same as you when you molest the world! Since I do this with a little ship I am called a pirate. You do it with a great fleet and are called an emperor"; as in George E. McCracken, trans., *City of God*, Volume 1 (Boston, MA: Harvard University Press, 1957); Augustine drew the anecdote about Alexander from the third book of Cicero's *On the Commonwealth*, but he employs it to very different ends; see also Clifford Ando, "Introduction," in *Piracy, Pillage, and Plunder in Antiquity: Appropriation and the Ancient World*, ed. Richard Evans and Martine De Marre (London: Routledge, 2020), 1–8.

71 Philip de Souza, "Greek Piracy," in *The Greek World*, ed. Anton Powell (London: Routledge, 1995), 180; De Souza, *Piracy*, 10–11; Chic García, "Violencia," 31–49; *contra*, Pascal Arnaud, "L'antiquité Classique et la Piraterie," in *Histoire des pirates et des corsaires. De l'antiquité à nos jours*, ed. Gilbert Buti and Philippe Hrodej (Paris: éditions CNRS, 2016), 27–28.

72 This means that this behaviour would be inherently wrong and not imposed by any court or created by society; for an overview, see John Finnis, *Natural Law and Natural Rights* (Oxford: Oxford University Press, 2011).

73 Lauren Benton, "Toward a New Legal History of Piracy: Maritime Legalities and the Myth of Universal Jurisdiction," *International Journal of Maritime History* 23, no. 1 (2011): 239–240.

idealization acted as a structuring feature of ancient life along its shores. Indeed, the legal regimes targeting violence at sea produced a dynamic connection between the conceptual categories of land and sea, with an utterly malleable application of jurisdiction over the sea itself. The sources included in this paper highlight that no individual could lay claim to or impose any right upon the sea itself and, therefore, that the sea was recognized as a free resource in the Roman world.[74] However, the different legal tools of public law employed to deal with violence at sea seem to define some limits and to extend not formally, but in effect, Roman governance over certain areas including land and sea.

In addition, the labels imposed on different conducts indicating what constituted sea violence were tied to the Roman political organization, which established the limits of legality and considered who was and was not part of a given social group, what counted as necessity, and what constituted violence.[75] Indeed, "the pirate" has featured prominently in Roman-centric conceptions of law, violence, and sovereignty that have been imposed onto other seas and oceans and in ways that continue to justify control.[76] The latter can be clearly appreciated when one reads Cicero and his statements on piracy, as well as later imperial dispositions on the matter.[77] Indeed, Cicero constitutes a single voice that perhaps has been echoed in excess and that, therefore, has created a one-sided idea of what was considered piracy and how to target it. Thus, how can we then read the imperial incursions on other lands and seas?[78]

By using the focus on violence reflected in legal sources targeting violence, it is possible to appreciate how that supposed fight against it guided the imperialistic efforts of Rome, first to extend their power and later to maintain their imperialistic propaganda of bringing the peace to

---

74 Johannes P. Hasebroek, *Staat und Handel im alten Griechenland* (Tübingen: Mohr, 1926), 126; Annalisa Marzano, *Harvesting the Sea: The Exploitation of Marine Resources in the Roman Mediterranean* (Oxford: Oxford University Press, 2013), 235–239; Gianfranco Purpura, "'Liberum mare' acque territoriali e riserve di pesca nel mondo antico," *AUPA* 49 (2004): 165–206.

75 This problem is timeless, as highlighted by Jatin Dua, "A Sea of Profit: Making Property in the Western Indian Ocean," in *Legalism: Property and Ownership*, ed. Georgy Kantor, Tom Lambert, and Hannah Skoda (Oxford: Oxford University Press, 2017), 178: "The concepts of resource piracy and defensive piracy remind us that in global coverage only certain actions are labelled as piratical: 'piracy' and 'legality' are loaded and polemical terms that are modes of legitimizing certain actions while condemning others."

76 Alfred P. Rubin, *The Law of Piracy* (New York: Transnational Publishers, 1998).

77 Cic. *Off.* 3.107–108; see De Souza, *Piracy*, 205–213.

78 August. *de civ. D.* 4.4.

the Mediterranean Sea.[79] Most probably, the main issue for the Romans was not sovereignty over the sea but, rather, the political implications that such an extraordinary command, and with it, unusual powers, would have. Therefore, even if they never elaborated on a doctrine of the law of the seas and even though in their texts the jurists maintained the idea of a sea belonging to humankind, at the same time they were in practice using different tools to handle sea hazards and to extend their rule at sea. Therefore, I propose to look at Rome as apparently defined and confined by the catastrophic sea but, ultimately, as spreading beyond its waves in search of their utopian maritime vision.

79 One of the best examples comes from the Augustan *Res Gestae* (*CIL* III.2.769–772), where the emperor claims to have defeated piracy in the Mediterranean.

Ancient Literature and Myth

CHAPTER SIX

The Seas are Full of Monsters: Divine Utopia, Human Catastrophe

Georgia L. Irby

Introduction

The Greco-Roman attitude toward the sea is ambiguous. The sea is a place of danger, a source of wealth (fish, pearls, murex purple dye), and a utopia where Nereids frolic, a paradise which categorically rejects human encroachment. The sea is the birthplace of catastrophe (disaster and destruction), where humans exist *un*naturally and only with the aid of tenuous technology. This potential for maritime catastrophe is given form by *kētē* (sea monsters) who corporealize the sea's more abstract dangers, its metamorphic qualities, storminess, and threats of death. The sea, moreover, is a sacred space, reserved for the divine and primal forces of nature. Here we shall investigate sea monsters in all their moods: honour guards of sea gods, winsome pets of Nereids, and harbingers or causes of disastrous storms at sea.

Greco-Roman literature is replete with accounts of storms at sea: Poseidon's vengeful squall that buffeted Odysseus;[1] Plato's cataclysmic flooding in the *Critias*;[2] and terrifying gales in Vergil,[3] Lucan,[4] and others. These storms, together with even the prospect of travel by water, are made all the more harrowing by the real or supposed presence of monsters in the depths as, for example, the ship-swallowing whale in Lucian's *A True*

This study emerges from my continuing work on watery matters, including the sea and sea creatures. I would like to thank Hamish Williams and Ross Clare for organizing this fascinating volume, and Duane W. Roller for his continued support, encouragement, and tireless reading of this draft (and countless others).

1 Hom. *Od.* 5.282–332.
2 Pl. *Critias* 111a–b.
3 Verg. *Aen.* 1.82–91.
4 Luc. 1.498–503.

Tale[5] and the huge sea monsters ("savage whales and watery dogs")[6] that in
15 CE Albinovanus Pedo imagined would ravage Germanicus' boats on the
distant, storm-tossed Amisia River (Ems) that debouches into the North
Sea.[7]

Giant sea creatures represent or create those very storms. Ocean was
the murky, tempestuous, unknown, and unknowable lair of *kētē*, large
and small. Ancient writers and artists, moreover, crafted denizens of the
deep as archetypes of an ocean that was a sphere of catastrophe (utter
destruction), a metaphor of death and disaster, a place where profound
danger lurks beneath the surface, an unknown, unknowable, non-human
place where existence is often returned to a primal, mixed state.[8] Ancient
writers and artists, furthermore, corporealized that fear in their vivid
accounts of real and imagined sea monsters. Sea creatures are churned
up by maritime squalls, but, owing to their sheer size, they are also
metonymic storms at sea. These biological and invented *kētē* were integral
to the tempests experienced by Greek and Roman sailors. *Kētē* caused
storms at sea, and storms churned *kētē* up from the depths.

Catastrophe in the Belly of the Whale

We start with the satirically exaggerated *kētē* from Lucian's *True Story*,[9]
set in imaginary locales beyond the Pillars of Heracles and full of tongue-
in-cheek parody. After returning from the Moon, Lucian's voyagers take
advantage of two days of calm seas (the sea can be a place of utopic
enjoyment, even for people), until their watery merrymaking is suddenly
interrupted by maritime beasts including *kētē*, the largest of which is 1,500

5 Lucian, *Verae Historiae* 1.30–2.2.
6 All translations of ancient sources are my own.
7 Sen. *Suas.* 1.15.
8 Gilgamesh, Perseus, Heracles, and Jason travel over Ocean in their dangerous
quests. Odysseus must sail north until his ship crosses Ocean's stream to reach Hades,
the land of the dead (*Od.* 10.507–515). Plato, moreover, pitched his hydrology as a
katabasis or descent into the underworld, as he explored the nature of the soul while
recounting Socrates' last day (*Phd.* 109b–113d; Malcolm Wilson, *Structure and Method
in Aristotle's Meteorologica* (Cambridge: Cambridge University Press, 2013), 179–180).
Cf. Marie-Claire Beaulieu, *The Sea in the Greek Imagination* (Philadelphia: University
of Pennsylvania Press, 2015); Sandra Blakely, "Maritime Risk and Ritual Responses:
Sailing with the Gods in the Ancient Mediterranean," in *The Sea in History: The
Ancient World*, ed. Philip de Souza and Pascal Arnaud (Woodbridge: Boydell & Brewer,
2017), 362–379.
9 Lucian, *Verae Historiae* 31–32.

stadia long (about 200 kilometres [125 miles]!). This incredibly giant *kētos* generates a gale, foaming up the sea over a great distance (πρὸ πολλοῦ). Lunging at the ship with its mouth open, it swallows the cast of characters together with their vessel. Its sharp teeth, white as ivory, just barely miss crushing the boat as it slips through the gaps. In the belly, the crew experience the whale's breeching, "carried swiftly to every part of the sea" (φερομένου αὐτοῦ ὀξέως πρὸς πᾶν μέρος τῆς θαλάττης). They see sky one moment, islands the next. The motion is frantic and chaotic, like a storm, threatening catastrophe, a stark reminder that humans do not belong on the sea. Lucian then recounts life in the whale's belly until he and his companions manage to kill the monster and escape.

In addition to causing storms, sea monsters also hunt under the cover of tempests. Lucian's whale had earlier taken advantage of a storm at sea to swallow another ship, whose survivors – an old man and his son – the narrator meets in the belly. That ship had been sailing to Italy, when a violent wind (ἄνεμος σφοδρός) drove it from Sicily out into the ocean (ἐς τὸν ὠκεανὸν) where the whale was waiting, swallowing the vessel and killing all the crew and other passengers.[10] Ocean, the circumambient river that delimits the *oikoumene* (inhabited human world) beyond the Pillars of Heracles, is where sea monsters dwell. According to one version, Heracles created the Pillars (the shallow, narrow spit of water between the westernmost promontories of Libya and Europe) deliberately to prevent sea monsters from encroaching into the Inner Sea (τὰ μεγάλα κήτη διεκπίπτειν ἐκ τοῦ ὠκεανοῦ πρὸς τὴν ἐντὸς θάλαττα).[11]

Poseidon: Saviour of Ships and Earthshaker

Ocean is also the realm of Poseidon, the Greek god of the sea. To the Homeric hymnist, Poseidon is the "saviour of ships" (σωτῆρά τε νηῶν), invoked to help those who sail (πλώουσιν ἄρηγε).[12] Because of his control over the sea, those who travel by water pray to Poseidon for calm passage.[13]

---

10 34.

11 Diod. Sic. 4.18.5. For terminology of the sea, see Beaulieu, *Greek Imagination*, 25; Georgia L. Irby, *Conceptions of the Watery World in Greco-Roman Antiquity* (London: Bloomsbury, 2021), 4–5.

12 *Homeric Hymns* no. 22.5, 7, "To Poseidon."

13 Alpheios of Mitylene prayed for calm weather from Rome to Syria (*Greek Anthology* 9.90). Theognis hoped that the god would return his friend Chaeon safely (691–692).

Poseidon is Ἀσφάλιός (*Asphalios*, "Steadfast"), bestowing his worshippers with gentle winds and rich harvests of fish.[14] Poseidon is also Σωτήρ (*Soter*, "Saviour"), the god who protects sailors during storms at sea. Poseidon Σωτήρ was supplicated by Greek sailors during a gale off Artemision (northern Euboea) in 480 BCE, which resulted in the loss of 400 Persian ships and an incalculable number of merchant ships carrying provisions (Herodotus does not report Greek losses). The squall came to an end when the Persian Magi propitiated Thetis and the other daughters of the minor sea god Nereus.[15]

At Rome, Poseidon's counterpart, Neptune, is also recognized for salvation at sea. At Corinth and Delos, worshippers invoked Neptune with small personal votives for unrecorded reasons (*Neptuno sacrum*).[16] At Carthage, Augustus honoured Neptune with a "small offering" as demanded by the people.[17] The sailor Caius Helvius Suavis and his wife, moreover, fulfilled a vow to the Augustan Neptune at Dougga (North Africa). Helvius explained that he had established his home in his ancestral seats and that his wife, Casia Faustina, had made offerings to the master of the waves and father of the Nereids. Helvius' bride, we assume, voyaged over water with her husband, perhaps after his discharge from service (Helvius did not record his rank or status).[18]

Poseidon/Neptune has the power to calm the waters and protect sailors at sea, but he is also the "Earthshaker" who causes earthquakes and storms at sea, speaking to the binary nature of Greco-Roman gods. Poseidon sent the gale that nearly destroyed Odysseus,[19] whereas Neptune quelled the squall that almost obliterated Aeneas' fleet.[20] Storms arise

14 Apollonius of Tyana 4.9; Ar. *Ach.* 682; Heliodorus 6.7; Oppian, *Fishing* 5.680; Paus. 7.21.7.

15 Hdt. 7.190–192.

16 *CIL* 8.2.2–3 (first century CE).

17 *AE* 1951, #71: *[N]eptun[o] / [Imp(erator) C]aesar divi [f(ilius) Aug(ustus)] / [po]nt(ifex) maxim[us] / trib(unicia) pot(estate) / [de st]ipe quam p[opulo p(ostulante)] / f(ieri) i(ussit) K(alendis) Ia[n(uariis)]*.

18 *CIL* 8.26491: *Neptuno Aug(usto) sac(rum) / C(aius) H[el]vius Suavis et Ca/sia Faustina coniunx eius / votum solverunt / Helvius haec voto suscepi munera divi / constituique larem sedibus in patr[i(i)s] / haec eadem coniunx mecum Faustina loca[vit] / undarum domino Nereidumque patri.* Vows to Neptune were also fulfilled at Timgad in Numidia (*AE* 1946, #71 = *AE* 1987, #1069), Capua (*CIL* 10.3813), and Rome (*CIL* 6.536). Details are omitted. A Neptune shrine was also incorporated into the Circus' *spina* where dangerous (and sometimes deadly) chariot races occurred.

19 Hom. *Od.* 5.282–332.

20 Verg. *Aen.* 1.142–156.

owing to the agency of Poseidon and the *kētē* who are naturally associated with the Earthshaker.

Gambolling *Kētē*: The Sea as a Utopic Paradise for the Divine

In literature and art, sea monsters gambol in Poseidon's company. In the *Iliad*, as Poseidon skims the waters on his way to Troy, *kētē* emerge from their deep watery lairs, skipping gleefully in the Earthshaker's path.[21] The Roman poet Statius (first century CE) echoes Homer's gambolling *kētē* in the *Achilleid*. A cheerful Neptune, returning from banqueting with Oceanus, causes the winds and storms to become silent, while rock-like sea monsters (*cete*) and Tyrrhenian flocks (seals) whirl about the god's chariot.[22] The sea here reflects the mood of its divine master, sometimes contented, sometimes raging. Additionally, the Greek rhetorician Philostratus the Elder (third century CE) describes a painting at Naples where Poseidon is escorted by hippocamps and *kētē*, fawning on him as they do in Homer.[23]

Kētē also gambol with Nereids in literature and art. According to Ovid, the artwork of the Sun's palace depicts the Nereids sunning themselves on rocks as they dry their green hair, or swimming and riding fishes.[24] The Greek poet Quintus Smyrnaeus (third century CE) replicates Ovid's Nereids who swim among *kētē*.[25] In addition, artwork shows charming images of Nereids with miniature pet *kētē*. Composites of fishes with lions, dogs, or bulls, these pets sport flippers, horse-legs, spiked ruffs, or snouts (furrowed, goateed, or tusked). On the Portland Vase (Figure 1), Thetis cuddles a tiny *kētos* with a scrunched snout and feathery dewlap. At the Villa Borghese, commensurately miniature sea-dragons and sea-lions are featured cavorting with cupids on the sarcophagus of a noble Roman lady who is depicted in a typical Aphrodite Anadyomene pose: crouching within a shell, holding a veil that billows like a sail (early third century CE).[26] Only by alignment with a goddess of the sea can our Roman lady participate in this utopic vision of the sea.

21 Hom. *Il.* 13.27–28.
22 Stat. *Achil.* 1.55–57.
23 Philostr. *Imag.* 1.8.
24 Ov. *Met.* 2.11–14.
25 Quintus Smyrnaeus, *Fall of Troy* 5.336–337.
26 See Illustration 110, in Paul Zanker and Björn C. Ewald, *Living with Myths: The Imagery of Roman Sarcophagi*, trans. Julia Slater (Oxford: Oxford University Press, 2012), 121.

Figure 1: Thetis and *kētos*, Portland Vase, BM 1945,0927.1.

Kētē are furthermore employed as vehicles for Nereids as early as the fifth century BCE.[27] On her way to deliver Achilles' new armour, for example, Thetis holds a cuirass as she rides a fierce-looking, toothy fish with spiky scales.[28] The Nereid on a sea monster is also a popular theme on cosmetic

27 John Boardman, "Very Like a Whale. Classical Sea Monsters," in *Monsters and Demons in the Ancient and Medieval Worlds: Papers Presented in Honor of Edith Porada*, ed. Ann E. Farkas, Prudence O. Harper, and Evelyn B. Harrison (Mainz: P. von Zabern, 1987), 74.

28 J. Paul Getty Museum, Malibu 86.*AE*.611: Apulian red-figure Pelike.

pallets. One silver piece found in a woman's tomb at Canossa, for example, shows a semi-nude Nereid clinging to the neck of an elegant scaly *kētos* with a spiky, webbed ridge along his back and feathery pectoral fins.[29] Like Aphrodite, the Nereids symbolize female beauty, and, like Aphrodite, they were popularly depicted on toiletry items. Like our Roman lady at the Villa Borghese, the lady of Canossa can enjoy the sea as a utopic sphere only by association with the Nereids.

Nereids are also shown riding all manner of sea beasts. On the Great Mildenhall Dish, for example, four Nereids are pulled along by four different mythical sea creatures: a sea-stag; a merman with a trifurcated tail and a crab-claw emanating from his belly; a hippocamp with the torso of a horse; and a serpentine *kētos* with an upturned snout and trifurcated tail.[30] Hippocamps and dolphins are especially prevalent, but we shall consider the more fearsome varieties: bulls, cats, centaurs, and dragons. The relief frieze on the Altar of Domitius Ahenobarbus, for example, shows a procession of guests on their way to the wedding of Peleus and Thetis. With a spiny piscine tail, a gentle sea-bull, almost smiling, conveys a placid Nereid holding a boxed wedding gift.[31] Bulls are violent creatures, associated with powerful deities of weather and storms, Zeus (Jupiter) and Poseidon (Neptune), representing primal forces of fertility and destruction. Despite the placid demeanor of the Ahenobarbus sea-bull, there is an underlying tension: a potentially dangerous animal ferries a Nereid over a capricious track of sea, which can be calm one moment and devastatingly catastrophic the next. Furthermore, the hippocamp on the far right of the panel rears up, throwing off its Nereid as a cupid tries to restrain it. Clinging to the hippocamp's mane, the Nereid seems to be slipping through its coiling tail. Even Nereids, born to the sea, can suffer from the sea's catastrophic forces.

Like sea-bulls, sea-centaurs are also frightful and dangerous. Nonetheless, they serve as mounts for many Nereids. Mosaic floors depict revelling ichthyocentaurs (with human torsos, equine forelegs, and fishy tails) holding torches or playing flutes while they ferry serene, semi-nude Nereids.[32] Notorious for their lust and drunkenness, centaurs embody the forces of untamed nature that threaten orderly Greek society and the Greek hero (Theseus and Heracles, in particular). The centaur thus

---

29 Taranto Museum, fourth to third century BCE.
30 BM 1946, 1007.1.
31 122–115 BCE: München Glyptothek: Inv. 239.
32 House of Silenus in Thysdrus, Tunisia, late second/early third century CE.

encapsulates the resonance of the sea as a catastrophic place of danger where a violent death is a real possibility.

Cats also represent danger. They were hunted in the Roman arena, and they drew the chariots of ecstatic gods (Cybele's lions; Dionysus' panthers). Like hippocamps, ophiotauri, and ichthyocentaurs, sea-cats transport Nereids across mosaic floors. Galatea, for example, holding onto her billowing robe, reclines on a sea-leopard swimming along a mosaic floor.[33] One mosaic floor features two sea-cats: a snarling sea-leopard with a coiling, spotted fish-tail conveys a calm, semi-nude Nereid, accompanied by winged *erotes* (cupids); and a sea-tiger, swatting a paw at the water, transports an *eros*.[34] Yet another mosaic sea-tiger carries another semi-nude Galatea who admires herself in a mirror. The sea-cat seems to gaze at the Nereid's reflection with bemused feline curiosity.[35] As with other images, there is a tension between the lovely Nereid astride the feral sea beast, untamed and untamable, like the waters through which they travel. *Kētē* actualize this paradox between placidity and imminent danger, the unpredictable oscillation between calm, glassy seas, enjoyed by those who belong to the sea (Nereids), and the foamy churning of roiling swells, the standard experience for the land-anchored sailor.

The sea-dragon is the most common type, with elongated snouts, slender, serpentine, spiked necks, and braces of webbed pectoral fins that function as "legs." Some Nereids handle their mounts without tack, grasping them by the neck as they snarl.[36] Other *kētē*, such as a coiling, horned sea-dragon from Apulia, are tacked. Reigning her haltered Apulian *kētos*, Thetis rides side-saddle.[37] The *kētos*' focused stare belies Thetis' apparent mastery over the monster. The bridle allows for only limited control, as on the Ahenobarbus sarcophagus where a cupid struggles to control a rearing hippocamp.

Roman evidence underscores this tension between calm and catastrophe. For example, a Vatican statue group features the abduction of a struggling, semi-nude Nereid by a youthful, beardless sea-centaur. A brace of cupids complicitly pretend that they cannot hear her cries for help

33 Gaziantep in Anatolia, first/second century CE.
34 Piazza Armerina Villa baths (Lambaesis, Algeria), early fourth century CE; see Illustration 114 in Zanker and Ewald, *Living with Myths*, 126.
35 Villa Romana del Casale, fourth century CE.
36 Athenian red-figure stemless cup, BM London E130; Beazley Archive no. 250178, fifth century BCE. The Nereid holds one of Achilles' new greaves in her left hand.
37 Apulia, red figure, Museo Ruva Jatta.

over the violent waves crashing beneath.[38] Turbulent waters and a hybrid sea creature come together to represent an act of rape. This composition underscores the paradox between the ichthyocentaur's enjoyment and the victim's anguish. Emphasizing the tensions between monster and maiden, this sculptural group highlights the sea as a harbinger of catastrophe, where even those born to the sea might be victimized by its dangers.

This paradox is also evident on the Tellus panel of the *Ara Pacis* ("Altar of Peace") where one of Tellus' companions, a semi-nude female, is seated on a dragonesque sea monster. With a curling upper lip, the sea-dragon reveals a mouth full of interlocking, sharp, crocodile-like teeth. The sea-serpent's long neck coils, allowing the monster to observe the central scene, as its wing-like pectoral fins skim above the waves. This *kētos* works on dual registers, as a reminder that Octavian has vanquished a foreign "Egyptian" foe (Cleopatra, elicited by the crocodile-like *kētos*) in a significant naval battle that has secured the Augustan peace (Actium, 31 BCE); and as a link to the divine matriarch of the Julian family, Venus, a considerable goddess of the sea in her own right.[39] Tellus' other companion sits astride a swan or goose, also sacred to Venus. The *kētos*' snarling expression seems incongruous with the images of peace and prosperity foregrounded on the altar's reliefs, revealing underlying tensions between the calm of peace and the storm of war.

Into the fourth century CE, dragonesque *kētē* continue to convey Nereids, as on the Projecta Casket, where a sinuous sea monster with goatee, horns, and leonine forelegs carries a Nereid with a billowing veil. The Nereid smiles enigmatically while the *kētos* swats the water with his leonine paws and reveals teeth in his elongated snout, again suggesting the tension between land and water, human and beast, calm and gale. The box was probably a wedding gift intended to hold toiletries, bringing us back to the Canossa Nereid.[40] Wherever Nereids ride *kētē*, there is palpable tension between the sea as utopia of timeless enjoyment (the beautiful Nereid) and the sea as catastrophic sphere of disaster (populated by savage

---

38 See Illustration 101, in Zanker and Ewald, *Living with Myths*, 116.

39 Cf. Silvia Barbantani, "Goddess of Love and Mistress of the Sea: Notes on a Hellenistic Hymn to Arsinoe-Aphrodite (P.Lit.Goodsp. 2, I–IV)," *Ancient Society* 35 (2005): 135–165; Karl Galinsky, "Venus, Polysemy, and the Ara Pacis Augustae," *American Journal of Archaeology* 96, no. 3 (1992): 457–475, doi:10.2307/506068, accessed 8 August 2021; Irby, *Watery World*, 176–178.

40 BM 1866,1229.1; see Alan Cameron, "The Date and Owners of the Esquiline Treasure: The Nature of the Evidence," *American Journal of Archaeology* 89, no. 1 (1985): 135–145; Kathleen J. Shelton, "The Esquiline Treasure: The Nature of the Evidence," *American Journal of Archaeology* 89, no. 1 (1985): 147–155.

hybrids who navigate roiling swells). The Nereids, with their billowing veils, are themselves paradoxical: are they willing passengers or victims of rape? Do they also represent the savagery of their untamed realm, as wild as the beasts that they keep as pets and mounts?

Fear of the Unknown: The Sea as a Catastrophic Sphere for Humankind

Not all *kētē* were so benign, if the pets and mounts of the Nereids were so. We have already seen the ambivalence between the snarling *kētē* and the Nereids who ride them. *Kētē* are the materialized danger and violence that lurks beneath the surface of calm and choppy waters. *Kētē*, in fact, actualize the human angst of the unknown and unknowable depths which are made all the less comprehensible during storms. Odysseus, when he finds himself adrift in Poseidon's squall, dreads that some powerful god might send a *kētos* from the salt, "such as those nourished by Amphitrite,"[41] an anxiety perhaps greater than the threat of a returning storm surge. Sailors can see the storm, but they cannot see what lurks beneath the surface. Pandora's crown features "terrible monsters" nourished by "land and sea" (κνώδαλ', ὅσ' ἤπειρος πολλὰ τρέφει ἠδὲ θάλασσα),[42] and sea monsters are listed among the "numberless dangers" facing humankind: "the bent folds of the sea are bursting with hostile wild creatures" (πόντιαί τ' ἀγκάλαι κνωδάλων ἀνταίων βρύουσι).[43] Humans, however, do not belong in the sea, and they inevitably meet with such dangers when they encroach into forbidden zones.

The sea is not merely the source of an occasional sea monster, it is crowded with *kētē* and nautical *knodalia* (monsters), thus increasing both the terror and the imagined probability of a fatal encounter. Vergil's Anchises, explaining the origin of souls to his son Aeneas, had envisioned monsters lurking beneath marble-smooth Mediterranean waters (*quae marmoreo fert monstra sub aequore pontus*).[44] Avienius (fourth century CE) would later describe Ocean as monster-filled (*beluosi*).[45]

It is this unknown that enhances Ariadne's dread when she finds herself alone, abandoned by Theseus on the island of Naxos. She anticipates

41 Hom. *Od.* 5.421–422.
42 Hes. *Theog.* 582.
43 Aesch. *Cho.* 587–588.
44 Verg. *Aen.* 6.729.
45 Avienius, *Ora Maritima* 102.

threats from both land and sea.⁴⁶ In addition to the wolves, lions, and tigers that perhaps dwell on the island, Ariadne dreads the giant seals that might emerge from the coastal waters (*et freta dicuntur magnas expellere phoca*).⁴⁷ Naxos' giant seals – liminal creatures who dwell in water and on land – are a source of unarticulated peril that would cause Ariadne's doom if they were to be churned from the depths. Ariadne deliberately worries that she will become food for swift beasts,⁴⁸ including those speedy swimmers who no doubt will invade her beach, bringing with them all the dangers inherent in the sea.⁴⁹ A violent, stormy death is thought to be the inevitable result for those who travel by sea, as Ariadne had envisioned, fearing that the sea itself would invade her beach.

Such angst was not restricted to players in the mythscape. The Roman poet Albinovanus Pedo transferred this terror of unknown marine perils to the historical crew serving under Germanicus in 15 CE. The fleet was caught up in a turbulent storm on the Amisia River (Ems):

> *nunc illum, pigris immania monstra sub undis*
> *qui ferat, Oceanum, qui saevas undique pristis*
> *aequoreosque canes, ratibus consurgere prensis,*
> *accumulat fragor ipse metus, iam sidere limo*
> *navigia et rapido desertam flamine classem,*
> *seque feris credunt per inertia fata marinis*
> *iam non felici laniandos sorte relinqui.*

> Now they see that Ocean who bears huge monsters everywhere beneath its sluggish waves as well as savage whales and watery dogs – rises up against the ships caught (in the storm surge), the very din increases the sailors' fears. Now they believe that ships sink in the mire and the fleet is deserted by the breeze, and that they themselves are abandoned by helpless fate to be pulled to pieces by the sea-beasts. Unlucky lot!⁵⁰

---

46 Ov. *Her.* 10.94.

47 87.

48 96.

49 According to ancient wisdom, seals were redolent (Hom. *Od.* 4.398–455; cf. Arist. *Hist. an.* 2.1.498a31–b4) as well as destructive, sharp-clawed, violent (Oppian, *Hunting* 5.376–391; Lloyd Llewellyn-Jones and Sian Lewis, *The Culture of Animals in Antiquity: A Sourcebook with Commentaries* (London: Routledge, 2018), 407). Ariadne's despair was well-placed according to the scientific community, and Oppian would have recommended that she bludgeon them on the head.

50 Sen. *Suas.* 1.15.

Figure 2: Child's sarcophagus with *kētē*,
Ny Carlsberg Glyptotek Copenhagen; third century CE.

From the depths, the storm churns up savage whales (*saevas pristis*) and
watery dogs (*aequoreosque canes*), those very sea monsters (*marinis feris*) who
wait in the waves to mangle storm-tossed sailors. In Albinovanus Pedo's
imagination, the storm and predatory sea creatures are inextricable.
Together they pose hazards greater than their individual intensities.

Among other functions (disaster, idyllic peace controlled by Nereids
and other sea gods), *kētē* cause death, and they might accompany those
who have died. Moaning balefully, *kētē* mourn with Thetis after the death
of Achilles at Troy,[51] howling together with the Nereids who shriek like
cranes which were, in turn, thought to portend great storms (ὀσσομένης
μέγα χεῖμα).[52] *Kētē* in fact appear after the Nereids' crane-like wails
presage a storm of maritime mourners. In Seneca's *Phaedra*, Theseus,
moreover, fantasizes that sea monsters (*ponti monstra*) would usher
him to his own death, dragging him down into the deep whirlpools.[53]
Achilles and Theseus are both the sons of maritime deities, and it is
appropriate that *kētē*, whether benign or threatening, would serve as
their *psychopompoi*. Scylla, the shark-woman whose cave faces Erebos,

---

51 Quintus Smyrnaeus, *Fall of Troy* 3.591–592.
52 3.591.
53 Sen. *Phaedra* 1204–1206.

the darkness of night, furthermore, was conceived as a guardian of the underworld.[54]

Scenes of Jonah and the whale and other *kētē* were consequently common on sarcophagi, underscoring both the horrors of travel by water (where sea-dragons threaten ships) and the sea as a utopia of timeless enjoyment (where Nereids flirt and frolic with handsome human-bull-fish *kētē*).[55] The terrors of sea travel are shown on a third-century CE child's sarcophagus from Rome where two symmetrical sea-dragons swim in rough waters (Figure 2). One *kētos*, facing right, has already started to swallow a sailor who has fallen from the rightward ship into the water; another *kētos*, facing left, awaits at the leftward ship where a crewman tries to prevent another from falling into the deep. Opportunistically coming upon a fleet caught in a gale, the *kētē* find the conditions ideal for hunting.

54 Hom. *Od.* 12.81; cf. Hes. *Theog.* 123; Stat. *Silv.* 5.3.280; Stat. *Theb.* 4.533; Verg. *Aen.* 6.286.

55 Zanker and Ewald, *Living with Myths*, 112–122. The sea as a place of timeless enjoyment – a type that becomes especially prevalent in the third century CE – is featured, for example, on a sarcophagus in the Archaeological Museum, Naples (240 CE). A brace of symmetrical horned sea-centaurs together with Nereids accompany a deceased woman playing a lyre, as her cloak billows above her head like a sail. The waves below are swirling beneath them, but the danger is not imminent (see Illustration 100 in Zanker and Ewald, *Living with Myths*, 115). Such marine *thiasoi* (revellers celebrating a god) are embellished with cupids (a symbol of erotic love), shells (evoking Venus and her birth from the sea), and Nereids personalized to resemble the deceased.

Squall and *kētē* – summoned from their deep lair by the roiling, stormy waters – together threaten the fleet with catastrophe.

Mythical Sea Monsters

Sea monsters are richly represented in ancient artwork. Dwelling in the liminal, chaotic sphere of deep water, a boundary between the human and divine spheres, between life and death,[56] sea monsters of myth and legend were also vanquished by gods and heroes in quests to subdue the chaotic forces of the sea and thereby establish human order in the maritime world, at least symbolically, and control over it.

Typhoeus

The monstrous son of Gaia and Tartarus, the primordial edge of creation beneath the earth,[57] Typhoeus was a flame-breathing, serpentine monster with one hundred snaky, flaming heads emerging from his shoulders, from each of which came indescribable sounds which ranged from the bellowing of a bull, roar of a lion, yapping of puppies, or a whistle through a mountain pass. Typhoeus is the prototype for the sea monsters that we have already encountered: part fish, part bull or lion, sometimes winged (Figure 3). Typhoeus becomes the storm at sea that is in turn vanquished by a storm from the sky, vividly recounted in both Hesiod and Nonnus.[58] In Hesiod, Zeus thunders as he casts lightning bolts that generate scorching winds while Typhoeus' fire permeates the sea. The fiery clashes result in long waves that crash back and forth, as land and sky and underworld seethe and groan and the earth melts. Zeus is victorious, and Typhoeus becomes a storm at sea: the watery force of tossing winds that scatter ships and destroy sailors according to the season.[59] This storminess is enhanced by the wings depicted on our black-figure Typhoeus. In Nonnus, Zeus employs a combination of fire-storms and ice-storms to defeat Typhoeus. Zeus rains on his adversary, and he attacks Typhoeus with rocky clumps of hail. Zeus meets Typhoeus' slings of storm-swift rocks with his thunderbolts, sending the monster's projectiles back along stormy paths that rifle and bounce. Typhoeus suffers further onslaught from the four

56 Beaulieu, *Greek Imagination*, 2016.
57 Hes. *Theog.* 820–880.
58 Nonnus, *Dionysiaca* 2.364–564.
59 Hes. *Theog.* 875–876.

Figure 3: Zeus and Typhoeus, Attic black-figure vase.

winds, Zeus' allies. The beast is pelted by frosty whirlwinds from Euros (East Wind), hot winds from Zephyrus (West Wind) and Notus (South Wind), and jagged hail-stones from Boreas (North Wind) that pierce the monster's bruised body. In the end, Typhoeus is buried under a Sicilian mountain, consequently becoming the force that fuels volcanic, fiery, stormy Aetna.[60] Typhoeus is a maritime entity who poses a real threat to coastal communities and those who sail, a source of volcanic eruptions, earthquakes, and tsunamis. The story of Typhoeus' demise establishes Zeus' superiority over the sea and the primal forces represented by the earlier divine generations. Although Typhoeus continues to threaten land-based humanity, his potential to effect real catastrophe has been mitigated by the god of land-based *polis* civilization. Land has conquered the sea, at least on a divine level.

The Trojan Kētos
In addition to Typhoeus, the sea monster who literally causes storms at sea, *kētē* are sent to punish the *hybris* of mortals. When, for example, King Laomedon of Troy refuses to render payment for the divinely built impenetrable walls of Troy, Apollo sends a plague and Poseidon sends a sea monster who causes floodtides, destroys the crops, and snatches victims from the plains.[61] In Diodorus, Apollo's oracle advises the sacrifice

---

60 Pseudo-Apollodorus, *Library* 1.6.
61 Diod. Sic. 4.42; Ov. *Met.* 11.211–215; Pseudo-Apollodorus, *Bibliotheca* 2.103; Pseudo-Hyginus, *Fabulae* 89.

of a child (the king's daughter, Hesione, selected by lot) to appease the monster's hunger. The beast was graphically rendered in an ancient painting (now lost):[62] of incredulous size, the *kētos* has large eyes with an encircling glare, an overhanging brow covered with spines, and a sharp projecting snout with jagged teeth in a triple row,[63] and it creates storms with its motion, splashing loudly, raising waves with the force of its surges, dashing against the shore, and thrashing the sea far-aloft with its tail. Valerius Flaccus, moreover, vividly recounts the storm created by the *kētos'* movements:[64] on Neptune's mark, the beast emerges from his lair in the Sigean Gulf, heaping up the waters. Its mouth – with its triple row of pronged teeth – shakes with thunderous crashes, while its lofty neck snatches up the suffering bay. The serpentine neck presses forward through the sea with a thousand coils, and the very storm of its own creation (*sua hiemps*) drives the beast onward, rushing toward the agitated shores. It is a weather event more violent than those emanating from the cloud-bearing Notus and Africus. Hercules agrees to fight the *kētos* and save the princess Hesione, Laomedon's daughter, a sacrifice to the monster. Hercules fights not a *kētos* but a storm, comprised of a sea that had been moved from its foundation and the "ample coils of the lofty beast."[65] Sea, monster, and storm are one. Together they are compared with the Boreas as the storm is lifted from the chilly Hebrus River (Devoll in Albania). Like Zeus against Typhoeus, Hercules must fight the storm with a storm, that is to say with the "entire *cloud* of his quiver" (*totaque pharetrae* nube),[66] whose effect is compared with the rains that erode the great Eryx Mountain in Sicily. Hercules then abandons his arrows for rocks that had been loosened by the winds and storm-tossed sea until the beast is laid low in the shoals.[67] The sea monster, ironically, is defeated by the very storm that it had created.[68]

---

62 Philostr. *Imagines* 12.

63 Aristotle ascribed a triple row of teeth to "martichoras," striped, blue-eyed man-eaters that resemble lions in size and paws, but men in face and ears, with scorpion-like tails complete with stingers and spines (*Hist. an.* 2.3.501a27–28). But the literary sources are silent on the arrangement of shark teeth (Irby, *Watery World*, 218n20).

64 Valerius Flaccus 2.497–508.

65 2.515.

66 2.521–522.

67 2.528–530.

68 Hercules' conquest of the Trojan sea-dragon is repeated in Aithiopia where Perseus slays a *kētos* to save Andromeda, the beautiful princess, whose mother foolishly boasted that she was more beautiful than the Nereids (Ovid, *Metamorphoses* 4.687; Pseudo-Apollodorus, *Library* 2.43; Pseudo-Hyginus, *Fabulae* 64). Literary and

Poseidon's Ophiotaurus

Another stormy sea monster is sent by Poseidon, not to punish an act of *hybris* but at the request of his son Theseus. Poseidon's sea-bull emerges from the water to destroy Hippolytus, the boy who refuses to worship Aphrodite and whose devotion to the virginal Artemis is excessive. For this, Aphrodite punishes the youth with the unwelcome sexual advances of his step-mother, Phaedra, a princess of Crete, the land of bulls (animals that are also sacred to Poseidon). Hippolytus is then unjustly accused of trying to seduce Phaedra. Theseus demands vengeance, and Poseidon complies with a monster that emerges from the surf, frightening Hippolytus' horses. Caught up in the tack, Hippolytus is dragged to his death. In Seneca, the monster is explicitly born from a tidal wave. The monster is the storm: "its own storm [*propria tempestas*] drives the calm sea [*placidumque pelagus*]."[69] Seneca recounts the floodtide coming to land: the sea thunders, swelling towards the stars (*subito vastum tonuit ex alto mare crevitque in astra*),[70] raging more powerfully than the south wind in the Messenian Strait and the northwestern winds in the Ionian Gulf, when rocks quake in response to the waves and the white foam that strikes the summit of lofty Leucate (*saxa cum fluctu tremunt et cana summum spuma Leucaten ferit*).[71] In Seneca, the enormous sea swells and threatens the land as a huge mass of water. The surge rolls forth, pregnant (*gravis*) with the monster in its fold. The sea resounds and the cliffs boom as the monster emerges from the sea, dripping brine from its crest as it foams and spews water (like a spouting whale). Seneca also preserves the ophiotaurus' moment of birth: as the sphere of water bristles and breaks open, conveying to the shore an evil greater than terror. "The sea rushes to the lands and its own monster follows" – Poseidon's ophiotaurus, a snorting beast with a blue neck, a crest on its green forehead, bristling ears, and flame-darting eyes. Seaweed drips from its dewlaps and chest, and the scaly creature drags a huge "tail such as could smash boats in the distant sea."[72] The monster that destroys Hippolytus is literally a child of the sea, emerging from the

---

artistic accounts emphasize the love story, not the monster's storminess. Hercules fights a tempest; Perseus rescues a maiden.

69 Sen. *Phaedra* 1010.

70 1007–1008.

71 1013–1014.

72 1035–1049. See Kenneth F. Kitchell, *Animals in the Ancient World from A to Z* (London: Routledge, 2014), 199; Gottfried J. Mader, "'Ut pictura poesis:' Sea-Bull and Senecan Baroque (Phaedra 1035–49)," *Classica et Mediaevalia* 53 (2002): 289–300. Cf. Eur. *Hipp.* 415, 1210–1212 and Ov. *Met.* 15.11–13, where the sea-bull is presented more impressionistically. Cf. Irby, *Watery World*, 152.

depths, born from a storm. Here, as Ariadne had feared, the sea invades the coast, bringing catastrophe to bear.

Scylla *and* Charybdis

Sea monsters are also associated with maritime phenomena. Naturally occurring where contrary currents meet or where tides affect the fast currents of waters in narrow straits, whirlpools are stormy hazards for sailors at sea. The narrow Messina Strait, between Italy and Sicily, is particularly dangerous, posing a double peril for sailors: the Mediterranean's most famous whirlpool (Charybdis) together with the Mediterranean's most famous sea monster (Scylla).

Charybdis is a common catastrophic feature in myth,[73] spewing water and flames whenever Typhoeus switches his position beneath Mount Aetna. Pindar explains the phenomenon: water surges up through interconnected subterranean cavities because the entire strait is inflamed.[74] Charybdis spews and swallows her whirling waves, causing ships to sink. In Homer, she boils and swirls "like a cauldron set on a great fire,"[75] a paradoxical image of water and fire, whose opposite effects instead result in even greater catastrophe. In Vergil, Aeneas' crew experience first-hand the frightening roller-coaster effect of the whirlpool: "we were lifted into the sky on a curved stream, then we sank down to deepest Hades on the wave removed from underneath."[76] Charybdis seethes and roars incessantly while the seas boom against the rocks. It is a terrifying phenomenon, a destructive fire-storm exacerbated by storm surges and the south wind.[77]

Nearby dwells Scylla, the once-beautiful girl punished either by a jealous Amphitrite for catching Poseidon's eye,[78] or by Circe for attracting Glaucus, whom Circe loved.[79] The monster has the torso of a beautiful woman, but six dog torsos (water-dogs, sharks) also emanate from her belly. Scylla is the shark-woman, with "teeth in three rows,"[80] a sea monster who preys on sailors like those on our Geometric crater (Figure 5), a nautical beast whom the heroes of Greek and Roman myth and

---

73 Hom. *Od.* 12.104–105; Strabo 1.2.16, 36; Verg. *Aen.* 3.420–423.

74 Pind. *Pyth.* 1.15–28.

75 Hom. *Od.* 12.237–238; cf. Ov. *Met.* 7.62–65.

76 Verg. *Aen.* 3.564–565: *tollimur in caelum curvato gurgite, et idem / subducta ad Manis imos desedimus unda.* The imagery seems to anticipate the roller-coaster effect of Lucian's whale.

77 Hom. *Od.* 12.426–428.

78 Scholia Tzetzes, *On Lycophron* 650; Servius, *On Aeneid* 3.420.

79 Ov. *Met.* 13.900–968; Pseudo-Hyginus, *Fabulae* 199.

80 Hom. *Od.* 12.85–100.

Figure 4: Scylla brandishing a ship's rudder, red-figure krater, *circa* 450–420 BCE. © RMN-Grand Palais / Art Resource, NY.

legend must avoid.[81] Although Scylla is not the storm or the cause of it (in fact her cave is halfway up the sheer cliff that blocks the sky),[82] she is the opportunistic hunter who preys on the victims of catastrophe, those dislodged by the stormy Charybdis and the dangerous strait where two seas meet.[83] She "fishes there for dolphins or dogfish, or whatever larger fish she could take."[84] In artwork, however, Scylla is very much the destroyer of ships, brandishing a rudder like a club (Figure 4), an

81 Odysseus: Hom. *Od.* 12.54ff., 210–259; Lycoph. *Alexandra* 648ff.; Jason: Ap. Rhod. *Argon.* 4.825–832, 922; Ov. *Her.* 12.123–124; and Aeneas: Ov. *Met.* 14.44; Verg. *Aen.* 3.420–425.
82 Hom. *Od.* 12.76.
83 Ap. Rhod. *Argon.* 4.921.
84 Hom. *Od.* 12.95–97; cf. Strabo 1.2.14.

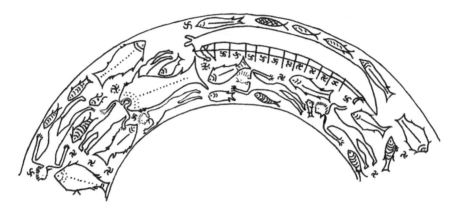

Figure 5: Sharks prey on shipwrecked sailors, Geometric crater, Ischia: Museo Archeologico, Pithekoussai 618813, as drawn by Georgia Irby.

image that Pompey's son and avenger, Sextus, would employ in 36 BCE to emphasize his own nautical superiority over his enemies.[85] Scylla's myth and form are inspired by the same sea creatures that provide the raw material of the more familiar types, and she becomes not only a metaphor for catastrophe at sea but also a foil for dangerous women.[86] The real threat to mariners at the Strait of Messina is transformed into a brace of sea monsters: one is a storm, the other is a predator who hunts under the protection of storms.

Sea Monsters as Metonymic Storms at Sea

Lucian's *kētos* is also a cataclysmic storm, and, despite the satirical exaggeration, Lucian's account parallels the historical observations and experiences of Greek and Roman blue-water sailors. Pliny describes whales in the Gallic Ocean (Atlantic) as "rearing up higher than a ship's rigging and disgorging a flood."[87] The storm, the flood, occurs owing to the whale's immense size.

85 Kathryn Welch, "Both Sides of the Coin: Sextus Pompeius and the So-Called *Pompeiani*," in *Sextus Pompeius*, ed. Anton Powell and Kathryn Welch (London: The Classical Press of Wales and Duckworth, 2002), 1–30.

86 For example, Clytemnestra (Aesch. *Ag.* 1233–1234) and Medea (Eur. *Med.* 1343).

87 Plin. *HN* 9.8; cf. Strabo 3.2.7. Pliny's whales may have been fin whales (averaging 20 metres in length, the second-largest cetacean): see Irby, *Watery World*, 137; cf. Arist. *Hist. an.* 3.12.519a23–25; Llewellyn-Jones and Lewis, *Culture of Animals*, 419–420.

Dread of the unknown deep and its sea-monster inhabitants was borne out by the real-life experiences of sailors who fell overboard during storms. For example, after a storm and shipwreck, two men, Antagoras and Pisistratus, fought over a single plank. Antagoras survived after pushing Pisistratus into the water. Pisistratus was then seized by a shark.[88] Pisistratus' shark was churned up by the storm that had wrecked the ship, and other sharks are churned by other storms that wreck other ships, as shown on a Geometric krater (Figure 5) where six shipwrecked sailors are hunted by a horde of predatory fishes: one victim has lost an arm, another is swallowed head-first, and still others try to escape.[89]

These large marine creatures were indistinguishable from catastrophic storms at sea, and ancient thinkers believed that the largest of them emerged from the Erythraean Sea (the Red Sea together with the Gulf of Aden and the northern Indian Ocean) at the solstices when violent whirlwinds and rainstorms (*tunc illic ruunt turbines, tunc imbres*) churned up the sea beds and brought the monsters to the surface (*vertunt maria pulsatasque ex profundo beluas cum fluctibus volvunt tanta*).[90] Oppian records the exaggerated dimensions of maritime creatures in the Erythraean Sea, dimensions that defy credibility: whales (*ballaenae*) of four *iugera* (about three acres), sharks (*pristes*) of 100 cubits (150 feet [46 metres]), and lobsters (*locustae*) of four cubits (six feet [about two metres]).[91] Such creatures are largely restricted to the ocean's floor owing to their bulk and weight, so it was thought, perhaps because sightings were rare. Nonetheless, in the Persian Gulf in 325 BCE, the crew of Alexander's admiral Nearchus encountered very large marine animals (25 *orguiae* [150 feet = 46 metres]) whose spray generated "great streams and a large body of mist from their eruptions, so that they could not see the area in front of them."[92] And they

88 Antipater of Thessalonica, *Greek Anthology* 9.269.
89 Ischia: Museo Archeologico, Pithekoussai 618813; John Boardman, *Early Greek Vase Painting, 11th–6th Centuries BC: A Handbook* (London: Thames & Hudson, 1998), Figure 161; Llewellyn-Jones and Lewis, *Culture of Animals*, 674. Under excavation since 2012, a mosaic floor at the synagogue at Huqoq, three miles west of the Sea of Galilee, shows several biblical scenes, including the story of Jonah who is swallowed by a fish. On the mosaic, the prophet's fish is swallowed by a larger one, in turn swallowed by yet a larger fish: see Kristen Romney, "Man-Eating Fish, Tower of Babel Revealed on Ancient Mosaic: Archaeologists Discover Even More Remarkable Biblical Scenes on the Floor of a 1,600-Year-Old Synagogue in Israel," *National Geographic* (15 November 2018): https://www.nationalgeographic.com/culture/2018/11/jonah-tower-babel-huqoq-ancient-synagogue-mosaic/.
90 Plin. *HN* 9.4–5.
91 Oppian, *Fishing* 5.46–49.
92 Strabo 15.2.12.

were terrified, despairing for their lives and imagining a violent death as the ships would be smashed by the incredibly large creatures.[93] The crew were handicapped as if in a storm, blinded by spouting and breeching whales. In order to repel the *kētē*, Nearchus and his crew created their own storm through noise and the violent displacement of water. They shouted, splashed their oars, and raised a clangor with their war trumpets, thus sending the pod back to the depths.[94]

Conclusion

Nearchus' crew could see the whales that appeared to threaten their fleet. That such prodigiously frightening creatures existed at all prompted the belief that even more terrible *kētē* might lurk beneath the surface, especially in turbulent waters where disaster and death seemed imminent. Sea monsters corporealize the real fear of the unknown watery depths. Sea monsters are born from storms, they create storms, and they utilize the cover of storms to hunt. Sea monsters, real and fabricated, inspire angst. Pirate ships, for example, might be rigged to look like *kētē* in order to strike greater terror into their victims: one such ship was brightly painted with grim eyes at the prow and a stern curving up into a thin crescent of a fish-tail.[95] But, unlike storms, sea monsters can be defeated. As such, *kētē* serve as the ultimate avatars of raw (oceanic) nature through which gods, heroes, and even regular folk could conquer and control the environment.[96]

The sea, however, was the natural environment of *kētē*, not human beings. As much as people tried to control the sea, they inevitably failed. Just as people hunted to destruction dangerous beasts who encroached

---

93　Diod. Sic. 17.106.6–7.

94　17.106.6–7; Arr. *Indika* 30; Plin. *HN* 2.5; cf. Strabo 3.2.7. Nearchus' whales were possibly blue whales (*Balaenoptera musculus*, ca 80 feet [25 metres]) or sperm whales (ca 65 feet [20 metres]): both species are native to the Erythraean Sea. Whales were also observed off Britain (Juv. 10.14) and in the Atlantic (Ausonius, *Mosella* 144–149). Mosella's whale was gentle compared to the typical Atlantic whales, which would displace large quantities of water and whose crests could block out the mountains. Their victory, like historical hunts of large sea creatures, was viewed as heroic: cf. Ael. *Nature of Animals* 13.6; Plin. *HN* 9.93; Llewellyn-Jones and Lewis, *Culture of Animals*, 678–679.

95　Philostr. *Imag.* 1.19.

96　See Ael. *Nature of Animals* 13.6; Plin. *HN* 9.93; Procop. *History of the Wars* 7.29.9–16; Irby, *Watery World*, 138–139, 143.

into human territory (for example, the Bull of Marathon, Calydonian Bull, and Geryon), sea monsters in their turn hunted and destroyed sailors who invaded the sea. The sea fostered sea monsters, and it was also the realm of sea gods: Poseidon, Proteus, Nereus, Amphitrite, her Nereid sisters, and others. Sea monsters accompanied Poseidon, and they attended the Nereids, as pets, as mounts, as honour guards. Human incursion into deep water was thus a violation of divine space, sacred spheres, forbidden territories, and stormy sea monsters thus exercised their prerogative to protect their domain by churning up storms and dislodging invaders from their realm.

CHAPTER SEVEN

Order among Disorder: Poseidon's Underwater Kingdom and Utopic Marine Environments

Ryan Denson

Introduction

The notion that there were any mythical abodes imagined in a submarine setting by ancient writers has, until recently, typically only been mentioned in passing by classicists. Scholars interested in mythological, utopic spaces of Greco-Roman antiquity have conventionally concentrated upon the terrestrial variety, such as the Ethiopians' and the Hyperboreans'. Ferguson, for instance, commenced his monograph on the subject with a chapter on the "Homeric beginnings" of such depictions, assessing the Homeric councils of the mortal heroes and Olympian gods as well as the society of the blameless Ethiopians.[1] Ferguson's expansive approach to ancient utopias considered utopianism as generally the idealization of values, pointing to the Homeric depiction of the Phaeacians as an idealization of a benevolent monarchy.[2] Yet even this wide-ranging consideration of ancient utopianism did not take notice of these underwater spaces. Scholarship on the ancient sea has conventionally overlooked this motif. It receives, for instance, only a passing mention in Lesky's monograph on the

I would like to thank the editors, Hamish Williams and Ross Clare, for graciously inviting me to contribute to this innovative volume. My gratitude also goes to Daniel Ogden for providing much helpful feedback on an earlier draft of this chapter.

  1 John Ferguson, *Utopias of the Classical World* (London: Thames and Hudson, 1975), 9–15. See also, Moses Finley, "Utopianism Ancient and Modern," in *The Critical Spirit: Essays in Honor of Herbert Marcuse*, ed. Kurt H. Wolff and Barrington Moore (Boston: Beacon Press, 1967), 6–12; James Romm, *The Edges of the Earth in Ancient Thought* (Princeton, NJ: Princeton University Press, 1992), 45–77 (esp. 49–54).

  2 Ferguson, *Utopias*, 14–15. On the subject of paradisiacal narratives, Ferguson seems to have deemed those as also a subset of ancient utopianism (146–147).

ancient Greek sea,³ though, more recently, Beaulieu has called attention to the topic with regard to the two myths of katapontic journeys.⁴ Otherwise, scholarly mentions of these underwater spaces have been relegated to passages of the modern commentaries on the key Homeric and Hesiodic passages or to scholarship on Bacchylides' seventeenth Ode. There is, perhaps, valid reason for the scattered and piecemeal nature of modern scholarship on the topic as, unlike the terrestrial utopias, ancient texts seldomly glance downwards at the underwater world. After Homer, the depictions of the utopic Ethiopians found a variety of other expressions, from Herodotus' tales about them as an extremely prosperous culture to Heliodorus' substantial portrayal of Ethiopia as the final destination for his protagonists.⁵ By contrast, Poseidon's underwater palace never became the major setting of any extant ancient Greek novel, nor did it ever receive any elaborate literary embellishments. The attribution of such a place to Poseidon has presumably seemed to many as merely a generic extension of the notion that many deities had specific abodes of their own, with that of the sea god appropriately being constructed in a submarine setting.

This chapter, then, intends to foreground these otherwise underappreciated depictions of utopic underwater spaces. "Utopic" here denotes a general idealization of a human-like world that is typically suffused with regal or paradisiacal imagery that, in turn, serves to elevate such a space as superior to the "normal" world. Furthermore, there are many similarities with the underworld in terms of katabatic (or better, katapontic) journeys, and the latter imagery serves to mark these spaces as specifically utopic. It will be shown that this motif habitually revolves around notions of marine divinities. It is not, however, that divinity is itself necessarily utopic but, rather, that notions of divine figures furnished the ancients with the only means to imagine such spaces within the underwater world; implicit notions of divine order play a substantial role in the characterization of these spaces as utopic within the usually chaotic and disordered sea. We can begin by establishing a conceptual similarity between marine utopic spaces and their terrestrial counterparts. Both are similar in terms of their spatial distance and separation from the "inhabited world" of

3 Albin Lesky, *Thalatta: Der Weg der Griechen zum Meer* (Vienna: Arno Press, 1947), 132–133.

4 Marie-Claire Beaulieu, *The Sea in the Greek Imagination* (Philadelphia: University of Pennsylvania Press, 2015), 71–79, 135–137. Beaulieu's analysis concerns primarily elements of this motif in Bacchylides and the myth of Enalus in contrast to the wider survey of the topic in this chapter.

5 Hdt. 3.23–25; Heliodorus, *Aethiopica* 10.5.

the *oikoumenē*, which Romm has shown to signify something akin to the "familiar world," the realm of daily life.[6] The mythical utopian societies of the Hyperboreans and Ethiopians are unseen by and unacquainted with the peoples of the *oikoumenē* (that is, the portions of Africa, Asia, and Europe perceived to be in contact with the Mediterranean world) by virtue of being located in the extreme north and south, respectively. Such a distance along a horizontal plane can, then, also be expressed along a vertical axis with imagined realms being distinguished from the *oikoumenē* by being below it, a common trait shared by both the underworld and the depths of the sea.[7] Such imagined spaces flourished in antiquity along the vertical axis in the other direction as well, as with the dwellings of the gods atop Mount Olympus and the occasional utopic expressions regarding the Moon.[8]

The surface of the sea floor, no more accessible for the ancients than the lunar surface, afforded an isolated location onto which one could fashion an imaginative space.[9] Relative to this marine context, the *oikoumenē* can best be considered as the sea's surface, the space frequented by mortal sailors. The depths of the sea, however, were generally imagined in literary contexts as the preserve of the divine, a reflection of the impossibility of ancient, deep-sea exploration. Such a disparity between the actual human experiences of the sea and imagined experiences of the divine, however, did not necessitate a complete disconnect between the two spheres; rather, ancient authors, clearly aware of this vertical dimension of the sea, projected into it a utopia, familiar in many ways to their world.

---

6 Romm, *The Edges of the Earth*, 37n73, 53–55.

7 On this vertical axis of the sea and allusions to the underworld, see Beaulieu, *Greek Imagination*, 26–32.

8 On the former, especially comparing Bellerophon's failed anabasis to Olympus with Theseus' katabasis, see Alexandros Kampakoglou, "Crossing Boundaries in Bacchylides 17," in *Vivre et penser les frontières dans le monde méditerranéen antique: Actes du colloque tenu à l'Université Paris-Sorbonne, les 29 et 30 juin 2013*, ed. Hugues Berthelot (Bordeaux: Ausonius, 2016), 149–150. On the latter, see Karen ní Mheallaigh, *The Moon in the Greek and Roman Imagination: Myth, Literature, Science, and Philosophy* (Cambridge: Cambridge University Press, 2020), 194–197. More generally, vertical aspects have been considered also in the context of *loci sublimes*, especially as the Greek term typically used for the sea's depths, *bathos*, can equally be utilized with reference to astral bodies; on which, see James Porter, *The Sublime in Antiquity* (Cambridge: Cambridge University Press, 2016), 531–536n452.

9 The exception to this is, of course, the shallow areas around coastlines, where ancient divers sought out pearls and sponge; on which, see Frank Frost, "Scyllias: Diving in Antiquity," *Greece & Rome* 15, no. 2 (1968), 180–185.

The first part of this chapter begins by tracing a history of the scant ancient references to such underwater spaces. Similar to the utopian Ethiopians, the underwater palace of Poseidon has a Homeric beginning, though this marine *locus amoenus* develops along a different trajectory, becoming more closely associated with other marine divinities in later texts, and even referenced as a kingdom in a pair of Latin texts. The second part addresses the katapontic journeys of Theseus and Enalus, myths equally as rare, but which, nevertheless, offer a better understanding of the ancient underwater world being imagined as a dimension typically only ventured into with the aid of divinity.

Ancient Underwater Abodes and Populating Poseidon's Palace

The earliest reference to such an underwater space associated with Poseidon comes in a fleeting mention from the *Iliad*: "Three times he [Poseidon] stretched out and on the fourth stride he came to his goal, Aegae, and there was built his famed golden palace [*dōmata*] in the depths of the sea, always gleaming and imperishable."[10] The subsequent lines portray Poseidon's journey across the water as sea monsters (*kētē*) frolic around him,[11] a scene that inspired later literary depictions.[12] Some of these later portrayals have him accompanied by other marine deities, though all omit any reference to an underwater space. The poet of the *Odyssey* includes an even more succinct mention of this space when Poseidon, returning from Ethiopia, travels there after having stirred up a storm against Odysseus: "So he spoke as he lashed his beautiful-maned horses, and he came to Aegae, where is his famed palace [*dōmat'*]."[13] This underwater palace has long been recognized as recalling the generic, appropriate spaces for the gods, such as Hephaestus' own golden and imperishable palace.[14] Descriptions of the palace of Hades in

10 Hom. *Il.* 13.20–23. Unless otherwise noted, all translations are my own. Here and elsewhere, I interpret the plural form *dōmata* as a poetic plural. While the notion is also sometimes expressed in the singular, there is never any clear indication of multiple structures being imagined.

11 13.24–38.

12 Ael. *On the Nature of Animals* 14.28; Philostr. *Imag.* 1.8; Quintus Smyrnaeus, 5.88–96; Stat. *Achil.* 1.52–60; Verg. *Aen.* 5.816–826. For further discussion of this motif, see Georgia Irby's paper in this volume.

13 Hom. *Od.* 5.381–382.

14 Hom. *Il.* 14.238, 18.370. See, for instance, Richard Janko, *The Iliad: A Commentary. Volume IV: Books 13–16* (Cambridge: Cambridge University Press, 1994), 14.

the underworld and those of the gods on Mount Olympus are generally phrased in like manner.[15] This was evidently recognized by ancient commentators as well. One scholium on these Iliadic lines, attributed to Aristonicus, remarks that, like the dwellings of the gods on Olympus, it is a place "unseen to humans."[16] These two brief references furnish the only glimpses of Poseidon's underwater palace in Homer as a place that the sea god alone is depicted as travelling to. Yet its location specifically within the sea draws an implicit contrast with the surrounding environment. The sea is, of course, an element elsewhere known for its catastrophic and fluctuating nature. Although journeys across the sea were acknowledged as being perilous and fraught with uncertainty for humans, this is not so for Poseidon, for whom the sea itself jubilantly parts.[17] In a similar manner, travelling along the sea's vertical axis and dwelling within its depths pose no difficulty for divinities as compared to mortals. Thus, the underwater palace, being "always gleaming and imperishable," is another expression, within an impossible location, of the sea god's mastery and control over this element.

In the world of the *Iliad*, Poseidon is not the only marine divinity depicted as dwelling in some underwater location. At one point, Thetis is said to reside alongside her father at some non-specified location within the depths of the sea,[18] while another Iliadic passage has Iris diving down to the depths to visit Thetis, where we are told that she and her sisters are found "in a hollow cave."[19] Some such cave is also referenced in *Iliad* 18 following the catalogue of the Nereids:

> But he [Achilles] groaned aloud terribly, and his queenly mother, seated in the depths of the sea next to the old man her father, heard him. Thereafter, she shrieked aloud and all the goddesses, the Nereids down in the depths of the sea, gathered around her [...]. And with them the silver-shining cave was filled.[20]

---

15 Hom. *Il.* 2.13, 12.21. It is in such divine contexts, particularly with such places often being referenced as "golden" in nature, that the term *dōma*, elsewhere a generic term for a "house" or "dwelling" (*A Greek–English Lexicon*, ninth edition (1968), s.v. "δῶμα"), has generally been translated as the more regal "palace."

16 Aristonicus, ad loc., in Harmut Erbse, ed., *Scholia Graeca in Homeri Iliadem (scholia vetera)*, Volume 5 (Berlin: De Gruyter, 1974), 399.

17 Hom. *Il.* 13.29.

18 1.357–358.

19 24.80–84.

20 18.33–38, 49–51.

The silvery quality of the Nereids' cave is perhaps generically similar to the shimmering and golden nature of Poseidon's palace,[21] and the element of luminescence with the Nereids will be seen again with Theseus' katapontic journey. This passage also offers an early, though brief, instance of the phenomenon of an interaction between the surface world and the depths as Achilles' grief is perceived by Thetis, whose own cry of anguish parallels that of her son. The final significant reference to this habitat of the Nereids also occurs in *Iliad* 18. Thetis tells her sister Nereids to go to Nereus, specifying their destination as the "palace of our father [*dōmata patros*],"[22] seemingly implying that Nereus has his own underwater palace as well (or at least, this is how the cave of the Nereids is expressed in these lines).

The cave or the *dōmata*, whatever the case may be, of the Nereids and Nereus is never expressed in the same terms as the palace of Poseidon in *Iliad* 13, nor is there ever any indication of a connection between these two *loci* in Homer. We have sufficient reason to suspect that these abodes of marine divinities were separate from each other in Homer. As with the Iliadic scene of Poseidon's journey across the sea, he is accompanied only by the *kētē*, and it is only in the later instantiations of the scene (for example, in Vergil and Statius) that more marine divinities come to be accumulated around Poseidon/Neptune. Likewise, while Poseidon in later centuries was also known for having the Nereid Amphitrite as his wife, Larson has recently argued that the Homeric Poseidon did not have a wife since Amphitrite is absent from the catalogue of the Nereids in the *Iliad*, and the *Odyssey* poet uses the name *Amphitrite* only to personify the sea itself, not in reference to a fully anthropomorphic goddess.[23] Just as the god himself has not yet been tied to other marine divinities, I would assert that the Homeric incarnation of Poseidon's palace as a utopic space has not yet been imagined as linked to the other marine figures.

The ensuing stage in the development of Poseidon's underwater palace, however, substantially alters its aspect as exclusive to the sea god alone. It comes, crucially, alongside a development that Larson has shown to be central to the conception of Amphitrite as the wife of Poseidon.

21   Moreover, just as Poseidon wears golden raiment (13.25–26), similar to his palace, the silvery quality of divine female figures can be seen elsewhere in connection to the Nereids with the term "silver-footed" as an epithet for Thetis at 1.538 and elsewhere.

22   18.138–141.

23   Jennifer Larson, "Amphitrite in and out of the Olympian Pantheon," *Les Études Classiques* 87, no. 1–3 (2019), 29–30. On Amphitrite as personifying the sea, see Hom. *Od.* 3.91, 5.422, 12.60, 12.97.

Amphitrite, finding herself now listed in the Hesiodic catalogue of the Nereids in the *Theogony*,[24] is explicitly accorded a place with Poseidon in his underwater palace: "And from Amphitrite and the loud-sounding Earthshaker was born great Triton of broad sway, who possesses the base of the sea [*thalassēs puthmen*]. An awe-inspiring [*deinos*] god, residing with his dear mother and father as lord, in the golden palace [*dō*]."[25] It should be noted that this passage comes from the latter portion of the *Theogony*, widely regarded as a later sixth-century addition, and, therefore, different from the work of the poet who first included Amphitrite in the Hesiodic catalogue of the Nereids.[26] Nevertheless, this passage remains the earliest reference to Poseidon's palace as inhabited by other marine divinities, and it seems through this appropriation of the Nereid Amphitrite as the wife of Poseidon that the Nereids as a collective become more associated with the sea god and, consequently, depicted as explicitly dwelling in Poseidon's underwater space. This passage of the *Theogony* is, moreover, noteworthy for being the earliest reference to Triton in a marine context. Triton is absent in Homer and, though elsewhere known as the son of Poseidon, seems to have had a more pervasive tradition in the ancient Greek world as a Libyan river/lake deity encountered by the Argonauts,[27] later becoming pluralized by the Hellenistic period. Here, Triton, as a singular deity, has been displaced from his more traditional habitat in Libya, coming instead to dwell at the "base of the sea," doubtlessly referring to the sea floor. This fashioning of a wife for Poseidon, along with the transferral of his son into the depths, presumably attempting to emulate the genealogical structure of the earlier portions of the poem, exerted a strong influence on later traditions, most prominently with the presence of Amphitrite, a key feature of Theseus' myth.

After Hesiod (or rather, after the author of the latter portion of the *Theogony*), there remain only scattered references to underwater dwellings in ancient literature from classical Greece to late antiquity (apart from our two katapontic myths, below). Much as with the Homeric and Hesiodic passages, these are characteristically succinct, offering only tantalizing glimpses of such an underwater world. The abode of Nereus is mentioned twice in Euripides' *Andromache* as the place where Thetis dwells.[28] From

24 Hes. *Theog.* 243; Larson, "Amphitrite," 30–31.
25 Hes. *Theog.* 930–933.
26 Martin West, *Hesiod. Theogony* (Oxford: Clarendon Press, 1966), 414–415.
27 The major literary instances of this occur at Ap. Rhod. *Argon.* 4.1547–1619; Hdt. 4.179–180; Pind. *Pyth.* 4.17–42.
28 Eur. *Andr.* 1231–1235, 1257–1258.

Euripides, though, also comes a much more interesting instance in which Poseidon alludes to this space, introducing himself at the start of *Trojan Women*: "I, Poseidon, have come from briny depths of the Aegean, where choruses [*choroi*] of Nereids move round with graceful footsteps."[29] The Homeric Aegae becomes more generalized as the Aegean Sea, but, more substantially, we can note these lines as the earliest instance of Poseidon coming from a place explicitly populated with the Nereids. Another passage comes from Apollonius of Rhodes' *Argonautica*: "So she spoke, and Iris immediately darted from Olympus and cut through the air, having fanned out her nimble wings. She plunged into the Aegean Sea, where the home [*domoi*] of Nereus is."[30] Thus, Apollonius also continues the tendency to locate such spaces generally in the Aegean, albeit attributing it to Nereus instead of Poseidon. These Euripidean and Apollonean references are essentially Homeric in form, functioning simply as a location ascribed as the departure or arrival point of some god or goddess (significantly, always with the same deities as the *Iliad* – Poseidon, Thetis, and Iris), yet these also contain occasional elements of later developments not found in the *Iliad*, such as the Nereids arranged as choruses (repeated in Bacchylides).

A trio of more creative, though no less brief, treatments of these underwater spaces come from late-antique literature. In one poem by Claudian (fl. fourth century AD), recounting the Gigantomachia, the attempt of the giant Porphyrion to uproot the island of Delos and hurl it into the sky precipitates a disturbance in the underwater realm: "The Aegean was frightened [*horruit Aegaeus*]; Thetis with her ancient father fled from their watery caves, and the palace of Neptune [*regia Neptuni*], revered by the handmaidens [*famulis*] of the depths, lay abandoned."[31] The emotive reaction of fear ascribed to the Aegean Sea itself serves as metonymy for the disturbance felt by its inhabitants. Claudian places the caves of the Nereids as alongside the palace of Neptune, seemingly implying a link between the two, especially with the reference to the *famulae* of the depths seeming to cast the Nereids as servants in this underwater utopia. Claudian elsewhere refers to this space, though not mentioning the Nereids, but rather Ino-Leukothea, a figure who was closely associated with the Nereids at times.[32] The journey of Venus across

29 Eur. *Trojan Women* 1–3.
30 Ap. Rhod. *Argon.* 4.770–773.
31 Claudian, *Gigantomachia* 117–119.
32 On instances of Ino-Leukothea associated with Nereids, see Callistratus, *Descriptions* 14; Pind. *Pyth.* 11.1–6; Sen. *Oedipus* 445–446 (discussed below). Nonnus' *Dionysiaca* offers two more brief references to her in the "dwelling [*oikon*] of Poseidon"

the surface of the water on the back of what he refers to as a Triton is complemented by a brief glance at the underwater world:

> The abode of Neptune [*Neptuni* (...) *domum*] is wreathed throughout. Leucothoe, the daughter of Cadmus, frolics, and Palaemon reins in dolphins with roses; Nereus sows violets alternatingly with sea-weed; Glaucus binds his grey hair with undying plants. Hearing the story, the Nereids also came, carried on various beasts.[33]

The floral imagery here is derived from the conception of this space in terms similar to a terrestrial sacred garden (*alsos*), a feature made explicit in Bacchylides.[34] The scene continues to describe the Nereids, and the marine beasts they ride (aquatic versions of a tiger, ram, lion, and calf), presumably having come from the underwater utopia, as they encircle Venus for several lines.[35] Nonnus (fl. fifth century AD), finally, provides us with one more noteworthy scene of Poseidon's palace:

> Meanwhile, the god, the lord of water, prepared himself for battle. And there was turmoil [*klonos*] among the Nereids. The damp deities came from the surface of the sea [*thalassaiōn apo nōtōn*] to assemble a battle array. The palace [*dōma*] of Poseidon, the water of the sea, was lashed with branching ivy clusters.[36]

Although it can generally refer to any state of confusion, *klonos* in this militaristic context more probably signifies a battle rout.[37] Just as the underwater palace of Poseidon is here creatively incorporated as one battlefield in the war with the forces of Dionysus, so too do we see the Nereids uniquely fashioned in terms appropriate to describe forces in battle.

While the above passages can be regarded as straightforward references to these underwater *loci*, owing to terms such as *dōma*, *domus*, and *regia*,

---

(9.80), and "in the court [*aulēs*] under the waves" (21.170). In a sense, we may regard Ino-Leukothea as similar to Theseus and Enalus as she was herself once a surface dweller, though her katapontic journey seems a permanent one. On her myth in general, see Beaulieu, *Greek Imagination*, 161–166.

33 Claudian, *Epithalamium dictum Honorio Augusto et Mariae* 155–156.

34 Significantly, floral imagery is not unknown with regard to other ancient utopic spaces such as the gardens around Alcinous' palace (Hom. *Od.* 7.112–132).

35 Claudian, *Epithalamium* 160–179.

36 Nonnus, *Dionysiaca* 43.34–39.

37 *A Greek–English Lexicon*, ninth edition (1968), s.v. "κλόνος." Cf. Nonnus, *Dionysiaca* 6.292, where the Nereids are arrayed in phalanxes.

there remain some instances in Latin literature where such an underwater space is alluded to in more subtle ways. In Seneca's *Oedipus*, in reference to Ino-Leukothea, we have the line *ponti regna tenet nitidi matertera Bacchi*, rendered in one translation as "the aunt of bright Bacchus rules the sea."[38] Yet I would assert that, in line with other instances of Ino-Leukothea as one inhabitant of the underwater palace, and the text's subsequent lines, we may better understand *ponti regna* as an explicit invocation of an underwater space:

> Ino, the daughter of Cadmus, aunt of shining Bacchus, occupies the kingdom of the sea [*ponti regna*] and she is encircled by a chorus of Nereids; an inexperienced boy, related to Bacchus, has power over the waves of the great sea, being no paltry divinity, Palaemon.[39]

Thus, we have another glimpse at this space, populated by this period with several marine deities, peculiarly phrased as a kingdom. A similar interpretation can also be put forth for the phrase *Neptunia regna* in Silius Italicus' *Punica*. This is rendered in the Loeb translation as "Neptune's realm,"[40] seeming to understand it as a mere poetic expression for the sea. The full context of the passage, however, reveals that it is referencing the underwater world specifically:

> And the kingdom of Neptune [*Neptunia regna*] was alarmed by the new storm. Then, the sea resounds with voices, and the echo of shouting reverberates from the cliffs [...]. The war-trumpets rattled with a terrible sound of violent air through the empty depths with an extensively echoing song. A Triton was disturbed, roused from the sea by the rumbling competing with that of his twisted conch-shell.[41]

We see, here, a substantial instance of the vertical aspect of the sea and its interaction with the surface, wherein the auditory disturbances of the chaotic battle between the Roman and Carthaginian fleets on the plane of the sea's surface impact the denizens of the deep, overwhelming the characteristic trumpeting of a Triton. Such a brief scene is illustrative of

---

38 Sen. *Oedipus* 445. Anthony Boyle, trans. and ed., *Seneca: Oedipus* (Oxford: Oxford University Press, 2016), 35.
39 Sen. *Oedipus* 445–448.
40 James Duff, trans., *Silius Italicus, Punica Volume I (Books 1–8)* (Cambridge, MA: Harvard University Press, 1934), 299.
41 Silius Italicus, *Punica* 14.364–365, 372–374.

the occasional reactive nature of the depths to events on the surface that we have seen in this concise history of ancient underwater spaces, wherein the foremost development is this amalgamation of marine divinities around the underwater utopia of Poseidon/Neptune.

Venturing into the Underwater Utopia: The Myths of Theseus and Enalus

While journeys to and from underwater spaces were primarily ascribed to deities, it was a much rarer feat in ancient mythology for mortals to be portrayed as crossing down into this marine sphere.[42] We can relate these katapontic journeys to a specific folkloric motif recorded in Thompson's folktale-motif index, wherein someone travels to an otherworldly realm and returns, gifted with some precious object, typically made of gold.[43] This basic structure can also be seen in one passage of Herodotus, describing a brief story of a journey of an Egyptian pharaoh to the underworld:

> They say that later this king while living went down [*katabēnai katō*] to what the Greeks refer to as Hades, and here he played dice with Demeter, and after both winning some games against her, and losing some to her, he returned once more bearing a golden hand towel as a gift from her.[44]

---

42 Aside from the myths explored here, the only other submarine ventures in ancient literature are the narrator of Lucian's *True History* and his crew being swallowed by an enormous sea monster (1.30–2.1) and the diving-bell episode of the *Alexander Romance* (2.38). The former is clearly a satirical narrative, while the latter, a failed attempt nearly killing Alexander, deals precisely with the theme of the overreaching of human limits; on which, see Richard Stoneman, *Alexander the Great: A Life in Legend* (New Haven, CT: Yale University Press, 2008), 111–114.

43 Stith Thompson, ed., *Motif-Index of Folk Literature*, 6 volumes (Bloomington, IN: Indiana University Press, 1955–1958). "Golden cup (bowl, urn) as gifts from otherworld inhabitants" (F343.14). See also, Aisling Byrne, *Otherworlds, Fantasy & History in Medieval Literature* (Oxford: Oxford University Press, 2016), 20.

44 Hdt. 2.122. On another instance of this folkloric motif with regard to a tale of Seleucus (Arrian, *Anabasis* 7.22.1–2), see Daniel Ogden, *The Legend of Seleucus: Kingship, Narrative, and Mythmaking in the Ancient World* (Cambridge: Cambridge University Press, 2017), 40–42n67. Theseus himself also has a (failed) katabatic journey to the underworld (Apollod. *Bibl.* 2.5.12); although with the drastically different goal of abducting Persephone, this is distinct from this folkloric motif underlying his katapontic journey.

There was no shortage of myths in classical antiquity that feature the more general idea of venturing to the underworld in some manner, such as with Odysseus and Orpheus. However, such tales with this specific folkloric motif of a journey into some otherworld and a return to the "normal world" occur with greater frequency in medieval literature, and the motif of returning with a valuable object has generally been noted as a marker of authority and proof of one's venture into such a space.[45] Not unrelated to this aspect of newfound authority associated with these folkloric returns from an otherworld is a feature of ancient dives into the sea that has been most strongly emphasized by Beaulieu. Journeys over or into the sea by male protagonists are generally associated with a type of coming-of-age story intimately bound up with notions of future political leadership.[46] Most significantly, Beaulieu equates Bacchylides' depiction of Theseus' katapontic journey to the underwater utopia with the roughly contemporary depiction of Perseus' journey to the utopia of the Hyperboreans in Pindar *Pythian* 10.[47] This marks another similarity with utopias found in both vertical and horizontal directions. Yet, more so than these journeys along a horizontal plane, katapontic journeys, with their elements of a downward journey and overcoming of death, are conceptually allusive of katabatic journeys.

We may begin with the earliest extant version of Theseus' dive down to the underwater utopia. The story, as told by Bacchylides, is set as Theseus sails with the other Athenian youths to Crete as offerings to the Minotaur. During this voyage, Minos makes sexual advances on one of the young Athenian girls, and Theseus confronts him. The resulting conflict revolves around Minos and Theseus each asserting their own divine parentage. Attempting to disprove Theseus' lineage to Poseidon, Minos removes one of his own rings, tosses it into the sea, and offers Theseus a challenge: "If Troezenian Aethra begot you to the Earth-Shaker Poseidon, bring this bright golden ornament on my hand back from the depths of the sea, throwing your body to the home of your father [*patros es domous*]."[48] This ultimatum has been noted as one bound up with matters of Theseus' personal identity, along with Athenian identity as a

45 Byrne, *Otherworlds*, 107–112.
46 Beaulieu, *Greek Imagination*, 59–60, 87–89.
47 Beaulieu, 69. On the depiction of the Hyperboreans in Pindar and Bacchylides, see also Renaud Gagné, *Cosmography and the Idea of Hyperborea in Ancient Greece: A Philology of Worlds* (Cambridge: Cambridge University Press, 2021), 213–226.
48 Bacchyl. 17.57–63.

thalassocratic power.[49] Our primary concern here, though, need only
be with the nature of this task itself. For Minos, doubting Theseus'
divine parentage, fittingly challenges him to accomplish a feat manifestly
impossible for any mortal. As mentioned at the outset of this chapter, the
ancient experience of the sea in open waters was primarily confined to
the horizontal plane of the sea's surface. Theseus, however, with his ties to
Poseidon, shatters this conventional boundary:

> But his spirit did not waver. He stood on the well-built deck of the
> ship, and darted forward [*orouse*], and the sacred grove [*alsos*][50] of
> the sea readily accepted him [...]. But the sea-dwelling dolphins
> quickly conveyed great Theseus to the home [*domon*] of his father,
> the god of horses and he went to the hall of the gods [*theōn megaron*].
> In that place, he saw the famed daughters of blessed Nereus, and
> he was awe-struck [*edeise*]. For light shone [*lampe*] from their bright
> limbs like fire, and ribbons, interwoven with gold, whirled about
> their hair. They were delighting themselves in a dance [*chorō*] with
> their flowing feet. He saw the dear wife of his father, revered,
> ox-eyed Amphitrite in that lovely dwelling [*domois*]. She placed a
> purple cloak around him, and set upon his curled hair a flawless
> wreath, dark with roses, which deceptive Aphrodite had once given
> her for her marriage. Nothing that the gods will is unbelievable to
> reasonable mortals. Theseus appeared [*phanē*] at the slender stern of
> the ship. Ah! How he perturbed the thoughts of the ruler of Knossos
> when he arrived unwetted from the sea, a marvel for all, and the
> gifts of the gods shone [*lampe*] from his limbs. The bright-throned
> maidens cried aloud with newly found delight, and the sea rang
> forth. And nearby youths chanted a paean with lovely voices. Delos,
> may your heart be warmed by the choruses of the Ceans, and may
> you send forth god-sent, just fortune.[51]

While Kampakoglou has shown that the theme of crossing boundaries
is fundamental to this poem and functions at multiple other levels,[52] it
is Theseus' crossing over from the mortal world of the sea's surface to
the divine space of its depths that provides us with the most substantial
portrayal of an underwater utopia in ancient literature. This impossible

---

49 Beaulieu, *Greek Imagination*, 69–70, 71–73; Kampakoglou, "Crossing," 152.
50 On this link to sacred groves, see Beaulieu, *Greek Imagination*, 74–75.
51 Bacchyl. 17.81–85, 97–132.
52 Kampakoglou, "Crossing," 149–150.

feat is appropriately embedded by Bacchylides with a variety of miraculous elements and allusions to divinity. The movement of Theseus from the boat into the sea is curiously described with the same verb that denotes Iris' own dive to the depths in the *Iliad*, and although it denotes a generic movement of rushing forward, the connection seems significant here, given Bacchylides' penchant for deploying Iliadic material in this poem.[53] Similarly, when Theseus emerges, we further have the detail that he comes up from the water "unwetted," a comparable trait being ascribed to the axle of Poseidon's chariot in the *Iliad* as he ventures across the sea.[54] The marine element, the cause of death for many unfortunate sailors, has had no effect on Theseus. Just as the anthropomorphic sea gods are unaffected by the conventional hostilities of the sea, Theseus is afforded a similar privilege. Moreover, the manner in which he is described upon this return is reminiscent of the marine divinities themselves. The luminescence of the Nereids, which Bacchylides likens to the shining of fire (an intriguing comparison given the underwater setting), is allusive of the glowing quality of Theseus himself upon his reappearance, now clothed with his new cloak and crown. The gifts from Amphitrite function, as per the underlying folkloric motif, as sure proof of Theseus' visit and markers of his newfound authority, while simultaneously allowing Theseus to glow as the Nereids do.

One final aspect of Bacchylides' narrative is noteworthy for emphasizing a paradox. After Theseus plunges in, Minos' boat continues to sail on, propelled by a sudden wind,[55] yet Theseus somehow manages to resurface at the boat again, as if it had remained in place. This discrepancy can best be explained in relation to another generic similarity of underwater utopia with the underworld. For while both the realms were considered to be generally underneath the surface world of the *oikoumenē*, they do not map precisely onto the geography of the world above. Ogden has already written about such "spatial instability of the realm of the dead," arguing that the relationship between the underworld and the surface realm should best be understood with reference to science-fictional notions of alternate dimensions.[56] That is, while travel down to the underworld was similarly

---

53 Bacchyl. 17.84; Hom. *Il.* 24.80; *A Greek–English Lexicon*, ninth edition (1968), s.v. "ὀρούω"; Jacob Stern, "The Structure of Bacchylides' Ode 17," *RBPh* 45, no. 1 (1967): 43–45.

54 Hom. *Il.* 13.30.

55 Bacchyl. 17.86–91.

56 Daniel Ogden, "Dimensions of Death in the Greek and Roman Worlds," in *Weltkonstruktionen. Religiose Weltdeutung zwischen Chaos und Kosmos vom Alten Orient*

conceived of as a vertical journey, this crossing into the realm of the dead also constituted a transition into another world entirely. "Distance travelled in the underworld does not map onto distance travelled on the surface [...] nor was a given place in the underworld always correspondingly beneath a given place in the surface world."[57] The same is true here with the disjuncture in the spatial relationship of the underwater utopia and the sea surface, to be construed also as a transition to another realm.

Beyond Bacchylides, our evidence for this myth remains thin. Bacchylides does not actually include a line stating that Minos drops the ring into the sea; the action must be assumed by the audience, a sign that his contemporaries were already familiar with the story and, therefore, that it was not an invention of his own.[58] A few artistic depictions of the myth, predominantly from the fifth century BCE, are extant. A red-figure vase shows one possible variation of the story, where Theseus appears to be greeted by Poseidon himself.[59] However, the lack of any explicitly marine features makes it uncertain whether this meeting is actually set underwater. An Attic bell crater dated to around 420 BCE provides a more interesting example.[60] Here, Theseus is carried in the arms of a Triton (perhaps indicating a version where he was conveyed down by a Triton, instead of dolphins) as he clasps the knees of Amphitrite in supplication. She adorns him with a crown as Poseidon, identified by his trident, is depicted below them. One final noteworthy depiction is another red-figure vase, known as the Cup of Euphronios, wherein Theseus greets Amphitrite as Athena stands next to them and a Triton at the bottom holds his feet, as if to support him; the detail of dolphins in the background confirms the underwater setting.[61]

This katapontic myth of Theseus is extant in only two other ancient authors, Hyginus and Pausanias.[62] These versions broadly preserve the

biz zum Islam, ed. Peter Gemeinhardt and Annette Zgoll (Tubingen: Mohr Siebeck Verlag, 2010), 103–104.

57 Ogden, "Dimensions," 119.

58 Ruth Scodel, "The Irony of Fate in Bacchylides 17," *Hermes* 112, no. 2 (1984): 138n6; see also Herwig Maehler, "Theseus' Kretafahrt und Bakchylides 17," *Museum Helveticum* 48, no. 2 (1991): 117–120.

59 *LIMC* Amphitrite 78; redrawn in Arthur Hamilton Smith, "Illustrations to Bacchylides," *Journal of Hellenic Studies* 18 (1898): 279, fig. 9.

60 *LIMC* Amphitrite 79; redrawn in Smith, "Illustrations," 277, fig. 7.

61 *LIMC* Amphitrite 75 (= Triton 23, = Theseus 36); redrawn in Smith, "Illustrations," 281, pl. XIV. See also, Maehler, "Theseus' Kretafahrt," 121–122. Other depictions of this myth are: *LIMC* Amphitrite 77; Triton 22, 24–27; and Beaulieu, *Greek Imagination*, 70, fig. 8.

62 Hyg. *de Astronomica.* 2.5.3; Paus. 1.17.3.

same story, albeit with the additional detail, omitted by Bacchylides, that Theseus returns with Minos' ring, conveniently handed to him by the Nereids. With all versions, we can note that Theseus is always said to encounter one of the Nereids, either Amphitrite or Thetis (as Hyginus states of some versions). Therefore, we can surmise that this story, with its essential structure dependent upon Nereids being present in Poseidon's palace, arose at some point after the Nereids had become more associated with Poseidon and his underwater utopia.[63]

One final story of an encounter by a surface dweller with Poseidon's underwater utopia is the myth of Enalus, whose name appropriately means "in the salt (sea)" in Greek. The relevant version of this myth comes in a fragment from Anticleides of Athens (fl. third century BCE), preserved by Athenaeus, recording what was likely a local legend:

> Some people in Methymna tell a tale concerning a maiden cast into the sea, and they say that one of the leaders, by the name of Enalus, being in love with her, plunged in as he intended to rescue the young girl. Then, both of them were buried by a wave and they vanished [*aphaneis genesthai*]. But at some later time, when Methymna was already inhabited, Enalus appeared and set out how < ... > and that the maiden spent her time among the Nereids, and that he himself had tended to the horses of Poseidon. But once a great wave came forth, he swam with it and emerged, bearing a golden goblet, cast of gold so marvellous that in comparison ordinary gold seemed nothing more than bronze.[64]

Another variation of Enalus' story, recorded by Plutarch, has him being conveyed by dolphins to the shore of Lesbos in a manner more reminiscent of the myth of Arion.[65] With Anticleides' version, Beaulieu has already noted a central feature being that the couple are said to literally vanish when they are transported to the underwater utopia, an element

---

63 It was not, as Jane Harrison once suggested, a myth left over from a hypothesized, pre-patriarchal stage of Greek mythology; see Jane Harrison, "Notes Archaeological and Mythological on Bacchylides," *The Classical Review* 12, no. 1 (1898), 85–86.

64 Ath. 466d; (*FGrH* 140 F4). The latter portion of this story is drawn from the epitome owing to missing leaves of the manuscript, and a lacuna is indicated here by the bracketed ellipsis. On these manuscript issues, see S. Douglas Olson, trans., *The Learned Banqueters, Volume V: Books 10.420e–11* (Cambridge, MA: Harvard University Press, 2009), 238n11.

65 Plut. *Mor.* 163a–d, 984e (*FGrH* 477 F14; cf. BNJ ad loc.).

resembling Theseus' own disappearance and reappearance.[66] Yet, unlike Theseus' journey, the mechanism that conveys Enalus and the girl to the underwater utopia (and returns him) is a wave, rather than dolphins. We can, then, perhaps see another paradoxical element, as being submerged under a wave in open waters might ordinarily be regarded as having fatal consequences. Here, that deadly force itself plunges the couple into this alternate dimension. The fate of Enalus' love interest is never told, and we are perhaps meant to assume that her visit to the underwater utopia is a permanent one, as was the case with the dive of Ino-Leukothea, and generally of female figures.[67] Lastly, we can note the reoccurrence of the folkloric motif of returning with some precious object. This myth, however, amplifies the object's significance, it being crafted from gold so exceptional that it even belittles the gold of the surface world. Thus, we see another hint at the specifically utopic nature of the underwater realm (and the objects contained therein) as not only an alternate space to the surface world, but one that is also inherently superior.

Conclusion

This motif of utopic underwater spaces, despite its infrequency in Greco-Roman antiquity, nevertheless represents a key feature among the bundle of the contradictions inherent in the ancient sea. As with so many other elements of the anthropomorphic gods of Greco-Roman mythology, there is a tendency to reflect elements of human society. In this manner, the unknown void of the depths, perhaps only otherwise thought of as the haphazard playground of fish and sea monsters, was made comprehensible and orderly in human terms. The anthropic and mixanthropic denizens of the deep, beyond just their physical forms, often exhibited human elements intimately familiar to the surface world such as the familial structure accorded to Poseidon, Amphitrite, and Triton in the *Theogony*, and the choral arrangements of the Nereids. The divinity of such figures was the crucial factor in the elevation of these spaces as utopic, allowing for the regal imagery of divine palaces and, occasionally, the paradisiacal and floral features of the *alsos* to flourish within this turbulent element. The katapontic myths of Theseus and Enalus, then, serve to deepen the complexity of this motif; relying upon the paradox that

---

66 Beaulieu, *Greek Imagination*, 76n59.
67 Beaulieu, 137.

being immersed in the harsh and ever-shifting sea would have ordinarily meant death, these surface dwellers were instead admitted into a realm of divine splendour. Such crossings of boundaries, moreover, along with the variety of interactions between the marine divine and the surface were, in effect, a means of imagining and understanding the connection between the vertical and horizontal axes of the sea. In turn, the inclusion of such divine figures furnishes the otherwise unknown of the depths of the ancient sea with a measure of divine control, as being the abode within which such marine gods and goddesses dwelt.

CHAPTER EIGHT

The Women and the Sea: The Subjective Seascape in Ovid's *Heroides*

Simona Martorana

Introduction

> *hoc saltem miserae crudelis epistula dicat,*
> *ut mihi Leucadiae fata petantur aquae!*

> At least, it may be a cruel letter to tell me this,
> so in my misery I can seek my fate in the Leucadian *Sea*![1]

Upon ending the last letter of the *Heroides*, the Ovidian Sappho (the fictional writer of *Heroides* 15) mentions the sea: *Leucadiae* [...] *aquae* (Leucadian waters).[2] The adjective "Leucadian" indicates the sea surrounding the Leucadian rock, in present-day Lefkada, from which the poet Sappho allegedly took her suicidal leap, but the term has also been understood as generically indicating the sea around the small Greek islands.[3] In Sappho's letter, the sea both articulates the catastrophic, dramatic outcome of her narrative, culminating in her suicide, and represents a place of solace, refuge, and literary creation.

This chapter grew out of my doctoral dissertation on motherhood within the *Heroides*. I would like to thank Jennifer Ingleheart and Ioannis Ziogas, my first and second supervisor at Durham University, who provided me with continuous guidance. I am also grateful to the editors of this volume, Ross Clare and Hamish Williams, for their feedback and support throughout the process, as well as my fellow volume authors for their insightful comments and discussion. Finally, I express my gratitude to the Alexander von Humboldt Foundation for providing me with financial support.

1 Ov. *Her.* 15.219–220. For the Latin text and English translation (with minor changes) of the *Heroides*, I draw from: Grant Showerman, trans., and G. P. Goold, ed., *Ovid. Heroides. Amores* (Cambridge, MA: Harvard University Press, 1977).

2 Ov. *Her.* 15.220.

3 See Peter E. Knox, *Ovid: Heroides: Select Epistles* (Cambridge: Cambridge University Press, 1995), 314–315.

The choice of "water" (and, metonymically, "sea") as the last word of the *Heroides* hints at how central the marine element is within this collection of fictional epistles.[4] The sea features prominently in Ovid's later poetic production, particularly his exile poetry, where the marine element notably marks the poet's isolation and distance from Rome; however, the sea is already a *Leitmotiv* within the quasi-subjective narrative of the *Heroides*, which have been said to anticipate the motifs (the recurring patterns) of abandonment and distress characterizing Ovid's exile production throughout.[5] A blend of elegy, tragedy, and epistolography, the *Heroides* are cast as epistles written by female characters of mythology to their partners, with the partial exception of Sappho, whose fame as a Greek Archaic poet had transformed her into a quasi-mythological figure.[6] Through the combination of literary genres and poetic personas, the *Heroides* merge the voice of the fictional author (the female heroine) and the voice of the poet (Ovid), with contradictory results: the (auto-)ironical attitude of the fictional personas makes the *Heroides* oscillate between self-complaint and self-empowerment; passivity and agency; submission and dissent.[7] This ambiguity also determines how the Ovidian heroines

4 It is worth mentioning that *Heroides* 15 has given rise to concerns about authenticity and attribution. While some scholars have presented valid arguments against Ovidian authorship based on external evidence and inconsistencies in style, Gianpiero Rosati ("Sabinus, the *Heroides* and the Poet-Nightingale: Some Observations on the Authenticity of the *Epistula Sapphus*," *CQ* 46, no. 1 (1996): 207–216) has made the most persuasive case to date in favour of authenticity. Even if we were to grant that *Heroides* 15 was not penned by Ovid, the text is nevertheless deeply characterized by Ovidian motifs, and a supposed imitator must have been aware of the most important themes featured in the other epistles. For an updated discussion, see Thea S. Thorsen, *Ovid's Early Poetry: From His Single Heroides to His Remedia amoris* (Cambridge: Cambridge University Press, 2014): 96–122.

5 Patricia Rosenmeyer ("Ovid's *Heroides* and *Tristia*: Voices from Exile," *Ramus* 26, no. 1 (1997): 29–56) examines the similarities between the *Heroides* and Ovid's exile works: "I interpret his [Ovid's] choice of the letter form for the exile poems as not only an allusion to, but also as an authorial statement of identification – on some level – with his earlier epistolary work, the *Heroides*" (Rosenmeyer, "Ovid's *Heroides* and *Tristia*," 29).

6 See P. Magno, "La Leucadia di Turpilio e Ovidio, *Heroides* XV, attraverso i loro modelli greci," *Sileno* 5–6 (1980): 81–92; also Gregory Nagy, "Phaethon, Sappho's Phaon, and the White Rock of Leukas: 'Reading' the Symbols of Greek Lyric," in *Reading Sappho: Contemporary Approaches*, ed. Ellen Greene (Berkeley, CA: University of California Press, 1996), 35–57; for Sappho's early reception, see Dimitrios Yatromanolakis, *Sappho in the Making: The Early Reception* (Washington, DC: Center for Hellenic Studies, 2007), esp. Chapter 4.

7 See, for example, Joe Farrell, "Reading and Writing the *Heroides*," *HSCPh* 98 (1998): 307–338; Laurel Fulkerson, *The Ovidian Heroine as Author: Reading, Writing, and Community in the Heroides* (Cambridge: Cambridge University Press, 2005); Duncan

engage with the surrounding natural world and, more relevantly to the aim of this chapter, the seascape.

   The sea is visually incorporated within the *Heroides* as a liminal feature between the exterior (landscape) and interior dimension (subjective poetry; feelings). Although a few studies examine the significance of landscape within the *Heroides*, these do not have a specific focus on the marine element as a site of subjectivization and, accordingly, the self-definition of the heroines.[8] By combining a philological approach to the Latin text with recent ecocritical readings of ancient literature,[9] this chapter navigates the relationship between the sea and the fictional authorial personas within Ovid's *Heroides*. Through the analysis of five case studies from the *Heroides* – namely Penelope in the first poem, Phyllis in the second, Dido in the seventh, Ariadne in the tenth, and Sappho in the fifteenth and final poem – I demonstrate that the heroines' engagement with the marine element articulates a blurring of boundaries between human and nature; between the heroines as poetic subjects and the sea as an external (landscape) feature. Substantiated by the posthuman-ecocritical notion of a continuum between human, nature, and natural (or artificial) objects,[10] my analysis

F. Kennedy, "The Epistolary Mode and the First of Ovid's *Heroides*," *CQ* 34, no. 2 (1984): 413–422; Duncan F. Kennedy, "Epistolarity: The *Heroides*," in *The Cambridge Companion to Ovid*, ed. Philip R. Hardie (Cambridge: Cambridge University Press, 2002), 217–232; Sara H. Lindheim, *Mail and Female: Epistolary Narrative and Desire in Ovid's Heroides* (Madison, WI: University of Wisconsin Press, 2003); Gianpiero Rosati, "L'elegia al femminile: le *Heroides* di Ovidio (e altre *heroides*)," *MD* 29 (1992): 71–94; Efrossini Spentzou, *Readers and Writers in Ovid's Heroides: Transgressions of Genre and Gender* (Oxford: Oxford University Press, 2003).

   8 See M. Catherine Bolton, "Gendered Spaces in Ovid's *Heroides*," *CW* 102, no. 3 (2009): 273–290; Isabelle Jouteur, "Le paysage marin des *Héroïdes*," in *Amor Scribendi. Lectures des Héroïdes d'Ovide*, ed. Hélène Casanova-Robin (Grenoble: Millon, 2007), 93–120; Luciano Landolfi, "Fondali del pathos elegiaco. Natura e lamento nelle *Heroides*," *RCCM* 42, no. 2 (2000): 191–214. For the role of landscape in the heroines' (subjective) literary construction, see Spentzou, *Readers and Writers*, 43–83.

   9 See, for example, Rebecca Armstrong, *Vergil's Green Thoughts: Plants, Humans, and the Divine* (Oxford: Oxford University Press, 2019); Brooke A. Holmes, "Situating Scamander: 'Natureculture' in the *Iliad*," *Ramus* 44, no. 1–2 (2015): 29–51; Christopher Schliephake, *Ecocriticism, Ecology and the Cultures of Antiquity* (Lanham, MD: Lexington Books, 2016); Christopher Schliephake, *The Environmental Humanities and the Ancient World: Questions and Perspectives* (Cambridge: Cambridge University Press, 2020).

   10 See Rosi Braidotti, *Metamorphoses: Towards a Materialist Theory of Becoming* (Cambridge: Polity Press, 2002), 1–10; Rosi Braidotti, *The Posthuman* (Cambridge: Polity Press, 2013); Rosi Braidotti, "Posthuman Critical Theory," in *Critical Posthumanism and Planetary Futures*, ed. Debashish Banerji and Makarand R. Paranjape (New York: Springer, 2016), 13–32; Francesca Ferrando, "Posthumanism, Transhumanism, Antihumanism, Metahumanism, and New Materialisms: Differences and Relations," *Existenz* 8, no. 2 (2013): 26–32.

shows how the blurring of boundaries between subject (the heroine; the poet) and object (the sea) contributes to the representation of the seascape as an extremely ambiguous, polysemous space. Within the *Heroides*, the sea appears as an external threat to the heroines' safety, a projection of their utopian desires, as well as a marker of their poetic agency.

Penelope and Ariadne: Between Distress and Self-Identification

Our exploration of the intersections between the sea and the poetics of the *Heroides* begins with the very first letter of the collection.[11] Imagined as an epistle written by Penelope to Ulysses, *Heroides* 1 stages a version of Penelope who seems to be waiting passively for the return of her husband and complaining about his absence. Her letter is, in fact, a masterpiece of rhetoric as it plays with and reshapes the most stereo-typical representations of Penelope as a faithful wife, which primarily drew on Homer's *Odyssey*.[12] In the view of some scholars, Ovid has Penelope merge previous epic tradition with the programmatic patterns of the *Heroides*: while still maintaining some of her Homeric and long-es-tablished epic features, the *faithful* Penelope is thus transformed into an elegiac lover, a knowledgeable reader, and a skilful poet.[13] An example

11   For the sequence of the epistles, see, for example, Heinrich Dörrie, *Untersuchungen zur Überlieferungsgeschichte von Ovids Epistulae Heroidum* (Göttingen: Vandenhoeck & Ruprecht, 1972); Howard Jacobson, *Ovid's Heroides* (Princeton, NJ: Princeton University Press, 1974), 407–409; Knox, *Ovid: Heroides*, 9–12; Martin Pulbrook, "The Original Published Form of Ovid's *Heroides*," *Hermathena* 122 (1977): 29–45.

12   The *Odyssey* has been acknowledged as the main source for *Heroides* 1; see Alessandro Barchiesi, *Epistulae Heroidum 1–3* (Firenze: Le Monnier, 1992), 53; Jacobson, *Ovid's Heroides*, 243; Knox, *Ovid: Heroides*, 86. However, the Ovidian version of Penelope departs in some instances from that of Homer, as noted by previous scholars; see, for example, Barchiesi, *Epistulae*, 53–55; Jacobson, *Ovid's Heroides*, 243–276; L. P. Wilkinson, *Ovid Recalled* (Cambridge: Cambridge University Press, 1955), 15; and for (the Ovidian) Penelope's manipulation of the *Odyssey*, see Sergio Casali, "Notizie da Nestore in Ovidio, *Heroides* 1 25–38," *Aevum(ant)* 176 (2017): 175–198.

13   Jacobson, *Ovid's Heroides*, 243–276. On the originality of Ovid's (re)use of previous sources and the mythological tradition in the *Heroides*, see Alessandro Barchiesi, "Narratività e convenzione nelle *Heroides*," *MD* 19 (1987): 63–90; Megan O. Drinkwater, "Which Letter? Text and Subtext in Ovid's *Heroides*," *AJP* 128, no. 3 (2007): 367–387; Genevieve Lively, "Paraquel Lines: Time and Narrative in Ovid's *Heroides*," in *Latin Elegy and Narratology*, ed. Genevieve Lively and Patricia Salzman-Mitchell (Columbus, OH: The Ohio State University Press, 2008): 86–102. Drinkwater maintains that Ovid provides "fresh perspectives on mythological stories while respecting their original framework" ("Which Letter," 369).

of Penelope's poetic mastery, and ironical discourse, can be found at the very beginning of her epistle, where the heroine addresses Ulysses as *lentus* (slow)[14] in returning. In the elegiac genre, this adjective is usually applied to the *puella* (the girl), the elegiac poet's beloved, who is not willing or eager to engage in a relationship with her lover.[15] This line anticipates what Penelope will say later on, namely that she suspects that Ulysses has been delayed by another, illegitimate lover.[16] The choice of such a word, however, also articulates a gender role reversal since the programmatic role of the elegiac *puella* is here attributed to Ulysses instead of Penelope – as the knowledgeable reader would expect.

Continuing consistently throughout her letter, Penelope's manipulation of well-established concepts and literary conventions also affects her subsequent portrayal of the waters of the sea. At lines 5–6, Penelope makes a reference to Paris and, accordingly, to his responsibility in the outbreak of the Trojan War. The heroine wishes that the *adulter* (adulterous man; Paris) had been submerged by the *insanis aquis* (furious waves)[17] while travelling towards Sparta,[18] where he subsequently had an affair with Helen. Along with the outbreak of the Trojan War, Paris' affair meant another unpleasant consequence for Penelope, namely the departure of Ulysses. The ambiguity of the adjective *insanus*, attributed to the waters of the sea, is the first expression of the complex relationship between the heroines and the marine element. While *insanis aquis* has commonly been translated as "furious" or "raging waters," the adjective *insanus* can also mean "unsound."[19] As *insanus* is most commonly used to qualify a person, particularly in its meaning of "unsound," "reckless," the choice of this adjective articulates Penelope's personification of the waters of the sea. Concurrently, the various meanings of *insanus* make the qualification of the sea extremely ambivalent. On the one hand, the sea is "raging" qua natural element; on the other hand, the sea is "unsound" since it allowed Paris to reach Sparta and have an affair with Helen, which ultimately provoked the Trojan War and Ulysses' consequent departure from Ithaca. Penelope's incorporation of the sea into her personal experience is our first

---

14 Ov. *Her.* 1.1.
15 Cf., for example, Ov. *Am.* 2.19.51; Prop. 1.15.4, 2.14.14, 3.8.20; see Barchiesi, *Epistulae*, 66; Knox, *Ovid: Heroides*, 88; cf. also Ov. *Her.* 2.23, where Phyllis uses this word to refer to Demophon.
16 Ov. *Her.* 1.75–76.
17 1.6.
18 1.5.
19 See *Oxford Latin Dictionary* (1968), s.v. *insanus*.

example of the blurring of boundaries between objectivity and subjectivity, between the sea as an external landscape feature and as part of the heroine's feelings and emotions. After seeing how the (Leucadian) sea closes the single *Heroides*, such an early engagement with the sea in the very first letter of the collection shows that the marine element prominently features within the heroines' writing and rhetorical strategies.

The seascape plays a very central role also in Ariadne's letter (*Heroides* 10), wherein the heroine complains about having been abandoned by Theseus on the desert island of Naxos: *vacat insula cultu; / non hominum video, non ego facta boum* ("The island is untilled. Of human traces I see none; of cattle, none").[20] While the wild natural landscape that characterizes Naxos serves to theatrically amplify the heroine's sense of loss and isolation, the lack of any other human beings leads Ariadne to establish a symbiotic and sympathetic relationship with the natural world.[21] When Ariadne wakes up in the middle of the night and discovers that she is alone on the island, she starts looking for Theseus and his comrades along the shores (*litora*),[22] running from one side of the beach to the other, with the sand slowing her down: *nunc huc, nunc illuc, et utroque sine ordine curro; / alta puellares tardat harena pedes* ("Now this way, and now that, and ever without plan, I run; the deep sand slows down my girlish feet").[23] Through this emphasis on elements of the landscape, Ovid has Ariadne start her dialogue and interactions with her natural surroundings, particularly the seascape: "the shores" (*litora*) and "the sand" (*arena*).[24]

At first, the shores are all Ariadne can see and, therefore, point out her loneliness: *quod videant oculi, nil nisi litus habent* ("so far as my eyes can see, they find nothing but shore").[25] Later, the elements of the seascape seem to sympathetically engage with Ariadne's distress and almost help her, as well as supporting and concurring with her in her sorrow. As the heroine cries the name of Theseus,[26] she receives back only the echo of

20 Ov. *Her.* 10.59–60. For the parallels between these lines and Ariadne in Catullus 64.177–178, see Knox, *Ovid: Heroides*, 243–244; for a summary of the main motifs and sources of *Heroides* 10, see Jacobson, *Ovid's Heroides*, 213–227.

21 For an analysis of Ariadne's isolation, see Nikoletta Manioti, "The View from the Island: Isolation, Exile and the Ariadne Myth," in *Insularity, Identity and Epigraphy in the Roman World*, ed. Javier Velaza (Newcastle: Cambridge Scholars Publishing, 2017), 45–67.

22 Ov. *Her.* 10.17.

23 10.19–20. Knox (*Ovid: Heroides*, 238) notes that repetitions and juxtapositions at line 19 suggest Ariadne's "state of complete confusion."

24 Ov. *Her.* 10.17, 20.

25 10.18.

26 10.21.

her own voice from the seashore: *reddebant nomen concava saxa tuum* ("the hollow rocks sent back your name to me").[27] The subject position of the *concava saxa* (hollow rocks) articulates the personification of the seashores, which seem to actively "send back" Theseus' name by echoing Ariadne's voice. A liminal landscape feature between land and the waters of the sea, the shores mark both visually and acoustically the separation between the heroine and her beloved. Geographical liminality coexists with the ambiguity of the sea as a subjective element within Ariadne's narrative. The sea represents the catastrophic outcome of the heroine's relationship as it allows Theseus' departure and, accordingly, "contributes" to Ariadne's abandonment; at the same time, it offers support to her suffering. As a result, the seascape becomes a personal, imaginary, and utopian space, where Ariadne can find solace and alleviate her isolation as the only human being left on the island.

The echo generated by the sea rocks makes it appear as though the whole "place,"[28] namely the shores, invokes Theseus' name, thus amplifying Ariadne's cry. The transformation of the seashores into a personified agent is completed at line 24, wherein Ariadne remarks that *ipse locus miserae ferre volebat opem* ("the place itself wanted to help her in her distress"). This personification of the seashores shows how Ariadne not only incorporates her feelings into the marine landscape but how the seascape itself holds an active agency within her narrative. By contributing to Ariadne's laments and amplifying them, the seascape partakes in the heroine's poetic construction.[29] As an internal focalizer and character within her narrative, Ariadne understands the sea rocks as resonating with her cry and, accordingly, helping her in the search for Theseus. As a fictional writer of her letter and quasi-heterodiegetic narrator of her story, Ariadne has the echo generated by the rocks choreographically amplify her sense of loss and abandonment.[30] This double level of focalization, and diegetic function, suggests that the sea(scape) not only plays a crucial role

27 10.22.

28 10.23.

29 According to Jacobson (*Ovid's Heroides*, 222), this personification and quasi-empathetic attitude of the sea denote the intrinsic pathetic fallacy of the epistle: "In a passing moment of self-deceit Ariadne takes this for Nature's sympathy [...], not quite seeing that the hollowness of the echo mirrors the vast empty solitude of the place"; see also Chiara Battistella, *P. Ovidii Nasonis Heroidum Epistula 10: Ariadne Theseo: Introduzione, testo e commento* (Berlin and Boston: De Gruyter, 2010), 56; Spentzou, *Readers and Writers*, 107.

30 For some general remarks on focalization, see Mieke Bal, *Narratology: Introduction to the Theory of Narrative* (Toronto: University of Toronto Press, 2017), 132–149; for narratological approaches to the *Heroides*, see, for example, Alessandro Barchiesi,

within the heroine's narrative; it also has a meta-literary function, as it serves to rhetorically intensify the heroine's distress. However, as a literary (and meta-literary) pattern, the sea is also profoundly ambivalent.

After being personified and depicted as Ariadne's collaborator, the sea becomes a hypostasis (a materialization) for the heroine's separation from her beloved. While scanning the "deep sea" to find traces of Theseus,[31] Ariadne sees his ship sailing away.[32] Like in other epistles of the collection, the sea suddenly becomes a threshold and a space of separation, which materializes the heroines' abandonment. In *Heroides* 6, for instance, Hypsipyle, having climbed upon a high tower, watches Jason's fleet sailing away through the sea;[33] in *Heroides* 2, lines 5–6, Phyllis reflects on the pointlessness of her hopes by addressing the waves of the sea: *nec vehit Actaeas Sithonis unda ratis* ("the Sithonian wave brings not the ships of Acte").[34] Since emotions such as love or grief were socially regulated and rhetorically constructed in the ancient world, the sea contributes in these instances to the performative representation of the heroines' feelings.[35] This oscillation between a personified agent that sympathetically engages with the heroines (cf. the seashores echoing Ariadne's cry) and a quasi-hostile natural element emphasizes the sea's ambiguity within the *Heroides*, wherein the sea appears as both a site of hope for the heroines and a place (and symbol) of their despair.

Furthermore, the depiction of the sea as a natural element and at the same time as a constructed component of a human-shaped environment articulates the notion of "natureculture," where the borders between natural and cultural features are extremely blurred and become indistinguishable.[36]

Speaking Volumes: Narrative and Intertext in Ovid and Other Latin Poets (London: Duckworth, 2001), 29–48; Liveley, "Paraquel Lines," 86–102.

31 Ov. *Her.* 10.28.

32 For an intertextual parallel, cf. Cat. 64.126–127.

33 Ov. *Her.* 6.67–70.

34 2.6. While *Sithonis* refers to the central of the three peninsulas of Chalcidice (Sithonia), the adjective *Actaeus* comes from the Greek Ἀκτή, an ancient name for *Attica*, and should therefore be understood as "Athenian"; see Knox, *Ovid: Heroides*, 114; also Barchiesi, *Epistulae*, 125–126.

35 See David Konstan, *The Emotions of the Ancient Greeks: Studies in Aristotle and Classical Literature* (Toronto: University of Toronto Press, 2006), 169–184, 244–258.

36 For the concept of "natureculture," see Donna Haraway, *The Companion Species Manifesto* (Chicago, IL: Prickly Paradigm Press, 2003), 25–32 and passim; Bruno Latour, *Facing Gaia: Eight Lectures on the New Climatic Regime*, trans. Catherine Porter (Cambridge: Polity Press, 2017), 16; for the collapse of distinctions between humans and non-human elements of the landscape, see Stacy Alaimo, *Bodily Natures: Science, Environment, and the Material Self* (Bloomington, IN: Indiana University Press, 2010).

This breach of the human–culture divide and the coexistence of human and non-human elements prominently feature in the *Heroides*. By incorporating the marine element within their hopes and feelings, the heroines sometimes self-identify with the seascape, as is the case for Ariadne.[37] As she scans the sea while sitting on the top of a sea rock, Ariadne slowly merges with the rock itself: *tam lapis ipsa fui* ("I myself became a rock").[38] This self-identification with the sea rock is an articulation of Ariadne's desperation, which causes her to lose her identity as a human being and merge with a natural element.[39] Bringing this self-identification further, in other epistles the sea is chosen as the site for the heroines' self-murder. Therefore, the sea marks the complete failure of the heroines' relationships, along with their annihilation, both as fictional narrators (since it sanctions the end of their writing/narrative) and as characters within their story (as it marks the end of their lives). Concurrently, by merging with a natural element such as the sea, the heroines accomplish their identification with the continuous flow of nature and so stress the connection between their poetry and the marine element as a perennially transforming flux.

Phyllis, Sappho, and Dido: Literary Manipulation and Ambivalence

In *Heroides* 2, a fictional letter addressed by Phyllis to Demophon, the heroine recasts the seascape surrounding her as the appropriate site for her self-murder. Her depiction of the bay as "gently curved to sickle shape with its bow-like lines"[40] and reference to "its outmost horns" as "rigid and in rock-bound mass"[41] blur the boundaries between an objective description of the seascape and how the heroine subjectively manipulates that seascape to make it both sympathetic to her feelings and suitable to her self-murder.[42] By incorporating the seascape into her personal experience, Phyllis reshapes the marine landscape through her subjective writing, thus depicting it as a place befitting her suicidal plans: *hinc mihi suppositas inmittere corpus in undas / mens fuit; et, quoniam fallere pergis, erit*

---

37 Ov. *Her.* 10.49–50.

38 10.50.

39 According to Spentzou (*Readers and Writers*, 93), Ariadne portrays herself as a statue at 49–50, thereby articulating her artistic prowess.

40 Ov. *Her.* 2.131.

41 2.132.

42 According to Knox (*Ovid: Heroides*, 136), from this point of the epistle onwards, the heroine "takes over so completely the role of the narrator that one almost expects a description of her hanging."

("my intention has been to throw myself from here into the waves beneath; and, since you still pursue your faithless course, so shall it be").[43] After her self-murder, the heroine wishes for her corpse to be delivered by the sea to the whereabouts of Demophon: *fluctus* [...] *portent* ("may the waves ... bring").[44] By hoping that the sea will then cast her dead body upon her beloved's shores, Phyllis seems to assign to the waves of the sea the agency that her body will lose after her death. Therefore, (what soon will be) Phyllis' de-personified, inert, and passive corpse transfers its agency and vital energy to a natural element, the sea. Phyllis' engagement with the seascape does not simply articulate her incorporation of the marine element within her feelings but also expresses her merging with, and almost transforming into, the sea, thereby actualizing what we can define, in posthuman terms, as a human–nature continuum.

As one can expect from a quintessentially fluid and liquid element, the sea is very changeable and ambiguous within Phyllis' letter. At lines 35–36, Phyllis claims that her beloved Demophon swore his faithfulness by the waters of the sea: *per mare, quod totum ventis agitatur et undis / per quod nempe ieras, per quod iturus eras* ("by the sea, all tossed by wind and wave, over which you had indeed sailed, and were to sail once more").[45] By attributing to the sea, along with Venus and Juno,[46] the role as the guarantor for Demophon's false oath, Phyllis relates this natural element to divine entities, thus further stressing its agency.[47] Concurrently, the sea's closeness to, and co-operation with, Demophon contradicts the heroine's previous and subsequent subjectivization of the maritime space. Once Phyllis has been abandoned, the seascape is addressed multiple times as the site which accompanies the heroine in her sorrow, alongside being the appropriate space for her suicide. While seeking Demophon, Phyllis walks along the shore and stares at "the broad sea" (*litora lata*).[48] Getting the impression of having seen something that resembles Demophon's ship, Phyllis runs into the waters of the sea, thus establishing a sensible contact with it: *in freta procurro, vix me retinentibus undis, / mobile qua primas porrigit aequor aquas* ("I rush forth to the waters, scarcely halted by the waves where the mobile sea

43 Ov. *Her.* 2.133–134.

44 2.135–136. For a similar wish, cf. *Her.* 18.197–199 (Leander to Hero); see also Ov. *Met.* 11.564–565.

45 Ov. *Her.* 2.35–36.

46 2.37–42.

47 According to Barchiesi (*Epistulae*, 135), the reference to the sea, a quintessentially changeable element, also serves to emphasize Demophon's unreliability.

48 Ov. *Her.* 2.122. Phyllis' attitude in these lines closely recalls Ariadne's walking along and watching the sea (*Her.* 10.26–30); see also *Rem. am.* 595; Knox, *Ovid: Heroides*, 135.

sends in its first tides").[49] While this sensible contact partially contradicts Phyllis' previous reference to the sea as sympathetically engaging with and supporting Demophon's (false) oath, it also anticipates the heroine's final union with and quasi-physical transformation into the waters of the sea after her suicide. Phyllis' contradictory depiction of the sea(scape) confirms the ambivalence that characterizes the sea in other epistles. The sea is a place of pain and troubles, as it reminds Phyllis of Demophon's false oath and subsequent abandonment; the sea is also a personified natural element, a site of subjectivization and transition for the heroine, whose body and identity merge with the marine waters. Through the establishment of a continuum between human and non-human, the sea somehow perpetuates Phyllis' existence – and bodily agency.

Not very distinct from Phyllis, the Ovidian Sappho in *Heroides* 15 constructs the waters of the sea as the site of her suicide, as well as merging her identity with the marine element. Before professing her intention to kill herself at the end of her epistle,[50] Sappho tells that she ran into the deep forest, seeking help from caves and groves.[51] The personification of, and attribution of active agency to, these landscape features blurs the boundaries between Sappho as a human poet (and a character within her narration) and natural elements, such as caves, forest, trees, grass, and tree branches, which seem to accompany Sappho in her sorrow by crying with her,[52] and birds, who stay silent to comply with Sappho's distress.[53] As I showed elsewhere,[54] this blurring of boundaries between Sappho and the surrounding natural objects, vegetables, and animals anticipates the heroine's engagement, rhetoric manipulation, and (eventually) appropriation of the marine element.

Appearing as an epiphany, a Naiad convinces Sappho that her passion can be healed only by throwing herself into the sea from the Leucadian rock.[55] After the Naiad's epiphany, the marine element becomes central within the

---

49 Ov. *Her.* 2.127–128.

50 15.219–220.

51 *Her.* 15.137. For the literary topos of the lovesick woman's wanderings, cf. Eur. *Hipp.* 215–222; Ov. *Ars am.* 1.311–312; and see Knox, *Ovid: Heroides*, 302.

52 Ov. *Her.* 15.141, 142, 144, 147, 150, 151–152.

53 *Her.* 15.152. For the natural world as empathetic towards the poet's emotion, cf., for example, Bion 1.31; Moschus 3.1; Theocritus 1.71, 7.74; Verg. *Ecl.* 10.13–15; see also Ov. *Met.* 11.44–49; Knox, *Ovid: Heroides*, 304.

54 Simona Martorana, "(Re)writing Sappho: Navigating Sappho's (Posthuman) Poetic Identity in Ovid, *Heroides* 15," *Helios* 47, no. 2 (2020): 135–160.

55 Ov. *Her.* 15.163–172. A woman committing suicide by throwing herself into the sea is a *topos*: cf., for example, Halia in Diod. Sic. 5.55.6.

letter of Sappho, who both includes the sea in her narrative and rhetorically manipulates it. In lines 179–180, the heroine asks *Amor*, the personification of Love, to support her fall so that she shall not die by jumping from the sea rock.[56] By saying that the *crimen* (crime) of her death might be attributed to the "waters of the Leucadian sea,"[57] Sappho personifies the sea and provides it with a certain agency. The personification of the Leucadian waters contributes to the incorporation of the sea, along with other natural elements, into her poetry. Like in other letters, Sappho's depiction of, and engagement with, the sea is highly ambivalent. In line 187, she maintains that her beloved's return would be "more health-giving" (*salubrior*) than the "Leucadian waves," thereby assuming that sea waters would have a beneficial effect on her.[58] Two lines after, she says that Phaon (her beloved) will be held as responsible for her death if he does not return, and he would therefore become "crueller" (*ferocior*)[59] than the rocks and waves of the sea[60] – thereby depicting the sea as a negative element.[61] Close to the end of her epistle, however, Sappho stresses again the benevolent nature of the sea vis-à-vis Phaon's cruelty. If Phaon were willing to return to her, Venus, the wind, and Cupid would support his sea journey.[62] However, as she knows already that her beloved will leave her deserted, Sappho anticipates that she is going to kill herself.

Marking the end of the epistle, the marine element prominently features in Sappho's foretold suicide: *ut mihi Leucadiae fata petantur aquae* ("so that my fates may be sought in the Leucadian waters").[63] According to some scholars, Sappho's leap into the water constitutes her self-annihilation. Sappho buries herself, together with her poetry, in the depths of

56 For a possible allusion to the scapegoat ritual that took place on the cliffs of Leucas, cf. Strabo 10.2.9; Knox, *Ovid: Heroides*, 309.

57 Ov. *Her.* 15.180.

58 The word *salubrior*, "healthier," reminds us of a medical context; see Knox, *Ovid: Heroides*, 311.

59 Ov. *Her.* 15.180.

60 15.189–190.

61 The comparison between hard-hearted lovers and hard sea rocks, and waves, is a recurring pattern within ancient love poetry; cf., for example, Ov. *Her.* 3.133; Ov. *Met.* 13.801; Verg. *Aen.* 4.365–367; also Hom. *Il.* 16.33–35.

62 Ov. *Her.* 15.213–216. In particular, Cupid is here metaphorically portrayed as the helmsman of the ship that would drive Phaon back to Sappho; see Knox, *Ovid: Heroides*, 314.

63 Ov. *Her.* 15.220. Jacobson (*Ovid's Heroides*, 299) notes: "Sappho (or Ovid) will take the leap, say farewell to love and at the same time to poetry. This line is not simply a metaphor of leave-taking, but its execution and fulfilment as well." This remark is highly suggestive if one thinks of *Heroides* 15 as the last epistle of the single *Heroides*.

the sea.[64] By contrast, through the proleptic description of her suicidal act, Sappho not only appears to engage with a natural element, as the sea is,[65] but her internal subjectivity is merged with the external environment, represented by the sea, thereby allowing the construction of a multi-dimensional (poetic) ego. Within this environment, Sappho's poetry plays a role both as a shaping force on a meta-literary level (since poetic language creates the natural settings) and as a means to increasingly blur the borders between human experience and non-human surroundings. Through the anticipation of her final suicidal act, Sappho merges her poetry with the continuous flow of the sea and stresses the connection between her poetry and the marine element in its form of flux in perennial transformation, which grants the perpetuation of her poetic memory throughout the ages. As a result, the sea both articulates the most evidently catastrophic outcome of Sappho's narrative (namely, her suicide) and, simultaneously, provides the heroine with a meta-narrative, imaginary, and quasi-utopian space for the transformation, and accordingly preservation, of her stature as a great poet.

Along with this (meta)poetic appropriation of the marine element as an articulation of their subjectivity, the heroines also manipulate the representation of the sea by using it to challenge the previous literary tradition, as emerges in *Heroides* 7, Dido's letter to Aeneas. It has long been established that the attitude of Ovid's Dido towards her Vergilian *Doppelgängerin* is extremely ambiguous and often antagonistic.[66] Scholars have argued that Ovid has Dido set up his own challenge and poetic *agōn* against Vergil and have decreed Vergil the victorious poet.[67] This challenge is articulated by the 'corrections' that Ovid's Dido makes to her Vergilian narrative, namely, the differences between her elegiac, Ovidian version from *Heroides* 7 and the epic one from the *Aeneid*.[68] After having been downplayed vis-à-vis her previous portrayal in Vergil, Ovid's Dido has

---

64 Lawrence Lipking (*Abandoned Women and Poetic Tradition* (Chicago, IL: University of Chicago Press, 1988), 67–69) argues that Sappho is the "fallen woman" and destroys herself with the help of a male poet.

65 Cf. Ov. *Her.* 15.177–180; 187–190.

66 Marilynn R. Desmond, "When Dido Reads Vergil: Gender and Intertextuality in Ovid's *Heroides* 7," *Helios* 20, no. 1 (1993): 56–68.

67 "In this poem we hear not simply Dido struggling with Aeneas, but Ovid waging war against Vergil; and he is doomed to defeat from the start because of his incapacity and unwillingness to appreciate the Vergilian position" (Jacobson, *Ovid's Heroides*, 90).

68 See Sergio Casali, "Further Voices in Ovid *Heroides* 7," *Hermathena* 177–178 (2004–2005): 147–164; Peter A. Miller, "The Parodic Sublime: Ovid's Reception of Virgil in *Heroides* 7," *MD* 52 (2004): 57–72.

increasingly received more positive judgments by scholars, who have seen precisely in the differences from her Vergilian account a hallmark of Ovid's highly refined poetic technique.[69] Among these differences, or "corrections," there are Dido's self-portrayal as generally more pitiful and forgiving towards Aeneas' decision to leave;[70] and, most notably, her allegation that she might be (*forsitan*)[71] pregnant with a child by Aeneas[72] – which supports her rhetorical argument aiming to convince Aeneas to stay with her in Carthage.[73] But how does Ovid's Dido engage with the sea? How is that manipulated in her literary construction? What is its rhetorical value?

First, the ambivalence and changeability of the sea are used as an argument to prevent Aeneas' departure. The turmoil of the sea, which is agitated by the Eurus (the southeast wind),[74] along with Aeneas' knowledge of how dangerous a sea journey can be,[75] should dissuade the hero from his resolution to leave Carthage. Both the reference to the sea as furious (*insana* [...] *aequora*)[76] and the definition of the "water" as "already experienced" (*expertae* [...] *aquae*)[77] contribute to Dido's rhetorical construction of the sea as a dangerous element. Concurrently, these references show her engagement with the previous literary tradition, wherein Aeneas goes through several shipwrecks.[78] Furthermore, Dido stresses the ambivalence of the sea, which might seem calm, and therefore "appealing" (*suadente*) for a journey,[79] but which, in fact, conceals many "risks" (*tristia*, literally "misfortunes").[80] This ambivalence is further developed when Dido portrays the sea as a potential ally, thus personifying it. The sea is said to be not forgiving of those whom "violated oaths"[81] but is inclined to punish the oath-breakers,[82] particularly when "love has been offended"

---

69 See, for example, Desmond, "When Dido Reads Vergil," 56–57: "Ovid explores the implications of a gender-based understanding of Vergil's narrative."

70 See Ov. *Her.* 7.61–64.

71 7.133.

72 7.133–138.

73 See Desmond, "When Dido Reads Vergil," 56–68; Jacobson, *Ovid's Heroides*, 76–93; Lisa Piazzi, *P. Ovidii Nasonis Heroidum Epistula VII, Dido Aeneae* (Firenze: Le Monnier, 2007), 248.

74 Ov. *Her.* 7.42.

75 7.53–56.

76 7.53; cf. 1.6: *insanis* [...] *aquis*.

77 7.54.

78 Most notably at Verg. *Aen.* 1.1–222.

79 Ov. *Her.* 7.55.

80 7.56.

81 7.57.

82 7.58.

(*praecipue cum laesus amor*).[83] This attitude of the sea is due to the fact that the goddess of love, *mater Amorum* (literally, the "mother of Love"),[84] is said to be closely related to its waters.[85] By appealing to the mythological and literary tradition of Venus' birth from the waters of the sea, Dido can justify her claim that the sea would support her by punishing Aeneas (ironically, Venus' son) for his reproachable behaviour. However, while depicting the sea as a potential ally of hers at 56–60, Dido in the following lines underlines again its hostility and dangerousness.

When Dido claims that she is afraid that a potential shipwreck may destroy Aeneas' fleet,[86] the heroine not only stresses how dangerous the sea can be but also contradicts, and challenges, her Vergilian *Doppelgängerin*, who curses Aeneas' journey and mission.[87] The sea is therefore used by (Ovid's) Dido to mark her departure from her Vergilian version and, later in the epistle, to emphasize her role as a rescuer of Aeneas (and his fleet). After Aeneas and his comrades had been shipwrecked on the African shores, Dido, reportedly, did not hesitate to help them and even entrusted her realm to Aeneas.[88] This mention of the "sea" (*fluctibus*)[89] as the cause for Aeneas' arrival at Carthage lends to the marine element a pivotal role within Dido and Aeneas' narrative. Along with this role as a catalyzer of Dido's narrative, the sea undergoes further personifications at line 73, where Aeneas' cruelty towards Dido is compared to the cruelty (*saevitia*)[90] of the agitated waves of the sea (*pelagi*).[91] Besides recalling Sappho's comparison between Phaon and the waters of the sea in *Heroides* 15.189, this reference further emphasizes the centrality of the marine element in Dido's letter.

This centrality persists towards the conclusion of the epistle, where Dido stresses once more the ambiguity and changeability of the sea as a

<hr/>

83 7.59. The Latin verb *laedere* (to damage) may indicate both a damage in most general, or legal, terms and each kind of damage caused by the beloved; for *laedere* in a legal context, see Adolf Berger, *Encyclopedic Dictionary of Roman Law* (Philadelphia: The American Philosophical Society, 1953), 536; for *laedere* within elegy, cf., for example, Ov. *Am.* 1.14.39, 2.9.4; *Her.* 20.126; *Rem. am.* 90, 293, 615; Tib. 1.9.1; Prop. 2.6.9, 2.15.48; see *Thesaurus Linguae Latinae*, s.v. *laedo*, accessed 16 August 2021. https://www.degruyter.com/serial/TLL-B/html.
84 Ov. *Her.* 7.59.
85 7.60. For the literary and artistic tradition referring to Venus' birth from the waters of the sea, see Knox, *Ovid: Heroides*, 213.
86 Ov. *Her.* 7.61–64.
87 Verg. *Aen.* 4.382–396, 607–629.
88 Ov. *Her.* 7.89–90; cf. Verg. *Aen.* 4.373–374.
89 Ov. *Her.* 7. 89.
90 7.73.
91 7.73.

natural element by claiming that the African sea, which she knows very well, sometimes prevents ships from leaving; at other times, conversely, it is benevolent and allows departures.[92] Therefore, the sea is a good argument for Dido to encourage Aeneas to delay his departure (*tempora parva peto*; "I am asking for a little time")[93] until the sea, along with her passion for him, becomes quiet (*dum freta mitescunt et amor*).[94] This overlap between the sea and her passion sanctions Dido's final appropriation of the sea as a literary and narratological element, as well as the incorporation of the sea in her feelings and rhetorical strategies. Like the sea, also Dido's love needs some time to become peaceful. A rhetorical element in support of Dido's argument, a marker of Aeneas' cruelty and, conversely, Dido's love, the sea in *Heroides* 7 appears as ambivalent as ever.

Conclusion

This depiction of the sea as an articulation of Dido's feelings, a site for subjective utopia and at the same time distress, complies with the representation of the sea that we saw in other epistles. The sea is a utopian space insofar as it reflects the heroines' hopes for the return of their partners, as well as offering a temporary escape from their doomed future. While it is a product of the heroines' literary construction, the sea also mirrors their feelings. Like their feelings, the sea is ambiguous, unpredictable, and ever-changing; overlapping with their emotions, the sea translates the heroines' sorrow as well as articulating their expectations; being the cause of shipwrecks and natural disasters, the sea is an uncontrolled force that can jeopardize the heroines and the lives of those they love, and therefore hypostasizes the powerfulness of nature. This power is perceived by the heroines both as a potential threat and as a way to express their subjectivity. As a threat, the sea materializes the catastrophic and tragic events of their life; as an expression of their subjectivity, it provides them with a (non-)place, a utopia, to voice their feminine, marginalized perspective. By appropriating the meaning of the sea and, conversely, letting the sea intervene in their writing, Ovid's *Heroides* exemplify the ambivalent conception of the sea in the ancient imaginary.

---

92 7.169–170.
93 7.178; cf. Verg. *Aen.* 4.433.
94 Ov. *Her.* 7.179.

CHAPTER NINE

The Anti-Tyrannical Adriatic
in Lucan's *Civil War*

Isaia Crosson

> "Where men can't live gods fare no better."
> Cormac McCarthy

Of Caesar and Nature

In her 2016 volume, *Your Soul is a River*, the Instapoet sensation Nikita Gill wrote:

> Your body was designed to contain a cosmic storm.
> It is no wonder that sometimes your head and heart hurt so
> much that you may just explode.
>
> It takes a nebula, a cosmic storm of epic proportions
> falling apart to create a star.[1]

No words could better encapsulate the indomitable nature of the fiction-alized version of Julius Caesar crafted by Lucan, the Corduban *enfant prodige* who, much like a storm spreading amid dark clouds, rapidly exploded in all his literary glory within and outside Rome in the age of the

I wish to thank professors Gareth D. Williams, Katharina Volk, Matthew Leigh, and Stephanie Frampton, who made me a more sophisticated reader of the Lucanian text. The idea for this paper originated from a class I taught at Columbia University in the fall of 2018, "The Artist and the Dictator": I invited my students to think about Caesar's megalomania as he crosses the Adriatic Sea in Lucan's poem, and we talked about the implications of his crossing, including the role of Nature in revolting against Caesar's quest for perpetual dictatorship. I wish to thank my students, whose enthusiasm, questions, and brilliant reflections make me forever grateful to be their teacher.
    1 Nikita Gill, *Your Soul is a River* (New York: Thought Catalog Books, 2016), 16.

Roman emperor Nero.[2] In Lucan's historical epic on the civil war between Caesar and Pompey, the *De Bello Civili*, Caesar the thunder-bearer also rages like a storm. He, subject to the continuous fluctuations of hope (*spes*) and anger (*ira*) – *acer et indomitus, quo spes quoque ira vocasset*[3] – crashes over his foes with the violence of an uncontrollable wave about to crash over helpless seafarers. The proportions of the storm that Caesar embodies and unleashes during the civil war will indeed contribute to make him into a star: the *sidus Iulium*, a cometary outburst observed a few months after Caesar's murder, in July 44 BCE, was interpreted by many as a sign of his deification.[4]

Cicero already described Caesar's uncontainable temper to his beloved Atticus in April 49 BCE: Caesar "is burning with rage and wickedness."[5] Lucan appropriates and enhances this type of negative characterization. Interestingly, our tempestuous Caesar survives the actual storm he traverses on the Adriatic Sea in Book 5 of the *De Bello Civili*. But, as we shall see, Lucan uses this episode to cast doubt on the human ability to embody and replicate the forces of Nature, and Caesar's survival after he braves the watery fury of the sea paradoxically symbolizes his defeat in controlling the kind of power his fearless countenance seems to evoke and channel.

My purpose in writing this paper is to demonstrate that the Adriatic Sea in Lucan's epic is at once an ominous *locus* of catastrophic accidents and an inspiring *locus* of utopian inspiration. More precisely, I argue that Lucan invokes the traditional epic imagery of sea storms and their murderous outbursts in order to conjure a prophetic reference to the demise of a quasi-divine tyrant: by highlighting the sheer force of the Adriatic, the poet suggests that Caesar – the near invincible *dictator perpetuus* whom no human or divine force is able to arrest within the poem as we have it[6] – *fails* to conquer Nature. His failure in turn hints at the hopeful, yet

2 Marcus Annaeus Lucanus, nephew of the Roman philosopher Seneca, lived a short yet successful artistic life (39–65 CE) before he was forced to atone by committing suicide for the sin of his participation in the Pisonian conspiracy to murder Nero. He produced at least fifteen works of literature, many of which the Latin poet Statius references in his *Silvae* (2.7) as proofs of a genius superior to Homer and Apollonius.

3 Luc. 1.146: "Alert and unvanquished, where hope and anger might call," Caesar would rush and strike a blow. All translations are my own.

4 See Plut. *Caes.* 69.3; cf. Plin. *HN* 2.93.

5 Cic. *Att.* 10.4.2: *ardet furore et scelere.*

6 Of course, the *quaestio* of the unfinished status of the *De Bello Civili* remains a vexing one, and the scope of this paper precludes a detailed analysis of the debate regarding whether or not Lucan ended his masterwork as he wished to. It will suffice to say that whereas the vast majority of Lucanian scholars believe that Lucan's suicide in 65 CE prevented him from adding more books to the ten we possess, a few disagree,

strictly utopian belief that the pro-Pompeians will succeed in reinstating the Republican government after Caesar's removal from absolute power. Thus, Nature symbolizes through the sea the temporary victory of the universe against a hubristic mortal who has committed impious acts without incurring divine nemesis. The Adriatic Sea becomes a twofold symbol in the *De Bello Civili*, as it exemplifies a sort of *utopian dystopia*: it is a terrifying, yet positive (natural) force, raging against Caesar, an even more terrifying (human) force whose megalomaniac quest for sovereignty ought to be halted. The tyrant's momentary defeat at sea foreshadows his historic assassination in the Senate House and gives a glimmer of hope to all the anti-tyrannical readers of Lucan's epic.

The polyvalent, if not oxymoronic, significance of the revolting sea in Lucan as a seat of catastrophe and utopia also hints at the notion of sublimity. In his magisterial study, Day is the first scholar to systematically read Lucan's epic in light of the aesthetics of the sublime in literature and art.[7] The sublime is a rather mercurial concept since the term is used to describe a form of ineffability that evokes and transcends conventional ideas of greatness in order to suggest to readers the overwhelming experience of *infinity*. An excellent example of this, as Sedley demonstrated, is Milton's *Paradise Lost*, a work of so vast a design as to seem "infinite" in its attempt to encompass "[h]eaven, hell, earth, chaos, *all*."[8] The notion of the sublime is also quite relevant when one classifies a

citing the possibility that the poem derives meaning from its incomplete state; see Isaia Crosson, *Lucan's Mutilated Voice: The Poetics of Incompleteness in Roman Epic* (New York: Columbia University, 2020); Jamie Masters, *Poetry and Civil War in Lucan's Bellum Civile* (Cambridge: Cambridge University Press, 1992), 244–247; Jonathan Tracy, "Evidence for the Completeness of the *Bellum Civile*," in *Brill's Companion to Lucan*, ed. Paolo Asso (Leiden: Brill, 2011), 33–79.

7   Henry J. M. Day, *Lucan and the Sublime: Power, Representation and Aesthetic Experience* (Cambridge: Cambridge University Press, 2013). Day devotes a subchapter to the Adriatic storm (*Lucan and Sublime*, 143–156) in which he refers to the long literary tradition of storms at sea as traditional *topoi* of the sublime: Edmund Burke, Immanuel Kant, Joseph Addison (the co-founder of *The Spectator*) – all agree that what causes the experience of the sublime is, in essence, the transformation of the fear caused by the seemingly boundless rage of the sea into a sense of delight on the part of the subject viewing and admiring the storm. Day (*Lucan and Sublime*, 152–156) argues that Caesar feels such a delight in Book 5 of the *De Bello Civili*, when he brags about how the mighty storm he is facing is worthy of his destiny. However, it should be stressed that Caesar's exultation is dictated by his megalomania. Thus, in contrast with the Lucretian devotees of Epicurus, Caesar learns nothing about the mysterious mechanics of the universe. As such, his experience of the sublime is limited and misguided.

8   David L. Sedley, *Sublimity and Skepticism in Montaigne and Milton* (Ann Arbor, MI: University of Michigan Press, 2005), 5 (italics added).

poem such as Lucan's, in which the *un*-representable is being represented: a civil war whose magnitude cannot be measured: [*f*]*ert animus causas tantarum expromere rerum,* / *inmensumque aperitur opus* ("my mind moves me to set forth the causes of such great events, / and an immeasurable task unravels before me").⁹ Within the immensity of the poet's work (*inmensum opus*), midway through the narrative readers face the immensity of the sea, an object that – fascinating and fearful – invites but also resists integration into symbolic frameworks of understanding.¹⁰ My argument posits that it is not possible to grasp the full meaning of Caesar's crossing on the humble vessel provided by the improbable ferryman Amyclas without presupposing a framework that evokes the tyrant's defeat and death as well as the subsequent hope of freedom from tyranny. I also posit that Caesar's inability to understand the threat posed by the raging sea attests to the elusive characteristics of the sublime: an overwhelming source of unsettlement confounding and transcending any frame of reference.¹¹

Caesar is not uplifted in any constructive manner by his experience of the immeasurable power of the sea, whereas other contemplators of sublime objects are: one thinks of Lucretius' enquirers, for whose minds the mysteries of the world are revealed after they attain Epicurean knowledge of the atomistic world they cannot measure with their wandering eyes.¹² What matters most for Lucan is that *we*, his readers, recognize in the Adriatic Sea the sublime, beautiful, and rational force of Nature precisely while Caesar is revelling in his heedless helmsmanship.

For Whom Mortals Fear

To better understand the narrative function and symbolic meaning of the Adriatic Sea in thwarting Caesar's route to power, we ought to first examine his characterization in the *De Bello Civili*. According to Marti's

---

9 Luc. 1.67–68.

10 See James I. Porter, "Ideals and Ruins: Pausanias, Longinus and the Second Sophistic," in *Pausanias: Travel and Memory in Roman Greece*, ed. Susan E. Alcock, John F. Cherry, and Jas Elsner (Oxford: Oxford University Press, 2001), 65.

11 See Philip Shaw, *The Sublime* (London: Routledge, 2006), 2; Slavoj Žižek, *The Sublime Object of Ideology* (London: Verso, 1989), 71–72.

12 Lucr. 3.14–17: *nam simul ac ratio tua coepit vociferari* / *naturam rerum, divina mente coortam,* / *diffugiunt animi terrores, moenia mundi* / *discedunt, totum video per inane geri res.* ("For as soon as your reasoning starts to proclaim / the nature of the universe, revealed by your divine mind, / the terrors within you dissipate, the walls of the world / vanish, and I behold action throughout the whole void.")

still poignant study, "[i]n Caesar, Lucan has created a superhuman figure endowed in almost equal degree with all the sins, an exemplar of evil, the incarnation of abstract Sinfulness."[13] This *Übermensch* Caesar, a devotee *ante litteram* of the Nietzschean doctrine of Zarathustra, creates new values and shatters old doctrines,[14] as the following passage highlights:

> *Inplicitas magno Caesar torpore cohortes*
> *ut vidit, primus raptam librare bipennem*
> *ausus et aeriam ferro proscindere quercum*
> *effatur merso violata in robora ferro:*
> *"Iam ne quis vestrum dubitet subvertere silvam,*
> *credite me fecisse nefas." Tam paruit omnis*
> *imperiis non sublato secura pavore*
> *turba, sed expensa superorum et Caesaris ira.*

> When Caesar realized that his cohorts were seized by
> great hesitation, he was the first to snatch and swing an axe, and
> dared to cut down with his steel a towering oak; as he plunged
> the blade into the desecrated tree, thus he cried:
> "That none of you should hesitate to cut down the forest,
> believe that I have committed blasphemy." Then all obeyed
> his orders; they were not a decisive crowd bereft of fear, yet they
> had weighed Caesar's wrath against the wrath of the gods.[15]

The act of violence against the oak is the culmination of a much-debated section of the *De Bello Civili* (3.298–455) in which Caesar approaches Massilia and, desirous of destruction for the sake of destruction, halts his march to build a wooden rampart and besiege the town. "Although I am hastening to the West, I have enough time to destroy Massilia,"[16]

---

13 Berthe M. Marti, "The Meaning of the *Pharsalia*," *AJP* 64, no. 4 (1945), 364.

14 I am solely referring to Nietzsche's rejection of otherworldly fulfilment: in *Thus Spoke Zarathustra: A Book for All and None* (1883), the German philosopher uses the character of Zarathustra to introduce the famous notion of the *Übermensch*, or "beyond-human." The *Übermensch* focuses on the earthly experience and strives to make it as fulfilling as possible, for he does not expect fulfilment from the afterlife promised by Christianity (hence the famous expression "God is dead"). Although Nietzsche focuses on the Christian god, a point of contact can be discerned between his idea of the *Übermensch* and Lucan's idea of Caesar: in Book 3 of the *De Bello Civili*, Caesar refuses to pay homage to the Druidic gods and strives to shape his own destiny on earth regardless of any otherworldly expectation.

15 Luc. 3.432–39.

16 3.359–360: *Quamvis Hesperium mundi properemus ad axem, / Massiliam delere vacat.*

he says before he invites his men to rejoice at this new opportunity: "by a gift of destiny" they will be able to perpetrate more violence.[17] Caesar himself makes no mention of this in his *Commentaries on the Civil War*: it is for his lieutenant Trebonius to handle all logistics related to the building of war machineries, and the only two references to the cutting of wood are concise, if unimportant.[18] Lucan's epic, instead, casts Caesar as the sole protagonist of a much-aggrandized scene to turn him into an active maker of nefariousness, or *nefas* (so Caesar cries at 3.437: *credite me fecisse nefas*), a tendency which Williams has most recently connected with the relentless unmaking of the Vergilian teleology on Roman *fata*, or else an inexorable retrogression to chaos: "Whereas Virgil narrates the *fata* of Roman destiny [...] Lucan sings of *nefas*, of what is not to be uttered (*ne-* + *fas*)."[19]

Caesar's bloodlust at Massilia, then, serves the purpose of highlighting the character's impiety, and it does so within a carefully crafted nexus of intertextual allusions: Keith argues that the grove in Lucan is modelled on Ovid's descriptions both of the Theban grove inhabited by the Dragon of Mars, a place "desecrated by no axe,"[20] and of the lifeless forest where Narcissus drowns.[21] An even more explicit parallelism sees Caesar in the act of violating sacred vegetation, just like the foolish Thessalian king Erysichthon did in a grove sacred to Ceres: a mighty oak, itself big as a grove (*robore quercus / una nemus*)[22] falls under the Thessalian's violating blow (*Ille etiam Cereale nemus violasse securi / dicitur et lucos ferro temerasse vetustos*).[23] While there are unmistakable linguistic parallels

---

17 3.360–361: *Gaudete, cohortes: / obvia praebentur fatorum munere bella.*

18 Caes. *B Civ.* 1.36.5, 2.15.1.

19 Gareth D. Williams, "Lucan's *Civil War* in Nero's Rome," in *The Cambridge Companion to the Age of Nero*, ed. Shadi Bartsch, Kirk Freudenburg, and Cedric Littlewood (Cambridge: Cambridge University Press, 2017), 97. On Lucan's antiphrastic gestures in regard to the *Aeneid*, see Sergio Casali, "The *Bellum Civile* as an Anti-Aeneid," in *Brill's Companion to Lucan*, ed. Paolo Asso (Leiden: Brill, 2011), 81–109; cf. Lynette Thompson and Richard T. Bruère, "Lucan's Use of Virgilian Reminiscence," *CP* 63, no. 1 (1968): 1–21.

20 Ov. *Met.* 3.28: *Silva vetus stabat nulla violata securi*. On this and other points of contact between the Massilian grove in Lucan and the Theban grove in Ovid, see Alison Keith, "Ovid in Lucan: The Poetics of Instability," in *Brill's Companion to Lucan*, ed. Paolo Asso (Leiden: Brill, 2011), 125–127.

21 Keith, "Ovid in Lucan," 125: "Lucan underscores the ominous nature of the setting by drawing on a second ecphrasis from Ovid's 'Thebaid' – the description of the pool at which Narcissus dies [...]. For the Massilian grove, like Narcissus', repels wildlife."

22 Ov. *Met.* 8.743–744.

23 8.741–742.

that span from the weapon (*ferrum*) to the verb signifying the execrable deed (*violare*) to the desecrated object (*robur*), one might argue that the comparison of two exemplary models of ungodliness, Erysichthon and Caesar, is flawed: the Gallic site where the latter by his own admission (*effatur*) stains his hands conceals no divine retribution, whereas the oak felled in Thessaly proves fatal to its desecrator. In fact, both in Ovid and in his most important source for the tale, Callimachus' sixth hymn, the goddess makes Erysichthon pay through a self-annihilating hunger that causes him to squander his own wealth and, in the Roman version of the myth, even devour his flesh. In recapitulating both accounts, Phillips adds that the stereotypical figure of the unholy grove-cutter *always* incurs nemesis:[24] for example, Halirrhothius was accidentally struck by his axe as he attempted to cut an olive tree sacred to Athena,[25] and the Herodotean Cleomenes died by his own hand "because, once he arrived at Eleusis, he cut down the precinct of the gods."[26] Phillips concludes that aside from a tenuous similarity between Erysichthon's literal hunger and Caesar's insatiable ambition, the latter amounts to a kind of cosmic monster to whom the gods give way with "disheartening regularity."[27] This apt description, reminiscent of Marti's, can be pushed further: since Caesar successfully replaces *fas* with *nefas*, a process beginning when Lucan first declares the ethical equation of *ius* and *scelus* in his proem,[28] he becomes more than a monster or the manifestation of the abstract notions of evil and sin, and he *de facto* supplants Jupiter himself. Nix describes the phenomenon: the climax of Caesar's portrayal in Book I of the *De Bello Civili* likens the man to the thunderbolt (*fulmen*), thus "displaying the power of a god over men."[29] Lovatt examines a battle scene in Book 7 in which Caesar emulates the watchful and supportive behaviour of epic gods, and just like Vergil's Venus does with her son

---

24 O. C. Phillips, "Lucan's Grove," *CP* 63, no. 4 (1968): 296–300.

25 The rather obscure story is mentioned in Servius' commentary on Verg. *G.* 1.18.

26 Hdt. 6.75: διότι ἐς Ἐλευσῖνα ἐσβαλὼν ἔκειρε τὸ τέμενος τῶν θεῶν.

27 Phillips, "Lucan's Grove," 300.

28 Luc. 1.2: *iusque datum sceleri canimus* ("we sing of legality conferred on crime").

29 Sarah A. Nix, "Caesar as Jupiter in Lucan's *Bellum Civile*," *CJ* 103, no. 3 (2008): 283; see also Denis C. Feeney, *The Gods in Epic: Poets and Critics of the Classical Tradition* (Oxford: Oxford University Press, 1991), esp. 295: in Lucan's hands, Caesar monopolizes everything by his inescapable presence, including all religious meaning. The effect of Caesar's godlike sway over the populace of Rome is manifest in two passages from Book 3: in the first (3.97–101), Caesar terrifies everyone while marching like an invincible presence and scattering away Rome's other deities (*sparsurusque deos*); in the second (3.437–439, quoted above), the general's anger is measured against that of the gods above, and Caesar convinces his men that he is more fearful.

Aeneas, Caesar is even capable of mending his men's wounds;[30] this furthers the impression that the man has been transfigured into his deified version *ante mortem*. However, according to Nix, who revamps Putnam's argument,[31] it is deceitful to think that the Roman dictator has appropriated with ease and success those divine attributes which Lucan pinpoints at different junctures of his poem: when the poet describes Caesar in the act of raging in his temples (*in sua templa furit*),[32] he may well be referencing the temple dedicated to *Divus Iulius* by Octavian in 29 BCE.[33] If this is the case (but the scholiast of the *Commenta Bernensia* thinks instead of the Capitoline hill),[34] Caesar's rage also turns against its source, following a trajectory reminiscent of Erysichthon's cannibalistic hunger. Is Lucan, then, hinting at the Ides of March? I believe so, and I agree with Nix's interpretation, since throughout the poem there are even more explicit references to the tyrant's demise in 44 BCE, for example when the Roman matron possessed by Apollo foresees it at the end of Book 1.[35] But what I find most interesting in relation to Caesar's godlike countenance is that, whether or not he falls short of those gods he strives to emulate, *no* gods ever try to oppose or resist him, whereas the Ovidian gods fail not to strike mortals who trespass against them. As the Druidic deities presiding over the Massilian grove in Book 3 are absent from the scene, so in general the gods of the Roman pantheon are conspicuously absent from the development of the plot, to the point that the narrator lets out a desperate cry in the midst of his gory reenactment of the decisive Battle of Pharsalus:

> *Sunt nobis nulla profecto*
> *numina: cum caeco rapiantur saecula casu,*
> *mentimur regnare Iovem. Spectabit ab alto*
> *aethere Thessalicas, teneat cum fulmina, caedes?*

---

30 Helen Lovatt, *The Epic Gaze: Vision, Gender, and Narrative in Ancient Epic* (Cambridge: Cambridge University Press, 2013), 118.

31 Michael C. J. Putnam, *Virgil's Aeneid: Interpretation and Influence* (Chapel Hill, NC: University of North Carolina Press, 1995), 228–229; cf. Masters, *Poetry and Civil War*, 2.

32 Luc. 1.155.

33 Nix, "Caesar as Jupiter," 283n11&12. For the dedication of the temple after Octavian's triumph on 18 August, see Stefan Weinstock, *Divus Julius* (Oxford: Oxford University Press, 1971), 399–400.

34 Hermann Usener, ed., *M. Annaei Lucani Commenta Bernensia* (Hildesheim: G. Olms, 1967), 21.

35 Luc. 1.690–691. On this and other references to Caesar's death, see Crosson, *Lucan's Mutilated Voice*, 27–29, 37n85.

Truly there are no gods for us:
as blind chance drags along century after century,
we deceive ourselves into thinking that Jupiter reigns.
Will he idly watch from high heaven the Thessalian
slaughter, though he controls the thunderbolt?[36]

Despite contradictions in the Lucanian *Weltanschauung*, which seems to oscillate between a disheartened scepticism towards the gods' providential interventionism and the more vehement, if not sarcastic antitheism displayed in the passage above,[37] one certainty remains: Caesar, who much like his successors in the imperial line enjoys being associated with the Olympians' symbols and their subsequent freedom of action, is indeed *free* to produce the *nefas* which propels the narrative of the *De Bello Civili*. The extent of this freedom is alarming and stains Lucan's hands, too: Malamud is keen to acknowledge that writing about Caesar makes Lucan "somehow complicit with and analogous"[38] to him or else a co-conspirator in the making of nefariousness. In the second half of this paper, I argue that mainly for this reason – and hence in an attempt to unburden himself from his share of guilt in immortalizing through a narrative reenactment the unutterable (*ne-* + *fas*) crimes perpetrated by Caesar – Lucan emphasizes the role of Nature in his poem, making the natural forces in the *De Bello Civili* temporarily victorious against the tyrant.

---

36 Luc. 7.445–448.

37 The bibliography on this topic is vast. Among those who posit the existence and, to some extent, presence of the gods in the *De Bello Civili*, see Elaine Fantham, "The Angry Poet and the Angry Gods: Problems of Theodicy in Lucan's Epic of Defeat," in *Ancient Anger: Perspectives from Homer to Galen*, ed. Susanna Braund and Glenn W. Most (Cambridge: Cambridge University Press, 2003), 229–249; Emanuele Narducci, *Lucano: Un'epica contro l'impero* (Firenze: GLF Editori Laterza, 2002), 42–74, 152–166; cf. Robert J. Sklenár, *The Taste for Nothingness: A Study of Virtus and Related Themes in Lucan's Bellum Civile* (Ann Arbor, MI: University of Michigan Press, 2003), who reads the poem through a nihilistic lens, leaving no space for divine providence, be it good or perverse; Shadi Bartsch, *Ideology in Cold Blood* (Cambridge, MA: Harvard University Press, 1997), esp. 108–130, where she resorts to Rorty's ironism to point out that in Lucan's poetic universe of perennial doubt (on the existence of the gods, on providence, and so on), the poet encourages his readers to choose to believe because a less bleak perspective grants more opportunities for action against the Caesars.

38 Martha A. Malamud, "Happy Birthday, Dead Lucan: (P)raising the Dead in *Silvae* 2.7," in *Roman Literature and Ideology: Ramus Essays for J. P. Sullivan*, ed. Anthony J. Boyle (Bendigo: Aureal Publications, 1995), 182.

For Whom Nature Seethes

In a world where men abuse their power, Nature finds its ways to turn against them. Take the story told in a *New York Times* article published in July 2021: the summer before, Melinda Webster, a researcher at the University of Alaska Fairbanks, crossed the Wandel Sea aboard an icebreaker and found plenty of open water instead of the thick sea ice that used to be there before global warming melted it.[39] Although a circular ocean current, the Beaufort Gyre, typically allows the region to retain ice in the summer months even as warming thins it elsewhere, it is possible that the Wandel Sea and the surrounding areas will not be a viable summer shelter for Arctic wildlife in future decades. These increasingly inhospitable conditions may soon affect not only wildlife in the Arctic but humans as well. Dr Webster is one of countless researchers who can speak to the disrupting effects of reckless – hubristic! – human-caused emissions of carbon dioxide and other heat-trapping gases, and to the devastating effects these have on humankind.

More than two thousand years before scientists started to observe the dramatic recession of ice in the North Pole through satellites and expeditions, Lucan recorded the far more explicit and more aggressive response of Nature to Caesar's hubris in his epic tale. Lucan hints at the arresting power of Nature already in Book I, when Caesar stops before the Rubicon River, the sacred boundary beyond which Roman legions should not march. Standing before the wavy waters of the tiny river (*parvi Rubiconis ad undas*),[40] Caesar beholds the apparition of his country Rome (*ingens visa duci patriae [...] imago*),[41] who tells him to stop, and he is suddenly pervaded by terror. For a moment, the ever-moving incarnation of Jovian bolts, ever growing with consuming anger and unmatchable speed, is unable to move:

> *Tum perculit horror*
> *membra ducis, riguere comae, gressumque coercens*
> *languor in extrema tenuit vestigia ripa.*

> Then terror shook
> the general's whole body, his hair stood on end, and a

---

39 Henry Fountain, "Arctic's 'Last Ice Area' May Be Less Resistant to Global Warming," *New York Times* (1 July 2021): https://www.nytimes.com/2021/07/01/climate/arctic-sea-ice-climate-change.html. Accessed 6 September 2021.
40 Luc. 1.185.
41 1.186.

weariness restrained his steps and kept him on the edge of
the river-bank.[42]

Although the epiphany of *Roma* by the Rubicon contributes to such a
dramatic reaction, the fact that the fearless and godlike Caesar displays
human emotions right after approaching the river is an important detail,
for it anticipates subsequent instances in which he will have a hard time
dealing with the natural element of water. Nor is it a coincidence that
the tiny rivulet (*parvus*) soon becomes more remarkable than it would
normally be: when Caesar sheds his terror, regains strength, and "undoes
the delay of war" (*moras solvit belli*), the Rubicon is swollen (*tumidumque per
amnem*)[43] because of wintry precipitations and, therefore, more problematic
to cross (*Tum vires praebebat hiemps, atque auxerat undas / tertia iam gravido
pluvialis Cynthia cornu*).[44] Masters argues that the poet's hypertrophic
representation of the Rubicon is a clever strategy to *delay* Caesar, thus
delaying through geographical obstacles the *nefas* he triggers all along
his march.[45] This is true, and to be fair, Lucan resorts to a vast array of
techniques to slow down his unravelling of *nefas*, including rhetorical,
moralizing outbursts that break off the sequence of events; as Bramble
theorizes, often the rhetorical moment, "seen whole, and interpreted for
its moral implications,"[46] becomes an essential unit of composition in
the *De Bello Civili*. Nevertheless, if one reads the scene at the Rubicon
in light of my previous observations on Caesar's unpunished impiety
and godlike freedom of action within the narrative frame of the poem,
one realizes that the role of natural forces in Lucan cannot be ascribed
to that of mere dilatory strategies, or *morae*. According to my view, the
turn of events set in motion by Caesar's crossing leads to a providential
crescendo reaction on the part of Nature, ranging from the swelling of
the Rubicon to the catastrophic storm on the Adriatic. Thus, Nature
is the sole providential substitute in the *De Bello Civili* for a lack of
divine providence. As such, it represents the poet's best instrument to
counteract the bleakness of a godless world disintegrated by so senseless
a strife that Nill takes the Caesarian disintegration through violence

---

42 1.192–194.
43 1.204.
44 1.217–218.
45 Masters, *Poetry and Civil War*, 2n2.
46 John C. Bramble, "Lucan," in *The Cambridge History of Classical Literature*, Volume
2: Latin Literature, ed. Edward J. Kenney and Wendell V. Clausen (Cambridge:
Cambridge University Press, 1982), 539.

(*Verwundungs- und Sterbenprozesses*) to be the poet's main criterion of composition: "Im *Unmaking* der Lucanischen Gewalt fallen somit *Struktur und Auflösung* zusammen su einer *Struktur der Auflösung*."[47]

Caesar and his army ultimately succeed at crossing the Rubicon, as if Lucan means to teach us that the impious get away with their impiety, regardless of all obstacles. Yet a more optimistic interpretation is warranted: the resistance of the tumid Rubicon, coupled with the dreamlike manifestation of personified Rome, shows us that Caesar is vulnerable, and that he *may* be vanquished. We get a similar impression in Book 10: the old priest Acoreus, prompted by Caesar, who at this point in the narrative is a guest at Cleopatra's banquet, lists in a lengthy speech the possible causes of the Nile's summer inundation;[48] he then proceeds to describe its known course from the beginning.[49] However, as Tracy sums up, the priest provides an incomplete account (interrupting his speech long before the river ramifies in the Delta region) because the Nile "is destined forever to confound the ambition of warlords who, following in the footsteps of Alexander and Cambyses, desire mastery over the natural universe through the penetration of its secrets."[50] Further opposition to Caesar stems from Acoreus' pointed reference to the victory of water over fire, the elemental force unleashed by the Caesarian thunderbolt:[51] the Nile River helps the world by rising against the burning mouth of Leo, that fire may not devour the earth (*neu terras dissipet ignis, / Nilus adest mundo contraque incensa Leonis / ora tumet*).[52]

---

47 Hans-Peter Nill, *Gewalt und Unmaking in Lucans Bellum Civile. Textanalysen aus narratologischer, wirkungsästhetischer und gewaltsoziologischer Perspektive* (Leiden: Brill, 2018), 86.

48 Luc. 10.219–267.

49 10.268–331.

50 Tracy, "The Completeness of *Bellum Civile*," 37–38. Acoreus frustrates Caesar's expectations (Luc. 10.268–285), commenting on the futile ambitions of those who tried to uncover a type of knowledge that was meant to stay concealed. Lucan is here conflating Julius Caesar and Nero, thus condemning altogether the imperial dynasty: thus Caesar boasts that it is a genuine "love for the truth" (*tantus amor veri*) (10.189) that leads him to uncover the secrets of the Nile, while in Seneca's *Quaestiones naturales* Nero is praised for his intellectual curiosity through an eerily similar language: *ut aliarum virtutum ita veritatis in primis amantissimus* (Sen. QNat. 6.8.3).

51 Emanuele Berti, *M. Annaeus Lucanus, Bellum Civile, Liber X* (Firenze: Le Monier, 2000), 213–214; Fritz König, "Mensch und Welt bei Lucan im Spiegel bildhafter Darstellung," in *Lucan*, ed. Werner Rutz (Darmstadt: Wissenschaftliche Buchgesellschaft, 1970), 451–471.

52 Luc. 10.232–234. For other references to the river overpowering heat and fire, see 10.215, 288, 307–308.

Whereas Caesar is shown to be in control when he makes history by crossing the Rubicon or when he scorns the gods by cutting the Massilian grove, he loses control in his attempt to master the mysteriously elusive nature of the universe. "Give me an assured hope to see the spring of the Nile, and I shall abandon civil war," he proclaims as he encourages Acoreus to share his knowledge with him.[53] At no other point in the *De Bello Civili* is Caesar ready to renounce his goal. His obsession with the Nile in Book 10 is as unique as his trepidation in front of the Rubicon in Book 1 (perhaps also a hint that Lucan intended Book 10 to be the last), and the clash between a hubristic mortal and Nature is manifest in both instances. However, the most egregious clash occurs in the middle of the epic poem, in Book 5, on the Adriatic Sea. All hands to quarter, then:

> Hark, now hear the sailors cry,
> smell the sea, and feel the sky,
> let your soul and spirit fly, into the mystic.[54]

In the Eye of the Storm

In contrast with the motionlessness characterizing the Rubicon scene and the Nile scene, in which Caesar is either paralyzed with terror or too curious to acquire new knowledge of the universe to move forward with his war plans, πολυπραγμοσύνη (*polypragmosunē;* officiousness) distinguishes his approach to the Adriatic Sea. The character's disquietude and eagerness to act are caused by Antony's sluggishness: in 48 BCE, after asking Antony, who was camped with his army at Brundisium, to cross the sea and join forces with him in Epirus so that they might both chase Pompey, Caesar did not obtain a rapid and satisfactory response. This is why Lucan has him fret alone, at night, awake and alert, as he plans to cross the Adriatic, reach Antony by surprise, and take the men Antony has failed to provide quickly enough:

---

53 10.191–192: *spes sit mihi certa videndi / Niliacos fontes, bellum civile relinquam.* These lines may be dismissed as an example of Caesar's deceitful rhetoric and attitude: that is, after getting what he wants from Acoreus, Caesar would resume his civil war project without hesitation; see Caesar's despicable display of hypocrisy in Book 9, when he sheds crocodile tears as he contemplates Pompey's beheaded *caput,* the pharaoh Ptolemy's ghastly gift to him (9.1035–1043).

54 Van Morrison, "Into the Mystic."

> *Caesar sollicito per vasta silentia gressu*
> *vix famulis audenda parat, cunctisque relictis*
> *sola placet Fortuna comes.*

> With anxious steps, through the vast silence,
> he plans to accomplish what slaves could hardly dare:
> he leaves everyone behind, entrusting Fortune as
> his sole companion.[55]

Narducci discerns in Caesar's anguished walk, or *sollicitus gressus*, the "sometimes swift, sometimes slow" criminal steps of Sallust's Catiline (*citus modo, modo tardus incessus*).[56] He adds that Lucan took inspiration from the nocturnal departure of Euryalus and Nisus in Book 9 of the *Aeneid*, contrasting the piety of heroes devoted to their men and country with the pathological self-absorption of Caesar, who chooses his Fortune as his taciturn fellow-traveller.[57] Within this rich intertextual setting, of special interest is the fact that an enterprise worth employing slaves (*vix famulis audenda*) befalls Caesar, to whom everyone bows in the poem. The easiest explanation is that so foolhardy is the attempt to traverse stormy waters at night with hardly any visibility that only a slave, whose life would be deemed worthless compared to Caesar's, would perhaps attempt this endeavour. But an alternative explanation is also possible: Lucan notes that Caesar was dressed like a slave in order to exit the camp unnoticed[58] and recasts this anecdote in his narrative of hubris. The poet's

---

55 Luc. 5.508–510.

56 Sall. *Cat.* 15.5; Narducci, *Lucano*, 250.

57 Luc. 5.508–510 is undoubtedly modelled on Verg. *Aen.* 9.922–923: *statione relicta / ipse comes Niso graditur.* The contrast between the altruistic heroism of the two friendly soldiers of Aeneas, who support each other in battle, and Caesar's solitary megalomania is stark. But before the storm narrative begins in Book 5 of the *De Bello Civili*, it is already possible to discern the detachment between *milites* and *dux*, as well as the latter's solipsism: back from Spain, after noticing his men's exhaustion and discontent on account of the unrelenting campaigns he has put them through, Caesar fears mutiny (*cum paene fideles* [...] *destituere ducem*) (Luc. 5.242–244), not so much because he feels hurt by his men's tottering loyalty, but mostly because he would lose the fruits of his crimes, and hence his personal glory (*timuit* [...] *perdere successus scelerum*) (5.241–242). For an overview of the instances in which Caesar's soldiers misunderstand their leader's intentions in Book 5, a symptom of incorrigible disunity in the Roman army, see Luke V. Pitcher, "A Perfect Storm? Caesar's Audiences at Lucan 5.504–702," *CQ* 58, no. 1 (2008): 243–249.

58 Plut. *Caes.* 38.2; Val. Max. 9.8.2; cf. App. *B Civ* 2.58, who does not mention the servile attire but reports that Caesar's men would later accuse him of having attempted what a soldier could perhaps try, but certainly not a general.

goal is to further the character's mythic transfiguration into a god: just as Jupiter and Mercury wander the earth after lessening their statuses to look like beggars and ask in servile fashion for food and a place to rest before the devout couple of Philemon and Baucis offer them hospitality in Ovid's tale,[59] so also godlike Caesar may act like a slave or camouflage himself in less authoritative clothes than his armour (*plebeio tectus amictu*).[60] The Ovidian couple, a flawless specimen of commendable poverty (*paupertas*), is indeed a key point of reference for the development of Lucan's story: poor and humble is the ferryman Amyclas, and he lives in a hut whose scant outfitting ought to make him safe from the harms of the civil war (*praedam civilibus armis / scit non esse casas*).[61] Unfortunately for him, Caesar still manages to be a disturbance. And unlike Jupiter and Mercury, who respectfully bowed their heads to enter their elderly guests' abode[62] (a gesture of humility also performed by Aeneas at the entrance of Evander's hut),[63] Caesar swells with arrogance. In her excellent commentary, Matthews meticulously deconstructs the antiphrastic gestures by which Lucan has Caesar behave in a manner opposite to traditional epic models of decency throughout his exchange with Amyclas.[64] It will suffice to say that, in overturning the argument made by Evander to Aeneas (to spurn riches in favour of divinely inspired poverty),[65] Caesar promises his interlocutor riches if only he entrusted his destiny *to a god* (*ne cessa praebere deo tua fata volenti / angustos opibus subitis inplere penates*).[66] According to Matthews, the term *deus* may here foreshadow Caesar's apotheosis in 42 BCE. But the soaring and systematic *crescendo* of unacceptable behaviour on Caesar's part – from his disregard for the Roman *pomoerium* in Book 1, when he crosses the Rubicon with armed men, to his self-declared endorsement of *nefas* while axing the Druidic oak in Book 3, to his disrespect of *paupertas* – suggests otherwise: Caesar already sees himself as a living god among the other (invisible, ethereal, heavenly) gods he himself sometimes invokes, and Book 5 constitutes the peak of

59 Ov. *Met.* 8.627–635.
60 Luc. 5.538. Quite possibly, Caesar was wearing the *lacerna*, a hooded mantle inappropriate for high-ranking society; see Emanuele Narducci, "*Pauper Amyclas*. Modelli etici e poetici in un episodio della *Pharsalia*," *Maia* 35 (1983): 183–194.
61 Luc. 5.526–527; see Narducci, *Lucano*, 258–261.
62 Ov. *Met.* 8.638–839.
63 Verg. *Aen.* 8.359–361.
64 Monica Matthews, *Caesar and the Storm: A Commentary on Lucan De Bello Civili, Book 5 lines 476–721* (Bern: Peter Lang, 2008), 87–114.
65 Verg. *Aen.* 8.364–365.
66 Luc. 5.536–537.

his hubris. And since the gods in heaven will not contradict his supremely blasphemous ego, not even on this occasion, only Nature can keep it in check by means of the sheer force of the Adriatic Sea.

The description of the storm is a rhetorical masterpiece. Amyclas sets the tone for it: his learned display of meteorological doxography draws from the manuals of Theophrastus and Aratus, via Vergil,[67] to illustrate what a terrible idea it is to set sail. The night,[68] signs from the Sun[69] and Moon,[70] and various other signs[71] should dissuade the boldest seafarers. Amyclas' technical expertise in listing these omens shows an attention to detail superior to that of Aeneas' helmsman, Palinurus.[72] Soon after Caesar chooses to ignore the signs and the two men embark on a small raft, the winds derail shooting stars from their ordinary course and shake even the fixed stars of the upper atmosphere,[73] as if the sky were about to crash down. Is this a storm? It rather resembles the Stoic ἐκπύρωσις (*ekpyrōsis*; conflagration) or, otherwise, the final hour of the universe as Lucan envisions it in Book I: the framework of the world will be shattered, constellations clash in confusion, and the fiery stars drop into the sea.[74] What the poet vividly imagines as a grim possibility if Rome keeps on its path of internecine strife *materializes* in the eye of this storm: winds rage against each other,[75] the waters may continue their own war even after the quelling of the winds,[76] mountains are buried,[77] and an apocalyptic confusion of boundaries symptomatizes the imminent possibility of a return to amorphous chaos:

> *Sic rector Olympi*
> *cuspide fraterna lassatum in saecula fulmen*
> *adiuvit, regnoque accessit terra secundo,*

---

67 Verg. *G.* 1.351–514; see Matthews, *Caesar and the Storm*, 114–116; cf. Mark P. O. Morford, *The Poet Lucan: Studies in Rhetorical Epic* (Oxford: Bloomsbury Academic, 1967), 38–39.

68 Luc. 5.540.

69 5.541–545.

70 5.546–550.

71 5.551–556.

72 Cf. Verg. *Aen.* 3.513–520, 5.25.

73 Luc. 5.561–564.

74 1.67–82. On Lucan's cosmic speculation over the phenomenon of *ekpyrōsis*, see the magisterial study by Michael Lapidge, "Lucan's Imagery of Cosmic Dissolution," *Hermes* 107, no. 3 (1979): 344–370.

75 Luc. 5.598–606.

76 5.606–607.

77 5.615–616.

cum mare convolvit gentes, cum litora Tethys
noluit ulla pati caelo contenta teneri.
Tum quoque tanta maris moles crevisset in astra,
ni superum rector pressisset nubibus undas.
Non caeli nox illa fuit: latet obsitus aer
infernae pallore domus nimbisque gravatus
deprimitur, fluctusque in nubibus accipit imbrem.
Lux etiam metuenda perit, nec fulgura currunt
clara, sed obscurum nimbosus dissilit aer.
Tum superum convexa tremunt, atque arduus axis
intonuit, motaque poli conpage laborant.
Extimuit natura chaos; rupisse videntur
concordes elementa moras, rursusque redire
nox manes mixtura deis: spes una salutis,
quod tanta mundi nondum periere ruina.

> Thus, the ruler of Olympus
> summoned his brother's trident to help in punishing
> mankind, when his own thunderbolt was weary;
> earth gave way to a second kingdom, when the ocean
> swallowed humankind and did not tolerate any limits,
> if not the sky. Now, again, so mighty a mass of waters
> would have reached the stars, if the ruler of the gods had not
> pressed it down with clouds.
> That was not the darkness of ordinary nights: the ether was
> hidden, veiled with the dimness of the infernal regions,
> vexed by clouds; and through a cloudy mist did the rain pour
> into the sea. All light, even if dreadful, died; no bright
> lightning gleamed, but the perturbed sky dimly flashed.
> Then, the seat of the gods quaked, the lofty sky rambled,
> and the heavens, jarred in their framework, toiled.
> Nature feared chaos: all elements seemed to have shattered
> their harmonious bonds; night seemed to return to enmesh
> the gods below with those above. Only a hope was left,
> that in so great a universal ruin they did not perish yet.[78]

Day argues in favour of the vividness of Lucan's language: its unique ἐνάργεια (*enargeia*), or else the "dynamic power" to concretize the

---

78 5.620–637.

unrepresentable into plastic, *living* descriptions, achieves sublimity by leaving us astonished (a sentiment both Burke and Kant point to in their speculation on the sublime).[79] Such a power of representation pervades the passage above, which transports readers out of themselves (εἰς ἔκτασιν ἄγει τὰ ὑπερφυᾶ)[80] and onto the written page of a cosmic conflict of cataclysmic scale (again, an *ekpyrōsis*).

Through the simile of the Ovidian flood, which Ovid unleashes to illustrate Jupiter's punishment against men's (and Lycaon's) moral sins,[81] Lucan finds a way to outdo the previous literary tradition, showing the superior magnitude of his tempest and reasserting the ineffectiveness of traditional anthropomorphized gods: in sarcastic vein the poet even questions their ontological status, positing that amid so great a cataclysm as Caesar and Amyclas dare to ride through, the gods above and below may *not* be immortal, and they are lucky to stay alive (*spes una salutis* [...] *nondum periere*). Conversely, the cosmic size of the storm at sea confirms Nature as Caesar's most powerful adversary.

Granted the literal representation of the *ekpyrōsis* in Book 5, right above the Adriatic Sea, I would add a caveat to Joseph's recent identification of Nigidius Figulus' "fatal day"[82] with the day of the Battle of Pharsalus. According to the seer, "the last days of many have conjoined into one time,"[83] but Lucan's scattered references to cosmic catastrophe forbid an easy identification with one specific day: it could be Pharsalus, as Joseph claims, or it could be the day of Caesar's attempted crossing of the Adriatic Sea, or it will most likely be some unspecified future day in the history of Rome and humankind:

> *Hos, Caesar, populos si nunc non usserit ignis,*
> *uret cum terris, uret cum gurgite ponti.*
> *Communis mundo superest rogus ossibus astra*
> *mixturus.*

79 Day, *Lucan and Sublime*, 82–92.
80 [Longinus], *Subl.* 1.4.
81 Ov. *Met.* 1.243–312. After Lycaon tries to deceive Jupiter, testing his omniscience, the god deliberates in a council that the human race deserves to be kept in check due to increased arrogance, and the flood ensues to submerge the world. For parallelisms between the Ovidian flood and Lucan's Adriatic storm, see Matthews, *Caesar and the Storm*, 195–196; Morford, *The Poet Lucan*, 62.
82 Timothy A. Joseph, "*Pharsalia* as Rome's 'Day of Doom' in Lucan," *AJP* 138, no. 1 (2017): 114.
83 Luc. 1.650–651: *extremi multorum tempus in unum / convenere dies.*

Caesar, if fire does not consume this host now,
it will hereafter, together with the earth and the waters of
the sea. There remains a conflagration which will destroy
all the world, commingling the stars and dead men's bones.[84]

The storm of the Adriatic threatens to anticipate Figulus' final hour, which is, however, yet to occur and, to be fair, will not even occur at Pharsalus. Whether or not Lucan wanted to end the *De Bello Civili* abruptly in Book 10, the open-endedness of the poem is ratified by the open-ended projection of the next Stoic *ekpyrōsis* into an unspecified future time that stretches beyond the physical boundaries of the narrative. Yet there is something to say for Lucan's effort to magnify the proportions of his sea storm in an unprecedented way, colouring it with the bleak strokes of a conflagration with no rebirth: that is, when Caesar's impiety leads him to call himself a *deus* in front of Amyclas, the poet responds by unleashing Nature's fury to keep him in check. Where the gods failed in the Massilian grove, Nature does not, and the tyrant fails to reach Antony's troops at Brundisium.

Thus, the Adriatic Sea becomes the ideal site of what I label *utopian dystopia*: it is at once a terrifying and a hopeful place. It is a *locus* that for its literal awesomeness and its symbolic underpinnings materializes on page the "disharmonious harmony" (*concordia discors*)[85] with which Lucan visualizes the whole world, the history of Rome, and the fragile equilibrium keeping the universe together.[86] In the description of the storm we see at work the subtle balance embedded in Lucan's oxymoronic expression: although the storm is so violent that the fabric of the κόσμος (*kosmos*) may crash down onto itself (*discors*), at last calm returns, and the sea does not leave its bed (*concordia*). If we transfer this tension on to the symbolic, meta-poetic level, we may rest assured that the discordant elemental force that is Caesar as the thunder-bearer will at last be quelled just like a storm, as indeed he was in 44 BCE. Caesar's partial defeat at sea, then, looks forward to the tyrant's murder in the Senate House, and provides some hope to the pro-Republicans.

As he witnesses the sublime phenomenon of the sea in revolt, rather than gaining greater insight into the human and universal condition (as Lucretius' devotees do in their experiencing of the sublime atomistic

84 7.812–815.
85 1.98.
86 Lucan borrows the expression from Ovid to describe the temporary peace among the triumvirs, but the expression aptly describes the Lucanian *Weltanschauung* in general.

universe they decipher through Epicurean enlightenment), Caesar is laser-focused on his megalomaniac ambition: all he cares about is the fact that future generations will fear him for his extraordinarily hubristic (mis)deeds: provided that he is feared, he cares not to die, nor for a funeral pyre or a sepulcher.[87] The tyrant's inability to learn from Nature and see beyond his own tyrannical ambition is a further symptom of his future, unavoidable slip from Fortune.

---

87 5.668–671.

Classical Receptions

How to Detain a Tsunami: Impassable Boundaries against Ocean Chaos in Ancient and Modern Imaginaries

Manuel Álvarez-Martí-Aguilar

Introduction

It would not be rash to claim that until Boxing Day 2004, most people were unfamiliar with tsunamis. The media images of tourists on the Thai beaches, puzzled but not alarmed by the rapidly retreating ocean and quite unaware of the approaching destruction with its violent return, reveal the lack of understanding of this natural phenomenon among those who do not live in high-risk, seismic hazard zones, such as the seaboards of Japan and Chile. The film *The Impossible* (2012) recounts the catastrophe on 26 December and perfectly illustrates the way in which the contemporary globalized society regarded that mega-tsunami as an inconceivable event.[1]

How have the cultures of the Mediterranean perceived the tsunami phenomenon over time? This question is the leitmotif of this chapter, which revolves around Fernand Braudel's idea of *longue durée*.[2] Specifically, it is suggested here that there was a long-standing cosmogonic and cosmological framework in the cultures of the Mediterranean, through

This research has been funded by the Spanish Ministry of Science and Innovation, the State Research Agency, and the European Regional Development Fund (ERDF) through the Grant PGC2018-093752-B-I00 ("Earthquakes and Tsunamis in the Iberian Peninsula during Antiquity: Social Responses in the *longue durée*"). I would like to express my gratitude to Hamish Williams for his invaluable help and assistance in the final drafting of this chapter.

1 Juan A. Bayona, dir., *The Impossible* (Madrid: Apaches Entertainment, Telecinco Cinema, 2012).

2 Fernand Braudel, "Histoire et sciences sociales: la longue durée," *Annales: Economies, Societes, Civilisations* 13, no. 4 (1958): 725–753.

which tsunamis were perceived in symbolic terms with common keys in both the Judeo-Christian and Graeco-Latin traditions. An attempt will be made here to show that in this tradition the sea was understood as a chaotic element, dominated and contained by the deity and separated from the land at the moment of creation, and on which cosmic limits were imposed with the command never to transgress them. Likewise, it will be demonstrated how the image of the flood, in both the Judeo-Christian and Graeco-Latin traditions, implies the transgression of those cosmic limits imposed on the sea. On the basis of these images, some of the representations of historical tsunamis, such as those occurring in the eastern Mediterranean in AD 365 and in the Atlantic in AD 1755, hinging on this symbolism, will be addressed below. To align this with the thematic focus of this volume, the concept of "catastrophe" that I use in this chapter refers to the immense tragedy and human suffering produced by extreme environmental events, perceived by ancient societies as an embodiment of chaos. Thus, the tsunami is perceived as representative of primordial chaos and, as a result, able (potentially) to cause human catastrophe, but as I demonstrate in this paper, they usually do not, due to "impassable barriers": a cultural, religious construction to guard against such catastrophes from the sea.

Chaos, Creation, and Cosmic Boundaries

The cosmogonic model on which this chapter is based is the famous *Chaoskampf*, recently defined as "a category of divine combat narratives with cosmogonic overtones, though at times turned secondarily to other purposes, in which the hero god vanquishes a power or powers opposed to him, which generally dwell in, or are identified with, the sea, and are presented as chaotic, dissolutory forces."[3] Indeed, that the sea is represented as a chaotic entity confronting the forces of cosmic order is a platitude in the cosmological frameworks and the cosmogonic accounts of the cultures of the ancient Middle East.

It is particularly interesting to highlight the "containing" of that chaotic entity and its "separation" from the land as actions linked to the creation of the cosmos. Although it is possible to glimpse some of those elements in the cosmogonic act associated with the battle between the hero god

---

3 Nick Wyatt, "National Memory, Seismic Activity at Ras Shamra and the Composition of the Ugaritic Baal Cycle," *Ugarit-Forschungen* 48 (2017): 560n35.

Marduk and Tiamat, the primordial deity incarnating the salty waters, in the *Enuma Elish*, the Babylonian creation poem (probably composed in the late second millennium BCE), the starting point here is the first part of the Ugaritic Baal Cycle (composed in the thirteenth century BCE),[4] which offers an account of the clash between Baal, the god of the land and the atmosphere, and Yam, the god of the sea. In the Ugaritic context, this conflict expresses what Paul K.-K. Cho has called the "sea myth"; this is "the story of divine conflict with and ultimate triumph over aquatic forces of evil and disorder," very widespread in the societies of the ancient Middle East during the Bronze Age.[5] Baal confronts Yam and Mot, the incarnations of the sea and death, respectively, and defeats the former, a deity identified with the monstrous Litan, "the fleeing snake, [...] the twisting snake, The powerful one with seven heads,"[6] in direct connection to the biblical Leviathan.[7] The logic behind the primordial battle between the cosmic deity and the sea, as a representation of the chaotic forces threatening humanity, is developed more extensively and with richer nuances in the Hebrew Bible in the images of Yahweh's confrontation with the sea.[8] It was precisely these biblical images that would serve as a frame of reference for the representation of historical tsunamis in the Judeo-Christian tradition. As can be deduced from the title of this chapter, in these images the concept of a "boundary" between the sea and the land established by God at the moment of creation would be of utmost importance. The hypothesis put forward here is not only grounded in a cosmogonic framework characteristic of the cultures of the ancient Middle East, but it also has evident parallels in the Graeco-Latin world. This model revolves around the concept of creation as the act of "separating"

---

4 *KTU* (*Keilalphabetische Texte aus Ugarit*) 1.1–1.2; see Mark S. Smith, ed., *The Ugaritic Baal Cycle. Volume I. Introduction with Text, Translation and Commentary of KTU 1.1–1.2* (Leiden: Brill, 1994); Mark S. Smith and Wayne T. Pitard, eds. and trans., *The Ugaritic Baal Cycle. Volume II. Introduction with Text, Translation and Commentary of KTU/CAT 1.3–1.4* (Leiden: Brill, 2009).

5 Paul K.-K. Cho, *Myth, History, and Metaphor in the Hebrew Bible* (Cambridge: Cambridge University Press, 2019), 1.

6 *KTU* 1.5 I 1–3; Smith and Pitard, *Ugaritic Baal Cycle*, 252.

7 Isa. 27:1; Ps. 74:13–14.

8 For the role of the sea in the Hebrew Bible and its conflict with Yahweh, see Cho, *Myth, History, and Metaphor*; John Day, *God's Conflict with the Dragon and the Sea: Echoes of a Canaanite Myth in the Old Testament* (Cambridge: Cambridge University Press, 1985); Carola Kloos, *Yhwh's Combat with the Sea: A Canaanite Tradition in the Religion of Ancient Israel* (Amsterdam: G. A. van Oorschot; Leiden: Brill, 1986); Mary K. Wakeman, *God's Battle with the Monster: A Study in Biblical Imagery* (Leiden: Brill, 1973).

previously existing cosmic elements[9] and confining them to a specific place by establishing boundaries that also occasionally serve – as we shall see later – as links.

The starting point of the arguments set out here – for whose development St Jerome's *Biblia Vulgata* will be frequently cited – is the passage of Genesis 1 in which, on the third day of creation, Yahweh commands the waters to recede so as to allow the dry land to appear: "And God said, 'Let the waters under the sky be gathered together into one place, and let the dry land appear'. And it was so. God called the dry land Earth, and the waters that were gathered together he called Seas [...]."[10] The acts of separation that comprise the process of creation in Genesis describe the withdrawal of the waters, which, in turn, allows for the appearance of the living space for humanity. This is depicted in a more complex and nuanced manner in Psalm 104:

> You set the earth on its foundations,
> so that it shall never be shaken.
> You cover it with the deep as with a garment;
> the waters stood above the mountains.
> At your rebuke they flee;
> at the sound of your thunder they take to flight.
> They rose up to the mountains, ran down to the valleys
> the place that you appointed for them.
> You set a boundary that they may not pass,
> so that they might not again cover the earth.[11]

The marking out of earth's foundations by Yahweh has connotations that could almost be called "anti-seismic." His action is dual. Firstly, he covers the land with the waters, an image that presents the sea "as a somewhat sinister force that, left to its own, would submerge the world and forestall the ordered reality we call creation,"[12] before commanding the waters to recede and forcing them to occupy the place reserved for them in the cosmos. That forced retreat of the waters is replete with underlying tension: the image of the sea is one of a contained, almost compressed

---

9 Cho, *Myth, History, and Metaphor*; John H. Walton, *Genesis 1 as Ancient Cosmology* (Winona Lake, IN: Eisenbrauns, 2011).

10 Gen. 1:9–10 (New Revised Standard Version translation [NRSV]).

11 Ps. 104:5–9 (NRSV).

12 Jon D. Levenson, *Creation and the Persistence of Evil: The Jewish Drama of Divine Omnipotence* (Princeton, NJ: Princeton University Press, 1994), 15.

body, in which it is possible to perceive a latent but clear will to expand and return to its previous state. Thus, Yahweh is obliged to impose a limit (*terminus*) on the waters that prevents them from returning. The image of the *terminus* imposed on the waters thus acquires a tremendous symbolic power; it represents the line of defence and protection of the land, the human habitat, against the permanent threat of the return of the waters.

The image of the boundary imposed on the sea by Yahweh acquires new nuances in other biblical passages in which to the physical boundary is added the prohibition to break His command. For instance, in Proverbs 8 there is a passage in which the personification of wisdom vindicates his presence during the acts of creation performed by Yahweh:

> When he established the heavens, I was there,
> when he drew a circle on the face of the deep,
> when he made firm the skies above,
> when he established the fountains of the deep,
> when he assigned to the sea its limit,
> so that the waters might not transgress his command,
> when he marked out the foundations of the earth [...].[13]

In this case, during those acts of creation Yahweh imposes not only a limit (*terminus*) on the sea but also a mandate (*lex*), preventing it from giving free rein to its expansionary tendencies and from transgressing the limits (*finis*) imposed on it. In St Jerome's *Biblia Vulgata*, the terms employed – *terminus, finis* – underscore the cosmological importance of that boundary, which is physically and spatially specified in Jeremiah 5:

> Do you not fear me? says the Lord;
> Do you not tremble before me?
> I placed the sand as a boundary for the sea,
> a perpetual barrier that it cannot pass;
> though the waves toss, they cannot prevail,
> though they roar, they cannot pass over it.[14]

For sustaining the aforementioned argument, it is important to stress the role of the sand (*harena*) as a physical barrier which Yahweh establishes as the boundary (*terminus*) of the sea. As in Proverbs 8:29 (*lex*), this

---

13 Prov. 8:27–29 (NRSV).
14 Jer. 5:22 (NRSV).

physical boundary is reinforced by a perpetual command (*praeceptus sempiternus*) that is necessary for preventing the sea, yet again depicted as a permanently aggressive and threatening body, from transgressing (*transeo*) that limit and invading the land.

Together with Psalm 104:5–9, Proverbs 8:29, and Jeremiah 5:22, the biblical passage that makes the greatest contribution to shaping this core narrative, which would subsequently be used to represent tsunamis in the Judeo-Christian tradition, is to be found in Job 38:8–11. In these verses, Yahweh reminds Job of His acts at the moment of creation, including the contention of the sea:

> Or who shut in the sea with doors
>   when it burst out from the womb? –
> when I made the clouds its garment,
>   and thick darkness its swaddling band,
> and prescribed bounds for it,
>   and set bars and doors,
> and said, "Thus far shall you come, and no farther,
>   and here shall your proud waves be stopped?"[15]

In the previous passages, Yahweh forces the sea to retreat to its proper place in the cosmos, before imposing an impassable limit on it, but in this case he is shown curbing and containing a sea that seems to have already transgressed those limits. The metaphor employed is that of a birth,[16] but it is a violent and threatening transgression. In response, Yahweh imposes not only a new limit (*terminus*) on the sea but also "physical" elements of contention – *vectes et ostia* ("bars and doors") – while issuing a powerful command which is now explicit: *usque huc venies et non procedes amplius* ("thus far shall you come, and no farther").

As Paul K.-K. Cho has rightly indicated, this series of biblical passages reflects the common belief in the ancient Middle East that the very existence of the land and life on it are the result of "the establishment and maintenance of a boundary between land and sea [...]. Creation is first and foremost an act of expulsion and exclusion, of building a wall and its maintenance."[17] In effect, the command that Yahweh delivers to the sea during the act of creation serves as a protective wall for humanity in

---

15 Job 38:8–11 (NRSV).

16 Collin R. Cornell, "God and the Sea in Job 38," *Journal of Hebrew Scriptures* 12 (2012): 1–15.

17 Cho, *Myth, History, and Metaphor*, 73–74.

the face of a threat as perpetual as His mandate and which is maintained thanks to His divine benevolence. As Jon D. Levenson has highlighted, this image is fraught with tension since "God has not annihilated the primordial chaos. He has only limited it."[18]

Floods and Boundaries

The flood with which Yahweh decides to eradicate life on earth implicitly signifies the elimination of that protective wall and a return to the status quo before the creation, when the elements were unseparated. However, in the passage in Genesis describing the Flood, this image is not explicit, with centre stage being given instead to "the springs of the great deep [...] and the floodgates of the heavens,"[19] which are opened to allow the rain to fall for 40 days and nights, and which are then closed following a flood lasting 150 days, once life on earth has been extinguished, the moment at which Yahweh restores the cosmic balance by forcing the waters to retreat.[20]

The covenant that Yahweh then establishes with Noah and his offspring, guaranteeing that "never again shall all flesh be cut off by the waters of a flood, and never again shall there be a flood to destroy the earth,"[21] also unreservedly implies the restoration of the cosmic wall protecting humanity from the sea. Be that as it may, the image of a flood breaking the boundary between the land and the sea is expressed more sharply and explicitly in the Graeco-Latin tradition, specifically, in Ovid's *Metamorphoses*. This work contains a cosmogonic episode and the account of a flood, both directly interrelated, which also revolve around the idea of a boundary between the cosmic elements, although in a tone differing from that of the biblical account.[22]

The passage describing the creation in the *Metamorphoses* starts by defining original chaos as "a shapeless, unwrought mass of inert bulk," characterized by the disconnection and discordance between the cosmic

---

18 Levenson, *Creation*, 123.
19 Gen. 7:11 (NRSV).
20 8:2.
21 9:11 (NRSV).
22 See Karen Sonik, "From Hesiod's Abyss to Ovid's *rudis indigestaque moles*: Chaos and Cosmos in the Babylonian 'Epic of Creation'," in *Creation and Chaos: A Reconsideration of Hermann Gunkel's Chaoskampf Hypothesis*, ed. Jo Ann Scurlock and Richard H. Beal (Winona Lake, IN: Eisenbrauns, 2013), 1–25.

elements – the land, the sea, and the air – which are "all heaped together in anarchic disarray."[23] In this case, the act of creation is also propitiated by "some god (or kinder nature)" and involves separating the cosmic elements – "earth from heaven, sea from earth and fluid ether from the denser air" – and associating them with a harmonic structure, bounding "the disentangled elements each in its place and all in harmony."[24] As Richard Tarrant observes, "the divine activity of creation consists in separating the elements, putting an end to their strife, and assigning a fixed place to each of them."[25]

In the cosmogonic model of the *Metamorphoses*, the idea of a boundary between the cosmic elements also acquires enormous structural importance, as can be seen in the account of the flood. In this case, there is indeed a direct reference to the disappearance of the boundaries between the cosmic elements once the flood has been unleashed:

> If any roof has managed to resist,
> untoppled, this unnatural disaster,
> the waves embrace above it nonetheless;
> its highest turrets lie beneath the flood.
> There are no longer boundaries between
> earth and the sea, for everything is sea,
> and the sea is everywhere without a shore.[26]

"There are no longer boundaries between / earth and the sea" (*Iamque mare et tellus nullum discrimen habebant*).[27] The cosmological importance of the boundary between the land and the sea is evinced in the scene depicting the end of the flood, when Neptune orders Triton to blow his shell so as to signal the start of the retreat of the waters:

> [...] the waters everywhere, on land and sea,
> all heard that sound, and were at once restrained.
> Now seas have shores [...] [*Iam mare litus habet*].[28]

---

23 Ov. *Met.* 1.7–9; Charles Martin, trans. and ed., *Ovid: Metamorphoses* (New York and London: W. W. Norton & Company, 2004). All subsequent translations from Ovid are Martin's.

24 Ov. *Met.* 1.21–25.

25 Richard Tarrant, "Chaos in Ovid's *Metamorphoses* and its Neronian Influence," *Arethusa* 35, no. 3 (2002): 350.

26 Ov. *Met.* 1.288–292.

27 1.291.

28 1.341–343.

The reappearance of the shores implies the restoration of the boundary and the bond of harmony between the land and the sea and, by extension, the restoration of cosmic order after the flood triggered a return to a form of original chaos, dominated by the state of disarray between the elements. Nevertheless, in the *Metamorphoses*, this flood is not the only catastrophe of cosmic dimensions – by "catastrophe," incidentally, I refer to the human toll or disaster which the watery chaos brings about in Ovid's passage ("If any roof has managed to resist, / untoppled, this unnatural disaster").[29] When Phaethon loses control of the horses drawing Helios' chariot, which is tantamount to transgressing the cosmic limits, this threatens to plunge the cosmos once again into shapeless, original chaos. In the face of the imminent danger, Tellus, the Earth, exclaims,

> Now if the sea, the lands, the heavens perish,
> all will be plunged in chaos once again [*in chaos antiquum*
> *confundimur*].[30]

As Richard Tarrant appropriately remarks in his commentary on this passage, "the verb *confundimur* is especially noteworthy, suggesting the collapse of boundaries keeping the realms of the cosmos distinct."[31] Indeed, in both this episode and that of the flood, the transgression of the limits between the cosmic elements and their possible disappearance implies a return to original chaos, namely, *chaos antiquum*.

The AD 365 Tsunami: Breaking the Boundaries

In the previous sections, a model of perception of the relationship between the land and the sea in cosmic terms has been identified. This model, which was widespread in the ancient Middle Eastern and Graeco-Latin traditions, revolves around the idea of the boundary established by the deity between both elements at the moment of creation. As has also been seen, in these traditions the images of the flood imply the disappearance of that boundary and a return to original chaos. The next section of this chapter demonstrates how this symbolic and narrative model served as a conceptual framework for constructing representations of

29 1.288–289.
30 2.298–299.
31 Tarrant, "Chaos in Ovid's *Metamorphoses*," 351.

the tsunami phenomenon in the Judeo-Christian cultural tradition, in a long-drawn-out process.

The first case addressed here entails representations of the best-known earthquake and tsunami in antiquity, which occurred on 21 July AD 365.[32] The epicentre of the earthquake, with an estimated moment magnitude of at least 8.5, was located close to Crete, where it has been associated with a nine-metre episodic uplift of the western part of the island. In turn, the archaeological evidence points to a broad horizon of destruction in the Cretan sites dating from the fourth century AD. In view of the reconstruction based on literary testimonies, archaeological evidence, and mathematical modelling, the tsunami generated by the earthquake affected the coasts of Crete, the Peloponnese, Sicily, Croatia, and North Africa, including Alexandria.[33]

The abundant literary references to the AD 365 earthquake and tsunami, dating from the last third of the fourth century AD onwards, are to be found in the works of both pagan and Christian authors. The excellent studies performed hitherto on these sources have identified, among other aspects, their important apologetic and political implications.[34] The most well-known portrayal of the AD 365 tsunami is provided

32 The Alexandria tsunami of AD 365 is also discussed in Middleton's chapter in this volume.

33 On the AD 365 earthquake and tsunami, see Nicholas N. Ambraseys, *Earthquakes in the Mediterranean and Middle East: A Multidisciplinary Study of Seismicity up to 1900* (Cambridge: Cambridge University Press, 2009), 151–156; Emanuela Guidoboni, *Catalogue of Ancient Earthquakes in the Mediterranean Area up to the 10th Century* (with the collaboration of Alberto Comastri and Giusto Traina) (Rome: Istituto Nazionale di Geofisica, 1994), 267–274; Emanuela Guidoboni and John E. Ebel, *Earthquakes and Tsunamis in the Past: A Guide to Techniques in Historical Seismology* (Cambridge: Cambridge University Press, 2009), 404–413. For a reassessment of the impact of the tsunami on Alexandria, see Stathis C. Stiros, "Was Alexandria (Egypt) Destroyed in A.D. 365? A Famous Historical Tsunami Revisited," *Seismological Research Letters* 91, no. 5 (2020): 2662–2673.

34 On the literary traditions about the catastrophe of AD 365, see Guidoboni, *Catalogue*, 267–274; Martine Henry, "Cassien et les autres: les sources littéraires et les événements géologiques du 21 Juillet 365," *Klio* 94, no. 1 (2012): 175–196; François Jacques and Bernard Bousquet, "Le cataclysme du 21 juillet 365: Phénomène régional ou catastrophe cosmique?," in *Tremblements de terre, histoire et archéologie: IVèmes Rencontres internationales d'archéologie et d'histoire d'Antibes, 2–4, novembre 1983* (Valbonne: APDCA, 1984), 183–198; François Jacques and Bernard Bousquet, "Le raz de marée du 21 juillet 365," *Mélanges de l'École française de Rome: Antiquité* 96, no. 1 (1984): 423–461; Gavin Kelly, "Ammianus and the Great Tsunami," *Journal of Roman Studies* 94 (2004): 141–167; Claude Lepelley, "Le presage du nouveau desastre de Cannes: la signification du raz de maree du 21 juilliet 365 dans l'imaginaire d'Ammien Marcelin," *Kokalos* 36–37 (1991): 203–214.

by the Roman historian Ammianus Marcellinus,[35] who offers a baroque account of its impact on Alexandria in Egypt,[36] plausibly describing the stages characterizing a tsunami, from the sea's initial retreat to its subsequent catastrophic return. In a previous work, I have attempted to show how in Ammianus' account the tsunami is perceived as breaking the *concordia elementorum*, like a disruption of the natural harmony between the land and the sea.[37] It is an image that connects with the model of the orderly cosmos through its references to notions of harmony, as has been seen in Ovid's work.

However, in the works of Christian authors in the fourth century referring to the AD 365 tsunami, the image that is systematically repeated is that of the sea's anomalous transgression of its own boundaries. The first Christian author to offer such an image was St Jerome, when referring to the cataclysm in three of his works. In Jerome's *Chronicon* (written ca AD 380; a continuation of Eusebius' *Chronicon*, compiled in the early fourth century AD), he states as follows: "There was an earthquake throughout the world, and the sea flowed over the shore [*terrae motu per totum orbem facto mare litus egreditur*], causing suffering to countless peoples in Sicily and many other islands."[38] A similar image can be found in St Jerome's *Commentary on Isaiah*, which relates how the inhabitants of Areopolis recalled a major earthquake occurring when he was a child: "And the sea swept in over the shores of the whole world [*totius orbis litus trangressa sunt maria*], and the city walls collapsed that same night."[39] The third reference to the tsunami by St Jerome appears at the beginning of a passage in a chapter of his biography on St Hilarion, to which the following section will be exclusively devoted. Yet again, the same image is repeated: "At that time there was an earthquake over the whole world [*terrae motu totius orbis*], following on the death of Julian, which caused the sea to burst its bounds [*maria egressa sunt terminos suos*], and left ships hanging on the edge of mountain steeps [...]."[40]

---

35 Amm. Marc. 26.10.15–19.

36 Kelly, "Ammianus"; cf. Stiros, "Was Alexandria (Egypt) Destroyed?"

37 Manuel Álvarez-Martí-Aguilar, "Talismans against Tsunamis: Apollonius of Tyana and the *stelai* of the Herakleion in Gades (*VA* 5.5)," *Greek, Roman, and Byzantine Studies* 57, no. 4 (2017): 979.

38 Euseb. *Chron.* 244 c; Guidoboni, trans., *Catalogue*, 268.

39 Hieronymus (Jerome), *Commentary on Isaiah* PL 24; Guidoboni, trans., *Catalogue*, 266.

40 Hieron. *Vita Hilarionis* 40; William Henry Fremantle, trans., *Jerome: Letters and Select Works* (NPNF2-06), ed. Philip Schaff and Henry Wace (New York: The Christian Literature Company; Oxford and London: Parker & Company, 1893), 313.

This same image, that of the tsunami understood as the sea's transgression of the limits (*termini*) that have been imposed on it, crops up time and again in later authors. In the case of the passage appearing in the *Consularia Constantinopolitana* (fifth century AD), in the compilation attributed to Hydatius, the following can be read: "In 365 during the consulship of Valentinian and Valens, the sea burst its bounds [*mare ultra terminos suos egressum est*] on the twelfth day before the Calends of August."[41] John Cassian (ca AD 399) says much the same in a passage describing the area around the mouth of the Nile, which was affected by the flood: "Panephysis, the lands of which and indeed the greater part of the neighbouring region [...] had been covered by the sea which was disturbed by a sudden earthquake and overflowed its banks [*repentino terrae motu excussum mare transgressis limitibus occupavit*] [...]."[42] Very similar descriptions appear in Socrates Scholasticus' *Ecclesiastical History* (written ca AD 439) and in the homonymous work of the Byzantine historian Sozomen (written ca AD 443):

The sea also changed its accustomed boundaries [*horoi*], and overflowed to such an extent in some places, that vessels might sail where roads had previously existed. And it retired so much from other places, that the ground became dry [...].[43]

A great calamity occurred near Alexandria in Egypt when the sea receded and again passed beyond its boundaries [*horoi*] from the reflux waves, and deluged a great deal of the land, so that on the retreat of the waters, the sea-skiffs were found lodged on the roofs of the houses [...].[44]

The finding of boats on the roofs of buildings after the waters had receded – an image highlighted in other descriptions of the tsunami, such as that of Ammianus Marcellinus (26.10.15–19) in the case of Alexandria

41 Hydatius, *Descriptio consulum* 910; Guidoboni, trans., *Catalogue*, 270.

42 Ioannes Cassianus, *Conlationes* XI, 3; Edgar C. S. Gibson, trans., *The Conferences of John Cassian. Part II* (NPNF2-11), ed. Philip Schaff and Henry Wace (Buffalo, NY: Christian Literature Publishing Co., 1894), 416.

43 Socrates Scholasticus 4.3; A. C. Zenos, trans., *The Ecclesiastical History of Socrates Scholasticus* (NPNF2-02), ed. Philip Schaff and Henry Wace (Buffalo, NY: Christian Literature Publishing Co., 1890).

44 Sozomen, *Ecclesiastical History* 6.2; Chester D. Hartranft, trans., *The Ecclesiastical History of Sozomen*, ed. Philip Schaff and Henry Wace (NPNF2-02) (Buffalo, NY: Christian Literature Publishing Co., 1890).

– is a perfect representation of the disorder unleashed upon ordered human society, the material upside-down catastrophic results of the tsunami. Another similar account, influenced by Socrates Scholasticus, is included in the anonymous *Life of Athanasius of Alexandria*, in the version preserved through Photius: "The sea, having exceeded its boundaries, flooded certain places, so that many areas which were previously farmland became navigable, which was most unusual; in other places it merely flowed out, so that ships were left high and dry [...]."[45] There are further examples up until the ninth century AD, when in his *Chronicle* the Byzantine monk George Hamartolos observes as follows: "When many people came running out to see this extraordinary wonder, the sea flowed back beyond its accustomed limits, and 50000 people were drowned [...]."[46]

In this long tradition of news about the AD 365 tsunami, the Christian authors focus on the sea's transgression of the "boundaries" – *termini*, in the Latin texts; ὅροι, in the Greek ones – imposed on it. *Terminus* is the key term in this symbolic model, which St Jerome himself translates into Latin in the passages in which he describes how Yahweh imposes perpetual limits on the sea.[47] The transgression of that *terminus*, embodied by the *litus* (the coast), thus has huge cosmic implications, for, as will be seen below, it implies the return to original chaos and a repetition of the Flood episode.

AD 365: The Miracle of St Hilarion

The representation of tsunamis in the Judeo-Christian sources must be seen in the context of the biblical model, which depicts the transition from original chaos to the act of creation through distinguishing cosmic elements and through the imposition of limits on the sea. This model served as a structural framework for developing traditions in which the tsunamis were miraculously detained by divine intervention. In this

---

45 Photius, *Bibliotheca* 258, *Life of Athanasius*, 484b; Ambraseys, trans., *Earthquakes*, 154.

46 Georgios Monachos, *Chronicon* 9.7; Ambraseys, trans., *Earthquakes*, 155.

47 Jer. 5:22; Job 38:8–11; Prov. 8:29; Ps. 104:5–9. I have dealt with the response (based on this same model of perception of the sea) of the Phoenicians in the southwest of Iberia to a tsunami that probably occurred in the area around the sixth century BCE; see Manuel Álvarez-Martí-Aguilar, "Melqart-Heracles and the Edge of the World: Religious Reactions to the Threat of the Ocean among the Phoenicians of Iberia," in *Transformations and Crisis in the Mediterranean: "Identity" and Interculturality in the Levant and Phoenician West during the 5th–2nd Centuries BCE*, ed. Giuseppe Garbati and Tatiana Pedrazzi (Rome: CNR Edizioni, 2021), 279–300.

section, the spotlight is placed on the episode appearing in the biography of St Hilarion (written ca AD 390), in which St Jerome describes the miraculous detention of the AD 365 tsunami by the saint on the beaches of the Croatian city of Epidaurus:

> At that time there was an earthquake over the whole world [*terrae motu totius orbis*], following on the death of Julian, which caused the sea to burst its bounds [*maria egressa sunt terminus suos*], and left ships hanging on the edge of mountain steeps. It seemed as though God were threatening a second deluge, or all things were returning to original chaos [*in antiquum chaos redirent omnia*]. When the people of Epidaurus saw this, I mean the roaring waves and heaving waters and the swirling billows mountain-high dashing on the shore, fearing that what they saw had happened elsewhere might befall them and their town be utterly destroyed, they made their way to the old man, and as if preparing for a battle placed him on the shore. After making the sign of the cross three times on the sand, he faced the sea, stretched out his hands, and no one would believe to what a height the swelling sea stood like a wall before him. It roared for a long time as if indignant at the barrier, then little by little sank to its level.[48]

In the passage in which he portrays the tsunami as a transgression of the limits imposed on the sea during the act of creation, the beginning of which has already been discussed above, St Jerome goes on to state something that should be obvious to all by now: that the transgression implies a return to the state of affairs prior to the creation, to wit, shapeless chaos.[49] Accordingly, for St Jerome the tsunami represents the threat of a new flood, perceived as a return to original chaos: *in antiquum chaos redirent omnia*. This expression connects, in turn, with some aspects of Ovid's portrayal of the flood in his *Metamorphoses* and with the idea of returning to original chaos as a result of Phaethon's ill-fated adventure, a transgression of the cosmic limits with catastrophic consequences, in light of which Tellus exclaims: *in chaos antiquum confundimur*.[50]

The threat of a return to *chaos antiquum* is a consequence of the sea's transgression of the *terminus* imposed on it by God during the act

---

48 Hieron. *V. Hil.* 40; Fremantle, trans., *Jerome*, 313.
49 See Jacques and Bousquet, "Le raz de marée," 450ff.
50 Ov. *Met.* 2.299.

of creation. It is no coincidence that St Hilarion readies himself on the beach as if he were preparing to do battle: a gesture reminiscent of the episodes in which Yahweh confronts the sea and its monstrous creatures, such as Leviathan[51] and Rahab, the fleeing serpent.[52] But the crowning moment of the miracle is when the saint, after making the sign of the cross three times on the sand, detains the waters by stretching out his hands: waters, represented as an enraged but impotent wall, which finally subside and recede. In an implicit manner, the saint conveys to the raging sea the message repeated in Psalm 104:6–9, Jeremiah 5:22, and Job 38:8–11, reminding it of the *terminus* and the *praeceptus sempiternus* that He imposed on it during the act of creation and which should never again be transgressed.

   Hilarion's message to the sea is more specifically that conveyed in Job 38:11, when the waters violently invade the land, as if bursting forth from the womb: "Thus far and no farther." We can be reasonably sure of this in view of the details of the next miracle in St Jerome's biography, which narrates how St Hilarion, overwhelmed by the fame that he has gained after the miracle of Epidaurus, decides to flee to Cyprus. During the crossing, some pirates bear down on his vessel, making the crew panic. The danger is again miraculously averted:

> Between Malea and Cythera, the pirates, who had left on the shore that part of their fleet which is worked by poles instead of sails, bore down on them with two light vessels of considerable size; and besides this they were buffeted by the waves on every side. All the rowers began to be alarmed, to weep, to leave their places, to get out their poles, and, as though one message was not enough, again and again told the old man that pirates were at hand. Looking at them in the distance he gently smiled, then turned to his disciples and said, "O ye of little faith, wherefore do ye doubt? Are these more than the army of Pharaoh? Yet they were all drowned by the will of God." Thus he spake, but none the less the enemy with foaming prows kept drawing nearer and were now only a stone's throw distant. He stood upon the prow of the vessel facing them with out-stretched hand, and said, "Thus far and no farther." Marvellous to relate, the boats at once bounded back, and though urged forward by the oars fell farther and farther astern. The pirates were astonished to

51   Ps. 74:13–17.
52   Job 26:10–13.

find themselves going back, and laboured with all their strength to reach the vessel, but were carried to the shore faster by far than they came.[53]

The expression with which Hilarion stops the pirates in their tracks – *hucusque, ait, venisse sufficiat* – connects with the command that God issues to the sea in Job 38:11, in St Jerome's own Latin version: *et dixi usque huc venies et non procedes amplius*. It is the same message that the saint conveys to the sea in the miracle of Epidaurus. The pirates can be seen here as embodying in human terms the catastrophic, chaotic nature of the sea, and their astonishing retreat, on hearing the saint's command, recalls the retreating waters after God has issued His own command, described in Psalm 104:6–9.

As claimed in the Christian tradition, the AD 365 tsunami was not only detained by Hilarion in Epidaurus. According to the account of the Egyptian bishop John of Nikiû (fl. AD 680–690), St Athanasius also detained it before it struck Alexandria:

And in those days [of Valens] there appeared a miracle through the intervention of the apostolic St Athanasius, the father of the faith, and Patriarch of Alexandria. When the sea rose against the city of Alexandria and, threatening an inundation, had already advanced to a place called Heptastadion, the venerable father, accompanied by all the priests, went forth to the borders of the sea, and holding in his hand the book of the Holy Law he raised his hand to heaven and said: "O Lord, Thou God Who liest not, it is Thou that didst promise to Noah after the flood and say: 'I will not again bring a flood of waters upon the earth.'" And after these words of the saint the sea returned to its place and the wrath of God was appeased. Thus the city was saved through the intercession of the apostolic St Athanasius, the great star.[54]

Also in this case, the tsunami is perceived as a new flood, a product of the wrath of God[55] – chaotic but punitive and ordered in a sense – and,

---

53 Hieron. *V. Hil.* 41; Fremantle, trans., *Jerome*.
54 Ioannes Nikiu, 21–23/84; R. H. Charles, trans., *The Chronicle of John, Bishop of Nikiu: Translated from Zotenberg's Ethiopic Text* (London: Williams & Norgate, 1916).
55 The anger of the gods is also the cause of tsunamis in the pagan tradition, as can be seen in the case of the Peloponnesian cataclysm of 373/372 BCE, which is discussed by Middleton in this volume. Diodorus states that it was the wrath of Poseidon that

therefore, Athanasius reminds Him of His commitment and alliance with Noah and his offspring in Genesis 9:11. The "borders of the sea" continue to serve as humanity's first line of defence against the threat posed by the watery chaos.

AD 1755: The Miracle of Our Lady of the Palm in Cadiz

The intention of the last section of this chapter is to demonstrate how the biblical narrative and the cosmological model that it contains – which, as has been seen, forms the core of the representations of the AD 365 tsunami – would yet again play a similar role in certain religious expressions emerging in the wake of the famous earthquake and tsunami of Lisbon in AD 1755. The earthquake on 1 November 1755 was one of the strongest in history. Occurring on the morning of All Saints' Day, its epicentre was located at an undetermined point some 400 kilometres southwest of Cape St Vincent. With an estimated moment magnitude of around nine, it caused widespread destruction in some areas of the Iberian Peninsula and Morocco. The earthquake destroyed the city of Lisbon, which was then ravaged by fire and the tsunami triggered by the earthquake. In addition to Lisbon, many places in the southwest of the Iberian Peninsula and on the Atlantic seaboard of Morocco suffered destructive floods, causing a great loss of life and property.[56]

The city of Cadiz, an ancient island off the southwest coast of Spain connected to the mainland by a narrow isthmus, did not suffer much damage from the earthquake but was indeed affected by the tsunami, which penetrated the western half of the city, destroying sections of its ancient defensive walls and flooding the popular quarter of the Viña. Moreover, the tsunami swept over the isthmus connecting the city with the mainland, killing all those making their escape to the locality of San Fernando.[57]

---

caused the disappearance of entire cities through an earthquake and a flood (Diod. Sic. 15.48.1, 15.49.3–4).

56 On the effects of the earthquake and tsunami of AD 1755 on the Iberian Peninsula, see José Manuel Martínez Solares, *Los efectos en España del terremoto de Lisboa (1 de noviembre de 1755)* (Madrid: Instituto Geográfico Nacional, 2001); Luiz A. Mendes-Victor, Carlos Sousa Oliveira, João Azevedo, and António Ribeiro, eds., *The 1755 Lisbon Earthquake: Revisited* (Berlin: Springer, 2009). On the representations of the catastrophe in European imaginaries, see Theodore E. D. Braun and John B. Radner, eds., *The Lisbon Earthquake of 1755: Representations and Reactions* (Oxford: Voltaire Foundation, 2005).

57 On the effects of the AD 1755 earthquake and tsunami in Cadiz and its impact on the religious life of the city, see José Antonio Aparicio Florido, *El maremoto que viene* (Cádiz:

The earthquake occurred when the people of Cadiz were celebrating the Mass of All Saints' Day, and the subsequent arrival of the tsunami plunged the city into a general state of panic and religious fervour. According to contemporary eyewitness accounts, recourse was had to sacred relics, objects, and images, several of which were displayed before the waters, while prayers were sent to God beseeching Him to save the city from the imminent catastrophe.[58] Notwithstanding the huge loss of life and the material damage, the general sensation transmitted by the sources is that the city was saved from complete destruction thanks to divine intervention.

Following this episode, a tradition about the miraculous detention of the tsunami thanks to the intercession of Our Lady of the Palm began to consolidate itself. The oldest version of the miracle has been tracked down by the researcher Antonio de la Cruz in an anonymous manuscript dating from the end of the eighteenth century, housed in the archive of the Archicofradía de la Palma.[59]

Different versions of this miracle, which all concur in the principal aspects, have come down to us. Following the earthquake, and faced with the horrific spectacle of the giant waves approaching the city, the inhabitants of the quarter of the Viña pleaded with two priests, who had just celebrated the Mass of All Saints' Day in the chapel of Our Lady of the Palm, to succour them. With one of them carrying a cross and the other the standard of Our Lady of the Palm, they made their way to the waters that had begun to flood the city. The crowning moment of the miracle occurred when one of the priests stopped in front of the waters and, driving the standard of Our Lady of the Palm into the ground, exclaimed:

Q-book, 2017); Ana Crespo Solana, "Manifestaciones culturales y actitudes religiosas ante las catástrofes naturales en la España de Antiguo Régimen. El Maremoto de 1755 en Cádiz," in *Naturalia, mirabilia & monstrosa en los imperios ibéricos (siglos XV–XIX)*, ed. Eddy Stols, Werner Thomas, and Johan Verberckmoes (Leuven: Leuven University Press, 2006), 143–168; Martínez Solares, *Los efectos en España*; Martínez Solares, "El Terremoto de Lisboa de 1 de noviembre de 1755," *Física de la Tierra* 29 (2017): 47–60.

58 Manuel Álvarez-Martí-Aguilar and Antonio de la Cruz, "Tsunamis y dioses en Cádiz: catástrofes naturales y respuestas religiosas en la *longue durée*," in *X Coloquio Internacional del Centro de Estudios Fenicios y Púnicos. Homenaje al Profesor José María Blázquez. Mare Sacrum. Religión, Cultos y Rituales Fenicios en el Mediterráneo*, ed. Ana Mª Niveau de Villedary (Sevilla, forthcoming).

59 Álvarez-Martí-Aguilar and de la Cruz, "Tsunamis y dioses en Cádiz"; Ana Mendoza "'¡Hasta aquí, Madre mía!' Cádiz conmemora el aniversario del maremoto de 1755," *La Voz de Cádiz* (1 November 2015): https://www.lavozdigital.es/cadiz/lvdi-hasta-aqui-madre-201510311855_noticia.html#vca=mod-sugeridos-p1&vmc=relacionados&vso=hasta-aqui-madre-mia&vli=noticia.foto.provincia. Accessed 26 April 2021.

¡Hasta aquí, Madre mía! ("So far, Mother!"). According to the tradition, after the priest had uttered this command, the waters were detained and began to retreat, thus saving the quarter and the city from destruction. Over the years, the account of the miracle has been embellished with further details, revolving around the same climax. In an article published in 1844, it is explained how the priest issued the command: *¡Hasta aquí, madre mía, y no más* ("So far and no farther, Mother!").[60]

The story line and, in particular, the mandate prohibiting the threatening waves of the tsunami from going any further are inspired by the biblical passages discussed in the second section of this chapter, specifically that of Job 38:11, in which Yahweh, after having imposed unpassable limits on the sea, reminds it, *usque huc venies et non procedes amplius*. In the account of the miracle of Cadiz, as in that of Hilarion in Epidaurus, the priests reinforce the cosmic limits imposed by Yahweh on the sea during the act of creation by using the cross and driving the standard of Our Lady of the Palm into the ground.

This account and its symbolic keys are still commemorated in the city of Cadiz. A monument with a niche that contained a painting depicting the miraculous detention of the waters (Figure 6), under the figure of Our Lady of the Palm, together with an inscription in verse summarizing the episode, was erected at the place where, according to the tradition, the miracle was performed. The painting, destroyed during the Spanish Civil War, was then replaced by a new one made by Félix Quijada in 1936 and still serves today as a memorial to the catastrophe through the performance of a popular religious ritual.[61]

Each year, on 1 November, the miracle is commemorated by a religious service in the Church of the Palm, after which a procession – a "Rosary of penance" – sets off for La Caleta Beach, the place where the tsunami entered the city, destroying its walls. There, the priest holds a cross over the waters to "bless them." Afterwards, the procession returns to the church, stopping to pay tribute at the place where, according to the legend, the miracle took place, in front of the picture and the inscription observing it. The video images of the 2018 procession[62] allow for suggesting that the

---

60 José María León y Domínguez, "La Estrella del Mar," *La Hormiga de Oro* XLV, 2ª semana de noviembre [second week of November] (1844): 708.

61 Adolfo Vila Valencia, *Episodios gaditanos: piadosa evocación del imponente maremoto que en el año de 1755 asoló por unas horas a la ciudad de Cádiz* (Cádiz: La Gaditana, 1955).

62 Cofrade del Amor, "Bendición de las aguas (La Palma), Cádiz 2018," YouTube (3 November 2018): https://www.youtube.com/watch?v=0mwSay2vdPY&t=23s. Accessed 29 November 2021.

Figure 6: Félix Quijada, *Miracle of Our Lady of the Palm in Cadiz, 1 Noviembre 1755*, 1936. The lower part of the painting shows the priests stopping the tsunami waves through the intercession of the Virgin.

priest holding the cross over the sea at La Caleta Beach is an annual reminder of Yahweh's message to it, showing it the cosmic limits that, under His perpetual command, it should never cross.

Catastrophes, Rituals, and Memory

In this chapter, I have attempted to summarize the symbolic keys of a very-long-standing model of perception of the sea among the cultures of the Mediterranean, which served as a framework for shaping representations of catastrophic sea floods, such as tsunamis. Besides its many versions in different places and times, this model includes a combination of events played out on a cosmogonic stage: the deity's domination over the sea as the incarnation of original chaos, the differentiation between the places belonging to the land and the sea, and the imposition of unpassable limits on the latter with the perpetual command that it should never transgress them. In the framework of this model, the tsunami phenomenon, like that of the flood, is understood as the sea's unlawful transgression of the limits imposed on it and as a return to original chaos, *chaos antiquum*.

The symbolic keys of that frame of representation of the sea, transmitted through the Hebrew Bible in the Judeo-Christian tradition, served as a conceptual framework to cope with the collective anxiety following catastrophic tsunamis throughout history. The keys of that model were employed to construct accounts explaining how the community had been saved thanks to divine intervention, as has been seen in the miracle of St Hilarion in Epidaurus in AD 365 and that of Our Lady of the Palm in Cadiz in AD 1755.

These examples enable us to delve deeper into why this symbolic model of perception of the sea in cosmogonic terms has prevailed over time. It seems that religious rituals and memory places played an important role in preserving the recollection of these major collective catastrophes. St Jerome's account of the miracle of St Hilarion in Epidaurus concludes by stating, "Epidaurus and all the region roundabout tell the story to this day, and mothers teach their children to hand down the remembrance of it to posterity."[63] For his part, Sozomen records the annual commemoration of the AD 365 earthquake and tsunami in Alexandria: "The anniversary of this inundation, which they call the birthday of an earthquake, is still commemorated at Alexandria by a yearly festival; a general illumination

63 Hieron. *V. Hil.* 40; Fremantle, trans., *Jerome.*

is made throughout the city; they offer thankful prayers to God, and celebrate the day very brilliantly and piously."[64]

Through the transmission of accounts of miracles and the periodic celebration of rituals of commemoration of catastrophes, the symbolic keys of the model of perception of the sea and tsunamis have not only survived the passing of time but also been updated in new sociocultural and religious contexts. In this connection, special mention should go to the interesting thesis put forward by Nick Wyatt, according to which an earthquake occurring in Ugarit in about 1250 BCE, which would have destroyed the Temple of Baal and would have been followed by a tsunami, would be related to the specific essence of the narrative of the conflict between Baal and Yam, appearing in the first part of the Baal Cycle.[65]

For his part, Ryan N. Roberts has offered a convincing reinterpretation of Psalm 29, generally considered to be the transposition of a Canaanite or Phoenician hymn, suggesting that it reflects the historical memory of an earthquake and even a tsunami, which would have affected the Phoenician coast.[66] Indeed, the "heavy earthquake imagery"[67] of its verses, together with images like that of "the voice of the Lord [...] over the waters" and that of Yahweh Himself "enthroned over the flood," makes it possible to consider that, also in this case, the recollection of historical catastrophic events might have been reflected in the Canaanite tradition which, in turn, served as inspiration for the biblical psalm. The same approach could be taken to the passages that I have analyzed in the second section of this chapter (Psalm 104:5–9; Proverbs 8:27; Jeremiah 5:22), in which Yahweh imposes a boundary on the sea, perceived as a threatening entity, especially in Job 38:8–11, in which He contains and represses the sea after its violent transgression of the established limits. It is also possible that these passages reflect, in a way, the recollection of some or other historical extreme wave event.

Throughout the history of the Mediterranean, earthquakes and tsunamis have triggered religious reactions that are reflected in mythical narratives and scenes in which the deity confronts and masters the sea and its creatures. The repetition of events of this type, albeit with long return periods, prompted the reformulation of the arguments originally deployed after previous catastrophic events, in a complex phenomenon

---

64 Sozomen, *Ecclesiastical History* 6.3; Hartranft, trans., *The Ecclesiastical History*.
65 Wyatt, "National Memory," 563ff.
66 Ryan N. Roberts, *Terra Terror: An Interdisciplinary Study of Earthquakes in Ancient Near Eastern Texts and the Hebrew Bible.* PhD dissertation (Los Angeles: UCLA, 2012).
67 Roberts, *Terra Terror*, 84.

of feedback over the centuries. The development of modern seismology, which gathered steam precisely as of AD 1755, led to a precise scientific knowledge of the triggering and propagation mechanisms of tsunamis. The memory of the AD 1755 earthquake and tsunami, in cases such as that of Cadiz, has gradually been restricted over the years to sectors associated with the celebration of religious rites commemorating the cataclysm. Broad sectors of the population living in the coastal communities of the Gulf of Cadiz are unaware of the possibility that a similar phenomenon might occur, something that geoscientists and specialists in natural hazards take for granted, given the seismic characteristics of the area.[68] If we take into account the opinion of these researchers, we can dare to say that, sooner or later, the ocean will try yet again to transgress the limits that, according to the Judeo-Christian tradition analyzed here, were imposed on it at the beginning of time.

68 Jörn Birkmann, Korinna von Teichman, Torsten Welle, Mauricio González, and Maitane Olabarrieta. "The Unperceived Risk to Europe's Coasts: Tsunamis and the Vulnerability of Cadiz, Spain," *Natural Hazards and Earth System Sciences* 10, no. 12 (2010): 2659–2675; Javier Lario, Cari Zazo, José Luis Goy, Pablo G. Silva, Teresa Bardají, Ana Cabero, and Cristino J. Dabrio, "Holocene Palaeotsunami Catalogue of SW Iberia," *Quaternary International* 242, no. 1 (2011): 196–200; Klaus Reicherter, David Vonberg, Benjamin Koster, Tomás Fernández-Steeger, Christoph Grützner, and Margret Mathes-Schmidt, "The Sedimentary Inventory of Tsunamis along the Southern Gulf of Cadiz (Southwestern Spain)," *Zeitschrift für Geomorphologie* 54 (Suppl. 3) (2010): 147–173.

CHAPTER ELEVEN

Classical Dimensions of the Robinsonade Pantomime: Neptune, Aphrodite, and the Threat to Civilization

Rhiannon Easterbrook

Introduction

In 1897, Daniel Defoe teamed up with Neptune. Captain F. W. Marshall's pantomime of *Robinson Crusoe*, at the Theatre Royal in the naval town of Plymouth, saw the author's ghost connive with the Roman sea god to end the eponymous hero's life and send him down to Davy Jones's locker.[1] If this seems like a departure from the original story, then Marshall was well aware: he has the long-deceased Defoe justify his murderous plan with the claim that Crusoe is no longer the character he created.[2] By this stage in the reception of Defoe's realist novel, liberties with the text are often part of the pleasure and also serve the ideological preoccupations of the moment. Several pantomime versions include light-hearted depictions of classical characters, especially Neptune, Venus, and the Amazons. While their appearances are usually limited to a minority of scenes, they carry a range of associations. With the late nineteenth century marinading in pro-imperial rhetoric, these figures connect the

I would like to thank the editors of this volume for their valuable insights and many helpful suggestions.

1 A note on authorship: pantomimes incorporated extemporaneous material and were adapted to topical and local concerns. They also featured a significant amount of stage "business," music, and dance as well as impressive sets and costumes. As such, the spoken word is only a small element of the overall impact of a pantomime. The relative unimportance of many pantomime authors compared to the producers is reflected in their omission from many manuscripts. Evidence for this chapter has been gathered from the manuscripts of the scripts in the British Library and from newspaper reviews.

2 "Amusements in Plymouth," *Era* (2 January 1897), 26.

productions to long-standing maritime traditions. They also signify both the potential for disaster that accompanies a sea voyage and the promise of encountering exotic lands and peoples that throw into relief the social and sexual mores of the metropole. In so doing, the pantomime stage transforms a narrative of catastrophe, perseverance, and survival into a kaleidoscope of terror, excitement, and wonder, with both the sea and the lands beyond it brought fully and fantastically alive.

Published in 1719, Daniel Defoe's fictional travelogue is a well-loved account that has been adapted into every format going. According to Ian Watt, by the end of the nineteenth century there had been at least 700 translations, editions, and imitations, not including an opera by Offenbach in 1867. Such has been its role in culture, particularly English self-image, that it has attained the status of myth.[3] It concerns a young man who goes to sea to seek his fortune. After several adventures, he eventually escapes and establishes his own plantation in Brazil. However, being greedy for more profits, as he notes, he sets out on a journey to acquire more enslaved people from Africa for himself and other local plantation owners.[4] On this journey, Crusoe is shipwrecked on an uninhabited island near Venezuela. With no means of escape, but an abundance of perseverance and ingenuity, he builds a decent life for himself, even making two residences and farming grain and goats. After 27 years on the island, he rescues a man who was about to be eaten by men from a warring nation. Crusoe names this man "Friday" and keeps him in his service. Some more time passes, and he then rescues Friday's father and a Spanish man, who were also about to be eaten. After he subsequently rescues a captain of a ship from mutineers, he sails away with Friday and returns to England.

The first pantomime version of the story was created by Richard Brinsley Sheridan for Drury Lane in 1781 and went down so well that it became a "mainstay of the English Christmas 'panto' repertoire through the Victorian period and into the twentieth century."[5] In the eighteenth century, pantomime looked very different from the type of performance that is familiar to modern audiences. They have their basis in the *commedia dell'arte* tradition, with harlequinades – stories about the stock characters Harlequin, Columbine, and Pantaloon – originally as

---

3 Ian Watt, "Robinson Crusoe as a Myth," *Essays in Criticism* 1, no. 2 (1951): 95–119, https://doi.org/10.1093/eic/I.2.95.

4 Daniel Defoe, *Robinson Crusoe*, ed. Michael Shinagel (New York and London: Norton, 1994), 29.

5 Andrew O'Malley, *Children's Literature, Popular Culture, and Robinson Crusoe* (London: Palgrave Macmillan, 2012), 2.

the main focus. John O'Brien considers a few ways in which pantomimes are partially the product of a classical inheritance. Firstly, the genre's name, originally referring to skilled individual performers of the Roman Empire, reflects the highly physical nature of early pantomime. Secondly, the stock harlequinade plot of a young man's frustrated attempts to form a relationship with a woman has something in common with Greek New Comedy. Lastly, and most importantly, when theatre-makers started adding an additional story to go with the harlequinade, these were often based on classical mythology. It is these secondary stories that developed into what we recognize as pantomime today.[6]

The main features of the Victorian pantomime were topical humour, breeches roles, in which women dress as young men, heroes and villains, a montage of spectacular changing scenery, known as a "transformation scene," and a happy ending. Many pantomimes of the nineteenth century continued to feature classical characters, particularly Greek and Roman gods such as the aforementioned Neptune. There may seem to be some overlap with Victorian classical burlesque here. Indeed, two writers of pantomime, James R. Planché and E. L. Blanchard, are remembered by classicists today for their mythological burlesques.[7] However, while the latter genre has received a considerable amount of attention from classicists, their contemporary, pantomime, has not.[8] Pantomime de- and re-contextualizes classical characters even more than burlesques, so that Psyche or Hymen, for example, might appear alongside fairies such as Titania or personifications such as Enterprise or Progress in anything from *Cinderella* to *Aladdin*. Nevertheless, both art forms made use of a general familiarity with classical antiquity that was seen to varying degrees across locations, classes, and genders.[9] Pantomimes can be used

6 John O'Brien, "Harlequin Britain: Eighteenth-Century Pantomime and the Cultural Location of Entertainment(s)," *Theatre Journal* 50, no. 4 (1998): 489–510.

7 Pantomime is generally closer to a fairy story, whereas burlesques are often less magical and instead focus on anachronistic and satirical retellings of familiar tales and serious theatrical productions.

8 For example, Edith Hall, "Classical Mythology in the Victorian Popular Theatre," *International Journal of the Classical Tradition* 5, no. 3 (1999): 336–366; Laura Monrós-Gaspar, *Victorian Classical Burlesques: A Critical Anthology* (London and Oxford: Bloomsbury, 2015); see also Rachel Bryant Davies, *Troy, Carthage and the Victorians: The Drama of Classical Ruins in the Nineteenth-Century Imagination* (Cambridge: Cambridge University Press, 2018).

9 Davies, *Troy, Carthage and the Victorians*; Edith Hall and Henry Stead, *A People's History of Classics: Class and Greco-Roman Antiquity in Britain and Ireland, 1689 to 1939* (London and New York: Routledge, 2020); Richard Jenkyns, *The Victorians and Ancient Greece* (Oxford: Blackwell, 1980).

to make topical comment, play with time and temporality, or express anxieties about social roles.

As with all forms of popular performance in the Victorian period, lavish spectacle was absolutely critical to an audience's enjoyment, with artists and producers making the most of the technology available to them as well as employing large numbers of supernumeraries (that is to say, the theatrical equivalent of extras) in order to build a scene.[10] The designers' skill was highlighted in the transformation scene, which would often be advertized explicitly on posters and playbills and involved spectacular scenic and lighting effects. Therefore, stories were frequently adapted so that as extravagant and impressive a transformation scene as possible could be included. All these visual treats combined with a cornucopia of characters – classical and otherwise – to fully impress upon the audience any dangers or delights that lay in wait for a young sailor.

Inherent to a pantomime's pageantry was its celebration of nation and empire. As Jim Davis has argued, the genre became increasingly nationalistic during the nineteenth century and "endorsed current ideologies in a much more unquestioning way," and it was at this time that *Robinson Crusoe* attained its place as a "core narrative."[11] From the 1860s, pantomimes of *Robinson Crusoe* became increasingly popular and reached their zenith in the 1890s, along with similarly nautical pantomimes of *Sinbad the Sailor*.[12] *Robinson Crusoe* and Robinsonades (narratives similar to Defoe's) with their brave and enterprising colonist heroes were part of children's education, in the form of didactic "home theatre."[13] It was the perfect subject matter for an audience used to hearing "By Jingo" in the music halls. However, as Marty Gould has argued,

> While the earliest theatrical adaptations align Crusoe with coloni-
> zation and the creation of a distinctly English domestic space in an
> alien landscape, later plays de-emphasize Crusoe's efforts to create

10 Michael Booth, *Victorian Spectacular Theatre, 1850–1910* (London: Routledge and Kegan Paul, 1991); David Mayer, "Supernumeraries: Decorating the Late Victorian Stage with Lots (& Lots & Lots) of Live Bodies," in *Ruskin, the Theatre and Victorian Visual Culture*, ed. Anselm Heinrich, Katherine Newey, and Jeffrey Richards (Basingstoke: Palgrave Macmillan, 2009), 154–168.

11 Jim Davis, "Introduction: Victorian Pantomime," in *Victorian Pantomime: A Collection of Critical Essays*, ed. Jim Davis (Basingstoke and New York: Palgrave Macmillan, 2010), 9, 11.

12 Captain F. W. Marshall had already written a libretto for a pantomime of *Sinbad the Sailor* in 1895.

13 O'Malley, *Children's Literature*, 45.

a European settler society and instead highlight Crusoe's brief but culturally transformative encounter with indigenous peoples. As Britain began to embrace a new imperial mode, theatrical Robinsonades began to offer audiences a reappraisal of the Crusoe story, exchanging a vision of permanent colonial settlement for that of geographic discovery and the reform of savage societies.[14]

While a large part of Defoe's story is taken up with the laborious process of adapting the island into a habitable place, these pantomimes focus on the journey and the adventures. The result is that there are no true utopias either to be found or made, only hazards, variously divine, human, and marine, with which to contend.

Just like colonial settlement, Christianity, a theme central to the original novel, cedes its place to adventure. Originally not interested at all in religion, Crusoe rescues a Bible from the wreck, causing him to reflect on Providence, and he becomes a devout Protestant who attempts to convert Friday. This process of religious awakening is entirely absent from the pantomime. While Crusoe originally represents the "novel's once prodigal son, redeemed by piety and industry," this Christian dimension, particularly the reflections on the differences between Protestantism and Catholicism, are usually entirely absent from pantomimes.[15]

With the shift in focus away from Defoe's religious preoccupations comes a more chaotic cosmology with entrenched racial differences, reflecting changed approaches to imperialism. Defoe's work reflected that non-Christian societies' cannibalism was an unfortunate result of their not yet being admitted to the word of God. In fact, Crusoe, when wondering why God had not yet chosen to spread knowledge of Christianity to so-called "savages," sees in Friday the capacity to "make a much better use" of the "saving Knowledge" than his own society currently does.[16] Defoe institutes Providence as a defining organizational principle for the world, which creates savages and non-savages alike. It will doubtless surprise few to note that such ruminations are entirely absent from the pantomimes since a reflective mode is not characteristic of the genre. As will be seen below, these shows, which make free use of racial slurs and blackface, present the British Empire as the sole chance for civilization to

---

14 Marty Gould, *Nineteenth-Century Theatre and the Imperial Encounter* (New York and London: Routledge, 2011), 52.

15 O'Malley, *Children's Literature*, 117.

16 Defoe, *Robinson Crusoe*, 151.

be imposed on largely irredeemable groups. The world of the Robinsonade pantomimes in this chapter is run by competing forces: the modern, thalassocratic British Empire on the one hand and the ancient, classical gods on the other.

The threat of lawlessness in the world at large, and particularly on the sea and in exotic locales, reflects a specifically late-Victorian imperial mode. Mangan has remarked that the framing of imperialist activities, at least in the metropole, at the beginning of the Victorian era was of an honourable and rules-based approach. No matter how far imperialists strayed from these ideals in practice, the self-image of the British elite was that conducting empire was similar to the culture of sportsmanship at a public school.[17] However, as the nineteenth century progressed, a more playful and anarchic form of imperial ideology emerged – what McCorristine calls "ludic terrorism."[18] This is the playfulness of that other great pantomime castaway and classicized figure, Peter Pan, who is known as the "Great White Father" of his own colony but who still needs his mother.[19] The result is that the enterprising adventures of Robinson Crusoe, rather than his traditional domestic and agricultural activities, can be amusingly and joyfully subordinated into a vision of British supremacy against which ancient classical figures are antagonists.

In addition to this playful and boyish form of colonial enterprise, the pantomimes reflect the imperial logic of time and gender. Postcolonial scholars including Anne McClintock have argued that the geographical and cultural differences of societies that Britain saw as primitive were figured as temporal distances. While Britain ran on masculine, linear time, these places were regarded as feminine, anachronistic spaces existing outside of chronological or civilizational progression.[20] As discussed below, this gendered conceptualization of space even extends to the portrayal of exotic lands as "somatopias" or "porno-tropics": fantastical places figured in terms of female bodies, ripe for exploration by the male colonist.

These pantomimes foreground gender and sexual difference due to another innovation, namely the inclusion of romance. Although women

17 James A. Mangan, "Play up and Play the Game: Victorian and Edwardian Public School Vocabularies of Motive," *British Journal of Educational Studies* 23, no. 3 (1975): 324–335, https://doi.org/10.2307/3120191.

18 Shane McCorristine, "Ludic Terrorism: The Game of Anarchism in Some Edwardian Fiction," *Studies in the Literary Imagination* 45, no. 2 (2012): 27–46.

19 Bradley Deane, "Imperial Boyhood: Piracy and the Play Ethic," *Victorian Studies* 53, no. 4 (2011): 689–714, https://doi.org/10.2979/victorianstudies.53.4.689.

20 Anne McClintock, *Imperial Leather: Race, Gender and Sexuality in the Colonial Contest* (New York and Oxford: Routledge, 1995), 30–31, 40–42.

are relegated to barely a footnote in Defoe's original story, the rescuing of Crusoe's sweetheart becomes central to the happy ending in several pantomimes. Poll the talking parrot, Crusoe's one confidante on the island for two decades, becomes Polly Perkins, his girlfriend who must be pursued across the sea and exotic lands. The introduction of numerous female characters, along with cross-gendered casting, as is typical of pantomime, is met with jokes about "new women," transgressive sexuality, and gender roles, suggesting the instability of these categories. The presence of classical characters, with their very existence defying linear temporality, is, perhaps perversely, aligned with the chaos of uncivilized spaces. In that sense, they represent a catastrophic threat to the often-fragile order of British civilization.

Neptune

In the case of Captain F. W. Marshall's *Crusoe* pantomime, linear and colonial time are juxtaposed explicitly. Neptune and Defoe's conspiracy is to wreak revenge on Crusoe, whose character has been so altered that he is now a schoolboy who has run away. While the god and the author wish to keep things as they once were, the pantomime celebrates progress:

> On a series of cloths is shown pictures depicting the Birth, Growth, and Progress of the British Navy. Beginning with the coracles of the Ancient Britons, other types of vessels are depicted, including those of the Norman and Elizabethan periods, the "three-deckers" of more recent times, and, lastly, the modern warships of the Magnificent type.[21]

If the reviewer's focus on the types of vessels themselves rather than the exploits of the Navy itself (or its predecessors) is taken to be representative of the production's content, then this display can be seen as a celebration of British engineering skill in creating the modern warship. While the reviewer admits that this exact subject matter is unusual for a transformation scene, it would surely appeal to the populace of Plymouth, who would have expected local and topical references in pantomimes. As Jill Sullivan argues, "[d]uring the second half of the nineteenth century, the increased number of pointed references [...] had become highly indicative

---

21 "Amusements in Plymouth."

of the new civic status of many of the growing towns of the period, reflecting their assertive industrial pride and political status."[22] The audience at Plymouth, an ancient town boasting long-standing involvement with both commercial and naval shipbuilding and seafaring, would surely have appreciated this innovation. Furthermore, by alluding to a prehistoric past, the display naturalizes Britons as an inherently seafaring nation, suggesting that a combination of continuity and evolution has led to this point of British naval supremacy, in which Plymouth has played an important role.

While classical figures might be adversaries in these productions, the forces of tradition and progress have a relationship that varies between the complementary and the antagonistic. The use of Neptune in particular signals this, as can be seen in a Robinsonade pantomime performed at Exeter. Written by F. Leslie Moreton and produced by the impresarios H. H. Morell and Frederick Mouillot, *Robinson Crusoe, or Harlequin Man Friday and the King of the Cannibal Islands* enjoyed a successful four-week run before being transferred to Torquay.[23] At the beginning, Neptune's traditional activities are in decline, although his manner of expressing himself is decidedly modern. Known here fully as Tornado Neptune, his main purpose seems to be to manage the weather at sea:

> What ho! Is old Neptune quite forgotten?
> Trade may be slack above – down here its rotten!
> I've not had a customer for weeks
> There's not a mariner my aid now seeks![24]

The claim that he is doing less business is not fully explained. It is likely that it refers to the increased safety of sea travel. George Thorne and F. Grove Palmer's *Robinson Crusoe and the King of the Cannibal Islands*, which was produced in 1882 in yet another port city, Liverpool, has a similar complaint. Here, the malign sea spirit Davy Jones opines that because of the recent efforts of Liberal MP Samuel Plimsoll to force shipowners not

22 Jill A. Sullivan, "'Local and Political Hits': Allusion and Collusion in the Local Pantomime," in *Victorian Pantomime: A Collection of Critical Essays*, ed. Jim Davis (Basingstoke and New York: Palgrave Macmillan, 2010), 157.

23 "Provinces," *The Stage* (14 January 1897); "The Theatres," *Torquay Times, and South Devon Advertiser* (29 January 1897).

24 F. Leslie Moreton, "Robinson Crusoe, or Harlequin Man Friday and the King of the Cannibal Islands," Add MS 53622 M, Lord Chamberlain's Manuscript Collection (1897), 9.

to load vessels beyond safe levels, he does not receive as many wrecks and dead sailors into his locker these days.[25] Jones's efforts are thwarted further by the Fairy Queen Electricity, representing modern technology, such as the electric light and the telegraph. Just as the *Odyssean* Poseidon punished the Phaeacians for their expert seafaring and safe conveying of passengers,[26] it is likely that Moreton's Tornado Neptune is doing something similar. He seems to complain of developments in nautical safety and the consequent decline in sailors' reliance on his supernatural powers.

Amusingly, Neptune's services continue to be portrayed as commercial. When Crusoe's enemy, Will Atkins, appears looking to buy from Neptune a storm that will kill the hero, the Olympian vendor claims that he sells storms in his "warehouse" at the "lowest cash terms." Customers have the opportunity to purchase "forked lightning for a guinea extra."[27] Later on, there is a dispute after Atkins fails to settle his account when the storm Neptune raises fails to kill Crusoe. Atkins responds with "what a funny little man you are," and in response, Neptune raises another storm that wrecks the ship, leading to the characters' being swept to the Cannibal Island.[28] In some senses, these actions represent a modernization of the associations we see with divine patrons in ancient texts. Famously, in the *Odyssey* of Homer, Poseidon held a grudge against Odysseus for blinding his son Polyphemus. As revenge, he caused waves to smash the hero's raft. However, his supporter, Athena, calmed the winds in order to save him.[29] Later, Tiresias warned Odysseus that he must make further offerings to Poseidon in order to placate the god.[30] The dynamics at play are replicated to a certain extent by the pantomime, with the Good Fairy Coraline taking Athena's place as the hero's patron. However, while ancient myths require that sacrifices and other offerings be made in order to win a god's favour, Moreton's focus on cash brings relationships between men and classical gods within the sphere of the Victorian obsession with trade and its ethical implications.[31]

---

25 George Thorne and F. Grove Palmer, "Robinson Crusoe and the King of the Cannibal Islands," LCP 1882/296, Lord Chamberlain's Manuscript Collection (1882), fol. 5r.

26 Hom. *Od.* 13.146–152.

27 Moreton, "Robinson Crusoe," 10.

28 Moreton, 19.

29 Hom. *Od.* 5.356–390.

30 11.119–134.

31 A fascinating account of Victorian attempts to square trade and imperialism with Christian values can be found in Geoffrey Searle, *Morality and the Market in Victorian Britain* (Oxford: Oxford University Press, 1998).

Nevertheless, a more mystical relationship with the god remains, and it is one with which many of the audience members would have been familiar. When Neptune returns to retrieve his payment, he explains his presence thus: "Well, as you were crossing the line, I thought I might pop up and exact the usual homage."[32] Neptune refers here to sailors crossing the equator (or sometimes other boundaries such as the tropics), a moment that was observed through certain rituals. This is not the only reference in these pantomimes to the tradition. A pantomime of *Robinson Crusoe* staged at Leicester's Theatre Royal during the 1895–1896 season has Neptune complain in typical punning fashion: "First they cross me, and then they *cross the line*."[33] There are numerous accounts of such rituals, not just from British sea-goers but from travellers of many other countries and over a period of hundreds of years.[34] Audience members may not only have heard of this practice but participated in it, particularly audience members in a port city.

While the ceremony can vary, there are some common themes. According to Simon J. Bronner, the sailors are divided into the experienced ones who have previously crossed the equator and the novices who have yet to do so, with the former being called "shellbacks" and the latter "pollywogs" (tadpoles). Prior to the crossing of the equator, Davy Jones appears to warn the captain "that he is trespassing on Neptune's domain with slimy pollywogs aboard." After the shellbacks have assumed command of the vessel, King Neptune or Neptunus Rex arrives with Queen Amphitrite or Aphrodite, Davy Jones, and various other attendants, such as a royal barber or dentist and a royal baby or belly. Neptune often holds the traditional attribute of a trident and sports a long beard. The novices prostrate themselves during a trial before they are dunked in a tank and finally become shellbacks. While the experienced sailors are treated simultaneously as "superior" and "corrupted" and are answerable to King Neptune, the novices are often duped, humiliated, and violated in a variety of ways, and even treated as animals.[35]

32   Moreton, "Robinson Crusoe," 19.

33   Harry F. McLelland, "Robinson Crusoe," LCP 1895/397, Lord Chamberlain's Manuscript Collection (1895), fol. 4r.

34   Harry Miller Lydenberg, *Crossing the Line: Tales of the Ceremony during Four Centuries* (New York: New York Public Library, 1957).

35   Simon J. Bronner, *Crossing the Line: Violence, Play, and Drama in Naval Equator Traditions* (Amsterdam: Amsterdam University Press, 2006), 9–15, https://doi.org/10.5117/9789053569146.

Many of these pantomimes draw on similar themes and ideas to the line-crossing ritual, albeit in a different register and with the customary happy ending for the goodies and comeuppance for the baddies. As Bronner has claimed, the equator in Western contexts marks the division between the homely North and "exotic" South, something which is emphasized in the ceremony by the shellbacks' costumes as indigenous people, including cannibals of the South Pacific.[36] The practice signals a permanent change for the pollywog, having now transitioned for the first time from the safety of the home to the dangers of the seas and lands beyond. In these pantomimes, Crusoe and several of his companions are frequently portrayed as young or inexperienced in seagoing, particularly if it is Crusoe's mother or paramour who joins him. The trials that they undergo, including shipwreck and abduction by cannibals, then, represent an induction into maritime peril. These pantomime portrayals of indigenous people – often incorporating Man Friday and other characters in blackface – are necessarily steeped in racist stereotypes and represent caricatures of indigenous people that echo other forms of entertainment, such as minstrelsy.[37] In both the ceremony and the pantomime, performers temporarily adopt the signifiers of a racial other that are given meaning by specific performance traditions. As with the line-crossing ceremony, the characters' encounter with Neptune precipitates a development in identity that comes from the mortal danger of sea travel and engagement with fantastical projections of racial difference and hierarchy. They are far from the order of home, and Neptune's presence and the shipwreck signal their vulnerability to the real dangers of sea travel and foreign spaces.

One theme that appears in Victorian texts on the subject is the idea that the line-crossing ceremony is an ancient tradition. For example, a lieutenant of the US Navy in the late nineteenth century suggests the following:

This custom, still observed as a pastime among sailors, began as actual worship of some deity, and finally existing as mere customs, without significance. Anciently, the Greeks sacrificed, on nearing

---

36 Bronner, 26.

37 For a discussion of race in *Robinson Crusoe* pantomimes, see Jim Davis, "'Only an Undisciplined [Nation] Would Have Done It': Drury Lane Pantomime in the Late Nineteenth Century," in *Victorian Pantomime: A Collection of Critical Essays*, ed. Jim Davis (Basingstoke and New York: Palgrave Macmillan, 2010), 111–115.

any prominent cape, on many of which temples to the deities were placed.[38]

Meanwhile, the *Chambers' Book of Days* claims that this form of "saturnalia" began as Roman rituals and used to signal departure from the Mediterranean through the Pillars of Hercules.[39] Lisa Gaughan argues that each re-performance of the ceremony allows sailors to maintain links across time, whether with one's past self and comrades, with mariners in general, or with "the eternal notions of the sea and the mythical creatures that inhabit it."[40] While the ceremony has in reality varied enormously in all respects over the centuries, its status as a traditional ritual and its connection with the deeper mysteries of the ocean were understood by Victorians. Where pantomimes draw on similar imagery, they too can allude to these grander narratives and ancient ties.

In contrast, the innovations of the present put increasing limits on the capacity of both Neptune and the sea itself to act against our heroes. As we saw with the 1882 pantomime at Liverpool, the development of the Plimsoll line was celebrated by the production for its life-saving impact. Harry F. McLelland's 1895–1896 pantomime at the Leicester Theatre Royal is full-throated in its embrace of modernity. Here, Crusoe's helpers against the plots of Neptune are fairies named Invention, Progress, and Enterprise. The god himself is furious to have heard a "saucy land lubber declare / 'Britannia rules the waves!'" and wishes to prove that he is still the real master of the ocean.[41] His use of the epithet "land lubber" recalls Neptune's distaste for inexperienced sailors in the line-crossing ceremony and suggests that only those who have not been subjected to the full might of the sea can believe the claims of the English national anthem. However, the pantomime offers numerous examples of Britain's imperial strength as a counter. The fairy Progress "has come straight from Japan and beating the Chinese has borne good fruit";[42] this presumably refers to

38 Fletcher S. Bassett, *Sea Phantoms: or, Legends and Superstitions of the Sea and of Sailors in All Lands and at All Times*, revised edition (Chicago, IL: Morrill, Higgins & Co., 1892), 416–420, as quoted in Lydenberg, *Crossing the Line*, 172.

39 Robert Chambers, *Chambers' Book of Days*, Volume 2 (Edinburgh: W. & R. Chambers, 1864), 653–654, as quoted in Lydenberg, *Crossing the Line*, 73–76.

40 Lisa Gaughan, "'The God, the Owner & the Master' (Barthes, 1979): Staging Rites of Passage in the Maritime Crossing the Line Ceremony," in *Staging Loss: Performance as Commemoration*, ed. Michael Pinchbeck and Andrew Westerside (Cham: Palgrave Macmillan, 2018), 171, https://doi.org/10.1007/978-3-319-97970-0_10.

41 McLelland, "Robinson Crusoe," fol. 4r.

42 McLelland, fol. 4v.

British imperial dealings during the first Sino-Japanese War of 1894–1895. Meanwhile, when Friday offers to be Crusoe's slave, he is rejected with the explanation that "'neath Britain's flag, that floats o'er countries many, you'll find no slaves."[43] For all of Britain's profits from enslavement, its role in abolition allowed Britons to celebrate liberty as an "English gift" to be bestowed upon Black people and imperial subjects.[44] This allusion to the "English gift" of abolition is a reminder of the apparent utopianizing power of British thalassocracy. While British ideological and technological progress promises to utopianize distant seas and lands, the temporary success of Neptune puts Britons at the mercy of this apparently more primitive way of life.

Naval strength abroad is linked with social, technological, and financial developments at home. Gould argues that the "circular movement from metropole to periphery and back again is the defining characteristic of the Victorian Robinsonade," with the characters often returning having gained the ability to solve a problem at home.[45] Despite the fact that this structure is not present in all *Robinson Crusoe* pantomimes, and although Gould's argument implies a level of narrative coherence that is not customary among this performance genre, circular movement is central to the pro-imperial sentiment of this particular production. Having started off in the great port city of Hull, Crusoe and the rest of his friends are rescued, not back to the Humber estuary, but to the very centre of the metropole: Mansion House in the City of London, the "home of industry and wealth," where Crusoe is given the Freedom of the City.[46] Gould links the Victorian Robinsonade's emphasis on connections between periphery and metropole with Britain's increased interest in "wanting new markets for manufactured goods and new sources of raw materials."[47] The ending of the pantomime in such a way makes clear the economic dimension of imperialist enterprise. However, the maintenance of a new order or *Pax Britannia* is also key. The story closes with Crusoe's enemy, Will Atkins, desiring to meet with Neptune in order to continue his vendetta. He is thwarted by the appearance of Invention, who stands for "the party called Police."[48] The ancient god of the sea has no power against English law and order, not now that Victoria, "our empress,"

43 McLelland, fol. 17r.

44 Hazel Waters, *Racism on the Victorian Stage: Representation of Slavery and the Black Character* (Cambridge: Cambridge University Press, 2007), 131.

45 Gould, *The Imperial Encounter*, 60.

46 McLelland, "Robinson Crusoe," fol. 23r.

47 Gould, *The Imperial Encounter*, 61.

48 McLelland, "Robinson Crusoe," fol. 25v.

can be declared "mistress of the sea."[49] Indeed, the pantomime suggests that soon sea travel may not have to be endured at all: thanks to British technological skill, Invention rescues the castaways on "Maxim's Flying Machine." Created by Hiram S. Maxim, this propellor-driven vehicle, which had been exhibited to the public and covered extensively by the press, was one of many attempts at mechanical flight at this time.[50] In this way, pantomimes remind the audience of the potential for chaos that seagoing can lead to, while averting the ultimate catastrophe for their hero. Although Neptune wins the battle, Britain wins the war.

Aphrodite and the Amazons[51]

Nevertheless, meetings with classical characters are not uniformly unpleasant, and their presence in pantomimes can indicate the more seductive elements of the exotic. One such example is Wilton Jones's *Robinson Crusoe*, which was toured around England and Scotland between 1895 and 1900, having first been originated by the late Thomas W. Charles for the Manchester stage.[52] While the cast changed over the years, the same scenery – or at least the same designers and choreographer – was used to great effect, and the production as a whole was well received. In this version, Crusoe goes to sea after he and his mother are kicked out of their crumbling cottage by "pirate landlord" Will Atkins, who is angered that Polly prefers her fiancé, Crusoe, to him. Crusoe is joined on board by both his mother and his girl, who is disguised as a cabin boy. However, they are soon separated, and Crusoe's constancy is tested by Aphrodite.

The goddess first appears after Crusoe drowns in a shipwreck and he is rescued by her sea fairies, who attempt to seduce him. Her home is a cave beneath the sea and forms part of a scene of visual splendour:

[A]n exquisitely tasteful picture, designed and painted by Mr. K. J. M'Lennan, where amid clusters of coral branches and submarine vegetation, the skeleton of the once good ship is seen.

49 McLelland, fol. 24v.

50 See, for example, "Maxim's Flying Machine," *Illustrated London News* (25 August 1894), 230; C. V. Riley, "Mr Maxim's Flying Machine," *Scientific American* (6 October 1894), 217.

51 A small part of this section appeared in my doctoral thesis.

52 "'Robinson Crusoe' at the Prince's Theatre," *Manchester Evening News* (14 December 1895).

Here a grand shell ballet, arranged by M. Victor Chiado, takes place, and with its troops of daintily attired sea nymphs and rhythmic dance measures, forms one of the most gorgeously beautiful features of the production. At the conclusion, a bevy of sea maidens bear the lifeless body of Robinson Crusoe from the wreck.[53]

Since extravagant spectacle was an end in itself for Victorian pantomime, this scene satisfies that aspect of audience expectation.[54] Crusoe's retrieval is followed by a familiar image: the hero is taken to Aphrodite's home, a cave under the sea. The cave of Venus was well known from the numerous productions of Wagner's *Tannhaüser* that toured Britain at this time and were often enjoyed for their magnificent scenes of nymphs and satyrs dancing in the luxurious home of Venus, in which the title character becomes ensnared.[55] Meanwhile, the scene also echoes the Victorian interest in Atlantis, a fictional, submerged utopia whose decline is a dire warning against the *hubris* of the British Empire.[56] The pantomime draws on familiar imagery to create a space of temptation for hero and audience alike, in much the same way as Aphrodite's underwater paradise may represent the corrupting influence of foreign climes.

The incorporation of Aphrodite evidently builds on her association with love, beauty, and seduction. Of the various mythological traditions surrounding Aphrodite and Venus, this pantomime draws directly from the story of her birth from Uranus' genitals being thrown into the sea,[57] with the sea nymph Wavelet hailing her as "Goddess of love – born of the foam of the sea!"[58] One of the most enduring images of Aphrodite and the sea is Botticelli's painting, and the fact that there was a shell ballet in the pantomime suggests an allusion was being made to the painting of Venus on a shell, which is especially likely given the symbiotic relationship between Victorian theatre and visual art, including art on classical themes.[59] Crusoe

---

53 "Amusements in Edinburgh," *Era* (19 December 1896).
54 Booth, *Victorian Spectacular Theatre*, 92.
55 "The Carl Rosa Opera Company," *Standard* (21 January 1896).
56 Alexander McCauley, *Victorian Atlantis: Drowning, Population, and Property in the Nineteenth-Century Novel*, PhD dissertation (Seattle: University of Washington, 2020), 46, 144–149.
57 Hes. *Theog.* 176–206.
58 Wilton Jones, "Robinson Crusoe," Add MS 53591 L, Lord Chamberlain's Manuscript Collection (1896), 72.
59 Rosemary Barrow, "Toga Plays and *Tableaux Vivants*: Theatre and Painting on London's Late-Victorian and Edwardian Popular Stage," *Theatre Journal* 62, no. 2 (2010): 209–226.

is revived by the power of Aphrodite's love, and she expresses her feelings for him. Here, though, we can expect a happy ending which reasserts British greatness. Robinson Crusoe does not return Aphrodite's affection, despite her offer of his sitting beside her throne. After a short discussion, the goddess relents and says that she is so impressed by his devotion to Polly that she will reunite the two lovers as long as he manages to stay strong in the face of the temptations of the Spirits of the Isles. However, this Aphrodite, whose "heart is full of weariness" and whose "only hope is mortals' sore distress," seems to live a lonely life at the bottom of the ocean, waiting for a mortal man.[60] In some senses, then, she is a dangerous temptation to young sailors and could be compared to Circe or Calypso in the *Odyssey*, who, although powerful characters, encounter the hero as he wanders and then leaves them to return home and to his wife.

The use of Aphrodite and the Isles draws on long-standing sexual anxieties around colonial adventure. Although Crusoe refuses the offer to share her kingdom, he is revived by the kiss of life from the goddess. She is able to "make the chilled blood pulsate through every vein," which has more than a hint of inducing erotic arousal.[61] Her successful reanimation of Crusoe suggests that, for all his faithfulness to Polly, she holds some power over the inexperienced young man. Crusoe's voyage through the seas reflects the link in the colonial imaginary between settling land and male sexual dominance of women. The Spirits of the Isles are about as literal a version as can be made of the "somatopia" or "porno-tropics": fantasy lands for colonization identified with sexualized female bodies.[62] The Spirits of the Isles are both women and anthropomorphic lands. In Scene 8, Crusoe is met by these Spirits, who represent islands with various natural features and resources such as fir trees, reptiles, and "sparkling waters." In at least one iteration, this "radiant picture" has them appear "in a number of brilliantly-illuminated state barges with Venetian masts illuminated by the electric light in vari-coloured lamps."[63] Such an exciting scene combines the display of women's beauty with the exhibition of nautical artefacts and technological innovation in the form of electric lighting. However, Crusoe, while impressed by them, stays focused on his ultimate goal of finding his true love, Polly. Porno-tropics, as McClintock

60   Jones, "Robinson Crusoe," 72.

61   Jones, 71.

62   Darby Lewes, "Utopian Sexual Landscapes: Annotated Checklist of British Somatopias," *Utopian Studies* 7, no. 2 (1996): 167–195; McClintock, *Imperial Leather*, 21–28.

63   "Amusements in Bolton," *Era* (8 January 1898).

shows, while tempting, are unknown, potentially full of danger, and present a challenge to male supremacy. These Isles couple female and telluric fertility, thus evoking the potential for some undiscovered paradise. However, they are framed explicitly as distractions to Crusoe that must be resisted. Through Aphrodite and her associates, sea-voyaging in distant lands is presented as a threat to the family unit.

Pantomimes' casting conventions further complicate the portrayal of sexual and gender norms. Not only is Crusoe's mother the pantomime dame figure, but Crusoe himself is a principal boy, and the band of sailors were often portrayed by actresses too, making women the main performers of male heroism. Rebecca Weaver-Hightower argues that *Crusoe* pantomimes could subvert imperial ideology through this casting.[64] She cites one pantomime in particular, which appears to mock the purported civilizing mission of empire, suggesting that this, when combined with jokes about Crusoe's "manliness," satirizes empire's prizing of manly virtue.[65] There is no doubt that this could be the case in some instances, yet the gendered connotations of male impersonators were varied and complex. These figures were a common and highly popular sight in Victorian performance. Principal boys would often wear costumes that accentuated the female form, revealing their shapely legs and highlighting the hips and waist, which could suggest that they were merely intended as an opportunity for men to view women's bodies. On the other hand, they could also represent an idealized form of masculinity. Vesta Tilley, one of the foremost male impersonators of her time, played Crusoe in the debut production of the Wilton Jones pantomime and would later become involved in military recruitment for the First World War, while posing in uniform as a volunteer.[66] In general, the various gendered and sexual associations of breeches roles were probably as many as there were audience members.[67]

Elsewhere, *Robinson Crusoe* pantomimes do appear to associate masculine women with cannibalistic societies. Virtually every pantomime of this story, whether it includes other classical references or not, makes

---

64 Rebecca Weaver-Hightower, *Empire Islands: Castaways, Cannibals, and Fantasies of Conquest* (Minneapolis, MN: University of Minnesota Press, 2007), 81.

65 Weaver-Hightower, 171–181.

66 "Provincial Theatres," *Clarion* (28 December 1895); Elaine Aston, "Male Impersonation in the Music Hall: The Case of Vesta Tilley," *New Theatre Quarterly* 4, no. 15 (1988): 253–254.

67 Jim Davis, "'Slap On! Slap Ever!': Victorian Pantomime, Gender Variance and Cross-Dressing", *New Theatre Quarterly* 30, no. 3 (2014): 218–230.

a reference to "Amazon women" living on the cannibal islands. The true nature of these martial women relative to their depictions in Greek culture has been the subject of recent scholarly debate, given their usefulness as a scare story for a deeply misogynistic and xenophobic Athenian culture.[68] However, while there undoubtedly were ancient warrior women, these pantomimes seem only to be interested in the exoticism of such characters. It is difficult to know how they were represented on stage since scripts and reviews alike offer few details, and they have no written dialogue; it seems as though there was an assumed, shared understanding about their appearance. Nevertheless, their portrayal as an undifferentiated and unnamed, mass bodyguard on "savage" islands (there are no Penthesileias here) speaks to the colonial association between undiscovered land and the female body that must be subdued. The Amazons' origin in ancient cultures could only have added to the view of colonized land as an anachronistic space. On the other hand, the high likelihood, given contemporary stage representations of other "military" women, that pantomime Amazons sported revealing outfits means they could evoke a utopia that was simultaneously of the porno-tropics kind and a longed-for space of female freedom and power.

Where line-crossing ceremonies recalibrated typical gender norms, they also are open to a range of interpretations. Although played by a woman in the pantomime, the role of Aphrodite, and, where relevant, Amphitrite, were inevitably taken on by a man during the ritual. However, while Aphrodite is near the top of the hierarchy, male femininity does not usually connote a high status. Bronner argues that the feminization undergone by pollywogs during their rite of passage indicates innocence and inexperience.[69] In the case of pantomime, there is a link between male femininity and youth. Crusoe's boyishness was dependent on his being played by a young woman and was an admired quality at the end of the nineteenth century.[70] Yet the "ludic terrorism" of this period's imperialist activities is a boyish mode. No doubt, there was a fear in the late nineteenth century that colonists were in danger of "backsliding" and being seduced by the depravity of primitive cultures.[71] To some

---

68 Adrienne Mayor, *The Amazons: Lives and Legends of Warrior Women across the Ancient World* (Princeton, NJ and Oxford: Princeton University Press, 2014); Walter Penrose, *Postcolonial Amazons: Female Masculinity and Courage in Ancient Greek and Sanskrit Literature* (Oxford: Oxford University Press, 2016).
69 Bronner, *Crossing the Line*, 10–12.
70 Davis, "Slap On! Slap Ever!" 228.
71 Jennifer DeVere Brody, *Impossible Purities: Blackness, Femininity, and Victorian*

viewers, the opportunities for adventures with exotic "savages" could have represented such a lure. The return to the metropole, fiancée in tow, is not just a return to a physical safety but to a moral one.

Conclusion

Just as deities populated the sea in the ancient imaginary (see Denson's chapter in this volume) and helped to make sense of the relationship between the depths and the surface, Greek and Roman gods continued to fill the sea with life in the Victorian era. To the extent that utopias can be considered an "expression of desire," the dwellings of Aphrodite and the Amazons also represent erotic utopias.[72] In this sense, there is yet another continuity with ancient attitudes, in that they express the hope of finding a utopia beyond the sea (see Beek's chapter in this volume). However, ancient utopic ideals ultimately cede place to the modernizing impulse of industrial Britain.

While Robinsonade pantomimes depict the triumph of British might (with the help of a good fairy) over dangerous, classical characters, Neptune and Aphrodite are figures in the game of empire, variously to be vanquished (but never finally) or to be enjoyed for the challenge the catastrophes they induce or threaten present to modernity and order. Just as the drowned utopia of Atlantis is a warning to the British Empire, whatever dangers the ancients might represent, they return night after night and at crossing after crossing: a reminder that the line between savagery and civilization is as fragile as the sea is powerful.

Culture (Durham and London: Duke University Press, 1998), 131–169.

72 Ruth Levitas, *The Concept of Utopia* (Hemel Hempstead: Syracuse University Press, 1990), 8.

CHAPTER TWELVE

Minoan Utopias in British Fiction, after the Thalassocracy: Lawrence Durrell's *The Dark Labyrinth* and Robert Graves' *Seven Days in New Crete*

Hamish Williams

Introduction: From Sea Paradise to Modern Utopia

"Neo-Minoanism" or "Cretomania":[1] a modern, mythmaking phenomenon which draws on Bronze Age Cretan civilization, which is known to us through archaeological finds (infrastructural ruins, works of art, other aspects of material culture) and scholarship, and/or its apparent memory in ancient Greek texts (histories, mythology, epic), and which refashions these through contemporary representations and discourses ("cultural texts") as "the Minoan" – the Minoan civilization, the Minoan people, the Minoan landscape, Minoan legends, and Minoan symbols, entailing iconic figures such as the Minotaur, the labyrinth, and the ritual *labrys* (double axe). This modern mythmaking exercise has been prevalent in a wide array of different cultural texts, practices, and objects since the start of the twentieth century:[2] speculative archaeological writings, such as Sir Arthur Evans'

---

1 For use of the noun "Cretomania" to describe the movement/phenomenon, see Nicoletta Momigliano, "Introduction: Cretomania – Desiring the Minoan Past in the Present," in *Cretomania: Modern Desires for the Minoan Past*, ed. Nicoletta Momigliano and Alexandre Farnoux (London: Routledge, 2017), 1–2. For use of the adjective "Neo-Minoan" to refer to an architectural style, see Fritz Blakolmer, "The Artistic Reception of Minoan Crete," in Momigliano and Farnoux, *Cretomania*, 43; Nicoletta Momigliano, *In Search of the Labyrinth: The Cultural Legacy of Minoan Crete* (London: Bloomsbury, 2020), 76.

2 For general studies on receptions of the Minoan since the start of the twentieth century, see Gerald Cadogan, "'The Minoan Distance': The Impact of Knossos upon the Twentieth Century," *British School at Athens Studies* 12 (2004): 537–545; Cathy Gere, *Knossos and the Prophets of Modernism* (Chicago, IL and London: University of

seminal four-volume *The Palace of Minos* (1921, 1928, 1930, 1935);[3] psychoana-
lytical texts, such as the personal letters of Sigmund Freud;[4] costume design
in theatrical production, such as those of Léon Bakst, particularly in the
Art Nouveau period (ca 1900–1914);[5] autobiographic travel writing, such as
Henry Miller's *The Colossus of Maroussi* (1941), Lawrence Durrell's *The Greek
Islands* (1978), Barry Unsworth's *Crete* (2004), and Christopher Somerville's
The Golden Step: A Walk Through the Heart of Crete (2007); as well as various
fictional genres. These include the detective story, from Agatha Christie's
"The Cretan Bull" (1939) to Barbara Vine's[6] *The Minotaur* (2005); modernist
literary fiction such as Nikos Kazantzakis' *Zorba the Greek* (1946) and André
Gide's *Thésée* (1946); historical fiction such as Mary Renault's *The King Must
Die* (1958); science fiction, whether in literature such as Poul Anderson's
The Dancer from Atlantis (1971) or in television such as *Doctor Who*'s six-part
serial *The Time Monster* (1972); historical fantasy such as Moyra Caldecott's
The Lily and the Bull (1979); horror such as John Farris' *Minotaur* (1985) and
Stephen King's *Rose Madder* (1995); and "postmodern" or critical (often
feminist) literary fiction such as Steven Sherill's *The Minotaur Takes a
Cigarette Break* (2000) and Jennifer Saint's *Ariadne* (2021).

As part of this volume's thematic focus on the sea as a utopic sphere,
this chapter begins by exploring how the Cretan realm of King Minos
(and, later, "Minoan" Crete) was mythologized as a perfective thalassocracy, a great and noble sea empire, in the British imagination, from
Enlightenment intellectuals such as William Mitford to popular archaeologists such as Sir Arthur Evans at the start of the twentieth century. This
pre-classical civilization could provide a benevolent, mythic, "original"
paradigm for justifying Britain's own immense sea empire which reached

---

Chicago Press, 2009); Momigliano, *Search of the Labyrinth*; Momigliano and Farnoux,
Cretomania.

3   For scholarship on Evans' "construction" of a Minoan myth, see Joseph
A. MacGillivray, *Minotaur: Sir Arthur Evans and the Archaeology of the Minoan Myth*
(London: Jonathan Cape, 2000); Nanno Marinatos, *Sir Arthur Evans and Minoan Crete:
Creating the Vision of Knossos* (London: Bloomsbury Publishing, 2014); Ilse Schoep,
"Building the Labyrinth: Arthur Evans and the Construction of Minoan Crete,"
American Journal of Archaeology 122, no. 1 (2018): 5–32.

4   Gere, *Knossos*, 153–160.

5   Nicoletta Momigliano, "From Russia with Love: Minoan Crete and the Russian
Silver Age," in Momigliano and Farnoux, *Cretomania*, 84–91 (*quoque*, see images
of Bakst's work reproduced at the back of the edited volume, 216ff., "Chapter 5:
Momigliano"). For further examples of Neo-Minoan material culture, including the
interior design of cruise ships, in performance art, and Art Deco architecture, see
Momigliano and Farnoux, *Cretomania*.

6   The *nom de plume* of Ruth Rendell.

its zenith in the Victorian age after the Napoleonic Wars. Such nostalgic mythologizations of ancient civilizations as lost paradises of the past were part of the broader process of "national memory"[7] that was so prevalent in the nineteenth and early twentieth century: "the outbreak of nostalgia [in the eighteenth and nineteenth centuries] [...] enforced [...] the emerging concept of patriotism and national spirit [...]. In the mid-nineteenth century, nostalgia became institutionalised in national and provincial museums, heritage foundations, and urban memorials. [...]. The past became 'heritage' [...]."[8] Just as the memory of Minoan civilization was mythologized, refashioned, and "owned" by the British (both the physical land and ethnic identity, in a sense, were owned and copyrighted by Sir Arthur Evans), so too in the early part of the twentieth century the pre-classical Hittite Empire became an important figure in Turkish national identity,[9] as did the pre-European Mesoamerican civilizations for an emerging, postcolonial Mexican national identity.[10]

This chapter, however, is primarily interested in the evolution of this Minoan national mythmaking exercise in the twentieth century, in how this paradisiacal sea empire was reimagined by British writers after global power definitely shifted away from Great Britain in the post-Second World War period, and when Minoan Crete could, thus, no longer serve to inform a unified national myth of pacific, free-trading thalassocrats. To this end, the works of two British expatriate writers are examined: Lawrence Durrell's *The Dark Labyrinth* (1947) and Robert Graves' *Seven Days in New Crete* (1949).[11] As the subsequent analysis shows, both their depictions of "the Minoan" move beyond a nostalgic, British conception of idealized sea-trading islanders, a national myth. The actual sea around

7 For the term, see Wolf Kansteiner, "Finding Meaning in Memory: A Methodological Critique of Collective Memory Studies," *History and Theory* 41, no. 2 (2002): 181.

8 Svetlana Boym, "Nostalgia and its Discontents," *The Hedgehog Review* 9, no. 2 (2007): 11, 13.

9 Can Erimtan, "Hittites, Ottomans and Turks: Ağaoğlu Ahmed Bey and the Kemalist Construction of Turkish Nationhood in Anatolia," *Anatolian Studies* 58 (2008): 141–171.

10 Dylan J. Clarke and David S. Anderson, "1 Past is Present: The Production and Consumption of Archaeological Legacies in Mexico," *Archaeological Papers of the American Anthropological Association* 25, no. 1 (2015): 1–18.

11 Lawrence Durrell, *The Dark Labyrinth* (henceforth, *DL*) (London: Faber and Faber, 2001); Robert Graves, *Seven Days in New Crete* (henceforth, *SDNC*) (Oxford: Oxford University Press, 1983). On Durrell's admiration for Graves' work, especially *The White Goddess* (1948), see Miranda Seymour, *Robert Graves: Life on the Edge* (London, New York, etc.: Simon & Schuster, 2003), 328.

Minoan Crete is no longer a watery space of thalassocratic potential (yielding ideas of expansion, commerce) but, rather, one of danger and potential catastrophe, of cultural ruin. Conversely, the utopian potential of the Minoan is rearticulated with respect to particularly modern contexts: for Durrell, his Minoan utopia is ontological, a place of pure being, which mingles the twentieth-century fascination in psychoanalysis and spiritualism, the latter especially directed towards the cultural East and Buddhism – a kind of Creto-Freudian Shangri-La; for Graves, his Minoan utopia is, in differing respects, a perfect feminized milieu, a personal place for poets, but also a kind of modern, chaotic dystopia (aligning Graves with figures in utopian fiction such as Orwell).

Background: Britannia – and the Minoans – Ruled the Waves

For about a century, from the turning point in the Napoleonic Wars to the start of the First World War (1815–1914), the British Empire was the global superpower; while the reasons for such hegemony must always be multifactorial, the mastery over the seas through the navy and trade fleet was without doubt an essential means for achieving this end.[12] Imperial ideology could legitimize this grand thalassocracy to its public in different respects: for example, through Victorian children's literature which focused on sea exploits such as Stevenson's *Treasure Island* (1883) or theatrical performances, as Easterbrook's chapter in this volume explores in the case of popular Victorian pantomime. The political appropriation of classical and pre-classical, mythic history was also an important means of constructing national memory. While British imperial ideology was doubtless informed by parallels with ancient Roman power[13] and perhaps also with classical Athens,[14] the Greek story of the pre-classical Cretans under King Minos – an island monarchy and thalassocracy just like Britain – provided a potent archetypal paradigm for the British (pre-)imagination of its own sea power.

During the Enlightenment, several British historians of Greece and Rome tended to reimagine and, for the most part, to idealize the early realm

12 See, for example, Robert Johnson, *British Imperialism* (Basingstoke and New York: Palgrave Macmillan, 2003), 4, 19.

13 Rama S. Mantena, "Imperial Ideology and the Uses of Rome in Discourses on Britain's Indian Empire," in *Classics and Imperialism in the British Empire*, ed. Mark Bradley (Oxford: Oxford University Press, 2010), 54–74.

14 Arlene W. Saxonhouse, "Athenian Democracy: Modern Mythmakers and Ancient Theorists," *PS: Political Science and Politics* 26, no. 3 (1993): 487–488.

and rule of King Minos.[15] For William Mitford (1744–1827), "Minos is [...] the very model of an Enlightened Monarch, both within Crete and abroad. Minos' power and influence abroad [...] were based in the first instance on the efficient suppression of piracy [...] in seeing the importance generally of security for all in overseas trade."[16] Two points are worth noting here. Firstly, Mitford curtails Thucydides' famous assessment in his histories so as to avoid the negative side of imperialism abroad;[17] secondly, the notion of the necessary, violent suppression of destabilizing factors to promote the economic ideal of free trade across the seas (even when the trade was not manifestly built upon security for all subjugated peoples) was a stock rationale of British expansionism in, for example, India and China during the nineteenth century.[18]

For Mitford, the benevolence of Minos' foreign endeavours over the seas was a reflection of a certain social–legal utopia which was to be found in his domestic power in Crete: "Minos' important achievement was the creation of a highly advanced state at home in Crete, a state in which all free men enjoyed freedom and equality."[19] Likewise, for John Gillies (1744–1836), "Minos [...] created institutions which were a model, the first such [...] and secured respect for his laws by getting them, Moses-like, direct from Zeus."[20] In these imaginings, King Minos' empire becomes an ancient version of a monarcho-liberal state rather like seventeenth- and eighteenth-century Britain, with emphasis given to equality of laws and the stability of legal institutions (a classically liberal, Enlightened state), divine lineage for these laws (given the prominent role which the monarchy still played in Britain),[21] and the promotion of fair, free trade over the seas.

These receptions of the Greek stories of Minos and the ancient Cretans were, of course, highly selective, drawing on small, isolated fragments of data from, for example, Thucydides,[22] Homer,[23] and Aristotle.[24]

---

15 See Sterling Dow, "The Minoan Thalassocracy," *Proceedings of the Massachusetts Historical Society* 79 (1967): 15–22.

16 Dow, "The Minoan Thalassocracy," 16.

17 See Thuc. 1.4: "And it is reasonable to suppose that he did his best to put down piracy in order to secure his own revenues"; as in Rex Warner, trans., *Thucydides: History of the Peloponnesian War* (London: Penguin Books, 1972), 37. On Thucydides' implicit comment on Athenian sea power, see Dow, "The Minoan Thalassocracy," 15.

18 See Johnson, *British Imperialism*, 18–23.

19 Dow, "The Minoan Thalassocracy," 16–17.

20 Dow, 18.

21 See Dow, 23.

22 Thuc. 1.4.

23 Hom. *Od.* 19.171ff.

24 Arist. *Pol.* 1271b, 1328b, 1330a.

Ambiguous or even negative portraits of King Minos as an imperialist in ancient sources, such as in Herodotus' *Histories*[25] or on the Attic stage,[26] were not entertained. As Dow says, "in this bright setting [of Minos' Crete reimagined by Mitford], the dark monster has no place. There is no adultery with a bull, no Minotaur, no Daidalos and no labyrinth, no abandonment of the seduced Ariadne."[27] In accounts by later nineteenth-century historians of Greece and Rome such as Connop Thirlwall (1797–1875) and George Grote (1794–1871),[28] greater attention is paid to the sheer extent of the sea-based empire which King Minos acquired;[29] thus, for Thirlwall, "without a domain over which to exercise it, however, the power [of Minos] has no meaning. Crete itself is insufficient. Minos' power [...] must mean that he ruled the Islands."[30] The picture of a grand Minoan thalassocracy across the Mediterranean, as a precursor to the British global sea empire, began to be concretized.

The imagination of a grand, pre-classical thalassocracy in Crete was forever changed from 1900 by the archaeological discoveries of Sir Arthur Evans, who, with his considerable financial reserves, bought and excavated the ruins at Knossos. Evans owned not only the physical site of the Bronze Age Cretans in Knossos but also their legacy, which was canonized through his monumental four-volume work *The Palace of Minos* and through their ethnic identity as "Minoans." On the influence of Evans in archaeological and publishing circles, the complaints of his successor in the curatorship of the Palace of Knossos, John Pendlebury, should serve as a good indication:[31] "Why nobody should be allowed to write about Knossos but Evans I don't know. Of course all future work must be to a certain extent based on him [...]."[32]

Evans tended to fashion Minoan Crete as an imperial paradise, reminiscent of the sophisticated, gentlemanly grandeur of Victorian civilization. Importantly, he gradually de-emphasized any aggressive military installations on the island: while Evans' initial forays into Crete in the

25 Hdt. 1.171.

26 Plut. *Thes.* 15.

27 Dow, "The Minoan Thalassocracy," 17. On the creation of two Minoses to reconcile ambiguities of character in the ancient texts, see Dow, 21.

28 Dow, 20–21. On George Grote's (one of the "Philosophical Radicals") concerns with the all-too-human excesses of Minos' sea kingdom, see Dow, 20–21.

29 Dow, 19ff.

30 Dow, 19–20.

31 See Dilys Powell, *The Villa Ariadne* (London, Sydney, Auckland, and Toronto: Hodder and Stoughton, 1973), 86–89.

32 Quoted from a letter by John Pendlebury to his father, as in Powell, *Villa Ariadne*, 86.

1890s revealed to him the importance of walls, forts, and towers,[33] he later "lost his appetite for reconstructing ancient military installations [...]. Instead he selectively focused on the traces of the ancient Cretan past that were compatible with a more pacific interpretation of the Minoan world."[34] Cathy Gere views Evans' shift as a reflection of his personal, anti-war attitudes from witnessing violence in the Balkans (as a reporter) and, later, in Crete.[35] While Evans' characterization of his Minoans was doubtless, in part, personal, it was also national-minded and builds on earlier British benevolent characterizations of King Minos' sea empire. Like his predecessors in the Enlightenment, Evans refutes the negative, imperialist characterization of Minos by ancient Greeks: "It was, however, reserved for Athenian chauvinism so to exaggerate the tyrannical side of that early sea-dominion as to convert the Palace of a long series of great rulers into an ogre's den. [...]. The ogre's den turns out to be a peaceful abode of priest-kings, in some respects more modern in its equipments than anything produced by Classical Greece."[36]

In different respects, Evans points to a civilizational paradise in Minoan Crete, marked out by highly advanced, proto-modern technologies,[37] a sense of devout religiosity embedded in political society,[38] and sophisticated art and recreational activities.[39] Working outwards from this domestic standpoint, Evans shows that Minoan activities abroad in their thalassocracy are aimed at trade and the necessary dispersion around the Mediterranean of the first true Western civilization.

> It was certainly in pursuit of very solid commercial objects that Minoan or other Aegean merchants pushed forward into the West Mediterranean Basin. [...] [There was] a wholesale invasion of Mainland Greece by Minoan forms [...,] a sudden revolution involving the idea of actual conquest and settlement. [...] [T]he dominant element that now comes into view represents an incomparably higher stage of civilisation than anything that had existed before on the Helladic side.[40]

33 Gere, *Knossos*, 66–67.
34 Gere, 67.
35 Gere, 67.
36 Arthur Evans, *The Palace of Minos at Knossos*, Volume I (London: Macmillan and co, 1921), 1.
37 Evans, *Palace of Minos* (Vol. I), 2.
38 Evans, 3–6.
39 Evans, 2.
40 Evans, 22–23.

Evans' Minoan invasion is essentially pacific[41] and cultural – an "invasion of [artistic] forms." His Minoans are hypercivilized gentlemen, and the dispersion of their superior culture is a blessing on inferior peoples. "In other words, this comparatively small island, left on one side to-day by all the main lines of Mediterranean intercourse, was at once the starting-point and the earliest stage in the highway of European civilization."[42] This civilizational belief in the essential benevolence of the spread of Western civilization was widespread in Victorian attitudes to supposed racially, culturally inferior cultures[43] during the expansion of British culture – and military forces, supporting economic trade networks – around the coasts of the world; the necessary spread of essentially pacifist Minoan civilization was thus a strong mythic paradigm for the type of peaceful, trading, sophisticated British sea-empire which Evans yearned for.

Evans was, in fact, already living in a post-Edwardian period of imperial decline, but his nostalgic longings for a Victorian–Minoan Empire were shared by later British writers. In *The Lion Gate* (1963), Leonard Cottrell, a popularizer of the classical world, not only praises Evans' vision of Minoan Crete but also seems to connote the ruins at Knossos as a Victorian, Evansian milieu:

> In the forecourt of the Palace [of Knossos], near the southwest entrance stands a bronze bust of Sir Arthur Evans. It is a fine head, though lacking something of the humanity of the well-known photographs of Evans in his long, shapeless raincoat and battered hat, standing near the North Portico with "Prodger" – his famous walking stick – beside him. [...]. If every trace of the Knossian palace were obliterated tomorrow, future historians could re-create it, and

41 According to Momigliano (*Search of the Labyrinth*, 64–66), a kind of modern, scholarly myth has arisen in recent decades which, erroneously, views Sir Arthur Evans' Minoans as a peaceful, non-violent, non-aggressive society. In fact, Evans' characterization of a pacific society, his *Pax Minoica*, is to be aligned rather with imperial ideas of *Pax Romana* or *Pax Britannica* (cf. Momigliano, 64–66ff.). That being said, within the broader movement of Cretomania, there were certainly later feminist representations of Minoans, especially during the counterculture 1960s and 1970s, which depicted these mythic people in hippie, flower-power, spiritualist terms; see, for instance, Moyra Caldecott's *The Lily and the Bull* (1979).

42 Evans, *Palace of Minos* (Vol. I), 24.

43 For a discussion of Minoan skull structures (Alpine, Mediterranean, etc.), which was a stock of nineteenth-century racial anthropology, see Evans, *Palace of Minos* (Vol. I), 7–8; for further discussion of the (often confusing) racial constitution of Evans' Minoans, see Schoep, "Building the Labyrinth," 12–13.

the civilization it represented, from Evans' monumental book, *The Palace of Minos.*[44]

One presumes that the on-site loss of the statue of this typical Victorian aristocrat would have been equally catastrophic in Cottrell's imagined infrastructural, modern-Minoan disaster. Cottrell's Minoan melancholy is as much a nostalgic desire for a return to the threatened virtues of Victorian–Edwardian civilization – hats, walking sticks, and raincoats – as a genuine interest in pre-classical histories. A similar "trip down memory lane" is offered by film critic Dilys Powell, widow of a British archaeologist who worked at Knossos, in her memoir *The Villa Ariadne* (1973); for Powell, Evans' eponymous private house at Knossos is "stubbornly Victorian in the Mediterranean landscape,"[45] and "1914 was more remote to us than the Minoan Age."[46]

Yet such nostalgia for a Victorian past could not change the course of history. The Second World War definitely signalled the *terminus* of the vast thalassocracy which Great Britain had boasted in the nineteenth century; three leaders ostensibly ruled over the ruins of Europe (Truman, Churchill, and Stalin), but in reality the power at the dawn of the nuclear age had shifted to the United States and the Soviet Union.[47] Moving into the 1950s, the image of power at sea would no longer be the majestic ship of the line but the nuclear submarine, in which production race Britain, paralyzed by the economic and infrastructural damage of six years of devastating war, could hardly compete. These political changes, in turn, transformed the appropriation of the Minoan myth and the visions of paradise to be found there.

Lawrence Durrell's *The Dark Labyrinth*: A Landlocked, Minoan Shangri-La of Pure Being

Lawrence Durrell's novel *The Dark Labyrinth* (1947)[48] is set immediately after the Second World War and introduces us to a diverse cast of British characters, of varying dispositions, professions, and class affiliations, who

---

44 Leonard Cottrell, *The Lion Gate* (London: Pan Books, 1967), 207–208.
45 Powell, *Villa Ariadne*, 8.
46 Powell, 15.
47 See, for example, Johnson, *British Imperialism*, 171–172.
48 For Durrell's own low opinion of *The Dark Labyrinth*, see Gordon Bowker, *Through the Dark Labyrinth: A Biography of Lawrence Durrell* (New York: St. Martin's Press, 1997), 163, 174.

are brought together during a Mediterranean cruise, one of the stops on which is Crete. They disembark at Suda, having all signed up for a tour of the recently unearthed "Labyrinth of Crete,"[49] but disaster strikes inside the dark underground network due to a sudden rockfall and, indeed, their incompetent, jingoistic tour guide. Several of the travellers die in the labyrinth, while others find a way out. Such a plot summary belittles the brilliance of Durrell's early novel, which is, in different parts, a cynical reflection on the Minoan explosion in archaeology and the fascination for this lost civilization on the part of the contemporary public;[50] a biting social satire on out-dated manners and modes of thinking in Britain;[51] and, most important for the purposes of this chapter, a quest of interiority, of exploring and possibly overcoming the vagaries of the mind (the unconscious, the irrational) in order to arrive at some form of superior, utopian state of being.

Durrell's Minoan Crete is the home of archaeologists such as Axelos, a trickster-type character, who is bisexual and binational (Greek and Arabic, but educated in England) and who undertakes archaeological forgeries and hoaxes to promote his own fame and to show that "experts know nothing and that archaeology has developed into a science as dull as theology."[52] Through this trickster, a creative archaeologist with a fondness for distributing fake news, Durrell is commenting on the constructed, fictive, modern, mythmaking phenomenon of Minoan Crete, exacerbated by the local forgery business of fake antiquities in Crete which had thrived and co-existed with the archaeological work; by the fallibility of English experts such as Sir Arthur Evans, whose aristocratic version in the story, the impotent, self-deceiving Graecen, struggles to decipher scientific fact from creative deception; and by the blatant tourist-oriented marketing on site in Crete, represented by the Jannadis Brothers in the story.[53] Apart from the primitive artwork in the labyrinth itself, which is revealed first to be a fake[54] and later, disarmingly, to perhaps be genuine,[55] the other link to antiquity is

---

49 *DL*, 125.

50 Durrell's decision to become an exile from England and to live on the Greek islands was inspired, in part, by the "Minoan explosion," although his own fascination with them was characteristically idiosyncratic (Bowker, *Through the Dark Labyrinth*, 55).

51 On the trauma of Durrell's early childhood transition from the grandeur of the Buddhist Himalayas to gloomy London, see Bowker, 14–19. On Durrell's counter-cultural attitude to the moral, sexual conservatism of Victorian ways, see Bowker, 41–57.

52 *DL*, 7.

53 *DL*, 125.

54 *DL*, 6–7, 150–151.

55 *DL*, 242.

the apparent presence of "an animal of some kind in the labyrinth. No one has ever seen it. But they hear it roar."[56] Despite the growing evidence that there is indeed an actual minotaur in the labyrinth, this connection with the ancient world breaks down at the end of the story, when it is revealed that a young boy had been paid by the Jannadis Brothers to blow "a ram's horn down one of the tunnels of the labyrinth."[57]

Durrell's response to the glory of a Minoan past – of the quest of Englishmen such as Graecen and fellow tourists to identify grand monuments and to uncover the utopian-sounding "New Era"[58] in the depths of the past – always concludes in a bathetic undertone, with the crassness of the contemporary scene (tour guides, forgeries, tricks) consistently denying the desire to uncover an idealized past. This is not to say that utopia, of a kind, cannot be found on Durrell's Minoan Crete; it can, indeed, be realized through characters wrestling with their inner contradictions in the psychoanalytical gauntlet of the labyrinth and through arriving at an altered state of consciousness after this trial.

There is, then, no physically monstrous bull in Durrell's story but, rather, a psychoanalyst called Hogarth, who brings together several of the protagonists, such as Baird, Fearmax, and Graecen, and pushes them onto their trip of discovery in the labyrinth, and who, importantly, is described in bull-like terms when he first enters the stage of the story: "the newcomer [Hogarth] lowered his grizzled taurine head and started towards him [Graecen], with all the caution of a big man who fears that he will overturn something"[59] – the proverbial bull in a china shop. Durrell's bull–psychoanalyst acts as a symbolic guide into "the Minoan interior," standing behind a catalogue of English characters, each of whom is dealing with some kind of psychological disturbance: Graecen with the denial of his own chronic illness and his imminent death; Baird (an ex-soldier) traumatized by his murder of a German prisoner-of-war in occupied Crete; Fearmax (a clairvoyant) with his morbid fear of his own death; Campion (an artist) with a self-defeating, artistic narcissism which prevents him from committing to loving relationships.

Their experience of being lost in the Minoan labyrinth, a location with far greater epiphanic potential than any mundane shrink's couch,[60] puts the

56 *DL*, 133.
57 *DL*, 239.
58 *DL*, 28.
59 *DL*, 23.
60 In a letter to Henry Miller, Durrell described the story, in Freudian terms, as entailing being "lost in the womb" (quoted in Bowker, *Through the Dark Labyrinth*, 163).

characters into the immediacy of life-or-death situations where their various psychic problems are manifested to them. The aristocratic archaeologist Graecen (quasi-Evans) is characterized by his pervasive self-deception (an English quality which Durrell savages throughout the novel): his elevated, misplaced delight at his own marginal poetic success, his distancing himself from his own impending death, his misunderstandings of others' motives, and even his professional expertise. On the latter, after finding a way through the labyrinth, Graecen declares to the "Bacchic trickster" Axelos at the end of the novel: "I'm only sorry about the minotaur [...] you could have spared me that Silenus, at my age."[61] Graecen's attempts to recover an idealized [pre-]Minoan past are stymied: the utopian-sounding "New Era" which Axelos had promised Graecen turns out to be a deception, a fact which psychoanalyst Hogarth had earlier prefigured:

> "It's just possible that the New Era is—"
> "Faked?" said Graecen in alarm.[62]

Instead, the story affords Graecen another type of Minoan quest, which turns out to be far more real: a quest of interiority into realizing his own self-deceptions.

Other characters experience similar revelations. For the evangelical, proselytizing Miss Dombey, her entrapment by the rock fall in the labyrinth causes her to despair, overdosing on her sleeping tablets and so causing her own death; however, before she slips away, she realizes that her faith was a charade and that, in true psychoanalytic fashion, her Christian love was just the transference of love for her own lost father.[63] "In some vague way the Second Coming had been designed as a plot to bring him [her father] back."[64] Fearmax, the appropriately named clairvoyant, experiences a debilitating morbidity, an overwhelming belief in his imminent death which frequently leaves him lethargic and apathetic to life;[65] this is compounded by his professional belief in and fascination with the supernatural. The labyrinth, however, offers Fearmax a fairy-tale-like choice at the physical bifurcation of a subterranean passage: the one corridor presents a possible escape, with Fearmax's cigar smoke being sucked into it; in the other, "he heard the steely vibrations

---

61   *DL*, 243.
62   *DL*, 28.
63   *DL*, 170–172.
64   *DL*, 172.
65   *DL*, 100ff.

of the minotaur's voice"[66] – choosing to enter this corridor, "he felt fear, yes, but at one remove as if through the clouds of morphia injection. He was supported now by the vertical flame of this overmastering curiosity to know what exactly the minotaur could be."[67] Whether Fearmax is really killed by some (mythic) cave-dwelling animal or whether he is simply paralyzed by his own fear is left unclear since events are focalized through his own thoughts, and Fearmax himself had begun to doubt his sanity – "My poor man you are raving."[68] Nevertheless, his own morbidity, his fear-ridden fascination with his own death (the maximum fear), essentially masters him, with the labyrinth providing the necessary external conditions for the fulfilment of his internal pathology; Fearmax himself even realizes this at one epiphanic point, recalling his psychiatrist Hogarth's words: "We act our inner symbolism outwards into the world. [...] [W]e get exactly what we ask for, no more and no less."[69]

The notion that Minoan Crete could represent a utopia of self-reflection, an ideal space offering the chance of epiphanic experience, is reinforced by the journey of Mr Truman and his wife Elsie. Making their way through the labyrinth, the minotaur they hear bellowing turns out, in fact, to be a cow – another bathetic, Durrellian anti-climax to mythic expectations. The cow leads them out of the labyrinth, through an exit, and into an enclosed mountain-top domain; this lush, natural, self-enclosed, alpine utopia is first likened by Mr Truman to "the Garden of Eden,"[70] although he later refers to it as "The Roof of the Bloody World"[71] – a cultural reference to the imagined Shangri-La of the Himalayas. There, the couple meet Ruth Adams, an old American lady who has dwelt there in seclusion since 1926 and who convinces the Trumans of the complete isolation of their new home, surrounded by impregnable cliffs and canyons. The experience of living in this self-sustaining, landlocked physical utopia has taught Ruth to reject all externalities of human society and life, to focus on understanding her own mind in a kind of pure ontological manner (being divorced from the distractions of thought and emotion), and, in a neo-Buddhist-like[72] fashion, "becoming one" with her environment:

66 *DL*, 177.
67 *DL*, 178.
68 *DL*, 177.
69 *DL*, 175.
70 *DL*, 211.
71 *DL*, 228.
72 For Durrell's great interest in Eastern beliefs and, especially, Buddhism, see Bowker, *Through the Dark Labyrinth*, 473 (s.v. "Buddhism").

I remembered how life was before [...]. I was outside everything in a certain way. Now I participate with everything. [...]. In my own mind, inside (not as something I think or feel, but as something I am) inside there I no longer prohibit or select. [...]. The things you were telling me, Mr Truman, about the growth of the state as a concept, and the beginning of social conscience – all this is only a detour, a long and vicious detour through material amenities towards a happiness that will continue to elude men so long as they continue to elude themselves and each other.[73]

Mr Truman struggles to come to terms with this philosophy, yearning for outside, worldly experiences (social or state utopias, ideas which were pervasive in the 1930s and 1940s), but his wife assimilates into an interior mode of utopian existence, as promulgated by Ruth: "She [Elsie] had realized that the roof of the world did not really exist, except in their own imaginations!"[74] Here Elsie has returned to Hogarth's contention that we project our inner symbolic structures onto the world; however, by denying the essential entrapment of their physical location in the mountains and the system of thought which has projected such an image (a rooftop), Elsie has freed herself from the externality of her existence and so realized an interior, ontological utopia, divorced from the self-deceptions and pathologies which were tested in the proving grounds of the labyrinth.

In contrast to the "interiority" of Durrell's Minoan utopia – not only the psychological inwardness it offers characters but also its physically landlocked terrain like a Himalayan Shangri-La or the biblical Garden of Eden – the sea is nowhere to be found in this isolated Cretan location. Mr Truman, upon first entering this landscape, is disturbed by this absence: "I wonder where the sea is?";[75] his search is in vain because, as the narrator writes, "nowhere shone the sea. The landscape might have been part of a crater on the moon's surface";[76] "They might have been in Asia."[77] Given the previous manifestations of a Minoan thalassocratic paradise in the British imagination, Durrell's choice to move his Minoan utopia away from the sea is highly symbolic. The sea represents a kind of mental turmoil, an unwillingness to confront one's internal strife and to commit, instead, to worldly action. This restlessness is represented by Ruth Adams' brother Godfrey,

---

73 *DL*, 225–226, 230.
74 *DL*, 236; cf. Bowker, *Through the Dark Labyrinth*, 164.
75 *DL*, 209.
76 *DL*, 220.
77 *DL*, 239.

who could not abide the alpine isolation and died trying to escape from the interior: "he began to get upset when year succeeded year and there seemed less and less to do. He was a victim of activity."[78] The destructive connotations of the sea are also indicated by the suicide of Campion, who, although he cannot swim, chooses to leap into the sea and to his bloody death from an inescapable cliff-ledge: "he felt himself turning over and over as his body was poured down the ladder of blueness. A red roaring seemed to fill the horizon. Frightened kestrels fell with them from ledges of rock for a few metres and then planed out, whistling their curiosity and terror. The sea turned up its expansive shining surface and waited for them."[79]

Robert Graves' *Seven Days in New Crete*: Feminine, Poetic Retrotopia and Dystopia

Robert Graves' *Seven Days in New Crete* (1949) is a heady generic concoction of nostalgic mythmaking, science fiction, utopian treatise, and modernist dystopian fiction. The plot involves the transport through time of the poet–narrator, Edward Venn-Thomas, into a future civilization called New Crete, where he experiences the peculiar customs and character of this future utopia and its people through integration into a social class, or estate, known as magicians; during his visit he becomes involved in various communal misadventures, with his stay culminating in the collapse of New Cretan civilization. In the fourth chapter, "The Origin of New Crete," the historical developments which led to the founding of this future utopia are narrated. Several failed global utopian ideologies and periods in Graves' imagined post-twentieth-century history – "Pantisocracy," "Orthodox neo-communism," "logicalism," "the Sophocratic epoch"[80] – are described as precursors to the establishment of New Crete. Graves also firmly positions New Crete in the literary tradition of utopian and anti-utopian fiction, creating a fictitious philosopher in his story who pioneered the anthropological experiment which led to the establishment of New Crete:

> An Israeli Sophocrat named ben-Yeshu [who] wrote a book, *A Critique of Utopias* [...]. From a detailed and learned analysis of some seventy *Utopias*, including Plato's *Timaeus* and *Republic*, Bacon's

78 *DL*, 218.
79 *DL*, 196–197.
80 *SDNC*, 39–40.

New Atlantis, Campanella's *Civitas Solis,* Fénelon's *Voyage en Solente,* Cabot's *Voyage en Icarie,* Lytton's *Coming Race,* Morris's *News from Nowhere,* Butler's *Erewhon,* Huxley's *Brave New World,* and various works of the twenty-first to the twenty-fourth centuries, he traced the history of man's increasing discontent with civilization as it developed and came to a practical conclusion: "we must retrace our steps, or perish."[81]

Graves' New Crete is, thus, a retrospective utopia, one which retraces steps, which is created through an anthropological experiment which placed its subjects in a primitive, quasi-Bronze Age milieu, originally based on the island of Crete and then spreading to other regions of the world. While this futuristic civilization is nominally Cretan, it is characterized by a smorgasbord of cultural historical influences, from its hierarchical medieval society governed by guilds to an Edwardian fascination with competitive school sports. Yet Graves does include a clear Minoan flavour in his New Cretan utopia in two respects: namely, its status as a great seafaring empire and its maternal religious milieu:

Together the five communities [of New Crete] evolved a new religion, closely akin to the pre-Christian religion of Europe [...] but with the Mother-goddess Mari as the Queen of Heaven. The New Cretans, no longer the subject of anthropological research were now regarded as "the seed-bed of a Golden Age," and when their swan-necked wooden galleys put into the port of Corinth, where they traded food and handicrafts for metal ore, china clay and pedigree cattle, the sailors had great trouble in keeping off would-be immigrants. [...]. A generation later, the islands of Rhodes and Cyprus were set aside for colonization.[82]

Graves' New Cretans adhere to the British imagination of the Minoans as thalassocrats, who excel in trading goods across the seas and who extend their territory through, apparently, peaceful colonization; however, there is a key difference in Graves' representation of their sea power with respect to Evans' characterization of a culture-bearing sea people. For Graves' quasi-Bronze Age New Cretans, sea travel brings them into contact with the corrupting technologies of modern civilization – "explosives,

---

81   *SDNC,* 41.
82   *SDNC,* 43.

power-driven vehicles, the telephone, electric light, domestic plumbing and the printing press."[83] Accordingly, they start to limit their contact with the "incidentals of civilization" in order to maintain "the New Cretan system,"[84] which entails them sailing by night into foreign harbours, which are smaller than the main ports, to reduce contact.[85] This distance from the technological modern civilizations on the mainland is justified through a subsequent historical degeneration and corresponding dark age outside New Crete, whereby other people become savages and the New Cretans become the dominant system, a global retrotopia realized. Tellingly, Graves' narrator, Venn-Thomas, does not encounter the New Cretans as thalassocrats but as self-contained mainlanders, living in self-sustaining communities in France. Graves' retrotopia set in the future, thus, inverts Evans' civilizational logic of a Minoan, hyper-technological thalassocracy which spread outwards to become a model of Europe's first civilization; Graves' futuristic Minoan utopia shrinks back inwards into an idealized early-Bronze Age existence, essentially isolated from the rest of the world through the diminution of its intercultural seafaring endeavours. History has returned to its retrotopic origin, retracing its steps.

To match this retrospective return to prehistory, Graves' New Crete is also characterized symbolically by a biological, "omphalic return" to origins: women hold the power in his future utopia. This is represented in the dominant form of worship in New Crete for the Mother-goddess; Venn-Thomas even appears to meet a divine representative of the Mother or the Mother herself. While the society of New Crete is divided into different class-like estates, women, especially those in the magician estate, are generally regarded as superior, as reflected through Venn-Thomas' enquiries.

> "Where do women come into this system?"
> "We maintain it, because we act directly on behalf of the goddess. We appraise men; we don't compete with them. Naturally, they treat us as the superior sex."[86]

Venn-Thomas finds himself frequently the victim or, at least, an inferior object of pity at the hands of the women of New Crete, including Sally and Sapphire. And one of the climactic scenes of the novel involves an

---

83 *SDNC*, 43.
84 *SDNC*, 45.
85 *SDNC*, 43.
86 *SDNC*, 18.

elaborate theatrical performance which involves the ritualistic slaying of the Year King on stage by a female representative of the goddess.

In characterizing his New Crete as a feminine-controlled utopia, governed by worship of a mother goddess, Graves was drawing heavily on then-contemporary theories of early matriarchies in early civilizations across the Aegean and elsewhere in the world, particularly in anthropological and classical studies.

> Frazer's *The Golden Bough* is usually cited; [...] but the idea of a goddess who is both the murderess and the muse probably came [*sc.* to Graves] from Jane Harrison, the remarkable Cambridge Classics don who, at the turn of the century, argued for the existence of an original matriarchy.[87] She was not the first to do so; her own sources include the sturdy German historians who took matriarchy for their subject in the nineteenth century.[88]

Indeed, Sir Arthur Evans himself had pointed to the dominant feminine space of Bronze Age Crete and the prominent position of the Mother-goddess in his reconstructions of the Palace of Knossos.[89] Graves, writing in an admixture of speculative genres such as science fiction and historical fiction, idealizes this characteristic further by suggesting the magical, supernatural capabilities of women such as Sally, who has the telepathic ability to read the mind of Venn-Thomas and who can engage in a form of psychic shapeshifting, altering how Venn-Thomas perceives her physical form. We can, rightly then, place Graves' New Crete in a tradition of scholarly works and creative writings on Minoan Crete which reinforced its status as a mythic proto-civilization that precasts and, thus, validates modern feminist attitudes.[90]

However, for Graves, his representations of a Minoan utopia were as much personal and poetic as they were socially oriented to reflect general anti-modernist, retrotopic antipathies towards technology (a feature of modernist poetry in the wake of the First World War) and women's

---

87 For further discussion on Harrison's theories, see Gere, *Knossos*, 86–91.

88 Seymour, *Robert Graves*, 307.

89 Arthur Evans, *The Palace of Minos at Knossos*, Volume IV: Part I (London: Macmillan and co, 1935), 18ff. On the complexity and, indeed, the condescending attitude of Evans' Victorian-inflected feminism, see Gere, *Knossos*, 79–81; Momigliano, *Search of the Labyrinth*, 59–61.

90 Gere, *Knossos*, 214–217. For Graves' positive attitudes to "first wave feminism" (exemplified by his first wife, Nancy), see Seymour, *Robert Graves*, 59, 68.

liberation movements. His futuristic Minoan utopia is a bardic paradise, a place where poets, such as Venn-Thomas, are elevated to the highest social class, the magician estate. Graves draws on a classical analogy to situate this important character of his personal, poetic utopia:

> He [the fictitious scholar/philosopher Ben-Yeshu] pointed out that no writer of a Utopia had ever applied himself to make good the damage done by Plato, when he banished poets from his Republic and preached a scornful indifference to poetic myth. "If we strengthen the poets and let them become the acknowledged legislators of the new world [...] magic will come into its own again, bringing peace and fertility in its train [...]."[91]

For Graves, poetry is a polyvalent virtue: it is the proper way to worship the goddess and, thus, is involved in true mythic belief rather than the truth of scientific facts; in the latter antagonism, and also through a focus on the magical qualities of poetry in defeating physical might (reflected through the satiric character of the soldier-general in the novel), Graves' utopia is placed firmly in the modernist, post-Nietzschean return to the irrational and the spiritual.[92]

Yet Graves does not allow the reader to believe that his utopia is, in fact, a place of absolute perfection (eu-topic). Much of the narrative of *Seven Days in New Crete* is concerned with tokens of decline in this paradise, reflected, for example, by the presence of a ghost from the past (a brutch) (that is, from Venn-Thomas' present) who torments and confuses the inhabitants of New Crete; by the jealous Sally, who falls in love with Venn-Thomas and viciously punishes those who stand in the way of this unrequited love, such as her murder of Fig-bread and the out-casting of Sapphire. This declining feature of society is confirmed by Venn-Thomas' consultation with the Mother in a watery meadow, who reveals that it was she herself who ordered him to be transported to New Crete, for a particular purpose; in an epiphanic, inspired trance at the end of the novel, Venn-Thomas reveals to the New Cretans that they have declined in their religiosity and that a process of death and rebirth is needed: "She summoned me from the past, a seed of trouble, to endow you with a harvest of trouble, since true love and wisdom spring only from calamity;

---

91 *SDNC*, 44.

92 In a letter to Ricardo Sicre, Robert Graves stated that the book was designed to show "how to stabilize society without boredom or tyranny" (as quoted in Seymour, *Robert Graves*, 323).

and the first fruits of her sowing are the disasters that have emptied the Magic House at Horned Lamb."[93]

Conclusion

In the imaginations of British thinkers in the Enlightenment, King Minos' Crete had represented the possibility of an idealized mythic archetype for the type of peaceful thalassocracy which their own nation-state was trying to solidify. Sir Arthur Evans nostalgically endowed the ruins at Knossos with imagined ethical value, an ancient, pre-classical *ou/eu-topos*, an idealized, quasi-Victorian hypercivilization. In the wake of two global wars, where the (sea) power of the British Empire was drastically reduced, the image of Minoan Crete as a utopia for a hypercivilized, seafaring people began to crumble in the popular imagination. In its place, creative British writers and thinkers such as Lawrence Durrell and Robert Graves were drawn to the special, imagined benevolence of this mythologized island; however, their expressions and confrontations with utopia had changed. Durrell's Minoan Crete is an ontological utopia, a site where we can confront the confusing labyrinth of our minds and arrive, perhaps, at some state of being which is hindered less by the malleability of a rapidly evolving modernity, by external projects of social utopias – an externality which is represented by the dangerous movements of the sea in his story. Graves' Minoan realm is a retrotopic utopia (isolationist rather than thalassocratic) which could address the anti-technological, anti-war, anti-rational sentiments of the post-First World War period, while, at the same time, incorporating the more revolutionary aspects of feminism and even becoming a personal, poetic utopia for the writer.

One might say, then, that the British imagination of Minoan Crete in the course of the twentieth century has migrated from a paradisiacal to a utopian vision. Generally, the term *paradise* involves a retrospective "golden-age" temporality, pastoral or natural landscapes, and religious or supernatural mechanisms in the ethical framework of these texts; *utopias* involve a future-oriented temporality, landscapes which are urban, institutional, and social, as well as an ethical code which resides in the Renaissance, Enlightenment traditions of secularism, humanism, and progress.[94] But

---

93 *SDNC*, 279.
94 See Rhiannon Evans, *Utopia Antiqua: Readings of the Golden Age and Decline at Rome* (London and New York: Routledge, 2008), 3ff., 12, 17, etc.; Darko Suvin, *Defined by*

more importantly, behind these structural, semiotic divisions lies the politics of memory and temporality: paradises enact restorative nostalgia, a conservative longing to return to an idealized, static past, "a transhistorical reconstruction of the lost home,"[95] often embedded in national memories; modern utopias, like those of Durrell and Graves, progress towards future or different potentialities, providing an "alternative historical hypothesis."[96]

Several Anglo-American travel writers, such as close friends Henry Miller and Lawrence Durrell, have expressed the *utopic* potential of Minoan Crete in terms of its ability to provide sublime experiences, epiphanies, or revelations – transformative emotions which help the individual look forwards (to the future) or sideways (in the present) as much as backwards to a lost paradise. In *The Colossus of Maroussi*, Henry Miller expresses the essential modernity of the ruins at Knossos:[97] "However Knossos may have looked in the past, however it may look in the future, this one which Evans has created is the only one I shall ever know."[98] At the ruins at Phaistos, Miller, in the tradition of Romantic writer–travellers such as Byron, can undergo transformative experiences in the present – Miller conjectures that the Minoans lived in, and for, the present[99] – which speak to a gnomic, universal sublime:

> I felt that the earth was bearing me through a zone I had never been carried through before. I was a little nearer to the stars and the ether was charged with their nearness [...,] the atmosphere has undergone a subtle, perfumed alteration. [...].[100] The illusion of vast distances, the reality of great vistas, the sublimity of silence, the revelation of light [...].[101] It was one of the few times in my life that I was fully aware of being on the brink of a great experience. [...] It had culminated in this moment of bliss.[102]

---

a Hollow: Essays on Utopia, Science Fiction and Political Epistemology (Oxford, etc.: Peter Lang, 2010), 22–23, 39.
95 Boym, "Nostalgia and its Discontents," 13.
96 Suvin, *Defined by a Hollow*, 30.
97 See Gere, *Knossos*, passim.
98 Henry Miller, *The Colossus of Maroussi* (London: Penguin, 2016), 99. To be clear, the "Cretan narrative" in *The Colossus of Maroussi* is only one of several places (also Athens, Corfu, etc.) which Miller tours across the Aegean.
99 Miller, *Colossus of Maroussi*, 100.
100 Miller, 125.
101 Miller, 129.
102 Miller, 131.

Miller is conscious that his discoveries are risible to scholars of the past – "historians will smile"[103] – but such scientific thought is not his concern; like Durrell, he is moved by "the spirit of the place." In his travel book, *The Greek Islands*, Lawrence Durrell repeats the word *revelatory*: "its [Crete's] history is certainly more continuous and more revelatory than in any other island. It is more revelatory chiefly because of the discovery of the Minoan civilization and the brave attempt to date history backwards almost into the Neolithic Age."[104] But what about Minoan civilization is, precisely, "revelatory?" In his subsequent discussions of Evans' reconstructions of Minoan Crete, Durrell goes on to show a certain disdain for "historical interest"[105] – a "grim"[106] pursuit not fit for those who "hate dates"[107] – and a preference, rather, for the place's ability to "supply an aesthetic experience which cannot be matched elsewhere."[108] This aesthetic experience causes Durrell to look "sideways" to other cultures – "the spiritual temper of these faraway Minoan people [...] make[s] one think of China and sometimes of Polynesia"[109] – as well as to contemporary Cretan poets such as Nikos Kazantzakis[110] in order to supply the appropriate poetic mood for a "mute"[111] ancient civilization.

103 Miller, 131.
104 Lawrence Durrell, *The Greek Islands* (London: Faber and Faber, 2002), 71.
105 Durrell, *Greek Islands*, 71.
106 Durrell, 73.
107 Durrell, 73.
108 Durrell, 71.
109 Durrell, 75.
110 Durrell, 82–83.
111 Durrell, 82.

Bibliography

A

Abbate, Michele. "Gli aspetti etico-politici della Repubblica nel commento di Proclo (dissertazioni VII/VIII e XI)." In *La Repubblica di Platone nella tradizione antica*, edited by Mario Vegetti and Michele Abbate, 207–218. Napoli: Bibliopolis, 1999.

Adam, James. *The Republic of Plato*, 2 volumes. Cambridge: Cambridge University Press, 1902.

Africa, Thomas W. "Thomas More and the Spartan Mirage." *Historical Reflections* 6, no. 2 (1979): 343–352.

Alaimo, Stacy. *Bodily Natures: Science, Environment, and the Material Self*. Bloomington, IN: Indiana University Press, 2010.

Álvarez-Martí-Aguilar, Manuel. "Melqart-Heracles and the Edge of the World: Religious Reactions to the Threat of the Ocean among the Phoenicians of Iberia." In *Transformations and Crisis in the Mediterranean: "Identity" and Interculturality in the Levant and Phoenician West during the 5th–2nd Centuries BCE*, edited by Giuseppe Garbati and Tatiana Pedrazzi, 279–300. Rome: CNR Edizioni, 2021.

Álvarez-Martí-Aguilar, Manuel. "Talismans against Tsunamis: Apollonius of Tyana and the *stelai* of the Herakleion in Gades (*VA* 5.5)." *Greek, Roman, and Byzantine Studies* 57, no. 4 (2017): 968–993.

Álvarez-Martí-Aguilar, Manuel, and Antonio de la Cruz. "Tsunamis y dioses en Cádiz: catástrofes naturales y respuestas religiosas en la *longue durée*." In *X Coloquio Internacional del Centro de Estudios Fenicios y Púnicos. Homenaje al Profesor José María Blázquez. Mare Sacrum. Religión, Cultos y Rituales Fenicios en el Mediterráneo*, edited by Ana Mª Niveau de Villedary. Sevilla (forthcoming).

Ambraseys, Nicholas N. *Earthquakes in the Mediterranean and Middle East: A Multidisciplinary Study of Seismicity up to 1900*. Cambridge: Cambridge University Press, 2009.

"Amusements in Bolton." *Era* (8 January 1898).

"Amusements in Edinburgh." *Era* (19 December 1896).

"Amusements in Plymouth." *Era* (2 January 1897).

Anderson, John L. "Piracy and World History: An Economic Perspective on Maritime Predation." *Journal of World History* 6, no. 2 (1995): 175–199.

Ando, Clifford. "Introduction." In *Piracy, Pillage, and Plunder in Antiquity: Appropriation and the Ancient World*, edited by Richard Evans and Martine De Marre, 1–8. London: Routledge, 2020.

Ando, Clifford. *Law, Language, and Empire in the Roman Tradition*. Philadelphia: University of Pennsylvania Press, 2011.

Ando, Clifford. "Public Law and Republican Empire in Rome, 200–27 BCE." In *Empire and Legal Thought: Ideas and Institutions from Antiquity to Modernity*, edited by Edward Cavanagh, 105–124. Leiden: Brill, 2020.

Andrich, Gian-Luigi. "Naufragio." *Digesto Italiano* 15, no. 2 (1904–1911): 1303–1355.

Aparicio Florido, José Antonio. *El maremoto que viene*. Cádiz: Q-book, 2017.

Armstrong, Rebecca. *Vergil's Green Thoughts: Plants, Humans, and the Divine*. Oxford: Oxford University Press, 2019.

Arnaud, Pascal. "L'antiquité Classique et la Piraterie." In *Histoire des pirates et des corsaires. De l'antiquité à nos jours*, edited by Gilbert Buti and Philippe Hrodej, 27–74. Paris: éditions CNRS, 2016.

Aston, Elaine. "Male Impersonation in the Music Hall: The Case of Vesta Tilley." *New Theatre Quarterly* 4, no. 15 (1988): 247–257.

B

Babusiaux, Ulrike. "Legal Writing and Legal Reasoning." In *The Oxford Handbook of Roman Society and Law*, edited by Clifford Ando, Paul Du Plessis, and Kaius Tuori, 176–185. Oxford: Oxford University Press, 2016.

Bagnall, Roger, and Peter Derow. *The Hellenistic Period: Historical Sources in Translation*. Malden, MA, and Oxford: John Wiley and Sons, 2007.

Bal, Mieke. *Narratology: Introduction to the Theory of Narrative*. Toronto: University of Toronto Press, 2017.

Bal, Mieke, and Christine van Boheemen. *Narratology: Introduction to the Theory of Narrative*, third edition. Toronto: University of Toronto Press, 2009.

Barbantani, Silvia. "Goddess of Love and Mistress of the Sea: Notes on a Hellenistic Hymn to Arsinoe-Aphrodite (P.Lit.Goodsp. 2, I–IV)." *Ancient Society* 35 (2005): 135–165.

Barchiesi, Alessandro. *Epistulae Heroidum 1–3*. Firenze: Le Monnier, 1992.

Barchiesi, Alessandro. "Narratività e convenzione nelle *Heroides*." *MD* 19 (1987): 63–90.

Barchiesi, Alessandro. *Speaking Volumes: Narrative and Intertext in Ovid and Other Latin Poets*. London: Duckworth, 2001.

Barrow, Rosemary. "Toga Plays and Tableaux Vivants: Theatre and Painting on London's Late-Victorian and Edwardian Popular Stage." *Theatre Journal* 62, no. 2 (2010): 209–226.

Bartsch, Shadi. *Ideology in Cold Blood*. Cambridge, MA: Harvard University Press, 1997.

Battistella, Chiara. *P. Ovidii Nasonis Heroidum Epistula 10: Ariadne Theseo: Introduzione, testo e commento*. Berlin and Boston: De Gruyter, 2010.

Beaulieu, Marie-Claire, ed. *A Cultural History of the Sea in Antiquity*, Volume I. A Cultural History of the Sea. London, Oxford, and New York: Bloomsbury, 2021.

Beaulieu, Marie-Claire. *The Sea in the Greek Imagination*. Philadelphia: University of Pennsylvania Press, 2015.

Beckett, Andy. "The Age of Perpetual Crisis: How the 2010s Disrupted Everything but Resolved Nothing." *The Guardian* (17 December 2019). https://www.theguardian.com/society/2019/dec/17/decade-of-perpetual-crisis-2010s-disrupted-everything-but-resolved-nothing.

Bederman, David J. *International Law in Antiquity*. Cambridge: Cambridge University Press, 2001.

Bengston, Hermann. *Die Staatsverträge des Altertums. 3 vols.* Munich: Beck, 1975.

Benton, Lauren. "Toward a New Legal History of Piracy: Maritime Legalities and the Myth of Universal Jurisdiction." *International Journal of Maritime History* 23, no. 1 (2011): 225–240.

Berger, Adolf. *Encyclopedic Dictionary of Roman Law*. Philadelphia: The American Philosophical Society, 1953.

Berti, Emanuele. *M. Annaeus Lucanus, Bellum Civile, Liber X*. Firenze: Le Monier, 2000.

Beschorner, Andreas. "Das 'Opusculum' des Iulius Exuperantius." *Hermes* 127, no. 2 (1999): 237–253.

Betegh, Gábor. "Plato's Magnesia and Costa's Brasilia." In *Political Theory and Architecture*, edited by Duncan Bell and Bernardo Zacka, 59–77. London: Bloomsbury, 2019.

Birkmann, Jörn, Korinna von Teichman, Torsten Welle, Mauricio González, and Maitane Olabarrieta. "The Unperceived Risk to Europe's Coasts: Tsunamis and the Vulnerability of Cadiz, Spain." *Natural Hazards and Earth System Sciences* 10, no. 12 (2010), 2659–2675.

Blakely, Sandra. "Maritime Risk and Ritual Responses: Sailing with the Gods in the Ancient Mediterranean." In *The Sea in History: The Ancient World*, edited by Philip de Souza and Pascal Arnaud, 362–379. Woodbridge: Boydell & Brewer, 2017.

Blakolmer, Fritz. "The Artistic Reception of Minoan Crete." In *Cretomania: Modern Desires for the Minoan Past*, edited by Nicoletta Momigliano and Alexandre Farnoux, 39–68. London: Routledge, 2017.

Blumenberg, Hans. *Shipwreck with Spectator: Paradigm of a Metaphor for Existence*. Boston: MIT Press, 1979.

Boardman, John. *Early Greek Vase Painting, 11th–6th Centuries BC: A Handbook*. London: Thames & Hudson, 1998.

Boardman, John. "Very Like a Whale: Classical Sea Monsters." In *Monsters and Demons in the Ancient and Medieval Worlds: Papers Presented in Honor of Edith Porada*, edited by Ann E. Farkas, Prudence O. Harper, and Evelyn B. Harrison, 73–84. Mainz: P. von Zabern, 1987.

Bolton, M. Catherine. "Gendered Spaces in Ovid's *Heroides*." *CW* 102, no. 3 (2009): 273–290.

Booth, Michael. *Victorian Spectacular Theatre, 1850–1910*. London: Routledge and Kegan Paul, 1991.

Borrero, Jose C. "Tsunami." In *Encyclopedia of Marine Geosciences*, edited by Jan Harff, Martin Meschede, Sven Petersen, and Jörn Thiede. Dordrecht: Springer, 2014. DOI 10.1007/978-94-007-6644-0_146-3.

Bowker, Gordon. *Through the Dark Labyrinth: A Biography of Lawrence Durrell*. New York: St. Martin's Press, 1997.

Boyle, Anthony, trans. and ed. *Seneca: Oedipus*. Oxford: Oxford University Press, 2016.

Boym, Svetlana. "Nostalgia and its Discontents." *The Hedgehog Review* 9, no. 2 (2007): 7–19.

Braga, Riccardo, trans. (Italian). *La lex de prouinciis praetoriis*. Milan: EDUCatt Università Cattolica, 2014.

Braidotti, Rosi. *Metamorphoses: Towards a Materialist Theory of Becoming*. Cambridge: Polity Press, 2002.

Braidotti, Rosi. *The Posthuman*. Cambridge: Polity Press, 2013.

Braidotti, Rosi. "Posthuman Critical Theory." In *Critical Posthumanism and Planetary Futures*, edited by Debashish Banerji and Makarand R. Paranjape, 13–32. New York: Springer, 2016.

Bramble, John C. "Lucan." In *The Cambridge History of Classical Literature*, Volume 2: Latin Literature, edited by Edward J. Kenney and Wendell V. Clausen, 533–557. Cambridge: Cambridge University Press, 1982.

Braudel, Fernand. "Histoire et sciences sociales: la longue durée." *Annales: Economies, Societes, Civilisations* 13, no. 4 (1958): 725–753.

Braun, Theodore E. D., and John B. Radner, eds. *The Lisbon Earthquake of 1755: Representations and Reactions*. Oxford: Voltaire Foundation, 2005.

Bronner, Simon J. *Crossing the Line: Violence, Play, and Drama in Naval Equator Traditions*. Amsterdam: Amsterdam University Press, 2006. https://doi.org/10.5117/9789053569146.

Bruins, Hendrik J., et al. "Geoarchaeological Tsunami Deposits at Palaikastro (Crete) and the Late Minoan IA Eruption of Santorini." *Journal of Archaeological Science* 35, no. 1 (January 2008): 191–212.

Bruins, Hendrik J., Johannes van der Plicht, and J. Alexander MacGillivray. "The Minoan Santorini Eruption and Tsunami Deposits in Palaikastro (Crete): Dating by Geology, Archaeology, 14C, and Egyptian Chronology." *Radiocarbon* 51, no. 2 (2009): 397–411.

Brunt, Peter A. *The Fall of the Roman Republic and Related Essays*. Oxford: Oxford University Press, 1987.

Bryant Davies, Rachel. *Troy, Carthage and the Victorians: The Drama of Classical Ruins in the Nineteenth-Century Imagination*. Cambridge: Cambridge University Press, 2018.

Burstein, Stanley. *Agatharchides of Cnidus, On the Erythraean Sea*. London: Ashgate, 1989.

Buxton, Richard. *Myths and Tragedies in their Ancient Greek Contexts*. Oxford: Oxford University Press, 2013.

Byrne, Aisling. *Otherworlds: Fantasy & History in Medieval Literature*. Oxford: Oxford University Press, 2016.

C

Cadogan, Gerald. "'The Minoan Distance': The Impact of Knossos upon the Twentieth Century." *British School at Athens Studies* 12 (2004): 537–545.

Cameron, Alan. "The Date and Owners of the Esquiline Treasure: The Nature of the Evidence." *American Journal of Archaeology* 89, no. 1 (1985): 135–145.

Cameron, Alan. *Greek Mythography in the Roman World*. Oxford: Oxford University Press, 2004.

Campbell, Brian, ed. and trans. *The Writings of the Roman Land Surveyors: Introduction, Text, Translation and Commentary*. London: Society for the Promotion of Roman Studies, 2000.

Carandini, Andrea. "Urban Landscapes and Ethnic Identity of Early Rome." In *Urban Landscapes and Ethnic Identity of Early Rome*, edited by Gabriele Cifani and Simon Stoddart, 5–23. Oxford: Oxford University Press, 2012.

"The Carl Rosa Opera Company." *Standard* (21 January 1896).

Casali, Sergio. "The *Bellum Civile* as an Anti-Aeneid." In *Brill's Companion to Lucan*, edited by Paolo Asso, 81–109. Leiden: Brill, 2011.

Casali, Sergio. "Further Voices in Ovid *Heroides* 7." *Hermathena* 177–178 (2004–2005): 141–158.

Casali, Sergio. "Notizie da Nestore in Ovidio, *Heroides* I 25–38." *Aevum(ant)* 176 (2017): 175–198.

Casson, Lionel. *The Ancient Mariners: Seafarers and Sea Fighters of the Mediterranean in Ancient Times*. New York: Macmillan, 1959.

Ceccarelli, Paola. "Sans thalassocratie, pas de démocratie? Le rapport entre thalassocratie et démocratie à Athènes dans la discussion du Ve et IVe siècle av. J.-C." *Historia: Zeitschrift für Alte Geschichte* 42, no. 4 (1993): 444–470.

Centrone, Bruno. *Platone. Repúbblica*, translated by Franco Sartori, foreword by Mario Vegetti, and notes by Bruno Centrone. Bari: Laterza, 2011.

Charles, R. H., trans. *The Chronicle of John, Bishop of Nikiu: Translated from Zotenberg's Ethiopic Text*. London: Williams & Norgate, 1916; Merchantville: Arx Publishing, 2007.

Chester, David K., and Angus M. Duncan. "Geomythology, Theodicy, and the Continuing Relevance of Religious Worldviews on Responses to Volcanic Eruptions." In *Living under the Shadow: The Cultural Impacts of Volcanic Eruptions*, edited by John Grattan and Robin Torrence, 203–224. Walnut Creek: Left Coast Press, 2007.

Chester, David K., and Angus M. Duncan. "Responding to Disasters within the Christian Tradition, with Reference to Volcanic Eruptions and Earthquakes." *Religion* 40, no. 2 (2010): 85–95.

Chevitarese, A., and Gabriele Cornelli. "(Almost) Forgotten Complicity: Socrates (and Plato) between the Oligarchic Coup of 404 BC and the Democratic Restoration of 403." In *New Perspectives on the Ancient World*, edited by Pedro Paulo A. Funari, Renata Senna Garraffoni, and Bethany Letalien, 161–167. Oxford: Archaeopress/FAPESP, 2008.

Chic García, Genaro. "Violencia legal y no legal en el marco del estrecho de Gibraltar." In *Piratería y seguridad Marítima en el Mediterráneo Antiguo*, edited by Alfonso Álvarez-Ossorio Rivas, Eduardo Ferrer Albelda, and Enrique García Vargas, 15–29. Seville: Universidad de Sevilla, 2013.

Cho, Paul K.-K. *Myth, History, and Metaphor in the Hebrew Bible.* Cambridge: Cambridge University Press, 2019.

Cifani, Gabriele. "Aspects of the Origins of Roman Maritime Trade." In *Roman Law and Maritime Commerce*, edited by Emilia Mataix Ferrándiz and Peter Candy, 11–22. Edinburgh: Edinburgh University Press, 2021.

Clarke, Dylan J., and David S. Anderson. "1 Past is Present: The Production and Consumption of Archaeological Legacies in Mexico." *Archaeological Papers of the American Anthropological Association* 25, no. 1 (2015): 1–18.

Clarke, Katherine. *Between Geography and History: Hellenistic Constructions of the Roman World.* Oxford: Oxford University Press, 1999.

Clay, Diskin, and Andrea Purvis. *Four Island Utopias: Being Plato's Atlantis; Euhermos of Messene's Panchaia; Iamboulos' Island of the Sun; Sir Francis Bacon's New Atlantis, With a Supplement on Utopian Prototypes, Developments, and Variations.* Newburyport, MA: Focus, 1999.

Clay, Jenny S. *Homer's Trojan Theater: Space, Vision, and Memory in the Iliad.* Cambridge: Cambridge University Press, 2011.

Coats, John F. "The Trireme Sails Again." *Scientific American* 260, no. 4 (1989): 96–103.

Cofrade del Amor. "Bendición de las aguas (La Palma), Cádiz 2018." YouTube (3 Nov 2018). https://www.youtube.com/watch?v=0mwSay2vdPY&t=23s.

Constantakopoulou, Christy. *The Dance of the Islands: Insularity, Networks, the Athenian Empire, and the Aegean World.* Oxford: Oxford University Press, 2007.

Cooper, John M. *Plato: Complete Works.* Indianapolis and Cambridge: Hackett, 1997.

Cornell, Collin R. "God and the Sea in Job 38." *Journal of Hebrew Scriptures* 12 (2012): 1–15.

Cottrell, Leonard. *The Lion Gate.* London: Pan Books, 1967 [1963].

Crawford, Michael, trans. *The Roman Statutes, Vol. 1.* London: Institute of Classical Studies, School of Advanced Study, University of London, 1996.

Crawford, Michael, Joyce M. Reynolds, Jean-Louis Ferrary, and Philippe Moreau. "*Lex de provinciis praetoriis.*" In *The Roman Statutes, Vol. 1*, edited by Michael Crawford, 231–270. London: Bulletin of the Institute of Classical Studies Supplement 34, 1996.

Crawley, Richard, trans. *Thucydides, The Peloponnesian War.* London: J. M. Dent, 1910.

Crawley, Richard, trans., and Robert B. Strassler, ed. *The Landmark Thucydides.* New York: Free Press, 1996.

Crespo Solana, Ana. "Manifestaciones culturales y actitudes religiosas ante las catástrofes naturales en la España de Antiguo Régimen. El Maremoto de 1755 en Cádiz." In *Naturalia, mirabilia & monstrosa en los imperios ibéricos (siglos XV–XIX)*, edited by Eddy Stols, Werner Thomas, and Johan Verberckmoes, 143–168. Leuven: Leuven University Press, 2006.

Crosson, Isaia. *Lucan's Mutilated Voice: The Poetics of Incompleteness in Roman Epic.* New York: Columbia University, 2020.

Crouch, Dora P. *Water Management in Ancient Greek Cities.* New York: Oxford University Press, 1993.

Cuq, Edouard. "La Loi Gabinia contre la Piraterie de l'an 67 av. J.C. d'àprés une Inscription de Delphes." *CRAI* (1923): 129–150.

D

Davis, Jim. "Introduction: Victorian Pantomime." In *Victorian Pantomime: A Collection of Critical Essays*, edited by Jim Davis, 1–18. Basingstoke and New York: Palgrave Macmillan, 2010.

Davis, Jim. "'Only an Undisciplined [Nation] Would Have Done It': Drury Lane Pantomime in the Late Nineteenth Century." In *Victorian Pantomime: A Collection of Critical Essays*, edited by Jim Davis, 100–117. Basingstoke and New York: Palgrave Macmillan, 2010.

Davis, Jim. "'Slap On! Slap Ever!': Victorian Pantomime, Gender Variance and Cross-Dressing." *New Theatre Quarterly* 30, no. 3 (2014): 218–230.

Dawson, Doyne. *Cities of the Gods: Communist Utopias in Greek Thought.* Oxford: Oxford University Press, 1992.

Day, Henry J. M. *Lucan and the Sublime: Power, Representation and Aesthetic Experience.* Cambridge: Cambridge University Press, 2013.

Day, John. *God's Conflict with the Dragon and the Sea: Echoes of a Canaanite Myth in the Old Testament.* Cambridge: Cambridge University Press, 1985.

Deane, Bradley. "Imperial Boyhood: Piracy and the Play Ethic." *Victorian Studies* 53, no. 4 (2011): 689–714. https://doi.org/10.2979/victorianstudies.53.4.689.

de Angelis, Franco. "Ancient Greek Colonization in the 21st Century: Some Suggested Directions." *Bollettino di Archeologia Online* 1 (2010): 18–30.

de Angelis, Franco, and Benjamin Garstad. "Euhemerus in Context." *Classical Antiquity* 25, no. 2 (2006): 211–242.

Defoe, Daniel. *Robinson Crusoe*, edited by Michael Shinagel. New York and London: Norton, 1994.

De Jong, Irene J. F. "Introduction." In *Space in Ancient Greek Literature: Studies in Ancient Greek Narrative, Volume 3*, edited by Irene J. F. de Jong, 1–18. Leiden: Brill, 2012.

De Jong, Irene J. F., ed. *Space in Ancient Greek Literature: Studies in Ancient Greek Narrative, Volume 3*. Leiden: Brill, 2012.

Desmond, Marilynn R. "When Dido Reads Vergil: Gender and Intertextuality in Ovid's *Heroides* 7." *Helios* 20, no. 1 (1993): 56–68.

De Souza, Philip. "Greek Piracy." In *The Greek World*, edited by Anton Powell, 179–198. London: Routledge, 1995.

De Souza, Philip. *Piracy in the Graeco-Roman World*. Cambridge: Cambridge University Press, 1999.

De Souza, Philip. "Towards Thalassocracy? Greek Naval Developments." In *Archaic Greece: New Approaches and New Evidence*, edited by Nick Fisher and Hans van Wees, 271–298. London: Duckworth, 1998.

De Souza, Philip, Pascal Arnaud, and Christine Buchet, eds. *The Sea in History: The Ancient World*. Woodbridge, Suffolk: Boydell Press, 2017.

Destrée, Pierre, and Radcliffe G. Edmonds III, eds. *Plato and the Power of Images*. Leiden: Brill, 2017.

Destrée, Pierre, Jan Opsomer, and Geert Roskam, eds. *Utopias in Ancient Thought*. Berlin, 2021.

DeVere Brody, Jennifer. *Impossible Purities: Blackness, Femininity, and Victorian Culture*. Durham and London: Duke University Press, 1998.

Dilke, Oswald A. *The Roman Land Surveyors: An Introduction to the Agrimensores*. New York: Barnes and Noble, 1971.

Dominey-Howes, Dale. "A Re-analysis of the Late Bronze Age Eruption and Tsunami of Santorini, Greece, and the Implications for the Volcano-Tsunami Hazard." *Journal of Volcanology and Geothermal Research* 130, nos. 1–2 (15 February 2004): 107–132.

Dörrie, Heinrich. *Untersuchungen zur Überlieferungsgeschichte von Ovids Epistulae Heroidum (NAWG 6)*. Göttingen: Vandenhoeck & Ruprecht, 1972.

Dougherty, Carol. *The Poetics of Colonization: From City to Text in Ancient Greece*. Oxford: Oxford University Press, 1993.

Dow, Sterling. "The Minoan Thalassocracy." *Proceedings of the Massachusetts Historical Society* 79 (1967): 3–32.

Driessen, Jan. "The Santorini Eruption: An Archaeological Investigation of its Distal Impacts on Minoan Crete." *Quaternary International* 499 (2019): 195–204.

Driessen, Jan. "*The Troubled Island*... 15 years later." Paper presented at the January 2013 Heidelberg meeting on the relations between Crete and Santorini (2013). https://www.academia.edu/2971816/The_Troubled_Island._15_years_later.

Driessen, Jan, and Charlotte Langohr. "Rallying 'round a 'Minoan' Past: The Legitimation of Power at Knossos During the Late Bronze Age." In *Rethinking Mycenaean Palaces II*, edited by Michael L. Galaty and William A. Parkinson, 178–189. Los Angeles: Cotsen Institute of Archaeology, 2007.

Driessen, Jan, and Colin F. MacDonald. "The Eruption of the Santorini Volcano and its Effects on Minoan Crete." In *The Archaeology of Geological Catastrophes*, edited by W. J. McGuire, D. R. Griffiths, P. L. Hancock, and I. S. Stewart, 81–93. London: Geological Society, 2000.

Driessen, Jan, and Colin F. MacDonald. *The Troubled Island: Minoan Crete before and after the Santorini Eruption*. Liège: Université de Liège, 1997.

Driessen, Jan, and J. Alexander MacGillivray. "Swept Away in LM IA? Explaining Debris Deposition in Coastal Neopalatial Crete." In *Proceedings of the 10th Cretological Congress of Chania 2006*, edited by Maria Vlasaki-Andreadaki, 233–244. Iraklion: Society for the Study of Cretan Historical Studies, 2011.

Drinkwater, Megan O. "Which Letter? Text and Subtext in Ovid's *Heroides*." *AJP* 128, no. 3 (2007): 367–387.

Dua, Jatin. "A Sea of Profit: Making Property in the Western Indian Ocean." In *Legalism: Property and Ownership*, edited by Georgy Kantor, Tom Lambert, and Hannah Skoda, 175–202. Oxford: Oxford University Press, 2017.

DuBois, Page. "The History of the Impossible: Ancient Utopias." *Classical Philology* 101, no. 1 (2006): 1–14.

Duff, James, trans. *Silius Italicus, Punica Volume I (Books 1–8)*. Cambridge, MA: Harvard University Press, 1934.

Dunsch, Boris. "*Describe nunc Tempestatem*. Sea Storm and Shipwreck Type Scenes in Ancient Literature." In *Shipwreck in Art and Literature: Images and Interpretations from Antiquity to the Present Day*, edited by Carl Thomson, 42–59. London: Routledge, 2013.

Dunsch, Boris. "Why Do We Violate Strange Seas and Sacred Waters?" In *The Sea as Bridge and Boundary in Greek and Roman Poetry*, edited by Marta Grzechnik and Heta Hurskainen, 17–42. Cologne: Böhlau Verlag, 2015.

Düring, Ingemar. *Herodicus the Cratetean: A Study in Anti-Platonic Tradition*. Stockholm: Wahlström & Widstrand, 1941.

Durrell, Lawrence. *The Dark Labyrinth*. London: Faber and Faber, 2001 [1947].

Durrell, Lawrence. *The Greek Islands*. London: Faber and Faber, 2002 [1978].

E

The Economist. "Who rules the waves?" (17 October 2015): https://www.economist.com/international/2015/10/17/who-rules-the-waves.

Edgerton, Harold. "Underwater Archaeological Search with Sonar." *Historical Archaeology* 10, no. 1 (1976): 46–53.

Ellis, Richard. *Imagining Atlantis*. New York: Vintage, 1998.

Engel, Max, et al. "New Sediment Cores Reveal Environmental Changes Driven by Tectonic Processes at Ancient Helike, Greece." *Geoarchaeology: An International Journal* 31, no. 2 (2016): 140–155.

Erbse, Harmut, ed. *Scholia Graeca in Homeri Iliadem (scholia vetera)*, Volume 5. Berlin: De Gruyter, 1974.

Erimtan, Can. "Hittites, Ottomans and Turks: Ağaoğlu Ahmed Bey and the Kemalist Construction of Turkish Nationhood in Anatolia." *Anatolian Studies* 58 (2008): 141–171.

Evans, Arthur. *The Palace of Minos at Knossos*, Volume I. London: Macmillan and Co., 1921.

Evans, Arthur. *The Palace of Minos at Knossos*, Volume IV: Part I. London: Macmillan and co, 1935.

Evans, Rhiannon. "Searching for Paradise: Landscape, Utopia, and Rome." *Arethusa* 36, no. 3 (2003): 285–307.

Evans, Rhiannon. *Utopia Antiqua: Readings of the Golden Age and Decline at Rome*. London and New York: Routledge, 2008.

F

Fantham, Elaine. "The Angry Poet and the Angry Gods: Problems of Theodicy in Lucan's Epic of Defeat." In *Ancient Anger: Perspectives from Homer to Galen*, edited by Susanna Braund and Glenn W. Most, 229–249. Cambridge: Cambridge University Press, 2003.

Farrell, Joe. "Reading and Writing the *Heroides*." *HSCPh* 98 (1998): 307–338.

Fasching, Darrell J. *The Ethical Challenge of Auschwitz and Hiroshima: Apocalypse or Utopia*. New York: State University of New York Press, 1993.

Fauth, Wolfgang. "Utopische Inseln in den Wahren Geschichten des Lukian. (L'île utopique dans les Histoires vraies de Lucien)." *Gymnasium Helveticum* 86, no. 1 (1979): 39–58.

Feeney, Denis C., *The Gods in Epic: Poets and Critics of the Classical Tradition*. Oxford: Oxford University Press, 1991.

Fenn, Percy T. "Justinian and the Freedom of the Sea." *The American Journal of International Law* 19, no. 4 (1925): 716–727.

Ferguson, John. *Utopias of the Classical World*. London: Thames and Hudson, 1975.

Ferrando, Francesca. "Posthumanism, Transhumanism, Antihumanism, Meta-humanism, and New Materialisms: Differences and Relations." *Existenz* 8, no. 2 (2013): 26–32.

Ferrari, Franco. *Teognide, Elegie. Introduzione, traduzione e note*. Milan: Biblioteca Universale Rizzoli, 1989.

Ferrary, Jean-Louis. "Recherches sur la législation de Saturninus et Glaucia." *MEFRA* 89, no. 2 (1977): 619–660.

Ferrary, Jean-Louis. "Retour sur la loi des inscriptions de Delphes en de Cnide (Roman Statutes n.12)." In *Epigrafis 2006. Atti della XIVe Rencontre sur l'epigraphie in onore di Silvio Panciera*, edited by Maria Luisa Caldelli, Gian Luca Gregori, and Silvia Orlandi, 101–114. Rome: Quasar, 2008.

Ferrary, Jean-Louis. "Traités et domination romaine dans le monde hellénique." In *I trattati nel mondo antico*, edited by Luciano Canfora, Mario Liverani, and Carlo Zaccagnini, 217–235. Rome: L'Erma di Bretschneider, 1990.

Finley, Moses. "Utopianism Ancient and Modern." In *The Critical Spirit: Essays in Honor of Herbert Marcuse*, edited by Kurt H. Wolff and Barrington Moore, 3–20. Boston: Beacon Press, 1967.

Finnis, John. *Natural Law and Natural Rights*. Oxford: Oxford University Press, 2011.

Fotheringham, John K. "On the List of Thalassocracies in Eusebius." *The Journal of Hellenic Studies* 27 (1907): 75–89.

Fountain, Henry. "Arctic's 'Last Ice Area' May Be Less Resistant to Global Warming." *New York Times* (1 July 2021). https://www.nytimes.com/2021/07/01/climate/arctic-sea-ice-climate-change.html.

Fowler, Robert L. *Early Greek Mythography, Volume 2: Commentary*. Oxford: Oxford University Press, 2013.

Fremantle, William H., trans. *Jerome: Letters and Select Works* (NPNF2-06), edited by Philip Schaff and Henry Wace. New York: The Christian Literature Company; Oxford and London: Parker & Company, 1893.

Frost, Frank. "Scyllias: Diving in Antiquity." *Greece & Rome* 15, no. 2 (1968): 180–185.

Fuhrmann, Christopher. *Policing the Roman Empire: Soldiers, Administration, and Public Order*. Oxford: Oxford University Press, 2012.

Fulkerson, Laurel. *The Ovidian Heroine as Author: Reading, Writing, and Community in the Heroides*. Cambridge: Cambridge University Press, 2005.

G

Gabba, Emilio. "True History and False History in Classical Antiquity." *Journal of Roman Studies* 71 (1981): 50–62.

Gabrielsen, Vincent. "Economic Activity, Maritime Trade and Piracy in the Hellenistic Aegean." *REA* 103, no. 1 (2001): 219–240.

Gabrielsen, Vincent. "Naval Warfare: Its Economic and Social Impact on Greek Cities." In *War as a Cultural and Social Force: Essays on Warfare in Antiquity*, edited by Tønnes Bekker-Nielsen and Lise Hannestad, 72–89. Copenhagen: Det kongelige Danske Videnskabernes Selskab, 2001.

Gagné, Renaud. *Cosmography and the Idea of Hyperborea in Ancient Greece: A Philology of Worlds*. Cambridge: Cambridge University Press, 2021.

Galinsky, Karl. "Venus, Polysemy, and the Ara Pacis Augustae." *American Journal of Archaeology* 96, no. 3 (1992): 457–475. doi:10.2307/506068.

Garcia Moreno, Luis. "Paradoxography and Political Ideals in Plutarch's Life of Sertorius." In *Plutarch and the Historical Tradition*, edited by Philip A. Stadter, 132–158. London and New York: Routledge, 1992.

Gargola, Daniel J. *The Shape of the Roman Order: The Republic and its Spaces.* Chapel Hill, NC: University of North Carolina Press, 2017.

Gastaldi, Silvia. "L'allegoria della nave." In *La Repubblica. Vol. 5, Libri 6 e 7,* edited by Mario Vegetti, 187–216. Napoli: Bibliopolis, 2003.

Gaughan, Lisa. "'The God, the Owner & the Master' (Barthes, 1979): Staging Rites of Passage in the Maritime Crossing the Line Ceremony." In *Staging Loss: Performance as Commemoration,* edited by Michael Pinchbeck and Andrew Westerside, 159–173. Cham: Palgrave Macmillan, 2018. https://doi.org/10.1007/978-3-319-97970-0_10.

Geelhar, Clemens. "Some Remarks on the *lex de provinciis praetoriis.*" *RIDA* 49 (2002): 115–117.

Genette, Gérard. *Narrative Discourse: An Essay in Method.* Ithaca, NY: Cornell University Press, 1980.

Gerber, Douglas E. *Greek Elegiac Poetry.* Cambridge, MA: Harvard University Press, 1999.

Gere, Cathy. *Knossos and the Prophets of Modernism.* Chicago, IL and London: University of Chicago Press, 2009.

Gibson, Edgar C. S., trans. *The Conferences of John Cassian. Part II* (NPNF2-11), edited by Philip Schaff and Henry Wace. Buffalo, NY: Christian Literature Publishing Co., 1894.

Gill, Christopher. *Plato's Atlantis Story: Text, Translation and Commentary.* Liverpool: Liverpool University Press, 2017.

Gill, Nikita. *Your Soul is a River.* New York: Thought Catalog Books, 2016.

Goddio, Franck, and Andre Bernand. *Sunken Egypt: Alexandria.* London: Periplus, 2004.

Goddio, Franck, and David Fabre. "Port of Alexandria: Underwater Archaeology." In *Encyclopedia of Global Archaeology,* edited by Claire Smith, 6020–6027. New York: Springer, 2014.

Godley, Alfred D., trans. *Herodotus, The Histories.* Cambridge, MA: Harvard University Press, 1920.

Goodman-Tchernov, Beverly, et al. "Tsunami Waves Generated by the Santorini Eruption Reached Eastern Mediterranean Shores." *Geology* 37, no. 10 (1 October 2009): 943–946.

Gould, Marty. *Nineteenth-Century Theatre and the Imperial Encounter.* New York and London: Routledge, 2011.

Graham, Angus C., trans. *The Book of Lieh-tzu: A Classic of the Tao.* New York: Columbia University Press, 1990.

Graves, Robert. *Seven Days in New Crete.* Oxford: Oxford University Press, 1983 [1949].

Grose Hodge, Humfrey, trans. *Cicero IX: Pro Lege Manilia. Pro Caecina. Pro Cluentio. Pro Rabirio. Perduellionis Reo.* Harvard, MA: Harvard University Press, 1927.

Guidoboni, Emanuela. *Catalogue of Ancient Earthquakes in the Mediterranean Area up to the 10th century*, with the collaboration of Alberto Comastri and Giusto Traina. Rome: Istituto Nazionale di Geofisica, 1994.

Guidoboni, Emanuela, and John E. Ebel. *Earthquakes and Tsunamis in the Past: A Guide to Techniques in Historical Seismology.* Cambridge: Cambridge University Press, 2009.

Guillaumin, Jean-Yves. *Sur quelques notices des arpenteurs romains.* Besançon: Institut des Sciences et Techniques de l'Antiquité, 2007.

H

Haas, Christopher J. "Athenian Naval Power before Themistocles." *Historia: Zeitschrift für Alte Geschichte* 34, no. 1 (1985): 29–46.

Hall, Edith. "Classical Mythology in the Victorian Popular Theatre." *International Journal of the Classical Tradition* 5, no. 3 (1999): 336–366.

Hall, Edith, and Henry Stead. *A People's History of Classics: Class and Greco-Roman Antiquity in Britain and Ireland, 1689 to 1939.* London and New York: Routledge, 2020.

Hamilton, James. *Volcano: Nature and Culture.* London: Reaktion Books, 2012.

Hamouda, Amr Z. "A Reanalysis of the AD 365 Tsunami Impact along the Egyptian Mediterranean Coast." *Acta Geophysica* 58, no. 4 (2009): 687–704.

Haraway, Donna. *The Companion Species Manifesto.* Chicago, IL: Prickly Paradigm Press, 2003.

Hardwick, Lorna, and Christopher Stray. "Introduction: Making Connections." In *A Companion to Classical Receptions*, edited by Lorna Hardwick and Christopher Stray, 1–9. London: Blackwell, 2008.

Harman, Rosie. "Colonisation, Nostos, and the Foreign Environment in Xenophon's Anabasis." In *The Routledge Handbook of Identity and the Environment in the Classical and Medieval Worlds*, edited by Rebecca Futo Kennedy and Molly Jones-Lewis, 134–135. New York: Routledge, 2016.

Harris, William V., ed. *Rethinking the Mediterranean.* Oxford: Oxford University Press, 2005.

Harrison, Jane, "Notes Archaeological and Mythological on Bacchylides." *The Classical Review* 12, no. 1 (1898): 85–86.

Hartog, François. *The Mirror of Herodotus: The Representation of the Other in the Writing of History*, translated by Janet Lloyd. Berkeley, CA: University of California Press, 1988.

Hartranft, Chester D., trans. *The Ecclesiastical History of Sozomen* (NPNF2-02), edited by Philip Schaff and Henry Wace. Buffalo, NY: Christian Literature Publishing Co., 1890.

Hasebroek, Johannes P. *Staat und Handel im alten Griechenland.* Tübingen: Mohr, 1926.

Heidarzadeh, Mohammad, and Aditya R. Gusman. "Source Modeling and Spectral Analysis of the Crete Tsunami of 2nd May 2020 along the Hellenic Subduction Zone, Offshore Greece." *Earth Planets Space* 73, article no. 74 (18 March 2021). https://doi.org/10.1186/s40623-021-01394-4.

Henry, Martine. "Cassien et les autres: les sources littéraires et les événements géologiques du 21 Juillet 365." *Klio* 94, no. 1 (2012): 175–196.

Holmes, Brooke A. "Situating Scamander: 'Natureculture' in the *Iliad*." *Ramus* 44, no. 1–2 (2015): 29–51.

Holmgaard, Sanne B. "The Role of Religion in Local Perceptions of Disasters: The Case of Post-Tsunami Religious and Social Change in Samoa." *Environmental Hazards* 18, no. 4 (15 November 2018): 311–325.

Hornblower, Simon. "The Old Oligarch (Pseudo-Xenophon's Athenaion Politeia) and Thucydides. A Fourth-Century Date for the Old Oligarch?" In *Polis and Politics: Studies in Ancient Greek History Presented to Mogens Herman Hansen on His Sixtieth Birthday*, edited by Pernille Flensted-Jensen, Thomas H. Nielsen, and Lene Rubinstein, 363–384. Copenhagen: Museum Tusculanum Press, 2000.

Hornblower, Simon, and Anthony Spawforth, eds. *The Oxford Companion to Classical Civilization*, second edition. Oxford: Oxford University Press, 2014 [1998].

Howland, R. L. "The Attack on Isocrates in the Phaedrus." *The Classical Quarterly* 31, nos. 3–4 (1937): 151–159.

Humphries, Mark. "Religion." In *A Companion to Ancient History*, edited by Andrew Erskine, 301–311. Chichester: Wiley-Blackwell, 2009.

Hunter, Virginia J. *Past and Process in Herodotus and Thucydides*. Princeton, NJ: Princeton University Press, 1982.

Huxley, Henry. "Storm and Shipwreck in Roman Literature." *Greece & Rome* 21, no. 63 (1952): 117–124.

I

Irby, Georgia L. *Conceptions of the Watery World in Greco-Roman Antiquity*. London: Bloomsbury, 2021.

Irwin, Elizabeth. "The Politics of Precedence: First Historians on First Thalassocrats." In *Debating the Athenian Cultural Revolution: Art, Literature, Philosophy, and Politics 430–380 BC*, edited by Robin Osborne, 188–223. Cambridge: Cambridge University Press, 2007.

J

Jacobson, Howard. *Ovid's Heroides*. Princeton, NJ: Princeton University Press, 1974.

Jacques, François, and Bernard Bousquet. "Le cataclysme du 21 juillet 365: Phénomène régional ou catastrophe cosmique?" In *Tremblements de terre, histoire et archéologie: IVèmes Rencontres internationales d'archéologie et d'histoire d'Antibes, 2–4, novembre 1983*, 183–198. Valbonne: APDCA, 1984.

Jacques, François, and Bernard Bousquet. "Le raz de marée du 21 juillet 365." *Mélanges de l'École française de Rome: Antiquité* 96, no. 1 (1984): 423–461.

Jameson, Michael H. "Poseidon." In *The Oxford Classical Dictionary*, fourth edition, edited by Simon Hornblower, Antony Spawforth, and Esther Eidinow. Oxford: Oxford University Press, 2012. https://www-oxford reference-com.libproxy.ncl.ac.uk/view/10.1093/acref/9780199545568.001.0001/ acref-9780199545568-e-5270.

Janko, Richard. *The Iliad: A Commentary. Volume IV: Books 13–16.* Cambridge: Cambridge University Press, 1994.

Janni, Pietro. *Il Mare degli Antichi*. Bari: Dedalo, 1996.

Jenkyns, Richard. *The Victorians and Ancient Greece*. Oxford: Blackwell, 1980.

Johnson, Robert. *British Imperialism*. Basingstoke and New York: Palgrave Macmillan, 2003.

Jones, Horace L., trans. *The Geography of Strabo*. Cambridge, MA: Harvard University Press, 1924.

Jones, Stuart H. "A Roman Law Concerning Piracy." *JRS* 16, no. 2 (1926): 155–173.

Jones, William H. S., trans. *Pausanias: Description of Greece*, Volume III. Cambridge, MA: Harvard University Press, 1918.

Jones, Wilton. "Robinson Crusoe." Add MS 53591 L. Lord Chamberlain's Manuscript Collection, 1896.

Joseph, Timothy A. "*Pharsalia* as Rome's 'Day of Doom' in Lucan." *AJP* 138, no. 1 (2017): 107–141.

Jouteur, Isabelle. "Le paysage marin des *Héroïdes*." In *Amor Scribendi. Lectures des Héroïdes d'Ovide*, edited by Hélène Casanova-Robin, 93–120. Grenoble: Millon, 2007.

Jowitt, Claire, Craig Lambert, and Steve Mentz, eds. *The Routledge Companion to Marine and Maritime Worlds, 1400–1800*. London: Routledge, 2020.

K

Kallet-Marx, Lisa. *Money, Expense, and Naval Power in Thucydides' History 1–5.24*. Berkeley, CA: University of California Press, 1993.

Kampakoglou, Alexandros. "Crossing Boundaries in Bacchylides 17." In *Vivre et penser les frontières dans le monde méditerranéen antique: actes du colloque tenu à l'Université Paris-Sorbonne, les 29 et 30 juin 2013*, edited by Hugues Berthelot, 149–158. Bordeaux: Ausonius, 2016.

Kansteiner, Wolf. "Finding Meaning in Memory: A Methodological Critique of Collective Memory Studies." *History and Theory* 41, no. 2 (2002): 179–197.

Kantor, Georgy. "Property in Land in the Roman Provinces." In *Legalism: Property and Ownership*, edited by Georgy Kantor, Thomas B. Lambert, and Hannah Skoda, 55–74. Oxford: Oxford University Press, 2017.

Kapell, Matthew W. *Exploring the Next Frontier: Vietnam, NASA, Star Trek and Utopia in 1960s and 1970s American Myth and History*. New York and London: Routledge, 2016.

Kaplan, Philip. "Location and Dislocation in Early Greek Geography and Ethnography." In *The Routledge Handbook of Identity and the Environment in the Classical and Medieval Worlds*, edited by Rebecca Futo Kennedy and Molly Jones-Lewis, 299–314. New York: Routledge, 2016.

Kastens, Kim A., and Maria B. Cita. "Tsunami-Induced Sediment Transport in the Abyssal Mediterranean Sea." *GSA Bulletin* 92, no. 11 (1 November 1981): 845–857.

Keith, Alison. "Ovid in Lucan: The Poetics of Instability." In *Brill's Companion to Lucan*, edited by Paolo Asso, 111–132. Leiden: Brill, 2011.

Kelly, Benjamin. "Riot Control and Imperial Ideology in the Roman Empire." *Phoenix* 61, no. 1–2 (2007): 150–156.

Kelly, Gavin. "Ammianus and the Great Tsunami." *Journal of Roman Studies* 94 (2004): 141–167.

Kennedy, Duncan F. "Epistolarity: The *Heroides*." In *The Cambridge Companion to Ovid*, edited by Philip R. Hardie, 217–232. Cambridge: Cambridge University Press, 2002.

Kennedy, Duncan F. "The Epistolary Mode and the First of Ovid's *Heroides*." *CQ* 34, no. 2 (1984): 413–422.

Kennedy, Rebecca Futo, and Molly Jones-Lewis. *The Routledge Handbook of Identity and the Environment in the Classical and Medieval Worlds*. London and New York: Routledge, 2016.

Keyt, David. "Plato and the Ship of State." In *The Blackwell Guide to Plato's Republic*, edited by Gerasimos Santas, 189–213. Malden: Blackwell, 2006.

Kitchell, Kenneth F. *Animals in the Ancient World from A to Z*. London: Routledge, 2014.

Kloos, Carola. *Yhwh's Combat with the Sea: A Canaanite Tradition in the Religion of Ancient Israel*. Amsterdam: G. A. van Oorschot; Leiden: Brill, 1986.

Knox, Peter E. *Ovid: Heroides: Select Epistles*. Cambridge: Cambridge University Press, 1995.

Koelsch, William. *Geography and the Classical World: Unearthing Historical Geography's Forgotten Past*. London: I. B. Tauris, 2014.

Kolia, Erophile. "A Sanctuary of the Geometric Period in Ancient Helike, Achaea." *The Annual of the British School at Athens* 106, no. 1 (November 2011): 201–246.

Koloski-Ostrow, Anne O. *The Archaeology of Sanitation in Roman Italy: Toilets, Sewers, and Water Systems*. Chapel Hill, NC: University of North Carolina Press, 2015.

König, Fritz. "Mensch und Welt bei Lucan im Spiegel bildhafter Darstellung." In *Lucan*, edited by Werner Rutz, 451–471. Darmstadt: Wissenschaftliche Buchgesellschaft, 1970.

Konrad, Christoph F. *Plutarch's Sertorius: A Historical Commentary*. Chapel Hill, NC: University of North Carolina Press, 1994.

Konstan, David. *The Emotions of the Ancient Greeks: Studies in Aristotle and Classical Literature*. Toronto: University of Toronto Press, 2006.

Koukouvelas, Ioannis K., et al. "Earthquake-Triggered Landslides and Mudflows: Was this the Wave that Engulfed Ancient Helike?" *The Holocene* 30, no. 12 (August 2020): 1653–1668.

Koutsios, A., et al. "Sedimentological and Geophysical Observations in the Delta Plain of Selinous River, Ancient Helike, Northern Peloponnesus Greece." *Bulletin of the Geological Society of Greece* 43, no. 2 (2010): 654–662.

Kovacs, George. "Moral and Mortal in *Star Trek: The Original Series*." In *Classical Traditions in Science Fiction*, edited by Brett Rogers and Ben Stevens, 199–216. Oxford: Oxford University Press, 2015.

Kulick, Rachel. "Urban Micromorphology: A Microecological Narrative of a Neopalatial Neighborhood at Bronze Age Palaikastro, Crete." *Geoarchaeology* 34, no. 4 (2019): 430–447.

L

Lamb, Walter R. M., trans. *Plato in Twelve Volumes*, Volume 9. Cambridge, MA: Harvard University Press, 1925.

Lambert, Andrew D. *Seapower States: Maritime Culture, Continental Empires and the Conflict that Made the Modern World*. New Haven, CT: Yale University Press, 2018.

Landolfi, Luciano. "Fondali del pathos elegiaco. Natura e lamento nelle *Heroides*." *RCCM* 42, no. 2 (2000): 191–214.

Lapidge, Michael. "Lucan's Imagery of Cosmic Dissolution." *Hermes* 107, no. 3 (1979): 344–370.

Lario, Javier, Cari Zazo, José Luis Goy, Pablo G. Silva, Teresa Bardají, Ana Cabero, and Cristino J. Dabrio. "Holocene Palaeotsunami Catalogue of SW Iberia." *Quaternary International* 242, no. 1 (2011): 196–200.

Larson, Jennifer. "Amphitrite in and out of the Olympian Pantheon." *Les Études Classiques* 87, no. 1–3 (2019): 29–40.

Latour, Bruno. *Facing Gaia: Eight Lectures on the New Climatic Regime*, translated by Catherine Porter. Cambridge: Polity Press, 2017.

León y Domínguez, José María. "La Estrella del Mar." *La Hormiga de Oro* XLV, 2ª semana de noviembre [second week of November] (1844): 707–709.

Lepelley, Claude. "Le presage du nouveau desastre de Cannes: la signification du raz de maree du 21 juilliet 365 dans l'imaginaire d'Ammien Marcelin." *Kokalos* 36–37 (1990–1991): 203–214.

Lesky, Albin. *Thalatta: Der Weg der Griechen zum Meer*. Vienna: Arno Press, 1947.

Levenson, Jon D. *Creation and the Persistence of Evil: The Jewish Drama of Divine Omnipotence*. Princeton, NJ: Princeton University Press, 1994.

Levitas, Ruth. *The Concept of Utopia*. Hemel Hempstead: Syracuse University Press, 1990.

Levystone, David. "La constitution des Athéniens du Pseudo-Xénophon: D'un despotisme à l'autre." *Revue Française d'Histoire des Idées Politiques* 1, no. 1 (2005): 3–48.

Lewes, Darby. "Utopian Sexual Landscapes: Annotated Checklist of British Somatopias." *Utopian Studies* 7, no. 2 (1996): 167–195.

Lindheim, Sara H. *Mail and Female: Epistolary Narrative and Desire in Ovid's Heroides*. Madison, WI: University of Wisconsin Press, 2003.

Lipking, Lawrence. *Abandoned Women and Poetic Tradition*. Chicago, IL: University of Chicago Press, 1988.

Liritzis, Ioannis, Panagiota Preka-Papadema, Panagiotis Antonopoulos, Konstantinos Kalachanis, and Chris G. Tzanis. "Does Astronomical and Geographical Information of Plutarch's *De Facie* Describe a Trip beyond the North Atlantic Ocean?" *Journal of Coastal Research* 34, no. 3 (May 2018): 651–674.

Lively, Genevieve. "Paraquel Lines: Time and Narrative in Ovid's *Heroides*." In *Latin Elegy and Narratology*, edited by Genevieve Liveley and Patricia Salzman-Mitchell, 86–102. Columbus, OH: The Ohio State University Press, 2008.

Llewellyn-Jones, Lloyd, and Sian Lewis. *The Culture of Animals in Antiquity: A Sourcebook with Commentaries*. London: Routledge, 2018.

Lomas, Kathryn. *Rome and the Western Greeks 350 BC–AD 200*. London: Routledge, 1993.

Long, A. G. "The Ship of State and the Subordination of Socrates." In *Plato and the Power of Images*, edited by Pierre Destrée and Radcliffe G. Edmonds III, 158–178. Leiden: Brill, 2017.

Lovatt, Helen. *The Epic Gaze: Vision, Gender, and Narrative in Ancient Epic*. Cambridge: Cambridge University Press, 2013.

Lovejoy, Arthur O., and George Boas. *Primitivism and Related Ideas in Antiquity*. New York: Octagon Books, 1973.

Luce, John V. *The End of Atlantis*. London: Paladin, 1969.

Luce, John V., and Kathleen Bolton. "Thera and the Devastation of Minoan Crete: A New Interpretation of the Evidence." *American Journal of Archaeology* 80, no. 1 (Winter 1976): 9–18.

Luraghi, Nino. "Author and Audience in Thucydides' *Archaeology*. Some Reflections." *Harvard Studies in Classical Philology* 100 (2000): 227–239.

Lydenberg, Harry Miller. *Crossing the Line: Tales of the Ceremony during Four Centuries*. New York: New York Public Library, 1957.

M

MacGillivray, Joseph A. *Minotaur: Sir Arthur Evans and the Archaeology of the Minoan Myth*. London: Jonathan Cape, 2000.

Mack, John. *The Sea: A Cultural History*. London: Reaktion Books, 2013.

Mackil, Emily. "Wandering Cities: Alternatives to Catastrophe in the Greek Polis." *American Journal of Archaeology* 108, no. 4 (October 2004): 493–516.

Mader, Gottfried J. "'*Ut pictura poesis*': Sea-Bull and Senecan Baroque (*Phaedra* 1035–49)." *Classica et Mediaevalia* 53 (2002): 289–300.

Maehler, Herwig. "Theseus' Kretafahrt und Bakchylides 17." *Museum Helveticum* 48, no. 2 (1991): 115–126.

Magdy, Samy. "Rising Seas Threaten Egypt's Fabled Port City of Alexandria." *Associated Press* (30 August 2019). https://apnews.com/article/e4fec321109941798cdbefae310695aa.

Magno, P. "La Leucadia di Turpilio e Ovidio, *Heroides* XV, attraverso i loro modelli greci." *Sileno* 5–6 (1980): 81–92.

Makins, Marian W. "Dissenting Voices in Propertius' Post-War Landscapes." In *Landscapes of War in Greek and Roman Literature*, edited by Bettina Reitz-Joosse, Marian W. Makins, and Christopher J. Mackie, 131–154. London: Bloomsbury, 2021.

Malamud, Martha A. "Happy Birthday, Dead Lucan: (P)raising the Dead in *Silvae* 2.7." In *Roman Literature and Ideology: Ramus Essays for J. P. Sullivan*, edited by Anthony J. Boyle, 169–198. Bendigo: Aureal Publications, 1995.

Malkin, Irad. "Networks and the Emergence of Greek Identity." *Mediterranean Historical Review* 18, no. 2 (2003): 56–74.

Malkin, Irad. *The Returns of Odysseus: Colonization and Ethnicity*. Berkeley, CA: University of California Press, 1998.

Mangan, James A. "Play up and Play the Game: Victorian and Edwardian Public School Vocabularies of Motive." *British Journal of Educational Studies* 23, no. 3 (1975): 324–335. https://doi.org/10.2307/3120191.

Manioti, Nikoletta. "The View from the Island: Isolation, Exile and the Ariadne Myth." In *Insularity, Identity and Epigraphy in the Roman World*, edited by Javier Velaza, 45–67. Newcastle: Cambridge Scholars Publishing, 2017.

Mantena, Rama S. "Imperial Ideology and the Uses of Rome in Discourses on Britain's Indian Empire." In *Classics and Imperialism in the British Empire*, edited by Mark Bradley, 54–74. Oxford: Oxford University Press, 2010.

Marinatos, Nanno. *Sir Arthur Evans and Minoan Crete: Creating the Vision of Knossos*. London: Bloomsbury Publishing, 2014.

Marinatos, Spyridon. "Helice: A Submerged Town of Classical Greece." *Archaeology* 13, no. 3 (1960): 186–193.

Marinatos, Spyridon. "The Volcanic Destruction of Minoan Crete." *Antiquity* 13, no. 52 (December 1939): 425–439.

Marr, John L., and Peter J. Rhodes, eds. *The "Old Oligarch": The Constitution of the Athenians Attributed to Xenophon*. Oxford: Aris & Phillips, 2008.

Marti, Berthe M. "The Meaning of the *Pharsalia*." *AJP* 64, no. 4 (1945): 352–376.

Martin, Charles, trans. and ed. *Ovid: Metamorphoses*. Introduction by Bernard Knox. New York and London: W. W. Norton & Company, 2004.

Martínez Solares, José Manuel. *Los efectos en España del terremoto de Lisboa (1 de noviembre de 1755)*. Madrid: Instituto Geográfico Nacional, 2001.

Martínez Solares, José Manuel. "El Terremoto de Lisboa de 1 de noviembre de 1755." *Física de la Tierra* 29 (2017): 47–60.

Martorana, Simona. "(Re)writing Sappho: Navigating Sappho's (Posthuman) Poetic Identity in Ovid, *Heroides* 15." *Helios* 47, no. 2 (2020): 135–160.

Marty, Martin E. "'But Even So: Look at That': An Ironic Perspective on Utopias." In *Visions of Utopia*, edited by Edward Rothstein, Herbert Muschamp, and Martin E. Marty, 49–88. Oxford: Oxford University Press, 2003.

Marzano, Annalisa. *Harvesting the Sea: The Exploitation of Marine Resources in the Roman Mediterranean.* Oxford: Oxford University Press, 2013.

Masters, Jamie. *Poetry and Civil War in Lucan's Bellum Civile.* Cambridge: Cambridge University Press, 1992.

Mataix Ferrándiz, Emilia. "*De incendio ruina naufragio rate nave expugnata.* Origins, Context and Legal Treatment of Shipwrecking in Roman Law." *RIDA* 66 (2019): 153–195.

Mataix Ferrándiz, Emilia. "'Washed by the Waves'. Fighting against Shipwrecking in the Later Roman Empire." In *Seafaring and Mobility in the Late Antique Mediterranean*, edited by Antti Lampinen and Emilia Mataix Ferrándiz, 133–148. London: Bloomsbury Academic, 2022.

Mathes-Schmidt, Margret, Ioannis D. Papanikolaou, Klaus R. Reicherter, and Aggelos Pallikarakis. "Event Deposits in the Eastern Thermaikos Gulf and Kassandra Peninsula (Northern Greece): Evidence of the 479 BC 'Herodotus tsunami'." *Zeitschrift für Geomorphologie*, Supplementary Issues 62, Supplementary Issue 2 (2019): 101–125.

Matthews, Monica. *Caesar and the Storm: A Commentary on Lucan De Bello Civili, Book 5 lines 476–721.* Bern: Peter Lang, 2008.

"Maxim's Flying Machine." *Illustrated London News* (25 August 1894), 230.

Mayer, David. "Supernumeraries: Decorating the Late Victorian Stage with Lots (& Lots & Lots) of Live Bodies." In *Ruskin, the Theatre and Victorian Visual Culture*, edited by Anselm Heinrich, Katherine Newey, and Jeffrey Richards, 154–168. Basingstoke: Palgrave Macmillan, 2009.

Mayor, Adrienne. *The Amazons: Lives and Legends of Warrior Women across the Ancient World.* Princeton, NJ and Oxford: Princeton University Press, 2014.

McAlhany, Joseph. "Sertorius between Myth and History: The Isles of the Blessed Episode in Sallust, Plutarch and Horace." *Classical Journal* 112, no. 1 (2016): 57–76.

McCauley, Alexander. *Victorian Atlantis: Drowning, Population, and Property in the Nineteenth-Century Novel.* PhD dissertation. Seattle: University of Washington, 2020.

McClintock, Anne. *Imperial Leather: Race, Gender and Sexuality in the Colonial Contest.* New York and Oxford: Routledge, 1995.

McCorristine, Shane. "Ludic Terrorism: The Game of Anarchism in Some Edwardian Fiction." *Studies in the Literary Imagination* 45, no. 2 (2012): 27–46.

McCoy, Floyd W., and Grant Heiken. "Tsunami Generated by the Late Bronze Age Eruption of Thera (Santorini), Greece." *Pure and Applied Geophysics* 157, no. 6 (2000): 1227–1256.

McCracken, George E., trans. *City of God*, Volume 1. Boston, MA: Harvard University Press, 1957.

McGushin, Patrick, ed. and trans. *The Histories*, Volume 1 and 2. Oxford: Oxford University Press, 1992–1994.

McInerney, Jeremy, and Ineke Sluiter, eds. *Valuing Landscape in Classical Antiquity: Natural Environment and Cultural Imagination*. Leiden: Brill, 2016.

McLelland, Harry F. "Robinson Crusoe." LCP 1895/397. Lord Chamberlain's Manuscript Collection, 1895.

Meadows, Peter S., and Janette I. Campbell. *An Introduction to Marine Science*. New York: Springer, 1988.

Mendes-Victor, Luiz A., Carlos Sousa Oliveira, João Azevedo, and António Ribeiro, eds. *The 1755 Lisbon Earthquake: Revisited*. Berlin: Springer, 2009.

Mendoza, Ana. "'¡Hasta aquí, Madre mía!' Cádiz conmemora el aniversario del maremoto de 1755." *La Voz de Cádiz* (1 November 2015). https://www.lavozdigital.es/cadiz/lvdi-hasta-aqui-madre-201510311855_noticia.html#vca=mod-sugeri-dos-p1&vmc=relacionados&vso=hasta-aqui-madre-mia&vli=noticia.foto.provincia.

Middleton, Guy D. *The Collapse of Palatial Society in Late Bronze Age Greece and the Postpalatial Period*. Oxford: Archaeopress, 2010.

Middleton, Guy D. *Understanding Collapse: Ancient History and Modern Myths*. Cambridge: Cambridge University Press, 2017.

Miller, Henry. *The Colossus of Maroussi*. London: Penguin, 2016 [1941].

Miller, Molly. *The Thalassocracies*. New York: State University of New York Press, 1971.

Miller, Peter A. "The Parodic Sublime: Ovid's Reception of Virgil in *Heroides* 7." *MD* 52 (2004): 57–72.

Minoura, K., et al. "Discovery of Minoan Tsunami Deposits." *Geology* 28, no. 1 (1 January 2000): 59–62.

Molloy, Barry P., et al. "Of Tephra and Tsunamis: A Secondary Deposit of Tephra Sealing LM IA Activity at Priniatikos Pyrgos." In *A Cretan Landscape Through Time: Priniatikos Pyrgos and Environs*, edited by Barry P. Molloy and Chloë N. Duckworth, 43–53. Oxford: Archaeopress, 2014.

Momigliano, Arnaldo. "Sea Power in Greek Thought." *The Classical Review* 58, no. 1 (1944): 1–7.

Momigliano, Nicoletta. "From Russia with Love: Minoan Crete and the Russian Silver Age." In *Cretomania: Modern Desires for the Minoan Past*, edited by Nicoletta Momigliano and Alexandre Farnoux, 84–110. London: Routledge, 2017.

Momigliano, Nicoletta. *In Search of the Labyrinth: The Cultural Legacy of Minoan Crete*. London: Bloomsbury, 2020.

Momigliano, Nicoletta. "Introduction: Cretomania – Desiring the Minoan Past in the Present." In *Cretomania: Modern Desires for the Minoan Past*, edited by Nicoletta Momigliano and Alexandre Farnoux, 1–13. London: Routledge, 2017.

Momigliano, Nicoletta, and Alexandre Farnoux, eds. *Cretomania: Modern Desires for the Minoan Past*. London: Routledge, 2017.

Monaco, Lucia. *Persecutio piratarum. Battaglie ambigue e svolte costituzionali nella Roma Reppublicana*. Naples: Jovene, 1996.

Monro, Charles H., trans. *The Digest of Justinian*. Cambridge: Cambridge University Press, 1904.

Monrós-Gaspar, Laura. *Victorian Classical Burlesques: A Critical Anthology*. London and Oxford: Bloomsbury, 2015.

Morel, Jean-Paul. "L'expansion phocéenne en Occident: dix années de recherches (1966–1975)." *Bulletin de correspondance hellénique* 99, no. 2 (1975): 853–896.

Moreton, F. Leslie. "Robinson Crusoe, or Harlequin Man Friday and the King of the Cannibal Islands." Add MS 53622 M. Lord Chamberlain's Manuscript Collection, 1897.

Morford, Mark P. O. *The Poet Lucan: Studies in Rhetorical Epic*. Oxford: Bloomsbury Academic, 1967.

Morrison, John S., and John F. Coates. *The Athenian Trireme*. Cambridge: Cambridge University Press, 1986.

Morrow, Glenn R. *Plato's Cretan City*. Princeton, NJ: Princeton University Press, 1960.

Moschetti, Cesare Maria. "Naufragio." *Enciclopedia del Diritto* 27 (1977): 547–558.

Müller, Christel, and Claire Hasenohr. *Les Italiens dans le Monde Grec (BCH 41)*. Paris: Ecole française d'athènes, 2002.

Murray, Gilbert. *Aristophanes. The Knights*. London: George Allen & Unwin, 1956.

Myres, John L. "On the List of Thalassocracies of Eusebius." *The Journal of Hellenic Studies* 26 (1906): 84–130.

N

Nagy, Gregory. "Phaethon, Sappho's Phaon, and the White Rock of Leukas: 'Reading' the Symbols of Greek Lyric." In *Reading Sappho: Contemporary Approaches*, edited by Ellen Greene, 35–57. Berkeley, CA: University of California Press, 1996.

Narducci, Emanuele. *Lucano: Un'epica contro l'impero*. Firenze: GLF Editori Laterza, 2002.

Narducci, Emanuele. "*Pauper Amyclas*. Modelli etici e poetici in un episodio della *Pharsalia*." *Maia* 35 (1983): 183–194.

New York Times. "Discovery off Greece Stirring Hope in Quest for Ancient City." (1 December 1966). https://www.nytimes.com/1966/12/01/archives/discovery-off-greece-stirring-hope-in-quest-for-ancient-city-sonic.html.

Nicolet, Claude. *Space, Geography, and Politics in the Early Roman Empire*. Ann Arbor, MI: University of Michigan Press, 1991.

Nightingale, Andrea W. *Genres in Dialogue: Plato and the Construct of Philosophy*. Cambridge: Cambridge University Press, 1995.

Nill, Hans-Peter. *Gewalt und Unmaking in Lucans Bellum Civile. Textanalysen aus narratologischer, wirkungsästhetischer und gewaltsoziologischer Perspektive.* Leiden: Brill, 2018.

ní Mheallaigh, Karen. *The Moon in the Greek and Roman Imagination: Myth, Literature, Science, and Philosophy.* Cambridge: Cambridge University Press, 2020.

Nix, Sarah A. "Caesar as Jupiter in Lucan's *Bellum Civile.*" *CJ* 103, no. 3 (2008): 281–294.

Nomikou, P., et al. "Post-Eruptive Flooding of Santorini Caldera and Implications for Tsunami Generation." *Nature Communications* 7, article no. 13332 (8 November 2016).

Nozick, Robert. *Anarchy, State, and Utopia.* Oxford: Blackwell, 1999 [1974].

Nussbaum, Arthur. *A Concise History of the Law of Nations.* New York: The Macmillan Company, 1947.

O

Ober, Josiah. "Thucydides *Theoretikos*/Thucydides *Histor*: Realist Theory and the Challenge of History." In *Thucydides*, edited by R. J. Rusten, 434–478. Oxford: Oxford University Press, 2009.

Ober, Josiah. "Views of Sea Power in the Fourth-Century Attic Orators." *Ancient World* 1 (1978): 119–130.

O'Brien, John. "Harlequin Britain: Eighteenth-Century Pantomime and the Cultural Location of Entertainment(s)." *Theatre Journal* 50, no. 4 (1998): 489–510.

Ogden, Daniel. "Dimensions of Death in the Greek and Roman Worlds." In *Weltkonstruktionen. Religiose Weltdeutung zwischen Chaos und Kosmos vom Alten Orient biz zum Islam*, edited by Peter Gemeinhardt and Annette Zgoll, 103–131. Tubingen: Mohr Siebeck Verlag, 2010.

Ogden, Daniel. *The Legend of Seleucus: Kingship, Narrative, and Mythmaking in the Ancient World.* Cambridge: Cambridge University Press, 2017.

Oliver-Smith, Anthony, and Susanna M. Hoffman. "Introduction: Why Anthropologists Should Study Disasters." In *Catastrophe and Culture: The Anthropology of Disaster*, edited by Anthony Oliver-Smith and Susanna M. Hoffman, 3–22. Santa Fe, NM: School of American Research Press, 2002.

Olson, S. Douglas, trans. *The Learned Banqueters, Volume V: Books 10.420e–11.* Cambridge, MA: Harvard University Press, 2009.

O'Malley, Andrew. *Children's Literature, Popular Culture, and Robinson Crusoe.* London: Palgrave Macmillan, 2012.

Opsomer, Jan. "Plutarch and the Stoics." In *A Companion to Plutarch*, edited by Mark Beck, 88–103. Malden, MA: Blackwell, 2014.

Osborne, Robin. *The Old Oligarch: Pseudo-Xenophon's Constitution of the Athenians*, third edition. London: London Association of Classical Teachers, 2017.

P

Paden, Roger. "The Two Professions of Hippodamus of Miletus." *Philosophy and Geography* 4, no. 1 (2001): 25–48.

Papalas, Anthony. "Polycrates of Samos and the First Greek Trireme Fleet." *The Mariner's Mirror* 85, no. 1 (1999): 3–19.

Papathoma, M., and D. Dominey-Howes. "Tsunami Vulnerability Assessment and its Implications for Coastal Hazard Analysis and Disaster Management Planning, Gulf of Corinth, Greece." *Natural Hazards and Earth System Sciences* 3, no. 6 (31 December 2003): 733–747.

Pelling, Christopher B. R. *Plutarch and History: Eighteen Studies.* Swansea: Classical Press of Wales, 2002.

Penrose, Walter. *Postcolonial Amazons: Female Masculinity and Courage in Ancient Greek and Sanskrit Literature.* Oxford: Oxford University Press, 2016.

Phillips, O. C. "Lucan's Grove." *CP* 63, no. 4 (1968): 296–300.

Piazzi, Lisa. *P. Ovidii Nasonis Heroidum Epistula VII, Dido Aeneae.* Firenze: Le Monnier, 2007.

Pirazzoli, P. A., et al. "Historical Environmental Changes at Phalasarna Harbor, West Crete." *Geoarchaeology* 7, no. 4 (July 1992): 371–392.

Pitcher, Luke V. "A Perfect Storm? Caesar's Audiences at Lucan 5.504–702." *CQ* 58, no. 1 (2008): 243–249.

Polonia, Alina, et al. "Mediterranean Megaturbidite Triggered by the AD 365 Crete Earthquake and Tsunami." *Scientific Reports* 3, article no. 1285 (15 February 2013). https://doi.org/10.1038/srep01285.

Porter, James I. "Ideals and Ruins: Pausanias, Longinus and the Second Sophistic." In *Pausanias: Travel and Memory in Roman Greece*, edited by Susan E. Alcock, John F. Cherry, and Jas Elsner, 63–92. Oxford: Oxford University Press, 2001.

Porter, James. *The Sublime in Antiquity.* Cambridge: Cambridge University Press, 2016.

Powell, Dilys. *The Villa Ariadne.* London, Sydney, Auckland, and Toronto: Hodder and Stoughton, 1973.

Pritchard, David M. "The Fractured Imaginary: Popular Thinking on Military Matters in Fifth Century Athens." *Ancient History* 28, no. 1 (1998): 38–61.

"Provinces." *The Stage* (14 January 1897).

"Provincial Theatres." *Clarion* (28 December 1895).

Pulbrook, Martin. "The Original Published Form of Ovid's *Heroides*." *Hermathena* 122 (1977): 29–45.

Purpura, Gianfranco. "'Liberum mare' acque territoriali e riserve di pesca nel mondo antico." *AUPA* 49 (2004): 165–206.

Purpura, Gianfranco. "Rinvenimenti sottomarini nella Sicilia Occidentale." *Archeologia subacquea* 3, no. 37–38 (1986): 139–160.

Purvis, Andrea L., trans., and Robert B. Strassler, ed. *The Landmark Herodotus.* New York: Anchor Books, 2009.

Putnam, Michael C. J. *Virgil's Aeneid: Interpretation and Influence*. Chapel Hill, NC: University of North Carolina Press, 1995.

R

Ramsey, John T. *Sallust: Fragments of the Histories, Letters to Caesar.* Cambridge, MA: Harvard University Press (LCL), 2015.

Rehak, Paul, and John G. Younger. "Review of Aegean Prehistory VII: Neopalatial, Final Palatial, and Postpalatial Crete." *American Journal of Archaeology* 102, no. 1 (January 1998): 91–173.

Reicherter, Klaus, David Vonberg, Benjamin Koster, Tomás Fernández-Steeger, Christoph Grützner, and Margret Mathes-Schmidt. "The Sedimentary Inventory of Tsunamis along the Southern Gulf of Cadiz (Southwestern Spain)." *Zeitschrift für Geomorphologie* 54 (Suppl. 3) (2010): 147–173.

Reitz-Joosse, Bettina. "Land at Peace and Sea at War: Landscape and the Memory of Actium in Greek Epigram and Propertius' Elegies." In *Valuing Landscape in Classical Antiquity: Natural Environment and Cultural Imagination*, edited by Jeremy McInerney and Ineke Sluiter, 276–296. Leiden: Brill, 2016.

Richardson, John. "Imperium Romanum: Empire and the Language of Power." *JRS* 81 (1991): 1–9.

Richardson, John. "The Meaning of imperium in the Last Century BC and the First AD." In *The Roman Foundations of the Law of Nations: Alberico Gentili and the Justice of Empire*, edited by Benedict Kingsbury and Benjamin Straumann, 21–29. Oxford: Oxford University Press, 2010.

Riley, C. V. "Mr Maxim's Flying Machine." *Scientific American* (6 October 1894), 217.

Roberts, Ryan N. *Terra Terror: An Interdisciplinary Study of Earthquakes in Ancient Near Eastern Texts and the Hebrew Bible*. PhD dissertation. Los Angeles: UCLA, 2012.

Robertson, Archibald. *Select Writings and Letters of Athanasius, Bishop of Alexandria*. Edinburgh: T. & T. Clark, 1891.

Robinson, Eric W. *Democracy beyond Athens: Popular Government in the Greek Classical Age*. Cambridge: Cambridge University Press, 2011.

"'Robinson Crusoe' at the Prince's Theatre." *Manchester Evening News* (14 December 1895).

Rolfe, John C., trans. *Ammianus Marcellinus. Rerum Gestarum*. Cambridge, MA: Harvard University Press, 1935–1940.

Romano, Allen J., and John Marincola, eds. *Host or Parasite: Mythographers and their Contemporaries in the Classical and Hellenistic Periods*. Berlin and Boston: de Gruyter GmbH, 2019.

Romilly, Jacqueline de. *The Mind of Thucydides*. Ithaca, NY: Cornell University Press, 2012.

Romilly, Jacqueline de. "Le Pseudo-Xénophon et Thucydide. Étude sur quelques divergences de vues." *Revue de Philologie* 36 (1962): 225–241.

Romm, James. *The Edges of the Earth in Ancient Thought*. Princeton, NJ: Princeton University Press, 1992.

Romney, Kristen. "Man-Eating Fish, Tower of Babel Revealed on Ancient Mosaic: Archaeologists Discover Even More Remarkable Biblical Scenes on the Floor of a 1,600-Year-Old Synagogue in Israel." *National Geographic* (15 November 2018). https://www.nationalgeographic.com/culture/2018/11/jonah-tower-babel-huqoq-ancient-synagogue-mosaic/.

Rosati, Gianpiero. "L'elegia al femminile: le *Heroides* di Ovidio (e altre *heroides*)." *MD* 29 (1992): 71–94.

Rosati, Gianpiero. "Sabinus, the *Heroides* and the Poet-Nightingale: Some Observations on the Authenticity of the *Epistula Sapphus*." *CQ* 46, no. 1 (1996): 207–216.

Rosenmeyer, Patricia A. "Ovid's *Heroides* and *Tristia*: Voices from Exile." *Ramus* 26, no. 1 (1997): 29–56.

Rothstein, Edward. "Utopia and its Discontents." In *Visions of Utopia*, edited by Edward Rothstein, Herbert Muschamp, and Martin E. Marty, 1–28. Oxford: Oxford University Press, 2003.

Rougé, Jean. "Le Droit de Naufrage et ses limitations en Mediterranée avant l'établissement de la domination de Rome." In *Mélanges Piganiol 3*, edited by Raymond Chevalier, 1467–1479. Paris: S.E.V.P.E.N, 1966.

Rougé, Jean. *Recherches sur l'organisation du commerce maritime en Méditerranée sous l'Empire romain*. Paris: S.E.V.P.E.N, 1966.

Rowe, Christopher. "Plato and the Persian Wars." In *Cultural Responses to the Persian Wars: Antiquity to the Third Millennium*, edited by Emma Bridges, Edith Hall, and P. J. Rhodes, 85–104. Oxford: Oxford University Press, 2007.

Rubin, Alfred P. *The Law of Piracy*. New York: Transnational Publishers, 1998.

Rubin, Zeev. "The Mediterranean and the Dilemma of the Roman Empire in Late Antiquity." *MHR* 1, no. 1 (1986): 12–26.

Rusten, Jeffrey S. *Dionysius Scytobrachion*. Wiesbaden: Springer, 1982.

S

Şahoğlu, Vasıf, et al. "Volcanic Ash, Victims, and Tsunami Debris from the Late Bronze Age Thera Eruption Discovered at Çeşme-Bağlararası (Turkey)." *Proceedings of the National Academy of Sciences* 119, no. 1 (December 2021): e2114213118. https://doi.org/10.1073/pnas.2114213118.

Salama, Asema, et al. "Paleotsunami Deposits Along the Coast of Egypt Correlate with Historical Earthquake Records of Eastern Mediterranean." *Natural Hazards and Earth System Sciences* 18, no. 8 (17 August 2018): 2203–2219.

Santini, Veronica. *Il filosofo e il mare: Immagini marine e nautiche nella Repubblica di Platone*. Milan: Mimesis, 2011.

Saxonhouse, Arlene W. "Athenian Democracy: Modern Mythmakers and Ancient Theorists." *PS: Political Science and Politics* 26, no. 3 (1993): 486–490.

Schaff, Philip, and Rev. Henry Wallace, eds. *Nicene and Post-Nicene Fathers: Second Series Volume II Socrates, Sozomenus: Church Histories*. New York: Cosimo, Inc., 2007.

Schliephake, Christopher. *Ecocriticism, Ecology and the Cultures of Antiquity*. Lanham, MD: Lexington Books, 2016; Rowman & Littlefield, 2017.

Schliephake, Christopher. *The Environmental Humanities and the Ancient World: Questions and Perspectives*. Cambridge: Cambridge University Press, 2020.

Schoep, Ilse. "Building the Labyrinth: Arthur Evans and the Construction of Minoan Crete." *American Journal of Archaeology* 122, no. 1 (2018): 5–32.

Schofield, Malcolm, ed., and Tom Griffith, trans. *Plato: Laws*. Cambridge: Cambridge University Press, 2016.

Scodel, Ruth. "The Irony of Fate in Bacchylides 17." *Hermes* 112, no. 2 (1984): 137–143.

Searle, Geoffrey. *Morality and the Market in Victorian Britain*. Oxford: Oxford University Press, 1998.

Sedley, David L. *Sublimity and Skepticism in Montaigne and Milton*. Ann Arbor, MI: University of Michigan Press, 2005.

Segal, Charles. "*Kleos* and its Ironies in the *Odyssey*." *AC* 52 (1983): 22–47.

Seymour, Miranda. *Robert Graves: Life on the Edge*. London, New York, etc.: Simon & Schuster, 2003 [1995].

Shaw, B., et al. "Eastern Mediterranean Tectonics and Tsunami Hazard Inferred from the AD 365 Earthquake." *Nature Geoscience* 1, no. 4 (9 March 2008): 268–276.

Shaw, Philip, *The Sublime*. London: Routledge, 2006.

Shelton, Kathleen J. "The Esquiline Treasure: The Nature of the Evidence." *American Journal of Archaeology* 89, no. 1 (1985): 147–155.

Sherk, Robert K. *Roman Documents from the Greek East*. Baltimore, MD: Johns Hopkins Press, 1969.

Sherman, Charles L., trans. *Diodorus Siculus, Library of History, Volume VII: Books 15.20–16.65*. Cambridge, MA: Harvard University Press, 1952.

Shipley, Graham. *A History of Samos, 800–188 BC*. Oxford: Clarendon, 1987.

Showerman, Grant, trans., and G. P. Goold, ed. *Ovid. Heroides. Amores*. Cambridge, MA: Harvard University Press, 1977.

Shuckburgh, Evelyn S., trans. *The Histories of Polybius*. London and New York: Macmillan, 1889; Bloomington, IN: Indiana University Press, 1962.

Sibley, Chris G., and Joseph Bulbulia. "Faith after an Earthquake: A Longitudinal Study of Religion and Perceived Health before and after the 2011 Christchurch New Zealand Earthquake." *PLoS ONE* 7, no. 12 (5 December 2012): e49648. https://doi.org/10.1371/journal.pone.0049648.

Sijpesteijn, Petra M. "The Arab Conquest of Egypt and the Beginning of Muslim Rule." In *Byzantine Egypt*, edited by Roger S. Bagnall, 437–459. Cambridge: Cambridge University Press, 2007.

Sillitti, Giovanna. *Tragelaphos: storia di una metafora e di un problema*. Napoli: Bibliopolis, 1980.

Sklenár, Robert J. *The Taste for Nothingness: A Study of Virtus and Related Themes in Lucan's Bellum Civile*. Ann Arbor, MI: University of Michigan Press, 2003.

Slings, S. R., ed. *Plato. Platonis Rempublicam*. Oxford: Clarendon Press, 2003.

Smith, Arthur Hamilton. "Illustrations to Bacchylides." *Journal of Hellenic Studies* 18 (1898): 276–280.

Smith, Mark S., ed. *The Ugaritic Baal Cycle. Volume I. Introduction with Text, Translation and Commentary of KTU 1.1–1.2*. Leiden: Brill, 1994.

Smith, Mark S., and Wayne T. Pitard, eds. and trans. *The Ugaritic Baal Cycle. Volume II. Introduction with Text, Translation and Commentary of KTU/CAT 1.3–1.4*. Leiden: Brill, 2009.

Sonik, Karen. "From Hesiod's Abyss to Ovid's *rudis indigestaque moles*: Chaos and Cosmos in the Babylonian 'Epic of Creation'." In *Creation and Chaos: A Reconsideration of Hermann Gunkel's Chaoskampf Hypothesis*, edited by Jo Ann Scurlock and Richard H. Beal, 1–25. Winona Lake, IN: Eisenbrauns, 2013.

Soter, Steven, and Dora Katsonopoulou. "Submergence and Uplift of Settlements in the Area of Helike, Greece, from the Early Bronze Age to Late Antiquity." *Geoarchaeology: An International Journal* 26, no. 4 (July/ August 2011): 584–610.

Spann, Philip. *Quintus Sertorius and the Legacy of Sulla*. Fayetteville, AR: University of Arkansas Press, 1987.

Spann, Philip. "Sallust, Plutarch, and the Isles of the Blest." *Terrae Incognitae* 9, no. 1 (1977): 75–80.

Spentzou, Efrossini. *Readers and Writers in Ovid's Heroides: Transgressions of Genre and Gender*. Oxford: Oxford University Press, 2003.

Stanley, Jean-Daniel, Thomas F. Jorstad, and Franck Goddio. "Human Impact on Sediment Mass Movement and Submergence of Ancient Sites in the Two Harbours of Alexandria, Egypt." *Norwegian Journal of Geology* 86 (2006): 337–350.

Stanley, Jean-Daniel, and Marguerite A. Toscano. "Ancient Archaeological Sites Buried and Submerged along Egypt's Nile Delta Coast: Gauges of Holocene Delta Margin Subsidence." *Journal of Coastal Research* 25, no. 1 (1 January 2009): 158–170.

Starr, Chester G. *The Influence of Sea Power on Ancient History*. Oxford: Oxford University Press, 1989.

Starr, Chester G. "Thucydides on Sea Power." *Mnemosyne* 31 (1978): 343–350.

Stern, Jacob. "The Structure of Bacchylides' Ode 17." *RBPh* 45 (1967): 40–45.

Stiros, Stathis C. "The 8.5+ Magnitude, AD 365 Earthquake in Crete: Coastal Uplift, Topography Changes, Archaeological and Historical Signature." *Quaternary International* 216, nos. 1–2 (April 2010): 54–63.

Stiros, Stathis C. "The AD 365 Ammianus Tsunami in Alexandria, Egypt, and the Crete ca. 365 Fault and Tsunami." *Arabian Journal of Geosciences* 13, article no. 716 (23 July 2020): 716.

Stiros, Stathis C. "The AD 365 Crete Earthquake and Possible Seismic Clustering During the Fourth to Sixth Centuries AD in the Eastern Mediterranean: A Review of Historical and Archaeological Data." *Journal of Structural Geology* 23, nos. 2–3 (February 2001): 545–562.

Stiros, Stathis C. "Was Alexandria (Egypt) Destroyed in A.D. 365? A Famous Historical Tsunami Revisited." *Seismological Research Letters* 91, no. 5 (1 July 2020): 2662–2673. doi: 10.1785/0220200045.

Stiros, Stathis C., and Sofia Papageorgiou. "Seismicity of Western Crete and the Destruction of the Town of Kisamos at AD 365: Archaeological Evidence." *Journal of Seismology* 5, no. 3 (July 2001): 381–397.

Stoneman, Richard. *Alexander the Great: A Life in Legend.* New Haven, CT: Yale University Press, 2008.

Storey, Ian. *Fragments of Old Comedy. Vol. 1.* Cambridge, MA: Harvard University Press (LCL), 2011.

Sulimani, Iris. *Diodorus' Mythistory and the Pagan Mission: Historiography and Culture-Heroes in the First Pentad of the* Bibliotheke. Leiden and Boston: Brill, 2011.

Sulimani, Iris. "Imaginary Islands in the Hellenistic Era." In *Myths on the Map: The Storied Landscapes of Ancient Greece*, edited by Greta Hawes, 221–242. Oxford: Oxford University Press, 2017.

Sullivan, Jill A. "'Local and Political Hits': Allusion and Collusion in the Local Pantomime." In *Victorian Pantomime: A Collection of Critical Essays*, edited by Jim Davis, 155–169. Basingstoke and New York: Palgrave Macmillan, 2010.

Sun, Lei, et al. "Religious Belief and Tibetans' Response to Earthquake Disaster: A Case Study of the 2010 Ms 7.1 Yushu Earthquake, Qinghai Province, China." *Natural Hazards* 99, no. 1 (10 August 2019): 141–159.

Suvin, Darko. *Defined by a Hollow: Essays on Utopia, Science Fiction and Political Epistemology.* Oxford, etc.: Peter Lang, 2010.

T

Tarrant, Richard. "Chaos in Ovid's *Metamorphoses* and its Neronian Influence." *Arethusa* 35, no. 3 (2002): 349–360.

Tarwacka, Anna. "Piracy in Roman Law and the Beginnings of International Criminal Law." *Polish Review of International and European Law* 1, no. 1–2 (2012): 57–74.

Tarwacka, Anna. *Romans and Pirates: Legal Perspective.* Warsaw: Wydawnictwo Uniwersytetu, 2009.

Tarwacka, Anna. "Some Remarks on Piracy in Roman Law." *Annuaires de droit maritime et oceanique* 36 (2018): 295–309.

Taylor, A. E. *A Commentary on Plato's Timaeus.* Oxford: Oxford University Press, 1928.

"The Theatres." *Torquay Times, and South Devon Advertiser* (29 January 1897).

Theutenberg, Bo J. "Mare Clausum et Mare Liberum." *Arctic* 37, no. 4 (1984): 481–492.

Thommen, Lukas. *An Environmental History of Ancient Greece and Rome*, translated by Philip Hill. Cambridge: Cambridge University Press, 2012.

Thompson, Lynette, and Richard T. Bruère. "Lucan's Use of Virgilian Reminiscence." *CP* 63, no. 1 (1968): 1–21.

Thompson, Stith, ed. *Motif-Index of Folk Literature*, 6 volumes. Bloomington, IN: Indiana University Press, 1955–1958.

Thorne, George, and F. Grove Palmer. "Robinson Crusoe and the King of the Cannibal Islands." LCP 1882/296. Lord Chamberlain's Manuscript Collection, 1882.

Thorsen, Thea S. *Ovid's Early Poetry: From His Single Heroides to His Remedia amoris*. Cambridge: Cambridge University Press, 2014.

Tinkler, John F. "Praise and Advice: Rhetorical Approaches in More's *Utopia* and Machiavelli's *The Prince*." *The Sixteenth Century Journal* 19, no. 2 (1988): 187–207.

Tracy, Jonathan. "Evidence for the Completeness of the *Bellum Civile*." In *Brill's Companion to Lucan*, edited by Paolo Asso, 33–79. Leiden: Brill, 2011.

Trzaskoma, Stephen M., and R. Scott Smith, eds. *Writing Myth: Mythography in the Ancient World*. Leuven, Paris, Walpole: Peeters, 2013.

Tsagalis, Christos. *From Listeners to Viewers: Space in the Iliad*. Cambridge, MA: Harvard University Press, 2012.

Tsetskhladze, Gocha R., ed. *Greek Colonisation: An Account of Greek Colonies and Other Settlements Overseas*, 2 volumes (Mnemosyne Supplements 193.1/2). Leiden: Brill, 2006–2008.

Tuddenham, David Berg. "Maritime Cultural Landscapes, Maritimity and Quasi Objects." *Journal of Maritime Archaeology* 5, no. 1 (2010): 5–16.

Tuori, Kaius. "The Savage Sea and the Civilizing Law: The Roman Law Tradition and the Rule of the Sea." In *Thalassokratographie: Rezeption und Transformation antiker Seeherrschaft*, edited by Hans Kopp and Christian Wendt, 201–218. Berlin: De Gruyter, 2018.

U

Usener, Hermann, ed. *M. Annaei Lucani Commenta Bernensia*. Hildesheim: G. Olms, 1967.

V

Van Effenterre, Henri. "Querelles cretoises." *REA* 44, no. 1 (1942): 31–51.

Van Oyen, A. *The Socio-Economics of Roman Storage: Agriculture, Trade, and Family*. Cambridge: Cambridge University Press, 2020.

Vegetti, Mario. "Beltista eiper dynata. The Status of Utopia in the Republic." In *The Painter of Constitutions*, edited by Mario Vegetti, 105–122. Sankt Augustin: Academia Verlag, 2013.

Vegetti, Mario. *Um Paradigma no Céu: Platão político de Aristóteles ao século XX*. São Paulo: Annablume, 2010.

Vegetti, Mario. *Platone. La Repubblica. Vol. V, Libri VI–VII*. Napoli: Bibliopolis, 2003.

Velissaropoulos-Karakostas, Julie. *Les nauclères grecs: recherches sur les institutions maritimes en Grèce et dans l'Orient hellénisé*. Paris: Droz, 1980.

Vila Valencia, Adolfo. *Episodios gaditanos: piadosa evocación del imponente maremoto que en el año de 1755 asoló por unas horas a la ciudad de Cádiz*. Cádiz: La Gaditana, 1955.

W

Wakeman, Mary K. *God's Battle with the Monster: A Study in Biblical Imagery*. Leiden: Brill, 1973.

Walbank, Frank W., ed. *The Cambridge Ancient History, Volume VII, Part 1: The Hellenistic World*. Cambridge: Cambridge University Press, 1984.

Wallinga, Herman T. *Ships and Sea-Power before the Great Persian War: The Ancestry of the Ancient Trireme*. Leiden: Brill, 1993.

Walton, John H. *Genesis 1 as Ancient Cosmology*. Winona Lake, IN: Eisenbrauns, 2011.

Ward-Perkins, Bryan. *The Fall of Rome and the End of Civilization*. Oxford and New York: Oxford University Press, 2005.

Warner, Rex, trans. *Thucydides: History of the Peloponnesian War*. London: Penguin Books, 1972 [1954].

Waters, Hazel. *Racism on the Victorian Stage: Representation of Slavery and the Black Character*. Cambridge: Cambridge University Press, 2007.

Watrous, L. Vance. *Minoan Crete: An Introduction*. Cambridge: Cambridge University Press, 2021.

Watt, Ian. "Robinson Crusoe as a Myth." *Essays in Criticism* 1, no. 2 (1951): 95–119. https://doi.org/10.1093/eic/I.2.95.

Watts, Edward J. *The Eternal Decline and Fall of Rome: The History of a Dangerous Idea*. Oxford: Oxford University Press, 2021.

Weaver-Hightower, Rebecca. *Empire Islands: Castaways, Cannibals, and Fantasies of Conquest*. Minneapolis, MN: University of Minnesota Press, 2007.

Weinstock, Stefan. *Divus Julius*. Oxford: Oxford University Press, 1971.

Weir, Robert. "Exaggerated Rumours of Death and the Downdating of Helike's Coinage." In *Helike V: Ancient Helike and Aigialeia. Poseidon, God of Earthquakes and Waters*, edited by Dora Katsonopoulou, 33–61. Athens: The Helike Society, 2017.

Welch, Kathryn. "Both Sides of the Coin: Sextus Pompeius and the So-Called *Pompeiani*." In *Sextus Pompeius*, edited by Anton Powell and Kathryn Welch, 1–30. London: The Classical Press of Wales and Duckworth, 2002.

Werner, Vera, et al. "The Sedimentary and Geomorphological Imprint of the AD 365 Tsunami on the Coasts of Southwestern Crete (Greece) – Examples from Sougia and Palaiochora." *Quaternary International* 473, Part A (15 April 2018): 66–90.

West, Martin L. *Hesiod. Theogony.* Oxford: Clarendon Press, 1966.

Westerdahl, Christer. "Holy, Profane and Political. Territoriality-Extraterritoriality: A Problem with Borders." In *Papers in Cartography, Numismatics, Oriental Studies and Librarianship Presented to Ulla Ehrensvärd*, 467–495. Stockholm: Kungl. biblioteket, 2003.

Wilkes, John. *The Illyrians.* Chichester: Blackwell, 1992.

Wilkinson, L. P. *Ovid Recalled.* Cambridge: Cambridge University Press, 1955.

Williams, Gareth D. "Lucan's *Civil War* in Nero's Rome." In *The Cambridge Companion to the Age of Nero*, edited by Shadi Bartsch, Kirk Freudenburg, and Cedric Littlewood, 93–106. Cambridge: Cambridge University Press, 2017.

Wilson, Malcolm. *Structure and Method in Aristotle's Meteorologica.* Cambridge: Cambridge University Press, 2013.

Wilson, Nigel G., ed. *Aristophanis Fabulae.* Oxonii: E typographeo Clarendoniano, 1935–2007.

Winiarczyk, Marek. *Die hellenistischen Utopien.* Berlin: De Gruyter, 2011.

Winiarczyk, Marek. *The Sacred History of Euhemerus of Messene*, translated by Witold Zbirohowski-Kościa. Berlin: De Gruyter, 2013.

Woolf, Greg. *The Life and Death of Ancient Cities: A Natural History.* Oxford: Oxford University Press, 2020.

Wyatt, Nick. "National Memory, Seismic Activity at Ras Shamra and the Composition of the Ugaritic Baal Cycle." *Ugarit-Forschungen* 48 (2017): 551–591.

Y

Yatromanolakis, Dimitrios. *Sappho in the Making: The Early Reception.* Washington, DC: Center for Hellenic Studies, 2007.

Young, D., ed. *Theognis: Elegiae*, later edited by E. Diehl. Leipzig: Teubner, 1971.

Z

Zanker, Paul, and Björn C. Ewald. *Living with Myths: The Imagery of Roman Sarcophagi*, translated by Julia Slater. Oxford: Oxford University Press, 2012.

Zapf, Hubert, ed. *Handbook of Ecocriticism and Cultural Ecology.* Berlin: De Gruyter, 2016.

Zenos, A. C., trans. *The Ecclesiastical History of Socrates Scholasticus* (NPNF2-02), edited by Philip Schaff and Henry Wace. Buffalo, NY: Christian Literature Publishing Co., 1890.

Žižek, Slavoj. *The Sublime Object of Ideology.* London: Verso, 1989.

Zoran, Gabriele. "Towards a Theory of Space in Narrative." *Poetics Today* 5, no. 2 (1984): 309–335.

About the Authors

Manuel Álvarez-Martí-Aguilar is a lecturer in ancient history at the University of Malaga (Spain). His research interests include the historical process of Tartessos and Phoenician Iberia, as well as the modern historiography of the ancient world. In recent years, he has been leading a line of research on the impact of historical earthquakes and tsunamis on the human communities of the Iberian Peninsula, as the principal investigator of the projects "The Tsunami in the Cultural Representations of the Ancient World: Gadir-Gades and the Gulf of Cadiz as a Case Study" (HAR2015-66011-P) and "Earthquakes and Tsunamis in the Iberian Peninsula: Social Responses in the *Longue Durée*" (PGC2018-093752-B-I00). In these projects, he has analyzed the symbolic keys to the perception of tsunamis in the ancient world, studied the apotropaic responses to this type of phenomenon, and reviewed the catalogue of historical earthquakes and tsunamis in the Iberian Peninsula.

Vilius Bartninkas is Assistant Professor of Philosophy at Vilnius University. He received his BA in philosophy from Vilnius University, his MPhil and PhD in classics from the University of Cambridge. His main research interests are ancient philosophy, Greek religion, and political theory. His latest articles explore the interaction between religion, cosmology, and morality in Plato's works, and he has published Lithuanian translations of Plato's *Lysis* and *Alcibiades* (with introduction and commentaries).

Aaron L. Beek (North-West University, Potchefstroom, South Africa) is a classical philologist and ancient historian who has worked in classics, history, and theology departments including also at Massey University (New Zealand) and the University of Memphis (USA). His principal research area covers pirates, bandits, and other such outlaws and outcasts in the ancient Mediterranean as well as their portrayal in both ancient history and ancient literature. Secondary interests include Roman North Africa, New Comedy, and Latin patristics. Recent and forthcoming publications discuss the writings of Polyaenus, Josephus, and Cassius Dio as well as Latin authors' reflections on earlier Greek philosophy in both "Augustine's Pirate" (*Latomus*, 2022) and the present volume. He is also now completing an edited volume (with J. R. Hall), *Trickery, Treachery, and Deceit in Ancient Conflict* (De Gruyter), and continuing work on his monograph *The "Other" Roman Soldier*, a study of how the Romans employed "outsiders" in their armies.

Ross Clare is an honorary research fellow at the University of Liverpool. He also sits on the Scholars Board of History Studio. His research interests are primarily in the crossover between the ancient world and modern popular culture, with specialism in video games. He is author of *Ancient Greece and Rome in Videogames: Representation, Play, Transmedia* (Bloomsbury, 2021) and of the upcoming *Greece and Rome in Modern Science Fiction* (Liverpool University Press).

Gabriele Cornelli is Associate Professor of Ancient Philosophy at the Universidade de Brasília, Brazil. He was President of the International Plato Society (2013–2016), and he is currently the Director of the Archai UNESCO Chair on the origins of Western Thought. He is also editor of the journals *Archai*, the *Atlantis Journal*, and the *Plato Journal*. He is currently editing four monograph series: Brill's Plato Studies Series (Brill), Archai (Annablume, SP), Cátedra (Paulus, SP), and Filosofia e Tradição (UNESCO, Brazil).

Isaia Crosson is a classics teacher and researcher at the Hun School of Princeton, as well as the Director of the National Junior Classical League and the Debate & Forensics Clubs. Isaia holds a PhD and an MPhil in classical philology from Columbia University, as well as a BA in Latin & Greek philology from the Catholic University of the Sacred Heart (Milan). Isaia is especially interested in Roman literature of the Early Empire, war poetry and trauma studies, the analogy between the body of text and the body politic, and the unfinished in literature and art. In his research, Isaia aims to show that the form of literary texts (including seemingly accidental ellipses, omissions, and asymmetries) can often be read as meaningful: there may be a message hidden in the formal imperfections of a nuanced text, especially when the narrative of such a text replicates the physical or psychological trauma inflicted upon human bodies by a disruptive phenomenon (such as war, an accident, or a natural catastrophe).

Ryan Denson is a PhD candidate in classics and ancient history at the University of Exeter. His research interests concern the supernatural in antiquity, folklore, and the ancient imagination, while his PhD thesis examines the ancient depictions of sea monsters and other imagined marine figures. His article "Divine Nature and the Natural Divine: The Marine Folklore of Pliny the Elder" has recently been published in the journal *Green Letters*, utilizing an interdisciplinary approach of classics, ecocriticism, and folklore. Other publications include an entry on the Sirens and Harpies for the forthcoming *Oxford Handbook of Monsters in Classical Myth*, and a chapter on Late Antique Christian attempts at delegitimizing folkloric conceptions of ghosts for the forthcoming edited volume *Erasure in Late Antiquity*.

Rhiannon Easterbrook is an honorary research associate at the Institute of Classical Studies. Having previously studied at the University of Cambridge and UCL before working for a charitable housing association, she received her PhD in classics from the University of Bristol for her dissertation "Performing Classical Antiquity on the Popular Stage in Britain, 1895–1914." Subsequently, she was a postdoctoral writing fellow with Women in the Humanities at the University of Oxford. A founder member of the Women's Classical Committee UK, she specializes in classical reception studies in relation to gender, performance, and consumer culture.

Georgia L. Irby is a professor of classics at William and Mary and the editor of the *Classical Journal*. Her research interests include the history of Greco-Roman science, mythology, literature, and religion. Her recent books include *Epic Echoes in The Wind and the Willows* (Routledge, 2022), in which she explores Grahame's engagement with epic themes, imagery, and story arcs; two volumes on water in Antiquity, *Conceptions of the Watery World in Greco-Roman Antiquity* and *Using and Conquering the Watery World in Greco-Roman Antiquity* (Bloomsbury, 2021); *A Companion to Science, Technology and Medicine in the Ancient World* (Wiley-Blackwell, 2016), *A Little Latin Reader* (Oxford, 2017), and *A New Latin Primer* (Oxford, 2015; both with Mary English). She is currently working on a translation and commentary of Pomponius Mela.

Simona Martorana is an Alexander von Humboldt research fellow at Kiel University and the University of Hamburg. Email: smartorana@email. uni-kiel.de. She completed her PhD in July 2021 at Durham University (UK), after spending some time at Harvard University as a visiting fellow. She is a scholar in classical and medieval Latin literature, and combines a rigorous philological reading of the texts with modern theoretical approaches, particularly from gender, posthumanism, medical humanities, and ecocriticism. Her publications include several articles on Latin poetry and medieval Latin philology. She is currently working on a monograph that explores motherhood within Ovid's *Heroides* through feminist readings. Her co-edited volume, *Body and Medicine in Latin Poetry*, is forthcoming with De Gruyter.

Emilia Mataix Ferrándiz is currently a postdoctoral researcher at the University of Helsinki Center of Excellence Eurostorie (law, identity, and the European narratives) and a fellow of the Käte Hamburger Kolleg in Münster (Germany). Emilia was also a fellow at the Helsinki Collegium for

Advanced Studies from 2018 until 2020. She holds a PhD in Roman law (University of Alicante and Facolta di Giurisprudenza Palermo) and a second PhD in archaeology (University of Southampton and Lyon 2 La Lumière). Her research interest lies in Roman law and archaeology, especially on its commercial and maritime focus. By studying legal evidence and its material manifestations, she investigates the ways societal practices helped generate new regional cultures and, in turn, the way in which these cultures helped define the faces of Rome.

Guy D. Middleton is a visiting fellow in the School of History, Classics and Archaeology at Newcastle University. His research interests include the archaeology, history, and historiography of collapse and transformation, in particular the end of the Mycenaean states of the Late Bronze Age Aegean and the eastern Mediterranean more widely. This includes an interest in ancient natural hazards, including earthquakes, tsunamis, and volcanoes, and the impacts of these on human communities and on ancient cultures. His books include *The Collapse of Palatial Society LBA Greece and the Postpalatial Period* (Oxford, 2010) and *Understanding Collapse: Ancient History and Modern Myths* (Cambridge, 2017). He also edited and contributed to *Collapse and Transformation: The Late Bronze Age to Early Iron in the Aegean* (Oxford, 2020).

Hamish Williams is a guest researcher at the University of Groningen. He has previously held a junior fellowship at the Polish Institute of Advanced Studies in Warsaw and a Humboldt postdoctoral fellowship at the Institute of English and American Studies, Friedrich Schiller University Jena. His main research area is classical reception studies, on the post-classical afterlives and reimaginations of ancient Greek and Roman thought, but he is broadly interested in modern literary studies, covering topics such as utopianism, hospitality, the sublime, and collapse. His previous project explored classical reception in fantasy writings, with the edited volume *Tolkien and the Classical World* (2021) and the upcoming monograph *J.R.R. Tolkien's Utopianism and the Classics* (2023), while his current project focuses on modern receptions of Minoan Crete.

Index

Printed and bound by CPI Group (UK) Ltd, Croydon, CR0 4YY

19/04/2023

03211934-0001